August Valentine Kautz, USA

AUGUST VALENTINE KAUTZ, USA

Biography of a Civil War General

Lawrence G. Kautz

McFarland & Company, Inc., Publishers
Jefferson, North Carolina

The present work is a reprint of the illustrated case bound edition of August Valentine Kautz, USA: Biography of a Civil War General, *first published in 2008 by McFarland.*

LIBRARY OF CONGRESS CATALOGUING-IN-PUBLICATION DATA

Kautz, Lawrence G., 1933–
August Valentine Kautz, USA : biography of a
Civil War general / Lawrence G. Kautz.
p. cm.
Includes bibliographical references and index.

ISBN 978-1-4766-6279-4 (softcover : acid free paper) ∞
ISBN 978-0-7864-8269-6 (ebook)

1. Kautz, August V. (August Valentine), 1828–1895.
2. Generals— United States— Biography. 3. United States.
Army— Biography. 4. United States— History— Civil War,
1861–1865 — Cavalry operations. 5. Soldiers— Northwest,
Pacific — Biography. 6. Northwest, Pacific — History, Military —
19th century. 7. Frontier and pioneer life — Southwest, New.
8. Southwest, New — History, Military — 19th century.
9. German Americans— Biography. I. Title.

E467.1.K22K38 2016   973.7'41092 — dc22   [B]   2008011658

BRITISH LIBRARY CATALOGUING DATA ARE AVAILABLE

On the cover: August Valentine Kautz, 1864, courtesy Virginia (Kautz) Borkenhagen

Printed in the United States of America

*McFarland & Company, Inc., Publishers
Box 611, Jefferson, North Carolina 28640
www.mcfarlandpub.com*

To Nancy

Table of Contents

Preface

For many years, I have had a keen interest in American history, especially in the American Civil War. Occasionally, when reading of that war, I would come across the name of a Union Army officer who bore the same surname as I, Kautz. It took little research to show that the officer, August Valentine Kautz, and I are related. He and my great-grandfather were second cousins. Knowing this, I made an effort to learn as much as I could about August Kautz and found that he led a most interesting life and played a role, although a minor one, in a number of chapters of American history. I came, over time, to admire the man from afar.

Several years ago, I read a book entitled *Richmond Redeemed: The Siege at Petersburg* by Richard J. Sommers. This book is a detailed, well-researched and perceptive account of one of the several Union attempts to capture the Confederate capital in 1864. Then a brigadier general and commander of a cavalry brigade, August Kautz took part in that offensive, but he was ineffectual in attempting to carry out the mission assigned to him in the action.

In the opening chapter of his book, Sommers offers brief biographies of several of the participants in the battle. His very negative paragraph on August Kautz includes the following:

> Vanity, boastfulness and disingenuousness marked him; tactical competence did not. Although he had shown administrative ability in the West in 1863, he had performed poorly since returning to the field in April 1864. In the succeeding five months his record included three ineffective raids, one of which ended disastrously; a severe defeat at the First Battle of Deep Bottom, loss of 2500 cattle and most of one regiment to Confederate raiders far behind Union lines, and the dubious honor of immortalizing his name in the Kautz-Gillmore Fiasco of the Ninth of June.

I knew that Kautz had performed well in all of the operations which Sommers mentioned — even superbly in some. If most of these operations were failures, it was not because Kautz had "performed poorly." That, however, was not the part of Sommers' statement which drew my attention. It was that "Vanity, boastfulness and disingenuousness" part.

Vain? He probably was. Boastful? He may have been at times, but to read some of his over-modest official reports written during the Civil War one would not think so. Disingenuous? He certainly was not.

Of course, Sommers is a professional historian with a Ph.D. from a prestigious university and, at the time he published *Richmond Redeemed* (1981), he was archivist/historian at the U.S. Army Military History Institute. It was because of Sommers' impressive credentials that I set out to search for clues to Kautz's true personality. I reread everything I had previously found written about or by Kautz looking for evidence to support Sommers' opinion of him. In addition, I have struggled through the nearly 5000 pages of Kautz's personal journals. I have found a man who is far too complex to accurately describe in just a few words.

The result is this book. I have attempted to rely as much as possible on contemporary documents and the reader will find that I have leaned heavily on Kautz's own journals. I feel I have laid out a fair biography of August Valentine Kautz without being excessively judgmental. I leave it to the reader to form his or her own opinion of the man.

A work such as this could not be possible without help from one's friends. Special thanks for their contributions and encouragement are due to Virginia Borkenhagen, Kenneth Kautz, John Warren Kautz, Darrell Kautz, Gerd Hemminger, Donald James Robinson, Clara Lee Chapman, Lee Edwards of the Ripley (Ohio) Museum, Orville Stout of the Historic Fort Steilacoom Association, Bruce H. Tabb of the University of Oregon Library, Georgiana Kautz and Cecelia Svinth Carpenter of the Nisqually Indian Tribe, Gerhard Kautz of the *Familienverband Kautz* (Kautz Family Association in Germany), the staffs of the Cincinnati Historical Society Library, the Library of Congress and the National Archives, and my wife, Nancy.

1. An Immigrant Family

When her ship landed in Baltimore on October 13, 1828, the Widow Kautz felt her spirits buoyed by the hope of a new life for herself and her children. The 59-day voyage from Bremen had been decidedly unpleasant. Confinement aboard the sailing vessel had deepened the melancholy which had been her constant companion since the death of her husband two years before.

Katharina Lichtenberger had been born August 31, 1775, in the village of Ispringen in the Grand Duchy of Baden. She had married Christoph Kautz in 1800 in the Evangelical church in Ispringen and borne six children. One had died as an infant. The other five were with her on the voyage to America. Also with them was the wife of her eldest son Johann Georg, Dorothea Elisabetha (Löwing) Kautz, and their infant son, August Valentine, born on January 5 of that year.

Christoph Kautz had been a surveyor in Ispringen. He, like Katharina, had been born in Ispringen, on November 2, 1775. Members of the Kautz family had resided in Ispringen since the middle of the 16th century and their ancestry could be traced to a man named Albert Kautz who was born in 1328 in nearby Alsace and had fought with Holy Roman Emperor Charles IV in the Hundred Years' War.

Early in their marriage, Christoph and Katharina had dreamt of moving to America, and many of their friends and relatives shared that dream. The Napoleonic Wars had caused havoc in Baden and recurrent droughts in the early years of the 19th century had produced famine in the Duchy. As their children were maturing in the mid–1820s, Christoph was able to purchase a tract of 100 acres of partially-cleared farm land in Franklin Township, Brown County, in far-off Ohio in the United States of America.

That land was part of the Virginia Military Reservation, an area of about 10,000 square miles between the Scioto and Little Miami Rivers in southwestern Ohio. It had been set aside by the federal government to satisfy the bounties promised Virginia veterans of the Revolutionary War, 200 to 15,000 acres, depending upon the rank of the veteran. Many of the veterans who claimed their bounties had no intention of removing to the "wilderness" of Ohio. As a result, much of the land in the Reservation had been for sale for years—often for as little as $1 per acre.

According to custom in Baden, Christoph's death on October 17, 1826, left his son, Johann Georg, head of the household. Johann Georg maintained his desire to settle in America and, after his marriage to Dorothea Löwing on August 7, 1827, he set plans in motion to move to America. Birth of a son on January 5, 1828, did not deter his resolve to emigrate, and the family, including his mother and siblings, took a boat down the Rhine River to Rotterdam and set sail from Bremen on August 15 of that year. After a severe storm and a narrow escape from shipwreck off Cape Henry, they arrived in Baltimore on October 13.

George Kautz had but $10 to his name. George had been christened Johann Georg, but he is not known to have used the German version of his name after coming to America. George had apprenticed as a cabinetmaker in Pforzheim, a larger town near his native Ispringen, so he had little trouble finding work in Baltimore and "soon placed himself beyond the possibility of want."[1]

By 1830, the family, including George's mother and siblings, was living in Cincinnati. Dorothy had borne another son while in Baltimore. The boy, named Frederick, was born November 6, 1829. Another son, John, was born in Cincinnati on December 22, 1831.

George appears to have planned to become a farmer. He and Dorothy purchased 100 acres of farmland in Franklin Township on October 8, 1831, from Enoch Laycock, an early Brown County settler, and, on January 25, 1832, Laycock sold them another 50 acres—all for a total of $700. At about the same time (January 7, 1832), Katharina Kautz sold the 100 acres that she and Christoph had owned to Wendall (Wendel) Klein, another German immigrant.

Meanwhile, George's brother, Sebastian, had moved to Brown County. He was working as a carpenter and lived with the Klein family. He married Wendall Klein's daughter, Wilhelmina, on April 8, 1832.

It seems that some time in the year 1832, George decided against farming. On December 4, he bought a lot on the northwest corner of Main and Market (now OH-125) Streets in the heart of the town of Georgetown from Joseph Nichols for $100. Then, on Christmas Day, he sold all his farm land. The 100-acre parcel was sold to his brother-in-law, Matthew Rombach. The other fifty acres went to his brother Sebastian for $140.

In March 1833, George and Dorothy moved to Georgetown and lived with the family of David Ammen, a newspaper publisher and prominent member of the community. Several years later, they bought a small house on three acres on the west side of town, which George remodeled and expanded to fit his growing family. George constructed a carpenter shop on his Main Street property. Over the next eleven years, he had a very successful business as a cabinetmaker.

The village of Ispringen, Baden, as it appeared in the middle of the 20th century, little changed from 1828 when August Kautz was born.

George's sister Margaretha was married in October 1833 to Matthew Schneider, who had been born in Bavaria and was working in Cincinnati as a meat cutter. They moved to Illinois, where Schneider farmed and was engaged in a number of successful businesses.

George's sister Katharina was married in Cincinnati in July 1832. Her husband was Matthew Rombach, a native of Naikirch, Baden. As has been mentioned, Matthew and Katharina Rombach purchased a farm in Brown County from George Kautz. They later moved to a farm near Wilmington, Ohio, where Matthew became a very successful businessman and banker. Their daughter, Louise Rombach, married a lawyer named James Denver, who will appear later in this book.

The youngest of the Kautz children, Christina, was married on July 30, 1837, to Philipp Daum, a native of the village of Ellmendingen, Baden. Christina and Philipp were first cousins. Philipp's mother, Christina (Lichtenberger) Daum, was a sister of Katharina (Lichtenberger) Kautz. The couple later lived in Vicksburg, Mississippi, where Philipp was involved in some phase of the Mississippi River transportation industry.

Although Beers' *History of Brown County, Ohio* (1883) states that among the German settlers to Franklin Township in Brown County after 1830 were "Mrs. Kautz, with her sons, George and Sebastian, and three daughters,"[2] it fails to mention that Katharina died shortly after the family's arrival in Brown County, probably in 1833 or 1834. No record of her death has been found.

2. Boyhood in Ohio

The great majority of Germans who emigrated to Brown County in the 1830s and 1840s settled on farms in the northeastern part of the county, most in Franklin Township. By 1850, 71 of the 207 households in Franklin Township were headed by persons born in Germany. The only town of note in Franklin Township was Arnheim, a hamlet laid out in 1836 by Jacob Arn, who had been born in Dürnn, Baden. Arn was married to another of the Kautzes, Rosina Kautz, a cousin of George Kautz.

Much of the social life of these German families centered around the Evangelical Lutheran Church in Arnheim, a definitely German church. Although the church was founded in 1832, the first sermon in English was not given until 1888 and the last service in German occurred in 1912.

The very Germanness of the Franklin Township community was a major factor leading to George Kautz's decision to sell his Franklin Township property and move to Georgetown. He had left his native land to become an American and he wanted his children to be raised as "American" as possible. English was to be the language spoken in his home. There were economic reasons for the move also. Working as a cabinetmaker in the larger town of Georgetown would be more lucrative than farming in Franklin Township. Besides, at this stage of his life, George was not the least bit interested in farming.

George was a Democrat, although he was not interested in public office. Among his closest friends in Georgetown were the local tanner Jesse Root Grant, schoolmaster John D. White, local lawyer and politician Thomas L. Hamer, and David Ammen, with whom his family had lived when they first came to Georgetown. All were outspoken Democrats, active in politics.

August Kautz was five when his parents moved from Cincinnati to Georgetown. In the autumn of 1834 he was enrolled in the subscription school operated by John D. White. Such schools were expensive and the fact that George was able to afford tuition for his sons is evidence of the success of his business.

John D. White, the schoolmaster, had been born in Virginia and was a surveyor by trade. As a young man, he moved to North Carolina and, in 1823, to Maysville, Kentucky. When he settled in Georgetown in 1826, he saw the need for a school and, the following year, opened his subscription school in a shed behind his house. In 1829, he built a two-room brick schoolhouse on Water Street in Georgetown and taught there until the late 1840s. He also continued as a surveyor, was named Brown County Surveyor, and later was elected to the office of County Treasurer.

Among the students taught by John White were Hiram Ulysses Grant, Jacob Ammen, Daniel Ammen and Charles W. Blair.

Grant, of course, is well known under the later from of his name, Ulysses S. Grant. Jacob Ammen graduated from West Point and was an instructor at the Academy for most of the next six years. In 1837, he resigned to teach at a number of colleges. Reenlisting in the Civil War, he rose to the rank of brigadier general. Daniel Ammen graduated from the U.S. Naval Academy and was a career naval officer, retiring in 1877 as a rear admiral. Blair, who was one of August Kautz's closest friends, was also breveted brigadier general during the Civil War.

In addition, White taught his own sons, Carr B. White, who was breveted to brigadier general in the Civil War, and Chilton Allen White, who became an Ohio state senator and was a member of the U.S. House of Representatives throughout the Civil War.

White, described by Grant as "kind-hearted ... and much respected by the community," was also known to use the switch when necessary. According to Grant, "The rod was freely used there, and I was not exempt from its influence. Switches were brought in bundles, from a beech wood near the school house, by the boys for whose benefit they were intended. Often a whole bundle would be used up in a single day."[1]

There is no indication the young Kautz received the switch with any frequency, nor is there any available information what kind of a pupil he was.

The term of instruction was three months when White opened the school in 1827, but was lengthened in later years. The term was sufficiently short to allow time for the pupils to help their parents in their businesses and on their farms. From an early age, August worked in his father's carpentry shop. From about 1840 to 1844, he also worked as a typesetter in the printing office of David P. Palmer, who published *the Georgetown Democratic Standard*, one of the short-lived newspapers which appeared from time to time in Georgetown. During that time, Palmer was studying law in the office of Andrew Ellison, a local lawyer, who was later a member of Congress. August took an interest in Palmer's law studies and this interest would carry into his adult years.

Three more children were born while the family resided in Georgetown: George Adam, born January 27, 1834; Louis T., born February 26, 1836, and Albert, born January 29, 1839.

In 1844, George Kautz decided to become a vintner. On May 6, he purchased 36 acres of land on the outskirts of the village of Levanna from Thomas Rogers for $380.36. Levanna was a hamlet lying hard against the bank of the Ohio River in southern Brown County. Boat-building

U.S. Grant Schoolhouse, Georgetown, Ohio, as it appears today. During the time August Kautz attended John D. White's two-room schoolhouse, other students included three future Civil War generals, two admirals, one U.S. congressman and, of course, one president, Hiram Ulysses Grant.

George Kautz's home in Levanna, Ohio, in 2003. This photograph shows the wine cellar below the house.

was its chief industry. The Boyd brothers, Charles and Samuel, were then building a lumber business which would eventually employ more than 100 men and lead to expansion of the town. Steep bluffs, which rise not far from the river, prevented expansion to the north and the village eventually spread along the river for almost a mile.

George's property lay on the River Road (now US-52). He built a brick house beside the road just west of town and planted the steep bluff behind the house, known as Pisgah Ridge, in Catawba grapes. He was so successful that he purchased another 22 acres about a mile west of town in 1852 for $625. He built a larger two-story brick house on his new property and again planted grapes on the side of the bluff. The house was built over a large basement, consisting of two large rooms with high, arched ceilings, cut into the base of the bluff; this basement served as his wine cellar. Both houses remained in the family until well into the 20th century. The first house escaped a fire which almost completely destroyed the town and its lumber mill in 1886, but succumbed to fire in the 1970s. The second house is still standing and is being lovingly restored by its present owner.

In addition to wine-making, George continued as a cabinetmaker, but to a lesser extent than he had at Georgetown. A seventh child, and the only girl in the family, named Sophia, was born in 1847.

In this setting, August Kautz grew to manhood. He was of average height with what would now be called an athletic build. His hair was black and his eyes light blue. He continued to work for his father although he hired out to help on nearby farms, usually at half wages, which was the custom for boys of his age.

Both houses in Levanna had lovely views of the Ohio River, but not so fine a view as that from the tree house young August constructed high on the bluff.[2] We can only surmise that he would, from time to time, look out over that river and, viewing the growing steamship traffic, wonder whether he would ever travel beyond his boyhood home in Brown County.

3. Mexico

On March 2, 1836, a group of Texians gathered in a ramshackle house in Washington, Texas to declare their independence from Mexico. Over the following decade, sporadic efforts to annex the infant republic to the United States failed — or rather, languished — primarily because of inaction on the part of the U.S. Congress. Southern Democrats were licking their chops over the prospect of having another slave state, while Whiggish New Englanders, led by former President John Quincy Adams, remained opposed.

In 1844, Texas President Sam Houston resubmitted the question of annexation to the Texas Congress. It took two years of diplomatic legislative wrangling before the Annexation Ordinance came to a popular vote in Texas. It passed 7664 to 430. The U.S. Congress then lost no time in passing a resolution to admit Texas as a state, and the deed was done when President James Knox Polk signed the Joint Resolution on December 29, 1845.

These events were viewed with obvious interest in Mexico, but that country was torn by internal strife which prevented its taking action until Mariano Parades y Arrillaga took over the government in a coup early in 1846. Mexican troops were ordered to the border with Texas, and President Polk answered by ordering Major General Zachary Taylor to Texas with an army of 10,000 men, one-third of the U.S. Army. Taylor arrived on March 28, 1846.

On April 25, Mexican troops crossed the Rio Grande and ambushed a small detachment of American dragoons. Two more attacks occurred and both were soundly defeated by American troops under the command of General Taylor at the Battles of Palo Alto and Resaca de la Palma on May 8 and 9.

On May 11, President Polk sent a message to Congress stating that a state of war existed and, two days later, Congress declared war on Mexico, appropriated ten million dollars and authorized the activation of 50,000 volunteers to serve for twelve months to help fight that war.

The above events were viewed from Brown County with mixed feelings. Despite the fact that Brown County was one of the major stops on the Underground Railroad, the county had close economic ties to the slaveholding South. Brown County farm products and manufactured goods passed down the Ohio and Mississippi Rivers on steamships, many of which were built in the shipyards of Brown County. The strength of the Democratic Party in the county reflected that economic reality. So, when the issue of admitting Texas to the Union came up, Brown County was all for it. When Mexico invaded and war was declared, the echoes of "Remember the Alamo," which had faded somewhat over the years, could once again be heard almost as loudly along the Ohio River as beside the Rio Grande.

We can assume that the teenage August Kautz held political views in common with his neighbors if he held any at all. His father was a Democrat, as were all of George's closest friends. In addition, when August worked at the *Democratic Standard* in Georgetown, he was constantly exposed to the editorial comments of his employer, David Palmer. So, when President Polk issued a call for 20,000 volunteers (instead of the 50,000 Congress had authorized) to prosecute a war against Mexico, August was one of the first in line.

The president had requested Governor William Bebb of Ohio to supply three regiments—thirty companies—of volunteers. Even before the governor complied, Thomas Hamer took it upon himself to raise a company in his home county. The response was immediate thanks to Hamer's persuasiveness. A full company was recruited and others had to be turned away.

The Brown County company assembled at Georgetown on June 8 and was marched off to Camp Washington near Cincinnati amid some fanfare and not a few tears. At Camp Washington the company was joined by other companies from Cincinnati, Portsmouth, Dayton, Hamilton and Sandusky to form the First Regiment of Ohio Volunteers. The Brown County company became Company G of that regiment. Other companies from eastern and northern Ohio formed the Second and Third Regiments to complete the First Volunteer Field Brigade, also known as the Ohio Brigade or the Buckeye Brigade.

The first order of business was the election of officers. The members of each company were permitted to elect their own officers, then the company officers chose from among their ranks the field-grade officers. Company G chose Hamer's law partner and son-in-law, Sanders W. Johnson, as their captain and James P. Fyffe as their first lieutenant, with W.P. Stewart and Carr B. White elected second lieutenants.

In the election for regimental officers, Hamer was chosen colonel, but declined the honor, choosing instead to take a lesser position at the rank of major. Alexander M. Mitchell of Cincinnati was subsequently named colonel of the regiment. Hamer's decision was not so magnanimous as the reader may believe. He felt certain that he would soon be named commander of the Buckeye Brigade and he received a letter from President Polk to that effect on the first day of August.

Three weeks seems hardly time enough to learn all there is to know about soldiering, but uniforms were issued, a little drilling took place and muskets were fired a few times. August Kautz and the rest of the First Volunteer Brigade were mustered into service on June 27 by Brigadier General John E. Wool, who had stopped in Cincinnati en route to Chihuahua, Mexico. Four days later the Ohio boys, too, were off to Mexico.

August's regiment marched through the streets of Cincinnati, where the steamer *New World* was waiting at the public landing to carry them to New Orleans. Cheering crowds lined the streets and many a young woman was seen to rush into the ranks for a last tearful embrace. Cannons roared as the *New World* slipped her moorings and the acrid smoke of gunpowder blended with the wood smoke from the steamer's boilers as she moved away from the landing into the channel.

The stay in New Orleans was brief and the regiment sailed in the second week of July amid more cheering and cannon fire for Port Isabel, Texas. From Port Isabel, which lies on a spit of land at the mouth of the Rio Grande, the regiment marched a few miles upriver to Camp Belknap.

It is hard to imagine a more desolate place than Camp Belknap as it is described by Major Luther Giddings. The camp, occupied by several thousand troops, lay about a mile from the river, and all supplies, including water, had to be hauled to the camp from the river through a swamp impassible by wagons. There, the usual camp diseases were augmented by a variety of tropical diseases, and daily sick call among the men of the First Ohio averaged almost 25 percent of the regiment. There was time, however, for the men to "earnestly commence upon a thorough system of instruction and discipline."[1]

On August 1, the First Ohio received its orders to depart Camp Belknap from General Taylor's headquarters in Matamoros, a place of "cow-pens and contemptible huts"[2] just upriver from Camp Belknap on the Mexican side. At the time, Taylor's army consisted of four brigades of the regular Army, two commanded by Brigadier General David E. Twiggs and two by Brigadier General William J. Worth and, in addition to the Ohio Brigade, a volunteer brigade from Indiana, regiments from Kentucky, Tennessee, Alabama and Georgia, and two regiments of mounted Texas Rangers. The Mexican army which opposed him had fallen back 200 miles west to the city of Monterrey after their defeats at Palo Alto and Resaca de la Palma and had been turned over to General Don Pedro de Ampudia. Ampudia, born in Cuba in 1803, was a veteran of the War for Texas Independence, having commanded the artillery at the capture of the Alamo.

Taylor was under pressure from Washington to move on Monterrey as quickly as possible. Although the regular Army troops under his command were well supplied logistically, Taylor did not have sufficient transportation to move all of the volunteers. He chose, therefore, to move on Monterrey with only a portion of his force. First, in mid–July, he ordered General Worth and his division of two brigades to Camargo, a village about halfway to Monterrey. Camargo was situated on the San Juan River, and that river, a tributary of the Rio Grande, was navigable as far as Camargo, but not beyond. His order of July 30 designated ten volunteer regiments to follow Worth, sending all of their heavy baggage and a contingent of their troops to Camargo by river steamer while the remaining men marched overland. According to his July 30 order only two regiments of the Ohio Brigade would go to Camargo under command of General Hamer. Hamer chose the First and Second Regiments. The march, according to Giddings (who went by steamer), "performed under midsummer suns, and through country but scantily supplied with water, was a severe and trying one."[3]

To complete the move to Camargo, General Twiggs's Division of regulars was the last to leave Matamoros. More accustomed to marching than were the volunteers, they arrived in Camargo just ahead of the volunteers.

On August 28, General Taylor issued an order which named, besides the two regiments of Texas Rangers, only four of the volunteer regiments for the continued march on Monterrey. The order began, "The limited means of transportation, and the uncertainty in regard to the supplies ... imposes upon the commanding general the necessity of taking into the field ... only a moderate portion of the volunteer force now under his orders," and then went on to explain that each of the regiments selected would be reduced to 500 men chosen as most able to undergo "the fatigues and privations of the campaign."[4]

The order named the First Ohio Regiment and the First Kentucky Regiment to form the First Field Brigade under the command of General Hamer, and the First Tennessee Regiment and the Mississippi Regiment to form the Second Field Brigade under the command of Brigadier General John A. Quitman. The two brigades became the Volunteer Division of Taylor's army, which was commanded by Brigadier General William O. Butler.[5] Taylor's army now numbered but 6000 opposed to more than 10,000 Mexicans waiting at Monterrey, a town with about 12,000 inhabitants.

September 6, the first day of the march, was the most difficult of the campaign for Kautz and his fellow Ohioans. Forced to set out around noon because of a delay in getting the pack animals loaded, they marched through the hottest part of the day without water. The water wagons had not been loaded and no water was found along the dusty route through the chaparral.

The volunteer division reached the small city of Cerralvo on September 10 and were at Marin on the 17th. The last 25 miles to Monterrey were through country less parched. Monterrey lay immediately at the foot of the lofty Sierra Madre Mountains and, even from afar, the men could clearly see the two peaks, the Saddle and the Miter, which flank the city on the west and east, respectively. There was little time to admire the mountain scenery as the column pressed on toward Monterrey. They arrived at a small forest called the Grove of Santo Domingo on September 19 and halted there, two miles north of Monterrey, to prepare for battle.

Monterrey was spread out for a little over a mile on the north bank of a small river, the Santa

Catarina, which flows out of the mountains from the west. The valley through which it drains provided, at that time, the route for the only road connecting the eastern plains (*Tierra Caliente*) and the central plateau of the country. Beyond the mountains on this road lay the city of Saltillo. Reconnaissance parties on September 19 and 20 could easily see that the road into the city was guarded by a formidable fortress, the Citadel, and that the eastern side of the city was guarded by a series of smaller fortresses, La Teneria, El Diablo and Libertad. The western approaches to the city and the road to Saltillo were commanded by two fortifications situated on the hill called the Miter. Fort Independence (*Fuerte Independencia*) was high on the hill. The Bishop's Castle was lower down. Both overlooked the city. Across the Santa Catarina River from Fort Independence were two smaller forts, Soldada and Federacion, which overlooked the Saltillo Road from a spur of the Sierra Madre. Hidden from the view of the reconnaissance parties was a small tributary stream that ran east-to-west through the city separating the northern suburbs from the city center. That stream was bridged at only one point and fortifications were thrown up the entire length of the stream. They also could not see that almost every street in the city was heavily barricaded.

The Battle of Monterrey got underway in earnest on the afternoon of September 20 when General Worth's Division (Fifth, Seventh and Eighth Infantry Regiments), supported by one regiment of Texas Rangers, was sent far to the west of the city to block the Saltillo Road and, if possible, carry the forts defending the road. Arriving about dusk, Worth halted and bivouacked just out of range of the guns of Fort Independence.

The next morning, Worth was to commence his assault of the western forts while the bulk of Taylor's army demonstrated against the eastern defenses of the city. After an early breakfast, August Kautz joined the remainder of the Volunteer Division on a march on the Marin Road to a low rise overlooking Monterrey from about a mile away. General Twiggs's Division (First, Third and Fourth Infantry Regiments and Second Dragoon Regiment) moved in line to the left of the Volunteer Division. Unfortunately the position was within range of the heavy guns in the Citadel, leaving the two divisions under a steady fire. The battery of light artillery assigned to the Volunteer Division returned the fire, but without effect.

Meanwhile, Worth had brushed aside two regiments of Mexican cavalry and had occupied the group of huts known as San Jeronimo on the Saltillo Road west of the Miter.

In order to prevent General Ampudia from reinforcing his defenses west of the city, Taylor sent the First and Third Infantry to the east of the city as a diversion and, if possible, to assault the outermost fortification (Fort Teneria). The movement of this strong brigade, commanded by Lt. Colonel John Garland, drew the fire of the cannoneers inside the Citadel, giving the Volunteer Division a break from the steady fire they had been under, allowing them to watch undisturbed as Garland's Brigade advanced on Teneria. Thinking that he might be able to more profitably assault Teneria from the rear, Garland moved his force to the right of the fort and began to circle around it to the west. This unfortunate move left the flank of his brigade under fire from the cannons at El Diablo and those hidden within the town in addition to that from the five guns in Teneria. So heavy was the fire that the smoke obscured from the view of the volunteers on the small rise the fact that Garland's Brigade was cut to pieces. Only when wounded and discouraged men began to pour to the rear did Kautz and his comrades realize that the assault had failed. The sound of fire coming from the cloud of smoke did, however, indicate that a large part of Garland's Brigade was still before the fortress.

General Taylor, from his position on the rise of ground, ordered three regiments of volunteers to the rescue. General Quitman with the Mississippi and Tennessee Regiments moved directly toward Teneria while General Hamer led the First Ohio into the northeastern suburbs. General Butler rode with the Ohio regiment.

As the Ohioans entered the town, they were exposed to heavy musket and cannon fire from their front. Unable to determine from where the fire was coming, they were powerless to respond.

They halted several blocks west of the stream running through the city. They were screened and somewhat protected by a thick hedgerow. Word reached them from an officer who had been with Garland's Brigade that Garland's attack on Teneria had been repulsed and he advised Butler to retreat from the city. Before the order to retreat could be carried out, Butler learned from General Taylor that Quitman's assault on Teneria had been successful and that the Mexicans had abandoned the fort and fallen back into the city. Butler then ordered the First Ohio to move to its left to a point east of the bridge, where they waded across the stream in good order, reaching an open area within sight of El Diablo about noon.

Kautz had been one of the first to cross the stream. Immediately after reaching the opposite bank, his rifle was knocked from his hand by a musket ball which "struck near the shank of the bayonet, wrenching it half way around over the ketch so tightly that I found difficulty in getting it off."[6]

Besides the small arms fire, his company had come under heavy fire from the cannons in the fort and from batteries near the bridge. The fire from their right flank was especially devastating and both General Butler and Colonel Mitchell were among the wounded, leaving the regiment nominally under the command of the regimental adjutant, Lieutenant Colonel John B. Weller, a former congressman from Ohio who would later be governor of California and minister to Mexico. General Hamer, however, was giving the orders.

The obvious move was to retreat, which they did with some difficulty. As they emerged from the city into open country they were attacked by two regiments of lancers from the direction of the Citadel. The lancers were repulsed with a single volley, but not before they "lanced" a great number of wounded soldiers who were being treated by surgeons in the open ground just to the west of the First Ohio's position.

The First Ohio then took up positions near Teneria and saw no more action on the 21st. After dark they returned to the Grove of Santo Domingo.

Worth's Division west of the city was also busy on the 21st. Beginning about noon, portions of his command stormed the two fortifications (Soldada and Federacion) south of the Santa Catarina River and occupied them shortly before dark.

Both armies felt satisfaction in a job well done after the fighting of the 21st. Both knew there was more work to be done. Casualty figures for the Americans on the one day totaled 394 killed and wounded.[7] The Mexicans' losses were smaller.

The next day, September 22, was quiet east of the city except for sporadic artillery fire. To the west, however, Worth had his regulars and some of the dismounted Texas Rangers in motion at 3 A.M. In fierce and exhausting fighting which lasted until nightfall, the rocky 800-foot-high Miter was scaled, Fort Independence was captured and, after a determined counterattack by the Mexicans, the Bishop's Castle was taken as well.

On the morning of September 23, Taylor learned that Ampudia had abandoned El Diablo and had set up strong lines around the city's center. Of the city's fortresses, only the Citadel was now occupied by the Mexicans. A slow and cautious advance on all fronts was ordered and much of Taylor's army was engaged in house-to-house combat throughout the day. Artillery fire from Fort Teneria and the forts atop the Miter was supplemented by light artillery batteries which accompanied the assaulting infantry. The Mexicans were driven back into the plaza in the center of the city. Shortly after noon, Hamer's Brigade was moved into Fort Teneria to replace Quitman's Brigade, and there they stayed through the night of September 23.

About 3 A.M. on the 24th, a messenger arrived at the Teneria under a flag of truce with an offer to surrender the city. General Hamer escorted him to Taylor's headquarters at the Grove of Santo Domingo, where the terms of surrender were negotiated throughout the day and into the night. On the morning of September 25, the terms of surrender were announced and August Kautz learned that the Battle of Monterrey was over.

After the surrender, Worth's Division garrisoned the city and the remainder of the army went into camp at Santo Domingo. Camp life was now more satisfying for August Kautz than it had been at the other camps his unit had occupied. Common dangers had engendered a camaraderie among the men of his company and, as the volunteers became more skilled at maneuvers and drills, an *esprit de corps* formed among them.

Early in November, General Taylor sent Worth's Division over the Sierra Madre to the city of Saltillo and marched off to the east toward Victorio with most of the remainder of his army, leaving the Fourth Infantry behind in Monterrey and First Ohio and First Kentucky Regiments at Santo Domingo.

Disease was again a problem, but not so severe as it had been at Belknap and Camargo. One of those who died, however, was Thomas Hamer. The Brown County men were dismayed to learn on the morning of December 3 of his death the evening before. In a letter home dated December 3, a private soldier of Company G wrote, "The whole camp to-day is shrouded in gloom. All seem to feel the greatness of their loss.... To me it seems I have almost lost a father."[8] According to Luther Giddings, "The whole camp, from the commander-in-chief down to the roughest soldier in the ranks, esteemed him and lamented his death."[9]

Hamer had contracted dysentery while at Camp Belknap, but was seemingly recovering at the time of the battle at Monterrey. The illness returned shortly after he learned that he had been reelected to the U.S. House of Representatives (the election had occurred on October 13) and grew steadily worse. He then developed yellow fever about November 30.

Kautz was present at Hamer's funeral which was conducted on December 4 with full military honors. Hamer's remains were later disinterred and returned to Brown County. George Kautz was in the crowd, estimated between 8000 and 20,000, who lined the streets of Georgetown to view the funeral procession from his home to the Old Georgetown Cemetery on February 15, 1847.

General Hamer seems to have been a positive influence in the life of August Kautz during these, his formative years. Of course, he was much admired and respected by many who knew him. According to U.S. Grant, "I have always believed that, had his life been spared, he would have been President of the United States during the term filled by President Franklin Pierce."[10]

After Hamer's death, Sanders Johnson, Hamer's law partner and son-in-law, resigned as captain of Co. G to return to his law practice in Georgetown. Carr B. White, the son of August's former schoolmaster, was appointed to the vacant post. He commanded the company for the remainder of its tenure in Mexico.

Less than two weeks after Hamer's death, intelligence reached Taylor that the Mexican Army was planning a move against Saltillo. He ordered General Butler, who commanded the volunteers, to hasten to Saltillo. The fifty-mile march to Saltillo was a difficult one, at first following the Santa Catarina River through a broad valley, then rising to cross the lofty Sierra Madre Mountains through two high passes. The First Ohio and First Kentucky made the 50-mile march without the aid of wagons or mules in three days.

Upon reaching Saltillo, it was learned that no Mexican troops were in the vicinity. The climate of the high plain on which Saltillo is located is far cooler than that at Monterrey. The men, having marched across the Sierra Madre without benefit of tents and without winter clothing, suffered severely from the cold. On the first day of January they began the return march to Monterrey, arriving on January 4. After their return, August Kautz and his regiment were comfortably housed in the city, which had been all but abandoned by its former inhabitants.

About the end of January, General Taylor was ordered to send all of his regular Army troops to the coast preparatory to a campaign against the city of Vera Cruz, leaving eight regiments of volunteer infantry and a few artillery under Taylor's command.

None of the Ohio regiments were involved in the Battle of Buena Vista (south of Saltillo) on February 23 in which Taylor, with but a few regiments of volunteers, defeated a Mexican army numbering almost 20,000. That action virtually ended the war in northern Mexico, although there were still major battles on the east coast and around Mexico City to be fought before the war was over.

The First Ohio remained at Monterrey until late in May. They then marched back to the Rio Grande and sailed to New Orleans, and were mustered out of the service on June 14, 1847. Kautz wrote that, as the Brown County men of Company G disembarked from the boat at Higginsport, they "found the banks black with people who were waiting to welcome us.... The enthusiasm of all was at its highest and I, myself, never felt so proud or so well repaid for the year's hardship as at that moment."[11]

Kautz's experiences in the Mexican War had so impressed him that he yearned to return to military life. He even considered attempting to enlist as a private in the regular Army. Finally, August's father sought the aid of Representative Jonathan D. Morris to have him appointed to the U.S. Military Academy. Morris, who had been elected to fill the seat in the U.S. House of Representatives vacated by the death of Hamer, agreed to nominate August. August received a letter of acceptance to West Point on March 20, 1848.

4. The Academy

Of the five Ohioans who graduated from the United States Military Academy on July 1, 1852, all would rise to the rank of major general or brevet major general in the Union Army during the Civil War. Despite their later successes, only one, David S. Stanley, ranked high academically while at the Academy. This should not surprise us. On the average, the "Western boys" had received less formal education prior to entering the Academy than their classmates from the East. The other Ohioans were George Crook, Charles R. Woods, Alexander M. McCook, and Kautz.

To this list of five young men might be added the name of Philip Sheridan, who began his West Point career with the class of 1852, but was set back a year for disciplinary reasons and graduated in 1853.

These were not the only future generals in the class of 1852. Others were George Hartsuff, Milo Hascall, John Hawkins and Henry Slocum of the Union Army, and George Anderson, George Cosby, Henry Davidson and John Forney, who fought for the Confederacy.

Kautz's class ranking (35th of 43)[1] reflects his humble preparatory education, limited to the seven or eight years in John White's 2-room schoolhouse. At the Academy, he did best in French, horsemanship and engineering.[2] He seems to have had a knack for languages and had ridden horses since early childhood. His good standing in engineering classes, taught by Professor Dennis Hart Mahan,[3] was due less to his understanding of engineering science than to his remarkable talent as a draftsman.

Also among Kautz's professors was Lieutenant George H. Thomas, who taught military tactics. Although Kautz did not score well in Thomas's class, the future "Rock of Chichamauga" left a lasting impression on Kautz. Thomas had distinguished himself in the Mexican War and had been breveted to captain and to major for gallantry exhibited at the Battles of Monterrey and Buena Vista. Thomas was known for his dignified manners and stately bearing, qualities which the young Kautz attempted to emulate.

The superintendent at the Academy during Kautz's time there was Captain Henry Brewerton, an 1819 graduate of the Academy, an engineer. He was appointed superintendent in 1845 and was replaced in September 1852 by Robert E. Lee.

While at West Point, Kautz was already developing a reputation as a hard worker and for his "methodical, analytical approach to problems."[4] His record of conduct in his four years as a cadet was almost spotless. He is known to have received no demerits in his first year (only four others in his class and fourteen members of all four classes shared this distinction). The only disciplinary action in surviving records appeared in October 1851. Kautz and Cadet Francis R.T. Nicholls were released from arrest and returned to duty on October 14, 1851, and they were to perform extra guard duty for offenses committed more than a month before. The nature of their offenses is not recorded.

Kautz's roommate for most of his time at West Point was Henry de Veuve, a Louisianan,

Among August Kautz's friends at the U.S. Military Academy were (*left to right*) George Crook, Philip Sheridan and John Nugen. Crook and Sheridan would continue to be Kautz's closest friends in the army throughout their lives. After John Nugen's untimely death in 1857, Kautz served as executor of his estate and also named his first-born son Nugen in honor of his friend. This photo, taken in the summer of 1853, shows Crook and Nugen in the uniforms of brevet second lieutenants in the army while Sheridan, having been set back for disciplinary reasons, still wears the uniform of an academy cadet. U.S. Military Academy Library Archives.

who retired from the army after one year and would later serve as a captain of engineers in the Confederate Army. His circle of friends included George Crook, Philip Sheridan, Alexander McCook, John Nugen, Charles R. Woods and George Mendell from his own class and John M. Schofield and Francis Nicholls of the class of 1853. It is noteworthy that two of the group (Sheridan and Schofield) would become commander-in-chief of U.S. Army before the end of the 19th century.

Probably only Crook and Sheridan could be called close friends and, although the relationship with Sheridan became somewhat strained in the 1870s, it survived.

During his years at West Point, Kautz picked up the nickname "Dutch." The name appears to have stayed with him — at least among his old friends— and appears in letters between Sheridan and William T. Sherman in the 1870s and in George Crook's autobiography written in 1888. Crook used the more familiar "old Dutch Kautz."

After his graduation, Brevet Second Lieutenant August Kautz was delighted to be assigned to the Fourth U.S. Infantry Regiment, the regiment of his West Point tactics instructor, George Thomas, and of fellow Brown Countian, Ulysses Grant. Kautz's Mexican War unit, the First Ohio Volunteers, had fought alongside the Fourth Infantry at the Battle of Monterrey, and Kautz was aware of the record of the regiment in subsequent battles of the Mexican War.

The Fourth Infantry had been authorized by an Act of Congress on May 30, 1796. It had participated actively in the War of 1812, the Seminole Wars and the Mexican War. In the summer of 1852 it was sent via the Isthmus of Panama to the West Coast and assigned to posts in

California and Oregon Territory. Cholera struck the regiment during the march across the Isthmus and 107 men died before reaching California.

Along with classmates John Nugen, John Mullan and George Crook, Kautz boarded a steamer at New York City on November 4, 1852, to begin the journey via the Isthmus of Nicaragua to join their regiments on the West Coast. Nicaragua was chosen to avoid the diseases which had stricken the Fourth Infantry in Panama. Crook, in his biography written in the late 1880s, somehow fails to impress us with the hazards of the journey, but stresses, sometimes humorously, the journey's discomforts. "The ocean steamer, smell of bilge water, the motion of the ship, and the vastness of the ocean — add to these the deathly sea sickness which overcame me near Sandy Hook — did not prepossess me in favor of that mode of travel.... Although I had my life yet before me ... so great was my aging during this sea sickness that I was indifferent to life, and could care but little whether the vessel went to the bottom or not."[6]

Arriving at San Juan del Norte, Nicaragua, the passengers were transferred to small river steamers for the trip up the San Juan River to Lake Nicaragua. The next 12-mile leg of the journey was a mule ride from Lake Nicaragua to San Juan del Sur on the Pacific Coast. The route was "one gigantic mudhole, places where mule and rider would almost sink out of sight. The most of us reached the port that evening one mass of mud from head to foot. Some time during the night Dutch Kautz came trudging along, carrying his carpet sack; said the last he saw of his mule was its ears sticking out of the mud. The next day we washed in the sea, clothes and all."[7]

The four young officers parted company in San Francisco on December 1, 1852. John Mullan, who had been assigned to the First Artillery, reported to the headquarters of that unit. George Crook and John Nugen were assigned to Companies F and B, respectively, of the Fourth Infantry at Benicia Barracks, California. Kautz was assigned to Company C of the Fourth Infantry, stationed, along with regimental headquarters, at Columbia Barracks[8] across the Columbia River from Portland, Oregon. He had arrived by mid-December.

5. The Fourth U.S. Infantry

The Fourth Infantry, commanded by Lieutenant Colonel Benjamin L.E. Bonneville,[1] was scattered in small detachments at facilities from San Francisco to Puget Sound. The largest was that of five companies at Columbia Barracks. August Kautz was elated to have an opportunity to meet First Lieutenant Ulysses Grant, the regimental quartermaster, and the two shared tales of their early lives and talked a bit of the Mexican War.

Before Kautz could become comfortable at his new post, he was ordered to carry some dispatches to the Wallawa Valley east of the Cascade Mountains. Setting off alone, he attempted to cross the mountains by the previously uncharted Natches Pass. The trail over the pass was hazardous even in summer. It was foolhardy to attempt the crossing in the dead of winter, but Kautz made the attempt. After losing one of his two horses and almost his life in the snow-covered mountains, he continued on. Upon reaching the valley of the Yakima River, he found his way via the Emigrant Road to the town of The Dalles. There is no indication that the dispatches were delivered.

On March 2, 1853, Washington Territory was created from the northern half of the previous Oregon Territory and, coincident with its creation, Company C of the Fourth Infantry was sent to Fort Steilacoom near the southern extreme of Puget Sound.

Fort Steilacoom had been occupied by a company of the First Artillery Regiment since 1849. Prior to that it had been an outpost of the Puget Sound Agricultural Company, a subsidiary of the Hudson's Bay Company, which had its headquarters at Fort Nisqually, seven miles to the north. According to Kautz's description, "The buildings were very primitive, being built of logs of small fir saplings with the bark on. The chincks were daubed with clay, which constituted the interior finish."[2] In addition to the buildings, the fort included a farm of about 600 acres.

The fort was located less than two miles inland from Carr Inlet near the mouth of the Nisqually River, which drains the southern and western slopes of Mount Rainier, forty miles to the southeast. That massive volcanic peak dominated the southeastern skyline. On a clear day, the snow-clad peaks of the Olympic Mountains could be seen on the western horizon. All of the area around Puget Sound from the Pacific Coast to the Cascade Mountains was dominated by virgin forests, mostly of evergreens. Here and there, over the centuries, forest fires had cleared spaces within the forest, forming openings in the forest called prairies. The Puget Sound Indians had for many years dug camas roots and harvested other edibles from the prairies and had helped to keep them open by controlled burning. After contact with white men of the Hudson's Bay Company, some of the Indians became proficient farmers.

The Nisqually Indians numbered fewer than 1000. Other closely related tribes and subgroups lived nearby, including the Puyallup, Colwitz, Chehalis, Squaxim, Yakama, Snoqualmie, Skagit and Kikealis. The lifestyle of the Nisquallies and their neighbors was far different from that of the nomadic Plains Indians. They were fishermen more than hunters and, to a lesser extent, farmers,

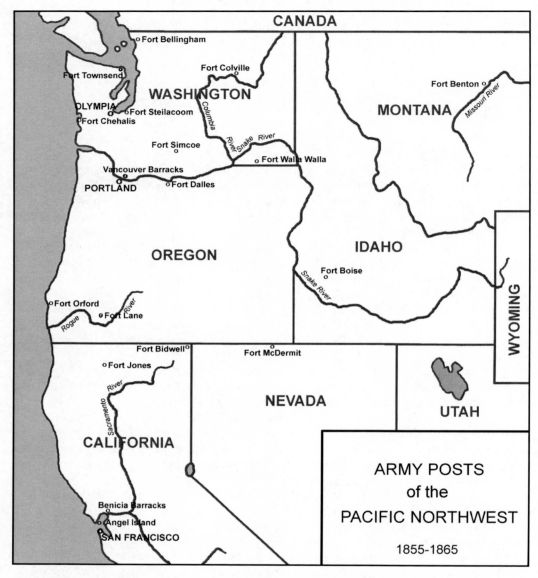

Map showing the location of most of the army posts in the Pacific Northwest during Kautz's stay there.

and lived in permanent settlements. For the most part, the various tribes lived at peace with one another. Only the Snoqualmies were of a warlike nature and were, therefore, feared by the other tribes. Intertribal marriages were common. The Indians tolerated the presence of the British fur traders and welcomed the trade goods which they received in exchange for pelts. They even accepted to some extent the religion brought by French Catholic missionaries who accompanied the fur traders. They rarely showed animosity toward the Americans, but they were not inclined to be overly friendly.

The day after his arrival at Fort Steilacoom, Kautz rode with "two gentlemen of the post" to take his first view of Puget Sound. He noted in his journal, "I could not control my admiration of the beauty of the scene."[3]

The spring passed pleasantly enough for Kautz. He received word of his promotion to the permanent rank of second lieutenant effective March 24, 1853. He had been appointed adjutant of the company and was responsible for guard duty and drilling of the company. He later said of this period,

> I began to have a realizing sense of what life in the army was likely to be. There was little to do, but it had to be done at certain hours and in a prescribed manner, and served to interrupt any self-imposed pursuit on the outside. A certain class of our visitors always caused the introduction of cards and playing for stakes. As I had forsworn cards, I was never included in the game, but in order to fill my leisure time I laid out a plan of reading and writing. I wrote a few letters to the New York Herald and the Spirit of the Times, but this was only a fraction of what I desired and mentally resolved to do. I soon realized that army life in garrison was one of laziness. It soon required effort to hunt or ride on the plains or go fishing.[4]

Kautz made friends quickly with the post's surgeon, Dr. John M. Haden, and with the company's quartermaster and commissary officer, Second Lieutenant William A. Slaughter, but had some trouble getting along with the haughty and aloof company commander, Captain DeLancey Floyd-Jones. Floyd-Jones was from an aristocratic Long Island family and had difficulty relating to either Kautz or Slaughter, a Kentuckian. According to Kautz, Floyd-Jones "was a man of good habits, and very reputable in his personal conduct. We only differed on one subject. He affected too much devotion to the conventionalities of aristocracy and family inheritance.... He was conspicuous for being the only man in the country who changed his shirt every day, which, in those days, certainly exhibited unpardonable pride.... He was rather devoid of tact."[5] Kautz failed to mention that Floyd-Jones had been promoted to captain to fill the vacancy created by the resignation of U.S. Grant.[6]

Slaughter, unlike Floyd-Jones, had a delightful sense of humor which endeared him to all who knew him. Ulysses S. Grant in his memoirs tells an interesting story about Slaughter which reminds us somewhat of George Crook. Grant says, "In the regiment there was a Lieutenant Slaughter who was very liable to sea-sickness. It almost made him sick to see the waves of a table-cloth when the servants were spreading it. Soon after his graduation, Slaughter was ordered to California and took passage by a sailing vessel going around Cape Horn. The vessel was seven months making the voyage, and Slaughter was sick every moment of the time, never more so than while lying at anchor after reaching his place of destination. On landing in California he found orders which had come by the Isthmus, notifying him of a mistake in his assignment; he should have been ordered to the northern lakes. He started back by the Isthmus route and was sick all the way. But when he arrived in the East he was again ordered to California, this time definitely, and at this date was making his third trip. He was as sick as ever, and had been so for more than a month while lying at anchor in the bay. I remember him well, seated with his elbows on the table in front of him, his chin between his hands, and looking the picture of despair. At last he broke out, 'I wish I had taken my father's advice; he wanted me to go into the navy; if I had done so, I should not have had to go to sea so much.'"[7]

Grant failed to mention that Slaughter was married during his return trip to the East. His wife, Mary, was the only white woman at Fort Steilacoom. She managed the officers' mess and Kautz enjoyed her company.

Besides the three officers and the surgeon, Company C was made up of about forty enlisted men. The nominal strength of an infantry company at the time was eighty men, but like almost all of the units of the frontier army, it was woefully under strength. The problem was magnified for the Fourth Infantry because of losses suffered in the Mexican War and on the journey across Panama.

"In April 1853, a number of reports of trouble with the Indians were sent to the commanding officer [Floyd-Jones] from the settlements along the lower Sound. White men had disappeared and were supposed to have been killed by Indians."[8]

In May, Kautz was ordered, along with a sergeant and ten men, to make a reconnaissance down Puget Sound. The party was supplied with a ship's launch with two sails and thirty days rations. Kautz was informed that the purpose of the expedition was to arrest any Indian suspected of murdering whites or any white man suspected of selling liquor to the Indians, but he thought the main "object of the expedition was to intimidate the Indians." He noted somewhat humorously, "When the strength of my command is considered in connection with the hordes of Indians then to be found along the shores of the waters of Puget Sound the absurdity of the order becomes apparent. This is more evident now than it was then, for at the time our mission seemed to partake merely of dangers, and not of folly."

On May 23, the party set out down the Narrows. They lunched at Day Island, "a beautiful piece of land covered by an impenetrable pyramidal forest," and camped that night on the eastern shore of Vashon Island. They then continued on to the Strait of Juan de Fuca. During the voyage, they learned from a settler that a man named Church had been murdered by an Indian named Sla-hai, who was half Kikealis and half Skagit.

By June 11, they had returned as far as Whidby Island, where it was learned that both George Sna-te-cum, chief of the Skagits, and Patch-ka-num,[9] chief of the Kikealis, were camped nearby. Kautz set about to capture the two chiefs to hold them responsible for having Sla-hai arrested. Patch-ka-num was indeed captured, but he quickly escaped by cutting a hole in the back of the tent in which he was being held prisoner.

On June 12, Kautz, "very anxious to make amends for my bungling," convinced the white settlers in the area to take up donations to use as a bribe to induce the Indians to turn Sla-hai in. Not able to wait longer, Kautz sailed over to Camano Island, where it was learned that the band to which Sla-hai belonged was encamped at the mouth of the Skagit River on the mainland. Feigning a return to Fort Steilacoom, Kautz and his party started south, then turned back north toward the mouth of the Skagit in an attempt to surprise and capture Sla-hai. The Indians got wind of the deception and hurriedly decamped. Kautz then gave up the search and started back to Steilacoom. The party reached the mouth of the Nisqually River at 1 A.M. on June 19.

Kautz was not satisfied with the results of the expedition, but later saw it as a valuable learning experience for the young, inexperienced officer that he was. The extract ends with the following: "Thus ended my first tour of independent duty, which has become an interesting memory. At that time I felt that we had failed in the object of the expedition, but considering that we were gone a month and that there was not a sailor in the party, it is a matter of wonder that we all returned alive and well, especially if we take into consideration the number of expert sailors who have since drowned in the same waters."

Soon events in Oregon would have Kautz on the move again.

6. Fort Orford

After Oregon Territory was annexed to the United States by treaty with Great Britain in 1846, its first territorial governor was the energetic, persuasive and self-promoting Joseph Lane. Lane, a native of North Carolina, had served in the Indiana House and Senate. He enlisted as a private in the Mexican War and rose to brevet major general. President Polk named him governor of Oregon Territory in 1848. With the governorship came an appointment as Superintendent of Indian Affairs, and Lane set about with some success to pacify the Indian tribes under his jurisdiction. He managed to make twenty-five treaties with various Indian tribes, none of which was ever ratified. In a letter to the Secretary of War in May 1850, Lane wrote, "I am happy to say that our relations ... with all the tribes, with the exception of the Shasta or Rogue River Indians, are of the most friendly character."[1] The Rogue River Valley and its native population would continue to be a problem.

Lane's assessment of the total situation was overly optimistic, but he was correct that the Rogue River area posed a problem. After Oregon gained territorial status, the influx of settlers arriving over the Oregon Trail increased exponentially. By 1851, the Rogue River Valley was beginning to fill with families of white settlers. When gold was discovered in 1851, prospectors and speculators further increased the white population. In addition, the major route to the gold country of California passed through the valley, adding a transient population of young, usually poor and often lawless men. That clashes would occur between the whites and Indians in the Rogue River Valley was inevitable.

In the spring of 1853, Anson Dart was replaced as Superintendent of Indian Affairs by Joel Palmer. Despite Palmer's attempts to maintain peace, tension increased. On June 7, 1853, a settler named Isaac Hill led a party of volunteers who attacked an Indian village near the town of Ashland, killing six of the Indians. The Indians retaliated by attacking a nearby immigrant camp. Through the summer, the conflict escalated until, in early August, companies of volunteers numbering about 300 men gathered all of the isolated families in the valley into a few locations and set off to capture the perpetrators of the latest Indian depredations. They were led by Captain Bradford Alden, who had come up from Fort Jones, California, with twelve members of the Fourth Infantry. On August 15, Alden, seeing that the volunteers under his command were lacking rifles, sent a request through the office of Governor George Curry to Colonel Bonneville at Vancouver Barracks for aid in the form of an artillery piece and additional rifles and ammunition. This request brought Lieutenant August Kautz to southern Oregon.

On August 24, Kautz was ordered to Vancouver Barracks, where he was put in charge of a 12-pounder howitzer and a crew of six artillerymen from the First Artillery and sent to the Rogue River. Governor Curry provided an escort in the form of a volunteer company raised by James W. Nesmith, who met Kautz at the town of Albany. "After a toilsome march, dragging the howitzer and other materials of war through the Umpqua Canyon, and up and down mountain trails, made slippery by recent rains, we arrived at General Lane's encampment on Rogue River ... on the 8th day of September."[2]

Meanwhile, Captain Alden had gotten his unruly volunteers organized and moved out on August 15 to pursue a band of Indians led by a minor chief known to the whites as Sam. A minor engagement took place near Evans Creek on August 17.

Four days later, Joseph Lane, temporarily back home from his congressional duties, arrived on the scene with a small detachment of volunteers from his home in Roseburg. Captain Alden deferred to Lane's volunteer rank of brigadier general and Lane took over the entire command.

After a pursuit of a few miles, Lane and Alden caught up with the main force of the Rogue River Indians about 15 miles north of Table Rock. On the morning of August 24, they surprised the Indian camp and fought a brief but bloody battle. In the initial engagement, Alden was severely wounded.[3] Lane then personally led an assault and was wounded by a rifle ball in his right arm near the shoulder. Despite the wounding of their two leaders, the Oregon volunteers prevailed. During the afternoon, the Indians called for a parley, asking for an end to hostilities. The two parties met at Table Rock on September 4 and a treaty was agreed to on September 8, the same day that Kautz arrived on the scene with the howitzer.[4]

On September 10, the Treaty of Table Rock was signed and, unlike the treaties made by Lane and Dart, it was ratified by the U.S. Congress the following April. The treaty bore the marks of several of the chiefs and the signatures of Palmer and Indian Agent Samuel H. Culver. August Kautz and Joseph Lane signed as witnesses. It provided cession of a large part of the Rogue River Valley to the whites for $60,000 and provided a temporary reservation for the Indians. Also included in the treaty were paragraphs dealing with the free passage of immigrant parties through the valley and for the arrest of persons, Indian or white, who might violate the treaty.

Unfortunately, the Treaty of Table Rock did not end hostilities. Through the winter of 1853–54, small bands of the Rogue River Indians and other Indians, nearing starvation, raided through the valley. Whites, most often gold miners, committed atrocities against the Indians as well and the Rogue River War continued.

In September 1853, it had been decided to construct a small fort in the Rogue River Valley in an effort to enforce the provisions of the Table Rock Treaty and to protect the uneasy peace that resulted from the treaty. The site chosen was the army encampment near Table Rock. The fort was named Fort Lane. The dragoon company of A.J. Smith was conveniently at hand and that unit was detailed to garrison Fort Lane.

August Kautz and a detachment of 25 men of Company M of the First Artillery were ordered to Fort Orford to fill the void left by the departure of A.J. Smith's dragoons and to offer support to the Indian Agent at Fort Orford, F.W. Smith. In the order, Kautz was named commander of the fort.

Fort Orford was on the coast 50 miles north of the Oregon-California border, midway between the mouths of the Coquille and Rogue Rivers. The fort had been built in 1851 to protect the adjacent town of Port Orford, established only a year before, after gold was found on the nearby beaches.

Kautz arrived at Fort Orford on October 17, 1853. Neither he nor Agent Smith had much to do. As a result of the lack of trouble around Fort Orford, most of Kautz's garrison were sent to other points where they were needed more. Nonetheless, Joel Palmer, in a letter dated December 3, 1853, warned Smith that it was "important to be on good terms with the Cis-ti-costas."[5] Within six weeks of Palmer's warning, trouble was brewing, but it came not from the Indians, but from the whites.

In late January 1854, a group of miners from Coos Bay induced a few of the Port Orford citizens to join them in an expedition to retaliate against the Coquille Indians, some of whom had raided farms near Coos Bay. Thirty vigilantes marched across the Coastal Range to the valley of the Coquille River and, on January 26, attacked a village near the ferry where the Oregon-California Trail crosses the river. Sixteen of the Coquilles were killed, including two women.

The miners reported that the Indians were heavily armed. The village attacked was guilty of no wrongdoing.

Three days later, Kautz and Sub-agent Smith departed for the Coquille River Valley to investigate reports that both the Indians and whites were preparing for hostilities. It was not until Kautz and Smith arrived on the Coquille that they learned of the killings. There they met a minor chief of the Coquilles and thirty of his followers, who denied the charges of the whites. In his report to Superintendent Palmer dated February 5, Smith noted that the Indians "gave up all their guns amounting to only three serviceable. As to powder and ball, I do not believe they have five rounds." Smith's report went on to complain that the whites, rather than the Indians, were the more responsible for the tension between the two races. He added, "If such murderous assaults continue, there will be no end of Indian wars in Oregon."[6]

Smith made the mistake of allowing portions of his report to be published in the newspapers of San Francisco. This so inflamed the miners that credible threats were made on Smith's life. Smith resigned.

Kautz, like Smith, was disturbed by the Coquille River massacre and he, too, had read the San Francisco papers. In his official report to General John E. Wool,[7] commander of the Department of the Pacific, Kautz remarked, "From all that we could gather ... there does not appear to have been sufficient cause to justify such a hasty attack." He added, "I make this statement in order that the Commanding General may not be misled by newspaper statements."[8]

Superintendent Palmer was becoming increasingly frustrated at the shortage of troops at the growing number of forts in Oregon Territory. In a letter to General Wool on May 12, 1854, Palmer made a request that additional troops be sent. He was careful to note that the whites were as responsible as were the Indians for the friction between the two races. Wool's adjutant answered on May 17 that additional troops were on the way, including "one sergeant, two corporals and twenty men to Lt. Kautz at Port Orford."[9] It is doubtful that this meager supplementation of the garrison was responsible for the period of relative peace which followed. More likely it was the presence of the new Indian agent, Ben Wright.

In the spring of 1854, Palmer appointed Ben Wright as the sub-agent at Fort Orford. It is difficult to understand why Palmer chose Wright. Wright was a native of Indiana who moved from his home at Yreka, California, to take the post at Port Orford. He had come west over the Oregon Trail in 1848 or 1849. Wright was as vehement an Indian-hater as anyone on the Pacific Coast. In 1852, he had organized a company of volunteers (not sanctioned by any federal, state or local government) which set out from Yreka to kill Indians. On November 8, 1852, near Lost River, the company met a party of Modoc Indians and invited them to dinner. When the Indians learned that the food served was poisoned, Wright's volunteers opened fire, killing 40 of the 45 Modocs.[10]

In the spring of 1854, Kautz and Wright held differing views on how to deal with Native Americans. It seems that Wright later came around to Kautz's way of thinking based on a description of Wright by post surgeon Rodney Glisan, who wrote, "After he became Indian Agent, his sympathies seem to lean, if either way, in favor of the Indian, and against the white man. He stood like a wall of adamant between the two races in their numerous quarrels on the coast, in the vicinity of Port Orford. There are many romantic stories related of this rude, but brave and very remarkable man. He was the Kit Carson of the Pacific Coast."[11]

The remainder of 1854 and the first half of 1855 were quiet times at Fort Orford. In fact, relationships between the white and red races were for the most part peaceful throughout all of Oregon and Washington Territories during this period. Doctor Rodney Glisan had arrived at Fort Orford as post surgeon on June 21, 1855, and he and Kautz became close friends. They fished for trout and enjoyed riding together, and both were interested in the mining which occurred along the coast and in the flora and fauna of the region.

In July 1855, Kautz got a taste of the animosity felt by many of the settlers toward those who might take the side of the Indians in any dispute. Some time earlier, he had arrested a citizen for threatening the Indians at the nearby reservation. Dr. Glisan noted in his journal on July 22, "Lieutenant Kautz has involved himself in a civil suit for putting a civilian, who had been creating disturbances among the Indians on the government reserve, in the guardhouse; he confined him six days. The civil authorities have brought a suit for false imprisonment against him. He left this morning to attend his trial at Coos Bay."[12] Unfortunately, Glisan failed to record the result of the trial in his journal.

Kautz and Glisan shared quarters at Fort Orford and as the only officers at the fort, they were responsible for entertaining visitors who might arrive on the steamers which plied the coast between San Francisco and Puget Sound on a regular schedule. One such visitor was John C. Van Tramp, an adventurer who arrived at Fort Orford in October 1855. Van Tramp, in a book describing his travels through the West, seemed surprised that "upon entering the house of Dr. Glisan and Lieutenant Kautz, we were soon engaged in conversation with a party of educated gentlemen, whose cultivated talents shone the more conspicuously in the wild region that duty had made the place of their residence."[13]

In August 1855, a council was planned between Superintendent Joel Palmer and the Tututni, Cis-ti-costa and other small Indian bands who lived along the coast. To be discussed was the setting aside of a reservation on which these Indians would live. Preparatory to the council, Ben Wright was assembling the tribes at a spot about three miles from the mouth of the Rogue River. On August 24, one of the Indians got into a quarrel with a white man and, in the scuffle which followed, the white man was wounded in the shoulder. Wright arrested the Indian. That night, while Wright and the Indian were asleep in a small shack nearby, someone fired into the building, wounding the Indian. The next day, Wright had to hold off a mob of sixty men who were threatening to lynch the Indian until a detachment of fifteen soldiers from Fort Orford arrived on the scene. The Indian was then arraigned by a civil magistrate and was sent up the river by canoe under guard of a squad of soldiers to be imprisoned awaiting trial. Three men appeared on the river bank and fired into the canoe, killing the prisoner and another Indian who was helping to paddle the canoe. The corporal in charge of the soldiers ordered a return of fire and the three offenders were killed. As a result all of the Indians fled the council grounds. After a delay of two weeks, a treaty was signed.[14]

This incident and one or two other minor conflicts so inflamed the Rogue River Indians that they took to the warpath and the bloodiest events of the Rogue River War were to follow.

On September 9, Company H of the Third Artillery,[15] commanded by First Lieutenant John G. Chandler,[16] arrived by steamer from San Francisco to replace the detachment of Company M, which had been under Kautz's command since his arrival at Fort Orford.

On October 8, Kautz commenced an exploration to the Oregon-California Trail intent on mapping a military road from Fort Orford to Fort Lane. He took ten men of the newly-arrived Third Artillery and a local man as guide. When the party neared the Big Bend of the Rogue River, they found the settlers hacking port-holes in the walls of their houses in anticipation of an attack by hostile Rogue River Indians. Those Indians were on the warpath and had killed some settlers, burning farmhouses and other buildings. The whole Rogue River Valley was gearing up for warfare and this was the first Kautz had heard of it.

Not having expected trouble on their mission of exploration, Kautz's men were poorly armed. He left his men to support the settlers and, along with the guide, returned the 45 miles to Fort Orford for additional rations, arms and ammunition. He arrived at the fort at midnight of October 15 and was off the next day with loaded pack animals.

Kautz and his party then continued on their way toward Fort Lane. They reached the Grave Creek Hills when an incident occurred which Dr. Glisen described as follows: "On his way to

Fort Lane, and within 45 miles of that place, he accidently came upon a hostile band of Indians, who attacked him, and killed 2 of his men, and wounded another and himself. He made good his retreat to Bates' Station, where he arrived on the twenty-fifth of October."[17]

Feeling that the settlers who had congregated at Bates' Station might benefit from military support, Kautz left his men there and, again alone, set off to Fort Lane for reinforcements. There he met with Captain A.J. Smith of the First Dragoons, who was still commanding officer at the fort. Smith ordered Captain Edward H. Fitzgerald to go to Bates' Station immediately with sixty of the dragoons.

Fitzgerald's detachment, accompanied by Kautz's small command, moved in the direction of the Indians, who were in the low hills between the valleys of Grave Creek and Wolf Creek. Finding the Indians in an excellent defensive position and far outnumbering his command, Fitzgerald chose to retire from the scene and send for additional reinforcements.

On October 30, A.J. Smith arrived from Fort Lane with about sixty more of the dragoons and 250 volunteers commanded by Colonel John E. Ross. The reason for Smith's delay in arriving is not explained. Perhaps it was due to the delay in getting the volunteers organized.[18] Smith began an assault before dawn on the 31st, but found that the Indians had moved about four miles away to a hill named Hungry Hill. After Smith was finally able to contact his enemy, the battle lasted the rest of the day, but no headway was made. One of the volunteers later recalled that "Owing to the lack of concert among ourselves, I think, the battle became a series of detached skirmishes and sharpshooting, continuing all day; and at night we counted our loss at about twenty-four, that of the enemy almost unknown."[19]

Sporadic firing continued through the night, preventing the soldiers from either eating or sleeping. The Indians launched an attack early the next morning, but were repulsed. Early in the afternoon, Smith, seeing his troops running out of ammunition as well as endurance and his horses and mules out of fodder, ordered a withdrawal.

In the two days of battle, five of the volunteers were killed and twenty wounded, and four of the regulars were killed and six wounded. One of those killed was from Kautz's small party.

The command set up camp along Grave Creek near where it empties into the Rogue River and spent most of November 2 resting and burying their dead before returning to Fort Lane to regroup.

A party of topographical engineers, led by Lieutenant Henry L. Abbot, who were exploring a possible route from the Willamette Valley to Yreka and Fort Jones, were passing through the Rogue River Valley and happened into the camp on November 2. With the engineers was Lieutenant George Crook. Kautz was able to spend several hours with his classmate.[20] Both Crook and Kautz then proceeded to Fort Lane, but they did not meet there. The engineer party was anxious to get on their way and out of danger.

Kautz didn't make it back to Fort Orford until November 18. Several days later, the mail steamer arrived with good news and bad. It seems that the uprising of the Rogue River Indians was part of a more general revolt. The Indians of Washington were also on the warpath and had gotten the upper hand in a number of engagements with the U.S. regulars. On December 4, Kautz's friend, William Slaughter, had been killed. Slaughter's death left a vacancy at the head of Company C of Kautz's Fourth Infantry Regiment. Kautz was offered the command of Company C, then stationed at Fort Steilacoom, Washington. If he should accept, the position came with a promotion to First Lieutenant.

Kautz accepted.

On January 7, 1856, the Steamer *Columbia* arrived at Port Orford from San Francisco. On board was Captain John F. Reynolds[21] of Company H, Third Artillery, who had come to relieve Kautz as commander of Fort Orford. With him he carried orders for Kautz to join his company at Fort Steilacoom. Kautz left on the next available mail steamer for Fort Vancouver.

Four months after Kautz departed, on May 27, 1856, the company of dragoons under Captain A.J. Smith and a company of the Fourth Infantry under Captain Christopher Augur,[22] aided by several hundred volunteers, defeated a large portion of the Rogue River Indians at the Battle of Big Meadows, ending what has become known as the Rogue River War.

7. Fort Steilacoom

On December 18, 1854, U.S. Senator James Shields[1] of Illinois, a member of the Senate Committee on Military Affairs, reported a bill in the Senate entitled "A Bill for the Increase and Better Organization of the Army, and for Other Purposes." The legislation, when finally enacted into law on March 3, 1855, provided a modest increase in pay for Lieutenant Kautz to fifty-seven dollars per month.

The bill also provided two new regiments of infantry, two new regiments of cavalry and four new batteries of artillery for the frontier regulars. One of the new regiments was the Ninth U.S. Infantry.

The Ninth Infantry had served in the Mexican War, but was disbanded in the reorganization of 1848. The Shields Bill authorized its reactivation under Colonel George Wright[2] and Lieutenant Colonel Silas Casey.[3] Recruiting finished, the regiment was ordered to the Pacific Northwest in December 1855. They traveled via the Isthmus of Panama to San Francisco and then on to Vancouver Barracks, where Colonel Wright took command of that post on his arrival. Companies D and H were detailed to Fort Steilacoom under Lieutenant Colonel Casey, who, as ranking officer at the fort, became its commander.

Kautz, having reached Vancouver Barracks by ship, accompanied Companies D and H on their overland march to Fort Steilacoom, arriving with them on January 29, 1856.

Since Kautz had departed Fort Steilacoom in August 1853, the fort had changed little physically, but now it quartered four regiments of infantry and one of dismounted artillery[4] plus eight or ten companies of volunteers. Both the fort and the nearby town were crowded with refugees, fearing possible depredations by the once-friendly Indians. Some of the refugees had built crude blockhouses in the open spaces around the fort. These changes could be attributed to one man, Isaac Stevens.

When Washington was made a separate territory in March 1853, Isaac I. Stevens was named governor of the territory.[5] Stevens, like Joseph Lane, his counterpart in Oregon, was also appointed Superintendent of Indian Affairs for the territory. Lane, as we have seen, respected the Indians as useful individuals and attempted to deal with them as fairly as government policy would allow. Stevens, on the other hand, saw the solution to the Indian problem to be the total annihilation of the Indians. Regardless of their personal opinions, the result would be the same: decimation of the Native American populations and settlement of the survivors on government reservations.

Stevens spent the first eight months of his governorship mapping a potential northern route for a transcontinental railroad. He finally took over as governor in November 1853. After organizing his government, he made a point of extinguishing the last of the British influence in Washington Territory by negotiating the purchase of all the property owned by the Hudson's Bay Company except nearby Fort Nisqually. Then he was off to Washington City to present the results of his railroad explorations and to lobby for funds to improve the infrastructure of

Washington Territory. Acting governor in his absence was Charles H. Mason,[6] the Secretary of the Territory.

In this setting, a minor episode occurred on October 19, 1854, which contributed in part to an eventual general uprising of the Puget Sound Indians. Four Indians who were being held prisoner at Fort Steilacoom escaped. At least one of the four was the alleged killer of the man named Church who had been murdered in May 1853. It is not certain, but among these may have been the men whom Kautz had attempted to capture while exploring the Sound. One of the men was recaptured immediately, but the other three were reported to be at a village named Ho-hum-an on the shore of Hood's Canal.

Lieutenant John Nugen requested the aid of Acting Governor Mason in recapturing the fugitives. Mason arranged for the treasury cutter *Jefferson Davis* to transport a detachment of Company A of the 4th Infantry down Puget Sound and up Hood's Canal to the site of the village. With the aid of the steam paddle-wheeler, SS *Major Tompkins*, the *Jefferson Davis* arrived at the village on November 26. Nugen ordered the surrender of the fugitives, but the Indians refused to comply and fled into the forest. A few rounds fired by the revenue cutter's cannons may have killed as many as five of the Indians. Nugen and his men then burned the village to the ground.

The incident probably would have ended there, but Governor Stevens arrived back from Washington City a few days later. The incident increased his desire to employ his solution to the Indian problem. He demanded that all of the Upper Puget Sound Indians (Indians who had, up to now, lived at peace with both the British and Americans in the area) meet with him at the old Nisqually council ground beside Medicine Creek, about halfway between Fort Steilacoom and Olympia. About 600 of the Indians showed up and Stevens brought with him a treaty which he expected the Indians to sign. On December 26, 1854, he cajoled, threatened and bribed various of the chiefs to sign this, the Medicine Creek Treaty, which ceded an area of Washington Territory on both sides of Upper Puget Sound from the Cascade Range to the Olympic Mountains to the United States in exchange for $32,500 and two reservations totaling about 2500 acres. Sixty-two Indians, hand-picked by Stevens, were signers of the treaty representing the Nisqually, Puyallup, Steilacoom and Squaxim Tribes. Few, if any, of the signers understood the implications of the treaty. They did understand that settlers were claiming land in the prairies which traditionally was used by the Indians for the digging of camas roots and for grazing their animals. To most of the Indians the concept of land ownership was new, but as time went by, some began to grasp its meaning. A treaty, they thought, would provide land ownership for both whites and Indians. The Stevens treaty would provide a meager share for the Indians.

One of those whose name appears on the treaty, Leschi of the Nisquallies, had actually refused to put his mark on the treaty, but an "X" was placed beside his name anyway. Leschi had requested a reservation which would include a portion of the Nisqually River for fishing and a section of prairie land for the tribal horses to graze. Neither need was addressed in the treaty.[7] Stevens was infuriated when Leschi stood up during the council and tore to shreds the paper which named him a "chief" of the Nisquallies and stomped from the treaty grounds.[8] One of those who did sign the treaty, a Nisqually Indian named Tyee Dick, later quoted Leschi as having said to the other Indians, "If you sign that paper, I will go away, but I will come back and get what I want."[9]

Leschi, born in 1808, was one of three children of a Nisqually father and a Klickitat mother. His father was a common man, but his mother was a member of an influential family from east of the Cascades. She was related by blood to Chief Kamiakin of the Klickitats. Her family was wealthy by Native American standards, so her dowry was impressive, including a large herd of horses and other valuables.

Although he was not truly a chief, Leschi was highly esteemed by his fellow Nisquallies and was frequently called upon to act as arbiter in domestic and intratribal disputes. An eloquent speaker in his native language, he spoke the languages of several other tribes, but did not learn English well.

The Nisquallies had previously had a hereditary chief by the name of Lahalet, who had lived within sight of Fort Nisqually. Lahalet died about 1850. At Lahalet's death, the people of the tribe had little respect for Lahalet's son and refused to accept him as a chief, so they had no chief.

Leschi's home was below the point where the small Mashel River enters the Nisqually River on the southern edge of what was called the Nisqually Prairie. There he kept a large herd of horses and cattle and planted some crops. A contemporary of Leschi by the name of Yelm Jim said of him many years later, "He had many horses scattered over the prairies, and had Indian boys to ride after them. He had much money in gold and hiaqua shells, and a good, big heart. He gave much to old sick men and women, and was kind to all people. Whenever there was a potlatch Leschi gave more than anybody."[10]

The King George men (British Canadians of the Hudson's Bay Company) had been at Fort Nisqually for a generation and had brought with them useful trade goods—machine-made clothing, firearms, iron tools, farming implements and medicines—but more importantly, they brought the knowledge of how to use these things. As the Boston men (American settlers) began to arrive on the Oregon Trail in small numbers, Leschi was one of the few members of the tribe to comprehend the potential for economic development which their presence represented. He was always willing to help the settlers. When the first Americans, the party led by James McAllister, arrived in 1845, Leschi rode out to greet them with gifts for the women, and when subscriptions were taken for work on a road over the Cascade Mountains at Natches Pass in 1853, Leschi donated horses to help with work on the road. It should have been clear to Governor Stevens that Leschi was one of the best friends the Bostons had in Washington Territory.

August Kautz, although he was not present at the treaty grounds at Medicine Creek, had this to say in February 1858: "Kanasket was at the council and was cognizant of the miserable piece of fir timber that was given to the Nisquallies. He saw how Leschi was spurned and spoke up in protest. They told him to go away. 'You are half Klickitat; you have nothing to say; the treaty is made.'"[11]

In the next month, Stevens negotiated three additional treaties with other Indian tribes west of the Cascade Range and surrounding Puget Sound. In each case, the Indians were given one year to move to designated reservations. Stevens then traveled east of the Cascades to treat with tribes living there. Although he did manage to get three treaties signed, he was unable to attain the acquiescence of all of those tribes.

A period of unrest followed both east and west of the Cascades. It was clear to the officers at Fort Steilacoom and to the settlers in the Puget Sound area and to the government that the Indians were dissatisfied, none more than the Nisquallies, and none more vocally so than Leschi.

Trouble started east of the Cascades. The Yakama Indian reservation lay along the route of the Oregon Trail and miners moving along the trail on their way to California committed outrages against the Indians. Miners were murdered in retaliation. In September 1855, the agent to the Yakama Indians was brutally murdered. In response, Governor Stevens sent a force of about 100 militia to the area to punish the offenders, but they were repulsed by the Yakamas. The regular Army was called upon to intervene. On October 2, Lieutenant Slaughter left Fort Steilacoom with about 50 men of his company. Captain Granville Haller[12] from The Dalles was to meet Slaughter on the Yakima River with about 100 men of the Fourth Infantry from Vancouver Barracks. Haller ran into a force of 500 to 1500 Yakama Indians under their chief, Kamiakin. When Haller was repulsed, Slaughter wisely retreated to Steilacoom.

Hostilities spread across the Cascades and, in late September and early October, raids by hostile Indians against settlements in the valleys of the Green and White Rivers caused the deaths of nine settlers and the burning of most of their homes.

Most of the settlers throughout the Puget Sound area fled to the towns or to blockhouses for protection. All non-hostile Indians were advised (and, in some instances, forced) to report to their reservations west of the Sound. It is likely that these two measures saved many lives during the hostilities which followed.

Leschi at first looked for ways to keep the Nisquallies out of the fray. In July 1855, he visited his old friend, William Tolmie, of the Hudson's Bay Company, to ask for advice on what action to take. He later met with Acting Governor Mason. He tried to explain to Mason that all he could personally do was to remain a non-combatant himself, but he could not keep others from going to war. His peaceful advances were repulsed. When Leschi and his brother, Quiemuth, were ordered arrested by Mason, they fled toward the Cascade Mountains. Other of the Nisquallies followed him and he, too, became a hostile, although, at first, an unwilling one.

The militia company which was sent to arrest Leschi and Quiemuth was that of Captain Charles Eaton. Eaton's Rangers, as they were called, went to Leschi's home several miles up the Nisqually River on October 24, but found that "the bird had flown, but that the prairie around about abounded with his horses, and other evidence that his absence was only temporary."[13] The pursuit of Leschi led across the Puyallup River toward the White River. On October 27, about two miles shy of the White River, two of Eaton's Company, Lieutenant James McAllister and Michael Connell, were killed by Indians. Eaton gave up the chase when his company was besieged near the Puyallup.

The bird had flown, indeed. Leschi and Quiemuth, forewarned of Eaton's approach, fled with their families to the east only hours before Eaton's arrival, hoping to cross the Cascades to seek refuge with their Klickitat relatives. Upon reaching the Green River, they met up with a camp of about 150 Indians, some of whom had themselves crossed from east of the Cascades to do battle with the soldiers who were attempting to invade their country. Among these were Chiefs Kanasket of the Klickitats and Kamiakin of the Yakamas. Both may have been distant cousins of Leschi on his mother's side of the family. A number of Nisqually Indians had already joined the hostiles and more were to follow behind Leschi. Eventually, between thirty and thirty-five of the hostiles would be Nisquallies and most of the rest would be Puyallups and Duwamish, whose homes were along the White River.

On October 28, the day after the death of James McAllister, several bands of Klickitat Indians from the hostile camp attacked the homes of settlers on the White River, killing nine persons, as mentioned above. Leschi was not involved in the massacre. There is no doubt that Leschi, when driven from his home on October 24, had every intention of going to war. He could, however, not condone the killing of noncombatants and demanded that the other leaders of the hostiles abstain from the practice as well. It is not clear whether it was because of Leschi's presence in the hostile camp or because most of the settlers had fled to the safety of the towns, but there were no more killings of civilians after that time.

As October 1855 ended, all of the U.S. regulars were in the field and were joined by 700 to 1000 volunteers, leaving but ten men under the command of Lieutenant Nugen at Fort Steilacoom. Captain Maurice Maloney[14] was on his way east of the Cascades with Company A, Fourth Infantry and a company of volunteers commanded by Captain Gilmore Hays. Company C, Fourth Infantry under Lieutenant William Slaughter was at a place called Bidding's Prairie one mile east of the Puyallup River. Volunteers were also sent to the Nisqually River and to rivers to the north. Heavy rains had swollen all of the streams and rivers, making operations difficult, and no headway was made.

On October 31, Maloney sent dispatches back to Fort Steilacoom advising of his position and the fact that he had encountered a force of Indians beyond the Cascades much too strong for his small party to engage. He notified Lieutenant Nugen, commanding the fort, that he intended to fall back into the valley of the White River to help protect settlers there. The dispatch rider who carried the message was William Tidd. Because Maloney knew that Tidd would be traveling through country occupied by hostile Indians, he provided an escort of six men: Joseph Miles, Andrew H. Bradley, Antonio B. Rabbeson, George R. Bright, Dr. Matthew P. Burns, and Maloney's volunteer aide-de-camp, A. Benton Moses. Near Connell's Prairie, the party met a group of about 150 Indians who claimed to be friendly and engaged them in conversation for some time. Shortly after leaving the area, the dispatch carriers were ambushed in a swampy area near the White River and two of their number, A. Benton Moses and Joseph Miles, were shot and killed. This brief encounter occurred near the spot where James McAllister and Michael Connell had been killed four days before.

As Maloney and Hays were falling back from their advanced position in the Cascades, they met the Indians who had murdered Moses and Miles. On November 3, they fought an all-day battle with these Indians in which the two small armies fired at each other across the White River at a point where the river could not be forded. After this battle, "which resulted in the expenditure of a good deal of ammunition, but not much blood,"[15] all of the regulars returned to Fort Steilacoom to regroup and resupply themselves. This brief encounter would seem to be of little importance. According to Ezra Meeker, however, it produced a leader among the Indians. Meeker explained, "It is doubtful if the force collected at this time would have ever been consolidated had not ... there suddenly [come] upon them the vanguard of Maloney's returning expedition. The Indians barely had time to get their main forces across the river before Maloney's command of 243 men were in full possession of the prairie without firing a gun.... The contentions of the chiefs suddenly ceased.... All eyes were turned to Leschi. He became commander of all the forces without a formal agreement. When the time came he went to the front in person, and asked no one to take any risks in which he and his immediate followers were not willing to share."[16]

Leschi led his small army in subsequent battles in November and December of 1855, none of which were substantial victories for either side.

On November 24, Lieutenant Slaughter fought a desultory all-day battle against a force of these Indians at Bidding's Prairie. There was little loss of life on either side. On the foggy night that followed the battle, the Indians ran off all of the company's horses. Slaughter moved his command over to the White River and, on December 3, had another battle with a mixed band of Nisqually, Puyallup and Klickitat Indians under the command of Leschi. That evening Slaughter and several other officers were in a small cabin belonging to one of the settlers, discussing their situation, when a party of Klickitat Indians led by Chief Kanasket raided the camp and shot Slaughter, another soldier and one of the volunteers dead and wounded six others.[17] The death of Slaughter brought Kautz back to Washington Territory.

Three days before Kautz arrived at Fort Steilacoom, Leschi and a large and determined band of hostile Indians attacked the town of Seattle in an effort to acquire additional arms and ammunition. Governor Stevens, back from his treaty-making on January 19, 1856, had scoffed at the idea that the Indians would attack Seattle or any of the other settlements of any size. Apparently, supposing the war nearly over, he was disbanding some of the volunteer militia forces in the territory.[18] Nonetheless, in a speech before the Territorial Legislature on the day of his arrival back to Olympia, he stated emphatically that "the war shall be prosecuted until the last hostile Indian is exterminated."[19]

The Indians moved on Seattle before dawn on January 26, 1856. The attack was easily repulsed, partly because the citizens of the town had been warned of the impending attack by friendly Indians, but primarily because of the guns of the USS *Decatur,* which was fortuitously lying at anchor in the harbor.

The "Battle of Seattle" struck fear into the whites. All who had not already done so fled to the towns around Puget Sound. Seattle, Olympia and Steilacoom were filled with refugees.

Lieutenant Colonel Silas Casey, upon his arrival at Fort Steilacoom, was quick to note the situation in the Puget Sound area. The Indians, with about 150–200 warriors, were firmly in position behind the White River. Just a few miles behind these hostiles were their families, numbering as many as 500, on either side of the Green River. An abundant supply of salmon taken from the Green River kept the Indians well fed, although they were in short supply of arms and ammunition. Through the months before Casey's arrival, the winter rains had kept the rivers almost impassable, making it extremely difficult to force the Indians from their position. But two things happened. First, the winter rainy season ended, making the White River fordable at many locations. Second, the annual salmon run was ending. The abundant food supply the Indians relied on was about to be interrupted. Casey saw instinctively that, if he could move the Indians from their position between the White and Green Rivers, the war around Puget Sound would be over. He took the offensive almost immediately.

Kautz's assessment of the situation at this time as quoted by Ezra Meeker was less military than that of Casey. Kautz wrote, "The Indians were at this time considerably disaffected among each other. The winter had given them time to reflect. They would willingly have made peace if they could have done so with safety to themselves. The winter passed without any act of hostility. No forays were made, no descent on the settlements, nothing of that hostile character which might be expected from such a foe took place during the winter; but frequent overtures of peace."[20] Elsewhere, Meeker said,

> At the suggestion of Leschi, a white child (one of their prisoners) was sent by way of an overture. That Leschi was the cause of this moderate policy is proved by his visit to the reservation, meeting on his way a number of white men whose lives he spared by interposing his influence against that of Kanasket. He returned without committing any acts of hostility, except to take off as many friendly Indians as he could induce to follow him to the hostile camp. His course in these matters created enemies for him in his own camp, and disaffection arose. But Leschi's name seems to have become unaccountably familiar in the mouths of the people, and obtained a notoriety beyond that of any other Indian in the war.[21]

Kautz shared the view of General Wool that, if the army bided its time and did nothing, the Indians would return to their homes and sue for peace. This was, indeed, the view of almost all of the officers in Washington Territory at the time. Casey, however, was a man of action.

On February 13, he sent three companies of volunteers to the Puyallup River and to Connell's Prairie to build blockhouses while he, himself, moved toward the White River with four companies of regulars. Casey crossed the Puyallup, then divided his force. He continued with two companies on the wagon road through Connell's Prairie and Lemon's Prairie to the crossing of White River above the Muckleshoot Prairie.

Casey sent Lieutenant Kautz with a company of the Ninth Infantry to the left by a more direct route to Muckleshoot. Kautz reached Muckleshoot Prairie on the last day of February, when he received a dispatch from Casey to meet him at the ford of the White River. Returning to the river crossing with about fifty of his men the following day, Kautz learned that a force of Indians much larger than his own was in his rear. He deployed his men in a defensive position among piles of driftwood on a bar in the river while the Indians surrounded him on both sides of the river. Kautz sent to Casey for help. Casey sent Captain Erasmus Keyes[22] on the double to the river crossing with about 100 men. Keyes arrived about 3 P.M. He and Kautz formed their men as skirmishers and began an advance. The Indians fired a single volley at the advancing regulars, then retreated. Almost all of the shots were high, but one struck Kautz, passing through his right leg below the knee. The Indians fell back about a half mile to an excellent defensive position atop a small, but steep, hill. Despite his wound, Kautz joined in a spirited assault which drove the Indians from the hill in disarray.

There are two contemporary accounts of this battle, one written by Kautz himself for Ezra

Meeker's *Pioneer Reminiscences*, the other, a longer version, written by Keyes in *Fifty Years' Observation of Men and Events*, but edited by Kautz. Both go into greater detail than we do here.[23]

Keyes added, "The hardship of that campaign, in which the pluck and endurance of Kautz, Sukely, Mendell, and several others were so severely tested, caused me afterwards to regard the seven days' fight before Richmond as a comparative recreation."[24]

In a later paragraph, Keyes added that Kautz and Mendell were "most efficient actors with me in the campaign of 1856, and are men of unimpeachable integrity. After writing my account of our operations, I received letters from those two officers corroborative of my descriptions."[25]

This brief battle represented, with the possible exception of the Battle of Seattle, the first victory of the entire war for the whites. It was also the final action between U.S. regulars and the Indians west of the Cascades. Kautz later received a commendation by General Winfield Scott for "conspicuous gallantry and devotion to duty" for his part in the battle.[26]

Two weeks later several companies of volunteers met the remains of the hostile Indians near Connell's Prairie and routed them. Immediately after that battle, Leschi, his brother Quiemuth, and their band of about thirty Nisquallies fled over Natches Pass to the Yakima Valley, and other of the Indians escaped to the safety of the reservations.

One last event of the war in the Puget Sound area occurred in April 1856 when a company of volunteers commanded by Captain Hamilton J.C. Maxon, while patrolling the upper reaches of the Nisqually River, surprised a group of Nisqually Indians who were fishing on the Mashel River near its confluence with the Nisqually River. Maxon and his men slaughtered the entire group of seventeen Indians, fifteen of whom were said to be women and children. Shortly after that Maxon's company found another, larger group and attacked them, killing as many as seventeen more, although some escaped. This tragic event, later known as Maxon's massacre, is considered even more despicable when it is known that the Indians killed had remained peaceable throughout the entire war. Late in April, Kautz was sufficiently recovered from his leg wound to lead Company C in a scout of the upper reaches of the Nisqually River. On reaching the Mashel River, he found the survivors of Maxon's massacre, mostly women, children and old men, and led them back to Fort Steilacoom to ensure their fair treatment.

By mid–March, Leschi's small army had disintegrated. A few of his men returned to their homes with their families, but most sought the refuge of the reservations. Leschi, Quiemuth and about twenty of their Nisqually followers fled with their families over the Cascades to join the Klickitats and Yakamas, who, credited by some with having started this war, had seen little of it. Casualties in Leschi's army had been few. Meeker states that, of the thirty-one Nisqually Indians who had followed Leschi, only one had died, and that was Leschi's brother-in-law, Stahi.

Leschi's journey across Natches Pass with his small party was a difficult one. They had fled the Connell's Prairie battlefield without food, blankets or tents. Eventually, they reached the camp of Kamiakin, who fed and sheltered them until they could care for themselves. Before summer came, these Nisquallies had moved to a camp on the upper Natches River.

The war wasn't over east of the mountains. Colonel George Wright's regulars fought a series of battles between March and July 1856 against the Klickitat, Yakama, Walla Walla and Pelouse Indians, who were led by Chiefs Kamiakin, Ow-hi and Te-i-as.

Kamiakin, Ow-hi and Te-i-as surrendered to Wright on July 9, 1856, and, at the suggestion of Kamiakin, Leschi and Quiemuth came in with them. Wright wrote to Governor Stevens on June 11 that Leschi and the others had surrendered and told the governor of Leschi's peaceful intentions.

The Governor, still rankled by Leschi's snub at Medicine Creek a year and a half before, responded on June 18, "I will, however, respectfully put you on your guard in reference to Leschi … and Quiemuth from the Sound, and to suggest that no arrangement be made which will save their necks from the executioner."[27]

Colonel Wright was deeply troubled by Stevens's attitude. He was convinced of Leschi's peaceful intentions and felt the Indian should be considered a prisoner of war. Fearful of what might happen if Stevens got hold of Leschi, Quiemuth and the others, Wright sought the support of his superior. In a letter to General Wool on July 25, Wright wrote, "I was visited by a party of Nisqually Indians ... probably seventy. They are poor, having lost nearly all their horses and property when they crossed the mountains last winter. They are very anxious to return to the Sound, either to the reservation or any other point which may be decided on.... Leschi is the recognized chief of these people.... They are all desirous of returning to the Sound, provided they can do so in safety. With regard to the three named [Nelson, Leschi and Kitsap], I sometime since received a letter from Governor Stevens, suggesting no terms should be granted them, but in as much as they came in and departed in security previous to that time, and appeared determined to be our friends, I would not take any harsh measures without having proof of their guilt."[28]

In October 1856, the reservations provided the Puget Sound Indians had been greatly expanded. The Puyallup Indians were given a reservation of about 18,000 acres on the Puyallup River and the Nisquallies were placed on one of about the same size on the Nisqually River south of Fort Steilacoom. This, of course, was much more to the Indians' liking and, ironically, the reservation provided for the Nisquallies was essentially what Leschi had asked for at the time of the Medicine Creek Treaty, including his own farm land.

With the enlargement of their reservation and the promise of safety provided by Colonel Wright, Leschi's band of Nisquallies recrossed the Cascades with the intent of moving onto their newly-created reservation. Upon their arrival, the Indian agent there, acting under the orders of Governor Stevens, refused to accept them. To clarify their position, they went to Colonel Silas Casey at Fort Steilacoom and, once again, surrendered. On October 20, Colonel Casey wrote to Governor Stevens requesting to be relieved of responsibility for the Indians.

The Governor's immediate reply was, "Although hostilities have for the present ceased on the Sound, yet in my judgement, the Indians at your post, most of whom have come from the east side of the mountains, are not in that condition of submission which makes it safe to incorporate them with the friendly Indians, nor will they be in that condition till the known murderers of that band are arrested for trial.... I have, therefore, to request your aid to assist me in apprehending Leschi, Quiemuth, Stahi, Nelson, and other murderers, and to keep them in custody awaiting warrant from the nearest magistrate, which being accomplished I will receive the remainder."[29]

Leschi went to Fort Nisqually to once again seek the advice of William Tolmie. After a long talk, Tolmie advised that the best course for Leschi was to go into hiding. This he did, moving with his family to the forested upper Nisqually River Valley, where he thought he would be safe. His forest sanctuary was betrayed by his nephew, Sluggia,[30] and he was captured on November 13 and taken to the governor's office at Olympia. Leschi was transferred immediately to the guardhouse at Fort Steilacoom and charged with the murder of A. Benton Moses.

When Leschi was captured, Quiemuth decided to turn himself in also. On November 17, Quiemuth surrendered to the Indian agent at the Nisqually Reservation. That night, he was held under guard at Governor Stevens's office in Olympia to await transfer to the guardhouse at Fort Steilacoom. Early in the morning of November 18, someone snuck into the governor's office and stabbed and shot Quiemuth to death. Although the identity of Quiemuth's murderer was well known in Olympia, he was never tried for the murder.

Some sources have said that Kautz was Leschi's jailor at Fort Steilacoom.[31] Whether that was truly the case or not, he had plenty of other duties to keep him occupied. When he arrived at Fort Steilacoom in January 1856, he had been named quartermaster of Fort Steilacoom, a duty which included serving as quartermaster for the entire Puget Sound District. Forts Bellingham and Townsend on the Sound and other small outposts came under his jurisdiction.

Kautz had mentioned earlier in his journal that he had "laid out a plan of reading and writing."[32] His reading included magazines, newspapers a wide range of fiction and nonfiction. Geography, geology and mineralogy fascinated him, as did the printed word itself. He was interested in newspaper publishing and, when Charles Prosch arrived at the town of Steilacoom to begin publication of the *Puget Sound Herald* in 1858, Kautz was a regular visitor to the newspaper's offices and, according to his journals, he wrote a number of articles for the paper.[33]

He was a prolific letter writer and, as a result, he received a considerable amount of mail in return. Mail ships were now coming up from San Francisco two or three times each week instead of weekly. Even on that schedule, it was rare for a mail steamer to arrive without letters for Kautz.

Much of Kautz's correspondence was with fellow officers, even those at posts near at hand. These men, especially the single officers, would often visit each other as well. On one occasion when Kautz, Sheridan and Nugen were ordered to Fort Bellingham for court-martial trials, Sheridan came up from Vancouver Barracks to visit with Kautz and Nugen for a week before departing for Bellingham. While at Bellingham, they socialized with Captain George Pickett[34] and other officers. When the trials were completed, the three, along with George Gibbs of the survey team, canoed over to Fort Townsend to visit Major Granville Haller before returning to Steilacoom.

It is occasionally alluded to in the literature, both fiction and nonfiction, that men who have shared the deprivations and dangers of war often form bonds of attachment as close as, if not more close than, those of family. So it seems with these young officers on the Northwest frontier. Kautz had been shaken by the death of William Slaughter in 1855. He was effected even more so by the death of John Nugen on October 22, 1857, stating in his journal of that day, "This is a great gloom upon us." Kautz and Nugen had suffered through the Academy together, had traveled together to the frontier and, when separated, had maintained their friendship through letters. Kautz had first mentioned in his journal entry of September 15 that Nugen was seriously ill with consumption. As his condition worsened, Kautz visited him for an hour or two each day. Nugen went into a coma on October 19 and died three days later. As will be seen in a later chapter, Kautz named his first-born son for his friend.

Kautz took it upon himself to write to Nugen's father, Colonel R.N. Nugen of Newcomerstown, Ohio, informing him of his son's death. He also served as executor of Nugen's estate, which duty occupied him off and on for more than a year. Among Nugen's effects at the time of his death was a letter he had written on July 31 to William Slaughter's widow, Mary, but had not mailed, in which he proposed marriage. Kautz sent the letter to Mary Slaughter, stating in his journal, "I shall send it to her as it may be valuable to her." He later received a reply acknowledging receipt of the letter. Kautz noted in his journal, "The same sadness that characterized the tone of her letters to Mr. Nugen pervades this one."[35]

Kautz was conservative in his personal habits. He drank little, more because of chronic dyspepsia which began to bother him in 1857 than for any other reason, but he tolerated drinking in others. He smoked more than he thought he should. Somewhat compulsive about getting his work done properly and on time, he was often troubled when he fell behind. He tried to exercise regularly, but was often frustrated when the demands of his job interfered with his physical activity. He was frugal in his personal finances as well as in those of his employer, the U.S. Army. When he received $708 in back pay in July 1857, he thought to invest it in real estate. His first investment was in twelve lots in the growing town of Steilacoom.

In his remarkable little book, *Customs of Service for Officers of the Army,* written in 1865 (see Chapter 34), Kautz outlined all of the duties of post quartermasters and commissary officers with clarity and insight. He finished the discussion of these two jobs with a statement that, if no commissary officer is available, the quartermaster has the prerogative, with permission from his superiors, to appoint a civilian as *acting* commissary, who will be "entitled to $20 per month, minus one ration, in addition to the pay as a Lieutenant."[36]

Kautz, with permission, appointed his brother Frederick acting commissary of the Puget Sound District, stationed at Fort Steilacoom.

Fred Kautz, along with younger brother George, had gone to the gold fields of California in 1850. Both had been quite successful. Fred probably came to Fort Steilacoom late in the spring of 1856. George, after returning to Ohio to help in his father's vineyards, spent some time in California, but was living in Illinois by 1860.

Lieutenant Kautz continued nominally in command of Company C, but his quartermaster duties consumed most of his time. His immediate superior as quartermaster was regimental quartermaster Rufus Ingalls, but he also answered to Lieutenant Colonel Thomas Swords, assistant quartermaster general at the War Department. As both quartermaster and commissary officer for a geographical region as large as the Puget Sound District, Kautz remained constantly busy. He could no longer complain, as he had in 1853, that there was little to do. He noted in his journal on June 1, 1857: "The duties of quartermaster and commissary keep me quite constantly employed, and I find little time for improving myself beyond the observations that I am daily able to make in the performance of my various duties."[37]

Captain Maloney was in command of Fort Steilacoom and Kautz complained often in his journal of Maloney's meddling in his quartermaster duties.

Kautz was required to handle quite large sums of money. Fred functioned to some extent as leg man for his older brother and it seems his duties were far more extensive and varied than the title "acting commissary" would suggest. In the pages of Lieutenant Kautz's journals, there is mention of Fred's carrying thousands of dollars from one post to another, including department headquarters at Vancouver Barracks. Fred later supervised the construction of a military road from Steilacoom to Seattle. The road was never finished because of a lack of funds. As can be expected, August Kautz was sincerely happy to have his brother working for him.

In his capacity as quartermaster, Kautz saw the immediate need for upgrading the buildings at Fort Steilacoom. The rough log buildings may have been adequate for the small detachment there in 1853, but were nowhere near so in 1856. At the insistence of Captain Maloney, he first arranged to make repairs to the existing buildings. This work did not get underway in earnest until the spring of 1857 because of a lack of funds. Throughout 1856 and well into 1857, he repeatedly requested funds from the chief quartermaster at the War Department to construct additional quarters, but was put off. Finally on October 15, 1857, he received a letter from Colonel Swords authorizing construction of additional buildings. As so often happens in the army, the order did not immediately provide funds sufficient for the project. Kautz drew the plans for all of the new buildings and, thanks to his frugality, he was able to completely upgrade the fort, including married officers' quarters, bachelor officers' quarters, quarters (including office space) for the commanding officer, a chapel, barracks for enlisted men and barns for the horses. The project was completed late in 1858, but not without delays which tried Kautz's patience. Despite the fact that vast amounts of lumber were being cut from the neighboring forests for shipment to San Francisco and elsewhere, building materials were not always available locally, causing delays to the project. Also, the available civilian labor pool was extremely limited and finding enough carpenters for the construction work was difficult. Gold had been discovered along the Fraser River in 1856 and Kautz competed with the gold fields for laborers to maintain a work force. Men were constantly abandoning his construction project to run off to the gold fields in hope of striking it rich. At one point, those men who remained went on strike for a pay raise to the incredible amount of $6 per day.

Although Captain Maloney remained at Fort Steilacoom, he was replaced as post commander by Lieutenant Colonel Silas Casey in December 1857, thus relieving Kautz of Maloney's interference.

Officers' Row at Fort Steilacoom about 1860. Kautz drew the plans for and supervised construction of all of the buildings.

Quartermaster's quarters, Fort Steilacoom, home to Lieutenant August Kautz and regimental surgeon Dr. Horace Wirtz. Both photographs courtesy Historic Fort Steilacoom Association.

Casey arrived this second time with his wife, Abby, two teenaged daughters and seven-year-old son, Edward. The Caseys moved into the house near the post hospital which Kautz and Horace Wirtz had occupied, forcing them to move to other quarters. Dr. Wirtz was "annoyed very much."[38] Although he was also disappointed, Kautz was willing to accept being dispossessed with equanimity. He had long before learned that rank has its privileges and one of those privileges is the choice of living quarters. The move was thought to be only temporary because one of the buildings Kautz was working on was a large house, including office space, for the commanding officer. Kautz admired Silas Casey and enjoyed the company of Mrs. Casey, whom he found "a very fine lady, but evidently strong minded,"[39] and two teenaged girls, who greatly enlivened the social life at Fort Steilacoom.

Casey was also the father of Kautz's classmate at West Point, Thomas L. Casey.[40] The younger Casey must have snubbed his less successful classmates while excelling at the military academy. When he was assigned to Fort Steilacoom briefly in 1860, Kautz wrote, "Tom Casey is here and seems to have improved in appearance and manners and he certainly treats me with a great deal more consideration than when we were cadets."[41]

When Kautz's construction project was completed in 1858, Fort Steilacoom took on the appearance of other frontier forts of the day, with a central parade ground surrounded by the post's buildings.

Throughout this two-year period, Kautz continued to act as the jailor for Leschi. So pervasive was Governor Stevens's power in Washington Territory, that he had arranged for Judge Francis A. Chenoweth to convene a special session of the Pierce County Court at Fort Steilacoom to try Leschi. A grand jury was hastily convened on November 17, 1856, and the trial before a just-as-hastily empaneled petit jury occurred on November 18.

Judge Chenoweth was careful to instruct the jury that, if they concluded that the killing of Moses was an act of war, the prisoner could not be convicted of murder. The only witness called was Antonio B. Rabbeson, a member of the party with Moses when he was killed. According to Meeker, who was a member of the jury, "He was a too willing witness to be truthful, and had not been on the witness stand five minutes until the guilt of perjury showed so plainly reflected in his eyes that no one really believed he was telling the truth."[42]

It has been implied that Rabbeson had been bribed to testify against Leschi, but there is no surviving evidence of this. Perhaps he had other motives to perjure himself. In defense of Rabbeson, perhaps he was honestly mistaken, but probably not. After all, the truthfulness of the witness really didn't matter, because as Meeker tells us, "The case had been tried outside the court and the prisoner found guilty."[43]

Meeker also gives an account of the jury's deliberations. Meeker and William M. Kincaid persisted in voting for acquittal. "Kincaid said, 'I never will vote to condemn that man,' and he never did. He and I stood out to the last against conviction and Leschi was saved for the time being. The jury was discharged and Leschi remanded into the custody of the military authorities at Fort Steilacoom for safe keeping until a regular term of court convened."[44]

It is likely that Lieutenant Kautz had known Leschi during his short tour at Fort Steilacoom in 1853, but the two had not become friends. They had also met on the White River battlefield, but neither was aware of the other's presence there. Now they were together on an almost daily basis and a strong bond formed between them. Kautz soon saw in Leschi the attributes of intelligence, self-confidence, firmness of purpose and clear reasoning power which made him a natural leader. Leschi had embraced the white man's Christian religion and Kautz admired him for the depth of his religious conviction. Kautz attributed his prisoner's stoic acceptance of his fate partly to that conviction and partly to his certainty that the course he had chosen in the recent war was morally correct. As time passed, Kautz became increasingly certain that Leschi was innocent, both of having started the war and specifically of the charge of murder. In February 1856, Kautz wrote, "...when Eaton's Rangers were sent to bring him in he fled with his brother (Quiemuth) to the enemy. His course during the war seems to be characterized by greater intelligence and humanity than that of any of the other chiefs. He protested against killing women and children, and against pillaging and plundering the settlements. On several occasions during the war he had individual white men in his power, and his influence saved them from being killed by Kanasket."[45]

Leschi's second trial was set for March 18, 1857. In the interval between the two trials, judicial districts had been redrawn and the second trial was held in Olympia, where Governor Stevens's influence was greatest. Kautz attempted to prepare Leschi for the trial, including acquiring the services of Olympia's most successful criminal lawyer, Frank Clark. This may have been a poor choice because Clark, although successful, had gained the reputation in Olympia as an unscrupulous protector of criminals. It seems that, in March 1857, it would have been difficult to find in Olympia twelve men who were not convinced of Leschi's guilt. Besides, someone had to be accountable for the deaths of innocent civilians and of volunteers like Moses. Quiemuth was dead, Kanasket was dead, Stahi was dead and Kamiakin had fled to Canada. Leschi would have to do.

The trial took but a day. Kautz led the detail which escorted Leschi from Fort Steilacoom to Olympia. A.B. Rabbeson again testified that he had seen Leschi on Connell's Prairie and, later, saw him shoot A. Benson Moses. According to Meeker, Rabbeson went into greater detail than in the first trial and added "that the road traveled by his party was three-quarters of a mile to the swamp and the trail [taken by Leschi] three or four hundred yards."[46]

This time other members of the Tidd party were called to testify. None said that they saw Leschi either at Connell's Prairie or at the swamp.

Unlike the first trial, the judge, in his charge to the jury, failed to mention that the killing of Moses might have been an act of war. He further explained that Leschi need not have actually fired the fatal shot. It was necessary only to show that he was present and abetting the actual killer in order to be found guilty of murder. The jury lost no time in pronouncing its decision. Leschi was found guilty and sentenced to hang on June 10, 1857. He was returned to Fort Steilacoom to await his fate.

Frank Clark pleaded on March 20 for a new trial for Leschi. The plea for a new trial was denied. Clark then filed an appeal to the Territorial Supreme Court. The appeal was granted.

The next session of the Supreme Court was not scheduled until December, 1857. For the next nine months Leschi remained confined at Fort Steilacoom awaiting his next court appearance. Kautz took a special interest in Leschi's case although he had many other duties. He and Leschi had many opportunities to discuss the case as well as other topics. Through their contact, each learned more of the other's language.

Leschi's appeal came before the Territorial Supreme Court on December 17, 1857. In the court's opinion, which Meeker suggests was written long before the case was heard, the decision of the District Court was correct and Leschi was once again sentenced to be hanged. The date of the execution was set for January 22, 1858.

Kautz immediately began to seek other means to save his friend from the gallows. His actions were opposed by Maurice Maloney, one of the few army officers who felt Leschi was guilty, as the following journal entry shows:

> Maloney made himself very officious today again. I had sent for Leshi [*sic*] to have some quiet conversation in my room with Dr. Tolmie. The Capt. found out that he was there and sent an order for me to have him taken back to the guard house, reprimanding me for taking him out of the garrison which is simply ridiculous. He, of course, can prescribe Leshi's limits but without some order to that effect, if I have occasion to communicate with Leshi or any other prisoner of the guard as Officer of the Day, I shall send for him to come to my quarters to do so, Captain Maloney to the contrary not withstanding.[47]

On December 21 and 22, Lieutenant Kautz and Dr. Tolmie traveled from the town of Steilacoom to Fort Nisqually and to Olympia testing public sentiment for or against Leschi. In the first two towns they found that some persons were opposed to Leschi and others favored him, but that most people were indifferent to Leschi's fate. At Olympia, however, many had strong feelings against Leschi.

While at Olympia, Tolmie and Kautz met with Governor Fayette McMullen,[48] who had been appointed to succeed Isaac Stevens in September 1857, to ask him to intercede in Leschi's favor. The governor refused to do so, but agreed to give Leschi "a sound hearing, which is all his friends can desire."[49]

This was the same day that Silas Casey arrived to replace Maurice Maloney as camp commander and Kautz was pleased to learn that Casey, unlike Maloney, had "a great leaning in favor of Leshi, he is going to do all he can to have him pardoned."[50]

On December 29 and 30, Kautz, William Tolmie and William Tidd, along with two Indians from the reservation named Luke and Porswiki, went to the scene of the killings and measured the distance on the military road which the Tidd party traveled from Connell's Prairie to the swamp where the shootings occurred. They also measured the distance an Indian would have had to travel over the path through the forest from the one point to the other. The distances were 68 chains and 104½ chains respectively, far from the "three-quarters of a mile" and "three or four hundred yards" which Rabbeson had testified. Kautz drew a rough map of the area showing the main features and the distances traveled and made a number of copies.[51]

The governor arrived at Fort Steilacoom on January 16 and heard arguments in Leschi's case. Kautz reported in his journal that the governor and Frank Clark "talked for about an hour. Clark presented quite a number of papers among them my survey of Connell's prairie and my affidavit."[52]

On January 20, "Clark went up to Olympia with a view to get the news of what the Executive was going to do in the case of Leshi. There was no doubt but what he will respite and [Sheriff George] Williams, who is in the Governor's confidence, stated as much."[53]

But it was not to be. Kautz described the following day:

> We were all much put out by the news today that the Governor has refused the Executive clemency. It seems that when the Governor reached Olympia he found a remonstrance awaiting him with about seven hundred signatures and some threats that the people would burn the Gov. in effigy if Leshi was respited decided him. There were no new features in the case simply a heavy pressure of public opinion put the Governor down. He sent for [Territorial Secretary Charles] Mason and obtained his written opinion which, of course, was adverse to Leshi except to prop up his decision on the side of seven hundred voters.
>
> Tolmie was exceedingly wrought up, he was desirous of entering a final protest. There was one hope and that was that if the Indian who committed the offense was to be found and his confession and voluntary surrender could be obtained Leshi might still be saved. [Indian Agent Michael] Simmons, Tolmie, Clark and I rode to the reservation on the Nesqually and had an interview with Puo-yon-is. He admitted that he was present when Moses was killed, that he fired but he would not say that his ball had killed Moses. He maintained that he was at war with the whites when he did this and thought he was doing right. But he would not surrender himself. So we had to return without him.[54]

When the day set for Leschi's execution arrived, Frank Clark, along with some of the men at Fort Steilacoom, hatched an elaborate plot to delay the hanging in hopes that a presidential pardon could be arranged with then-President James Buchanan. When Sheriff George Williams arrived at Fort Steilacoom on the morning of the planned execution, the fort's sutler, J.M. Bachelder, who was also a U.S. commissioner, issued a warrant for Williams's arrest, charging him with selling whiskey to Indians. Fred Kautz and Lieutenant David McKibbin served the warrant and Williams, who was a party to the plot, was taken to the jail in town. Williams, who was in possession of Leschi's death warrant, refused to hand the warrant over to the executioner, Charles McDaniel. When 2 o'clock, the legal time limit for the execution, had passed, Williams was released from jail. Colonel Casey, Clark and Bachelder were hanged in effigy in Olympia and Bachelder was later removed as U.S. commissioner for his part in the scheme.

The following day, in a move which muddies the relationships among the executive, legislative and judicial branches of government, Governor McMullen ordered the territorial legislature to pass a law requiring the state Supreme Court to hold a special session in order to again sentence Leschi to death. This was done and the date of execution was set for February 19, 1858. William Mitchell, the sheriff of Thurston County (Olympia), was appointed to carry out the mandate of the court. Charles Grainger was named by Mitchell to be the executioner.

If political propaganda, primarily in the form of the Territory's major newspaper, the *Pioneer and Democrat,* had played a role in enlisting public opinion against Leschi, Kautz decided to answer with a newspaper of his own. With the cooperation of Colonel Casey and others at Fort Steilacoom, Kautz published a newspaper entitled the *Truth Teller,* declaring on the masthead, "Devoted to the Dissemination of Truth and the Suppression of Humbug." Only two issues of the one-page paper were printed, using the presses at Charles Prosch's *Puget Sound Herald.* The first issue, published on February 4, contained articles and letters written by Kautz, Tolmie, and other supporters of Leschi and even had a crude woodblock print of Kautz's map of Connell's Prairie which Kautz made himself.

All was to no avail.

As the day of the execution approached, Silas Casey refused to permit the gallows to be placed within the limits of Fort Steilacoom. It was constructed on the prairie about a mile east of the fort and the execution went on as planned on February 19. Charles Grainger, the executioner, told about it many years later.

> I felt that I was executing an innocent man. I had had charge of Leschi for two weeks before he was taken to Steilacoom. He was as cool as could be—just like he was going to dinner. I used to take his handcuffs off and let him eat. On the scaffold he thanked me for my kindness to him. He said that people had lied about him and had given false evidence. I asked him if he wished to say anything further. He said again that he was not guilty; that Rabbeson had lied when he said he saw him in the swamp, and that he would meet him before his God and he would tell him there he lied. He said he was miles away when Moses was killed. He said he would not be the first man that lost his life on false evidence. If he was dying for his people he was willing to die; that Christ died for others. After he made his speech he turned and thanked me again for my kindness to him while a prisoner under my care, and said that he had nothing more to say and that he was ready. He died without a struggle. It seems to me he talked for fifteen minutes, but spoke very deliberate and slow; but he made very few gestures while speaking and had a dignified way that made a lasting impression on my mind.... He did not seem to be the least bit excited at all, and no trembling on him at all—nothing of the kind, and that is more than I could say for myself. In fact, Leschi seemed to be the coolest of any on the scaffold. He was in good flesh and had a firm step and mounted the scaffold without assistance, and as well as I did myself. I felt that I was hanging an innocent man, and believe it yet.[55]

August Kautz was among the crowd of 300 to 500 people who attended his friend's execution. His journal entry was simple, "Leshi was accordingly taken out and executed about 11 o'clock. He died manfully."[56]

Leschi was buried in a secluded spot not far from the site of the execution.

The second issue of the *Truth Teller* did not appear until after Leschi's death. Nonetheless Kautz and his fellow officers felt the need to release it in order to tell the story of the injustice which had been done. Kautz seems to have gained special satisfaction in sending a large bundle of the papers to Governor McMullen's home district in southwest Virginia.[57]

On July 4, 1895, Leschi's remains were removed to a burial ground on the Nisqually Reservation. The ceremony, attended by more than a thousand Indians, Nisquallies and others, and by almost as many whites, was impressive. As though his bones had not been disturbed enough, during World War I, the government confiscated a large part of the reservation in order to build Fort Lewis. The section of the reservation taken included Leschi's grave. His remains were then moved to a cemetery on the Puyallup Indian Reservation. An appropriate memorial stands above his grave.

In the first years of the 21st century, members of the Nisqually tribe, including Cecelia Svinth Carpenter, Nisqually tribal historian, Cynthia Iyall, a descendant of Leschi's sister, and others worked to have Leschi exonerated of the murder of Moses. As a result of their persistence, on December 10, 2004, a special court of seven noted judges, led by Washington State Supreme Court Chief Justice Gary Alexander, convened at the Washington State Historical Museum to reopen Leschi's trial. Before a crowd of about 200 spectators, eleven witnesses were called including tribal members, historians and an expert on military law from the U.S. Army. After a short deliberation, the judges returned a verdict completely exonerating Leschi on the grounds that a state of war existed at the time Moses was killed and, as an enemy combatant, Leschi could not be tried for murder.

There is no doubt that Leschi's life and tragic death contributed in large part to attitudes which would remain with Kautz for the remainder of his life. He would remain distrustful of the motives of the civil authority, especially of the Indian Bureau. He now saw the military as a potentially powerful tool in the spread westward of the American culture. He remained throughout the rest of his career devoted to the judicious use of that power.

8. Semiahmoo Bay

In the summer of 1857, Kautz took on an additional assignment that would add substantially to his work schedule.

The Pacific Northwest had been annexed to the United States by treaty with the British in 1846, but the actual boundary, the 49th Parallel, had never been marked or even surveyed. Early in 1857, teams from the United States and Canada, called the Northwest Boundary Commission, were appointed to mark off the boundary. Although the U.S. team was headed by Archibald Campbell, much of the field work was performed by Lieutenant John G. Parke[1] of the U.S. Army's Topographical Engineers, who was named chief astronomer and surveyor. Company F of the Ninth Infantry, commanded by Captain Dickinson Woodruff,[2] served as escort.

Campbell and the others who came from the East arrived at San Francisco on May 20, 1857. On June 18, Kautz received orders "to supply the Boundary Commission with any excess of stores that I may have on hand."[3] From that time on Kautz became *de facto* quartermaster and commissary officer to the commission's camp at Semiahmoo Bay near the border and was required to make occasional excursions to Fort Billingham and to Semiahmoo Bay with supplies.

The members of the commission arrived at Olympia aboard the U.S. Coastal Survey Steamer *Active* in the latter part of June. Kautz mentioned in his journal that the officers of the *Active* and the members of the commission were invited as guests to Fort Steilacoom to celebrate Independence Day on July 4. Also present were the officers of HMS *Satellite*. "They formed quite a large party.... They amused themselves riding Uncle Sam's horses over the prairie until they were nearly all lamed. We had dinner at six at which nearly fifty or more guests sat down.... The evening closed with dancing."[4] Kautz made an effort to mention in his journal all of the guests. Besides the officers of the two ships and those of the boundary commission, those mentioned were Dr. Tolmie, Miss Work (the sister-in-law of Tolmie), and Edward Huggins of the Hudson's Bay Company at Fort Nisqually.

The work of the commission began in August 1857 and continued into 1861. During the first year, only the U.S. team was present. They surveyed from Boundary Bay on Puget Sound to the crossing of the Skagit River. In 1858, they were joined by a British team led by Captain J.S. Hawkins and surveyed an additional 90 miles. In 1859, the Columbia River was reached and, by 1861, all 409 miles to the crest of the Rocky Mountains were completed. In all,161 survey markers were placed on the border. Around each marker a clearing was cut at least forty feet wide and one-half mile long, forming a dotted line in the virgin forest which stretched one-sixth of the way across the continent. Lieutenant Parke wrote an extensive report of the survey in 1862 but, by that time, the Civil War was underway and the report was never published.

In conjunction with his association with the Northwest Boundary Commission, Kautz made a point of studying everything he could find on the subject of international law. He had demonstrated such an interest in the activities of the commission that Archibald Campbell petitioned the War Department to have him transferred to the commission and the transfer was ordered. Kautz, despite Campbell's assumption to the contrary, had little interest in leaving Steilacoom. He was surprised when, on August 6, 1858, he received orders from Army Headquarters to report to Semiahmoo Bay, near present-day Blaine, Washington, for duty with the Boundary Commission's escort, Woodruff's company of the Ninth Infantry. Kautz noted, "This seems a little unexpected. It is flattering to me, but I don't think much to go and be on duty with another regiment away from my own."[5]

Kautz delayed somewhat in turning over his quartermaster and commissary duties at Steilacoom to his replacement, Lieutenant Edward J. Harvie, but finally departed down the Sound on October 15 and arrived at Semiahmoo Bay two days later.

The move, as Kautz had anticipated, did not satisfy him. The majority of the enlisted men were with the survey crew, leaving the small post all but deserted. He found serving under Captain Woodruff difficult. Woodruff, according to Kautz, had trouble deciding on any course of action. Kautz and the post surgeon, Dr. James H. Berrien, concluded that he was mentally disturbed. Woodruff interfered in Kautz's quartermaster duties in ways similar to those of Captain Maloney, although the personalities of the two men were in no way similar.

The officers' quarters were inadequate, so one of Kautz's first tasks as quartermaster was to provide living quarters for himself. Woodruff balked at the idea and interfered somewhat, but Kautz finished a small house by December 2 which was "far from comfortable."[6]

On December 12, he returned up the Sound and spent more than a month at Steilacoom and Olympia purchasing enough supplies for his new post to fill the holds of two small ships.

Captain Woodruff was away from January 19 to March 5, 1859, leaving Kautz in command.

Left: Louise (Rombach) Denver, first cousin of August Kautz and wife of James William Denver, ca. 1860. Through the years, she was one of Kautz's most frequent correspondents. *Right*: James William Denver in his uniform of a Civil War brigadier general (1861). Both photographs are from August Kautz's photograph album, courtesy Virginia (Kautz) Borkenhagen.

Kautz, Dr. Berrien and the others at the camp were delighted. Kautz noted in his journal that the men of the company had difficulty with the change of command: "I let some of the men off on leave and several of them came home drunk. They do not know how to appreciate ... light treatment. Woodruff is so irregular in his ... control of them that moderation is a relaxation they are disposed to abuse rather than economize." A day later, he added, "I shall be compelled to treat them more severely, otherwise they will be beyond control."[7]

Kautz had not seen his family for seven years. His health was beginning to concern him and he blamed this on the pressures of work. Since he had accumulated enough money, he decided to take a leave of absence to travel to Ohio and, subsequently, to Europe. He applied to Woodruff for a six-month leave of absence, but Woodruff refused to approve it. He then went over Woodruff's head and applied directly to the War Department, but heard nothing for months. On February 15, he wrote in his journal, "I find myself talking about a leave all the time and many of my thoughts are turned that way. I shall be disappointed if I don't hear something about it tomorrow." The steamer arrived about midnight that night and Kautz was awakened to receive the mail. Before he returned to bed, he added a supplemental note in the journal, "I could not sleep much on account of the exciting news.... There was a leave of absence for six months without any conditions or provisions." In the same mail there was a letter from James Denver. "Cousin Lou added a p. s. to Genl. Denver's letter. He no doubt was very influential in getting my leave for me."[8]

Kautz departed Semiahmoo Bay on April 10, 1859, and spent two weeks at Fort Steilacoom. There he learned that his brother Fred had been discharged. August and Fred left Fort Steilacoom for the East on April 25. Before we let him go, there were two events which occurred at Fort Steilacoom which demand our attention. Each deserves a chapter to itself.

9. Tacobet

When Brevet Second Lieutenant August Kautz came to Fort Steilacoom in 1852, he was impressed by the beauty of his surroundings. He noted in his journal that "Mount Rainier was in full view"[1] and said later, "On a clear day it does not look more than ten miles off, and looms up against the eastern sky white as the snow with which it is covered, with a perfectly pyramidal outline, except at the top, which is slightly rounded and broken. It is a grand and inspiring view." He "was ... fond of visiting unexplored sections of the country, and possessed of a very prevailing passion for going to the tops of high places." When he returned from Oregon in January 1856, that passion grew until his "resolution took shape and form about the first of July [1857]."[2]

Kautz learned all he could about the mountain's history. When, in June 1792, Captain George Vancouver of the Royal Navy sailed his ship *Discovery* into Puget Sound, he was in the second year of a three-year exploration of the Pacific Coast. Spanish explorers had been here before him and had named the entrance to Puget Sound the Strait of Juan de Fuca, but they had not entered the Sound. Vancouver named the Sound after one of his lieutenants, Peter Puget. Other landmarks, Mount Baker, Hood Inlet, Vashon Island and Whidbey Island, were named for other officers of the ship. The name Vancouver Island was reserved for the large island north of the Strait. By the time Vancouver reached the Upper Sound, he had run out of crew members for whom to name the massive "round snowy mountain"[3] to his southeast. Vancouver named it for his friend, Admiral Peter Rainier, who had never set foot on the American continent. Vancouver cared not that the Native Americans who lived on the shores of Puget Sound knew the mountain as Tacobet and held it in great reverence. They attributed great mystic powers to Tacobet. If there are gods who observe our lives or control our destinies, thought the Indians, they must reside at such a place as this.

It wasn't until 1833 that any white man approached Tacobet, and he, too, called it Mount Rainier. On August 27, 1833, young Dr. William Tolmie received permission to form a "botanizing excursion" to Mount Rainier. He was accompanied by five Indians, including Lahalet, the chief of the Nisqually Indians, and Lahalet's nephew, Lachmere, who served as a porter. After a difficult climb, Tolmie and one of the Indians, probably Lahalet, reached the summit of a peak lying about six miles northwest of the summit and halted there. Tolmie, as he had promised, collected some botanical specimens and departed.

Twenty-four years had passed since Tolmie's "botanizing excursion," but the memory of the trip was still fresh in his mind. He advised Kautz that the most promising route to the top appeared to be from the west. Kautz also consulted with his friend, Leschi, then imprisoned on a charge of murder. Leschi informed Kautz that he knew the route to the western slopes of the mountain well and volunteered his services as a guide. When Kautz answered that Leschi's release from prison was out of the question, Leschi suggested another Nisqually named Wapowety as a guide.

"I had expressed so often my determination to make the ascent, without doing it, that my fellow officers became incredulous," Kautz noted later. "Nearly all the officers had been very free to volunteer to go with me as long as they felt certain I was not going; but when I was ready to go, I should have been compelled to go alone but for the doctor [Dr. Robert O. Craig, surgeon at Fort Bellingham], who was on a visit to the post from Fort Bellingham." Also recruited were Privates William Carroll and Nicholas Dogue to climb the mountain and two soldiers named Doneheh and Bell who were to stay with the horses at the base camp on the Mashel River.

"We made for each member of the party an *alpenstock* of dry ash with an iron point. We sewed upon our shoes an extra sole, through which were first driven four-penny nails with the points broken off and the heads inside. We took with us a rope about fifty feet long, a hatchet, a thermometer, plenty of hard biscuit, and dried beef such as the Indians prepare."[4] Kautz failed to mention that they also carried tea.

On July 9, the party reached "Mishawl Prairie, where we camped for the night, this being the end of the journey for our horses, and the limit of our knowledge of the country." The Mashel Prairie was the site of Maxon's massacre, mentioned in a previous chapter, which Kautz had visited fifteen months before. Here they left the horses with Doneheh and Bell.

The next day they climbed to the ridge which parallels the Nisqually River, but finding no water and a very rough and irregular ridge top, they returned to the level of the river on July 11. The river was now a narrow stream falling precipitously from Mount Rainier. Kautz remembered, "That mountain proved a severer task than we anticipated." His journal noted that "the ascent of the river is very laborious."[5]

Climbing more steeply each day, they averaged less than ten miles per day. On the morning of the fourth day (July 13), Wapowety killed a deer, so they halted to dry the meat to supplement the dried meat they had started with. The fatigue of the hike, coupled with the elevation, to which they were unaccustomed, severely affected their appetites. Kautz had noted on the previous day, "With considerable cramming I managed to dispose of the most of my rations." The fresh deer meat seems to have been more palatable.

The fifth day saw them climbing within a cloud and through the narrow bed of the Nisqually River, "the torrent more and more rapid, and our progress slower and slower." ...

> For several miles before camping the bed of the stream was paved with white granite bowlders [*sic*], and the mountain gorge became narrower and narrower. The walls were in many places perpendicular precipices, thousands of feet high, their summits hid in the clouds. Vast piles of snow were to be seen along the stream — the remains of avalanches—for earth, trees, and rock were intermingled with the snow.... We followed thus far the main branch of the Nesqually, and here it emerged from an icy cavern at the foot of an immense glacier.
>
> On the morning of the sixth day, we set out again up the glacier. We had a little trouble in getting up the glacier, as it terminated everywhere in steep faces that were very difficult to climb. Once up, we did not meet any obstructions ... for several hours, although the slippery surface ... made it very fatiguing with our packs.... [There were] immense crevasses crossing our path, often compelling us to travel several hundred yards to gain a few feet. We finally resolved to find a camp. We found that the face of the lateral moraine was almost perpendicular, and composed of loose stones, sand, and gravel ... about fifty feet high. Wah-pow-e-ty and I finally succeeded in getting up, and with the aid of the rope we assisted our companions to do the same. When we reached the top we were a little surprised to find that we had to go down-hill again to reach the mountain side. Here a few stunted pines furnished us fuel and shelter, and we rested for the remainder of the day.

Kautz was describing crossing Wapowety Cleaver from Nisqually Glacier to Kautz Glacier.

> On the following morning [July 16] ... the sky showed signs of clear weather,[6] and we began the ascent of the main peak. Until about noon we were enveloped in clouds. Soon after midday we reached suddenly a colder atmosphere, and found ourselves all at once above the clouds, which were spread out smooth and even as a sea, above which appeared the snowy peaks of St. Helens,

Mount Adams, and Mount Hood, looking like pyramidal icebergs above an ocean. Above, the atmosphere was singularly clear, and the reflection of the sun upon the snow very powerful. The summit of Rainier seemed very close at hand.

About two o'clock in the afternoon the clouds rolled away like a scroll; in a very short time they had disappeared, and the Cascade Range lay before us in all its greatness. The view was too grand and extensive to be taken in at once.... We had no time, however, to study the beauties that lay before us.... The travel was very difficult; the surface of the snow was porous in some places, and at each step we sunk to our knees. Carroll and the Indian gave out early in the afternoon, and returned to camp. The doctor began to lag behind. Dogue stuck close to me. Between four and five o'clock we reached a very difficult point. It proved to be the crest of the mountain, where the comparatively smooth surface was much broken up, and inaccessible pinnacles of ice and deep crevasses interrupted our progress. It was not only difficult to go ahead, but exceedingly dangerous.... Dogue was evidently alarmed, for every time that I was unable to proceed, and turned back to find another passage, he would say, "I guess, Lieutenant, we petter go pack."

Finally we reached what might be called the top, for although there were points higher yet, the mountain spread out comparatively flat, and it was much easier to get along. The soldier threw himself down exhausted, and said he could go no farther. I went on to explore myself, but I returned in a quarter of an hour without my hat, fully satisfied that nothing more could be done.[7] It was after six o'clock, the air was very cold, and the wind blew fiercely.... Ice was forming in my canteen, and to stay on the mountain at such a temperature was to freeze to death, for we brought no blankets with us. When I returned to where I had left the soldier, I found the doctor there also, and after a short consultation we decided to return.

Kautz described the descent that evening with considerable detail. Dogue lost his footing and plunged down the mountain, but was only slightly injured. When Kautz, Dogue and Doctor Craig reached the campsite of the previous night, they found Wapowety to be snow-blind with his eyes swollen shut He had to be led down the mountain. Attempting the summit the next day was impossible because of exhaustion and the lack of food. Kautz noted that the water for tea boiled at 199 degrees, indicating an elevation of 7000 feet according to a graphic scale that Kautz carried with him. He estimated the elevation at the top to be about 12,000 feet.[8]

The return to Mashel Prairie and the horses took four days, but they had long since run out of food and ate only berries that they picked along the way. Kautz and Dr. Craig rode into Fort Steilacoom on July 21 so changed from their ordeal that their friends did not recognize them. "I felt the effects of the trip for many days, and did not recover my natural condition for some weeks. The doctor and I went to the village the next morning, where the people were startled at our emaciated appearance. We found that the doctor had lost twenty-one pounds in weight in fourteen days, and I had lost fourteen pounds. The two soldiers went into the hospital immediately on their return, and I learned that for the remainder of their service they were in the hospital nearly all the time.... The Indian ... barely escaped with his life after a protracted illness."

Later, in the *Overland Monthly* article, Kautz said that recently [1875] railroad surveyors had explored through the valley of the Nisqually River looking for a route to the upper Columbia River and concluded, "When the locomotive is heard in that region some day, when American enterprise has established an ice-cream saloon at the foot of the glacier, and sherry-cobblers may be had at twenty-five cents half-way up to the top of the mountain, attempts to ascend that magnificent snow-peak will be quite frequent. But many a long year will pass away before roads are sufficiently good to induce anyone to do what we did in the summer of 1857."

10. Tenas Puss

During his brief stay at Fort Steilacoom in 1853, Lieutenant Kautz met and was enamored of a young Nisqually woman named Tenas Puss (Little Kitten). They were married in an Indian ceremony either in 1853 or after he returned to Steilacoom in 1856.[1]

Tenas Puss was the daughter of Lachmere and Sicadalles and was possibly a cousin of Leschi. After her marriage, she Anglicized her name to Kitty Etta, a rough translation of Tenas Puss.

After Kautz's return from Oregon, Kitty shared his quarters at Fort Steilacoom, but their relationship was not quite that of equals. As a Native American living in the nineteenth century, Kitty could easily accept a subservient role in their relationship. Twice Kautz mentioned arguments between him and Kitty. His description of the first of these demonstrates that role quite well: "I had a row with my friend but nothing serious. Simply a little impudence repaid with a slap; and I went off, depending more on a system of coldness to produce subordination than by force."[2]

Kautz, like most army officers, considered himself a member of a privileged class and employed enlisted men, called strikers, as servants. His journal contains one entry which seems to show that he considered Kitty little more than a servant: "I am troubled about a servant, Farrely (an enlisted man) drinks our liquors and gets drunk and is confined in the guard house, and then I have no one to black my shoes. K. [Kitty] takes care of my room, but does it very indifferently."[3]

Kitty, as a reservation Indian, shared in the regular distribution of rations and funds according to treaty. On one occasion, Kautz noted that she returned to the reservation to attend Indian payment.

Kautz had a very full social life. He attended parties, dinners, dances and weddings as well as military functions and simple nights out, but at no time does his journal mention that Kitty joined him at any such event. He also entertained frequently in his own quarters, but the guests were always men. There is absolutely no mention of any woman except Kitty being present in his quarters.

On March 17, 1857, the marriage between Kautz and Kitty produced a son. He was named Nugen for Kautz's dear friend, John Nugen. While in Washington Territory, Kautz always referred to Nugen by his nickname, Lugie, although he called him Nugen in later years.

There are numerous entries in Kautz's journals which indicate that he was devoted to his little family. Lugie contracted whooping cough when he was six months old, an especially dangerous age for Native Americans who had not developed herd immunity to the disease. Kautz noted in his journal, "Lugie is quite sick. His lungs effected by the hooping [sic] cough and I fear he will have a wretched time." The following day, he added, "We had quite a time administering to the little patient." Over the next twelve days Kautz described Lugie's slow recovery.[4]

Among the officers of Kautz's acquaintance who had similar arrangements with Indian women was George Pickett, who was stationed at Fort Bellingham. In January 1858, Kautz received a letter from Pickett stating that he "has received a little recruit at his post, on New Year's Day." The following month Kautz was at Fort Bellingham for court-martial duty and noted, "Pickett has quite a fine little half breed boy."[5] Kautz would not learn until many years later that his friend, Phil Sheridan, had sired two daughters by an Indian woman while at Vancouver Barracks, one of whom, Emma, later married Franklin Pierce Olney, the son of an early settler.

When Kautz was transferred to Semiahmoo Bay in October 1858, Kitty, five months pregnant with their second child, did not join him. She and Lugie remained on the Nisqually Reservation. By mid–December, when Kautz had his new quarters completed to his satisfaction, he was required to return up the Sound to purchase supplies for the Semiahmoo Bay camp. The night after he arrived at Fort Steilacoom, he stayed with Kitty and Nugen on the reservation. He wrote, "I found Etta and Lugie very well and comfortably situated. The Indians here are becoming civilized very rapidly. Some of them live like ordinary white people of the country in log cabins with floors, chairs, tables, bedsteads, &c. It is a degree of improvement that surprises me not a little in the present conditions of Indians who a few years ago were as wild as any savage."[6]

Tenas Puss. After her marriage to August Kautz in an Indian ceremony, she Anglicized her name to Kitty Etta. Photograph taken about 1875.

Kautz returned to Semiahmoo Bay a month later with the holds of two sailing ships loaded with supplies. He described his departure on the schooner *Reporter* briefly: "After some delay ... we set out with a fine breeze about two o'clock P.M. A canoe came along just as we started by previous arrangement and Etta came on board with Lugie as passengers."[7] We can surmise that he had his family in mind when he wrote in his journal on the night of arrival at Semiahmoo Bay, "All is well and I am again established in my quarters."[8]

On February 9, Kautz wrote in his journal, "A brother to Lugie arrived in the world today about three o'clock P.M. The mother was not in labor more than an hour. I called in an old Lummi[9] but her practice of midwifery did not suit Kate and I brought in Dr. Berrien and in a short time after his arrival the boy was born, who I shall call Doctin in consideration of my numerous friends of the medical profession.[10] The mother is doing well. She is much better than a white woman would be under the most favorable circumstances, nature is a better mother than most."[11]

Kitty, did, however, have difficulties. Although Kautz did not explain what the problems were, his note two days after Doctin was born says, "Etta is quite unwell. She has not got through her labor so comfortably as we were led to expect." Doctin was eight days old when Kautz was able to write, "K.[ate] is quite well again."[12]

Kautz received news of his upcoming leave of absence shortly after Doctin was born and, about a week later, mentioned having had a talk with James Berrien about "the dependents." He wrote that Dr. Berrien "laughs about my proposition to have the little ones brought up as Boston children and ridicules the idea of their turning out like others."[13]

Kitty, Lugie and Doctin returned to Steilacoom with Kautz as he was starting east, but they stayed on the Nisqually Reservation. Kautz, in his attempt to provide for them in his absence, went to Fort Nisqually and made arrangements with William Tolmie "for taking care of my little family. I left a hundred dollars with him and shall send him ten more. They are to have a cow and the balance of the money is to be paid to them periodically." Kautz then returned to the Nisqually Reservation and stayed the night. "I saw Mr. Gosnell[14] who also has volunteered to look after my Indian friends. I like his views about Indians. He is down on Indian killing."[15]

The following day, he wrote that he "bid goodbye to my Indian friends on the reservation. Rode to Dr. Tolmie's where I made some additional arrangements with Dr. T. about my little ones."[16] August and Fred Kautz departed from Steilacoom on April 25.

11. To Europe and Back

When August and Frederick Kautz arrived at San Francisco on April 29, 1859, they took rooms at the Sherman House. In addition to attending to some quartermaster business, the older brother had time to take in a play, an opera and two minstrel shows before sailing for Panama and the East on May 5.

The day after arriving in San Francisco, August received a disturbing note from Lieutenant Horatio Gibson of the Third Artillery. It seems Gibson was upset that Kautz had "made remarks reflecting on his conduct" at the Hungry Hill battle four years before. Gibson "wished an explanation or retraction of the same."[1] Kautz answered in a note stating that what remarks he had made to friends were not intended as a personal attack, but only a statement of facts as he saw them. On the day before he left San Francisco, he received another note from Gibson, this one delivered by Erasmus Keyes, charging angrily that Kautz had stated that Gibson had been drunk during the Hungry Hill engagement.

Assuming that Keyes had been Gibson's informant, Kautz was more upset with Keyes than with Gibson. He left a note at the Sherman House for Gibson apologizing for speaking of the matter outside of Gibson's presence and explaining that he had not said that Gibson and Lieutenant Benjamin Allston of the Dragoons were drunk *at* the battle, but rather *before* the battle and stating that it "might have been an excusable error."[2] Because he was leaving for the East the following morning, Kautz gave Gibson his forwarding address, but thought his apology had closed the matter.

The twenty-one-day trip to New York via Panama would have been pleasant except for the seasickness. The brothers arrived in New York on May 26 and took rooms at the Metropolitan Hotel. Fred, anxious to get home, left for Ohio on May 30.

While in New York, Kautz was somewhat surprised but "gratified to meet Lieutenant Allston[3] formerly of the Army. I told him that I had been taken to task by Gibson and told him the substance of our correspondence."[4] If Allston was upset, Kautz failed to note it in his journal.

Kautz left on June 6 for Washington to complete his quartermaster paperwork and to make final arrangements for his leave of absence. On June 13, he was shocked to learn that his leave of absence had been granted, but permission to travel to Europe was denied on the grounds that he might be pressed into military service there "and give the State Department a great deal of trouble."[5] The following morning, he convinced Secretary of War John Buchanan Floyd that, under the terms of his father's manumission, the Grand Duke of Baden had no claim on him. The secretary was so impressed by his argument that he promised to bring the matter up with President Buchanan at a cabinet meeting the following day. The president allowed Kautz "to travel to Europe but, under promise of secrecy, I am to keep the fact that I have a leave out of the papers and especially the fact that I have permission to visit Europe."[6] He left Washington for Ohio the following morning.

On the way home, Kautz stopped in Newcomerstown, Ohio, to deliver a trunk filled with

John Nugen's personal effects. He learned that Nugen's father had died in the previous year, but he presented the trunk to Nugen's siblings, who were being cared for by an uncle. Kautz's journal rarely gives us more than a hint of his emotional feelings, but the family's gratitude and Kautz's own emotional response are recognizable in his journal pages.

Kautz then stopped briefly in Wilmington, Ohio, to see his aunt Katharina Rombach and her family. He arrived in Levanna on June 21 and remained a week. It had been seven years since Kautz had seen his family. He found his father looking as well as ever, but his mother appeared to have grown much older. He described his younger brothers as "strong, robust and sun-burnt" young men and noted that his sister, Sophie, had "grown into a large and radiant woman."[7]

Kautz's comments about meeting other family members and old friends are interesting. "I find people grown much older and many strange faces grown up to manhood and womanhood that I can only remember as children."[8] Later he added, "Everywhere familiar scenes met my eyes, changed and altered in many instances, but still familiar. I recollect everything in its connection with my childhood and the distances that were so great and the objects there so large are now to me so small that I can almost imagine that I have grown into a giant or that everything has been reduced on a smaller scale."[9]

Kautz and Francis Herbst, who had been a topographer with the Northwest Boundary Commission, had planned to begin their journey to Europe together, and Herbst was the first person Kautz met when he arrived in New York City. Kautz remembered that Secretary of War Floyd had enjoined him to maintain secrecy, so he told no one of his travel plans. He and Herbst purchased tickets on the steamer *Kangaroo*, which departed on July 2.

Kautz was seasick by the evening of the first day out, but recovered quickly and enjoyed the rest of the voyage. The *Kangaroo* arrived at Liverpool on July 14 and Kautz and Herbst were at the Royal Hotel Blackfriars Bridge in London two days later.

Kautz was at first impressed by the sin which pervaded the city. He had not previously been exposed to the practice of tipping and wrote, "I was much perplexed with the great many extra charges that are everywhere made by waiters, porters, etc."[10]

During three weeks in England, Kautz visited all of the usual tourist stops, but was most impressed by Westminster Abbey, saying, "I never saw anything so inspiring.... The knowledge that you are standing amidst all that remains of the great rulers, statesmen and poets of past ages and to have the knowledge forced upon you by the very character of the monuments that remain, their time worn appearance, many of them defaced and broken, contained within such a grand and antiquated building is impressive. There is no building that I have visited that has interested me so much."[11]

In London, Kautz met Colonel William Loring[12] of the Mounted Rifle Regiment and the two men toured Scotland, Wales and Ireland together. Owing, perhaps, to the difference in their ranks, Loring treated Kautz more as a servant than as a traveling companion. He displayed several remarkable outbursts of temper, which bothered Kautz, but Kautz complained little, other than to say, "I should not like to be damned to travel forever with him."[13]

At Sandhurst, they met former President Franklin Pierce.[14] Kautz described the encounter briefly: "I was introduced to him by Col. Loring. He immediately asked me about Gov. Stevens' health. I told him that as far as I knew nothing had ever ailed him except fondness for whiskey. He then admitted that that was the object of his inquiry and, as he continued the conversation Pierce expressed his disapproval of his course of martial law and gave me an opportunity of saying a few words against Stevens' general demeanor."[15]

Loring and Kautz returned to London on August 12 and, although both were going to Paris, they traveled separately. To Kautz's partial relief, they did not get together again except for one or two occasions when they were with a group of officers.

Kautz was in Paris for ten days and maintained as busy a pace as he had done in London. He met more than a dozen of his fellow army officers in the French capital, four of whom, Colonel Philip Cooke and Lieutenant John Pegram of the Second Dragoons, John Kelton of the Sixth Infantry and Major George Blake of the First Dragoons, would play important roles in Kautz's life in the next few years. Wanting to see as much of Europe as possible, Kautz was critical of some of the other officers who did not share his enthusiasm, saying in his journal, "I find the officers do not see much of Paris. They loaf about the Hotel de Louis and talk English and learn little French and see only a portion of Paris." Knowing that he would be returning to Paris later in his tour, he added, "When I return here I shall be very different. I shall take a room and isolate myself entirely from Americans and English."[16]

He was also upset with himself for falling in with the other officers in drinking parties which lasted well into the night. One such affair, more formal than the others, was hosted by his classmate, Jerome Bonaparte. It was a lavish dinner party attended by French, American and British diplomats, at least one U.S. senator, and most of the officers of the American and French armies in Paris at the time. Kautz enjoyed the party, but, seeing no end to it, "stole away" about 3 A.M. The following day, after his hangover had subsided, he wrote in his journal, "I am, however, getting tired of these dinner parties, besides I am losing so much time by them. However, I see one thing there; I see how Americans do in Paris and I don't like it and it is time I put an end to it."[17]

As he was putting an end to his stay in Paris, Kautz arranged to meet Lieutenants John Pegram and John Kelton at Cologne (Koln), Prussia, in about a week with plans to travel up the Rhine River to Switzerland together. Kautz then made a rapid swing through the Low Countries. The highlight was a full day spent on the battlefield at Waterloo.

While boarding the train from Amsterdam to Cologne on August 29, he noted that his stomach was upset, which he attributed to the water in Amsterdam. By the time the train reached the Prussian frontier at Emmerich, he described himself as "quite sick" and, afterwards, vomited in the rail car "much to the annoyance of the conductor. It was about six when I reached Oberhausen and two hours more would have taken me to Cologne, but I could not go. I called a boy who guided me to the Royal Hotel, the village inn, plain but comfortable."[18]

By the following morning, Kautz was so ill with fever, vomiting and diarrhea that he could not get out of bed. He managed to send a note to Pegram and Kelton telling them to go on without him. A doctor was called and he gave Kautz some medications which were of no benefit. Instead of going on with their sightseeing trip, Pegram and Kelton graciously came to Oberhausen to see what they could do to help.

Over the next three days, Kautz lay in the inn critically ill. The doctor visited him frequently, the innkeeper's wife nursed him and Pegram and Kelton were almost constantly at his bedside. On September 2, Kautz wrote, "As soon as I can be moved I will go to some hospital, otherwise Kelton and Pegram will not leave me and I feel that is asking too much from them."[19]

When he was stable enough to be moved, he was taken by carriage, accompanied by Pegram and Kelton, to the Convent of Saint Elizabeth at Essen where the Sisters of Charity kindly took him in. He bid Kelton and Pegram goodbye, hoping to meet again in Switzerland.

Kautz was cared for by one of the sisters. At first he couldn't leave his bed and had to be spoon-fed liquids. After about a week, he felt strong enough to travel and the doctor grudgingly gave his approval. It was not until then that he learned he had survived the deadly cholera.

Arriving in Cologne on September 10, Kautz commenced his excursion up the Rhine River. From Mainz on the Rhine, he took the train to Frankfurt and then to Heidelberg, two cities which he enjoyed very much.

He had planned to visit the town where he was born during his European tour and decided to do it at this time. He took the train south to Wilferdingen, then went by omnibus to the city of Pforzheim, arriving on September 18. This was the city where Kautz's father had served his apprenticeship as a carpenter forty years before. At nine the next morning he set out on foot for Ispringen, a distance of about eleven miles. The first building he saw as he entered town was the Gasthaus züm Adler,[20] now a small inn. He learned later that it had once been the private home in which he was born. He proceeded into the center of the village to the Angel, a tavern and inn. He tells us, "I called for a 'shoppen'[21] wine and made myself known, and soon the villagers flocked in, many of them distant relatives. An old man ... who was my godfather came in. He seemed most delighted to see me because I could tell him of his son who went to the United States and lived on my father's place for several years."[22]

Kautz stayed at the Angel that night and the next day he went to the funeral of a man named Joseph Grau.[23] He noted that at the funeral, "The women all wore black dresses and black caps.... The men wore the three cornered hats of the last century and short britches, with a long piece of rope tied to their hats.... It was an interesting spectacle to me."[24]

Kautz hired a photographer to go with him to photograph some of the homes of relatives, the local church and the public buildings. He also took pencil and paper and made sketches of some of the landmarks. He failed to accomplish much, writing, "I was stopped by the villagers so often to tell them about their relatives in America or about my own people in whom they all seem so interested. I am much interested in these simple people myself and much amused also at the simplicity of their questions. Perfect strangers come up and ask me how their Elisabeth is getting along, or whether we have bread, or horses, or wine, etc."[25]

On his 1859 tour of Europe, Kautz visited Ispringen, the village of his birth. By that time, the house where he had been born had become a country inn, the Gasthaus zum Adler.

Kautz continued up the Rhine to Switzerland, where he visited the major cities and was positively impressed. In Switzerland, he once again came in contact with other Americans, including Major George Blake and other officers. Of the Alps, he wrote, "The only effect they had upon me was to recall the snow peaks of Oregon and Washington."[26]

After spending two weeks in Munich and several days in Nürnberg, he proceeded to the Hessian city of Kassel (Cassel), which was his mother's place of birth. The only member of the Löwing family he could locate was the widow of Dorothy Kautz's brother, who lived in poverty with her eighteen-year-old son, Ferdinand.

Kautz met several times with the widow and her son over the next several days. He described one visit: "She wound up begging that I might render her some little assistance. I enquired as to what she stood in the greatest need of at present and she said a cloak for the winter."[27] Two days later, he met with Mrs. Löwing again and presented her with a warm cloak and twenty thalers.

Despite the fact that he was suffering badly from malaria during his stay in Kassel, he was able to write in his journal, "My recollections of Cassel, with the exception of the unpleasant circumstances of the Lewings, will be recalled with pleasure when I relate them to my mother."[28]

Kautz traveled to Hanover, Hamburg, Berlin and Dresden in Germany, and Prague in Bohemia, still bothered by the malaria. He then took the train for Vienna, arriving there on November 25.

A full six weeks were spent in Vienna. Kautz had had little difficulty with language on his European tour. He was fluent in German and was able to use the little French he had learned at the Academy to good advantage. Since he planned to go from Vienna to Italy next, he hired a tutor to teach him Italian, but made little progress.

Kautz left Vienna on January 4, 1860. During a quick swing through northern Italy, he visited the battlefield at Solferino where a major battle had been fought the previous June in what has come to be known as the War for Italian Unification. Kautz wrote, "There are few traces to be seen of the great battle that was fought there a few months ago. A few ball holes in the castle and bullet marks in the little cemetery walls is all that remains to be seen."[29]

The trip from Genoa to Leghorn (Livorno) was by boat and Kautz was again seasick. He enjoyed a week-long stay in Florence, a city he found fascinating. When he saw Antonio Canova's statue of Venus at the Pitti Palace, he compared it to the Venus de Milo in Paris, complaining, "The Venus de Milo disappointed me. The head is too small, but the lower extremities are exceedingly beautiful. Canova's Venus in the Pitti Gallery pleased me much more."[30]

After Florence, Kautz traveled to Rome, arriving January 28 and remaining four weeks. He mentioned in his journal meeting other army officers for the first time since Switzerland. There was much to be seen in Rome, including the Vatican, where he briefly saw the Pope conducting a religious ceremony. Keeping up a very busy schedule, he spent much of his time with his classmate, John Todd.

In addition to the usual tourist stops, Kautz visited the studios of a number of artists who were living and working in Rome. Among these was the sculptress Maria Louisa Lander, whose work Kautz admired more than that of the others. He noted that her statue of Virginia Dare would "be finished next summer for exhibition in the United States." He was so impressed by the statue that he returned later to see it again, saying, "I like the statue of Virginia Dare better than anything in stone that I have seen."[31]

From Rome, Kautz and Major Robert Garnett[32] of the Ninth Infantry went by steamer to Naples. Together they took a tour of Pompeii and, on February 25, rode on horseback to the foot of the lava dome of Mount Vesuvius and proceeded on foot to the crest of the crater. They cooked a lunch of eggs and "beef stake" over a crevice, rode round the crater and descended. Kautz went to bed early that night exhausted.

After a few days in Naples, Kautz began the long journey home. The first leg was a three-day voyage from Naples to Marseilles, France. Although the sea was choppy the first day out, Kautz was so little effected by seasickness that he didn't miss a meal. Passengers aboard the *Capri* included Mr. and Mrs. Fletcher Harper of New York. Kautz described Harper as "a very pleasant man, exceedingly dry in his manner, but evidently very good natured."[33] After arriving at Marseilles, Harper asked Kautz to prepare some articles for his magazine.

Kautz bid goodbye to the Harpers at Lyons and took the train alone to Paris on March 6. He seems to have forgotten the promise he had made to himself before he left Paris the previous August to isolate himself from Americans and avoid the luxury hotels because he took a room at the Louvre Hotel and immediately attempted to locate his friends, Pegram and Kelton.

Over the next two weeks, Kautz, often accompanied by Pegram or Kelton or by the Harpers, visited some sights he had missed on his first stay and a few he saw for a second time. His evening entertainments included a performance by Jean Eugene Robert-Houdin, considered the father of modern magic, which Kautz considered "very clever."[34]

Finally, he and Pegram began their journey home by taking the boat train to London. They arrived in London on March 19 and purchased tickets for seventy-five dollars each for cabins aboard the *Kangaroo*, which was sailing from Liverpool on March 21.

The *Kangaroo* stopped at Lancaster to pick up about 200 steerage passengers. Kautz, perhaps thinking about his own parents' journey to the New World, wrote, "The scene among the emigrants was remarkable and characteristic. Old women on the wharf were seen crying and gesticulating as long as we were in sight. The passengers on board seemed affected also coming on board, but the excitement of transhipment from the tender set them to thinking about other things."[35]

After a rough passage, the *Kangaroo* arrived in New York Harbor early on the morning of April 6. It was learned that a child on board had come down with smallpox. This required that the passengers and crew be vaccinated before they went ashore. Because of the delay, Kautz and Pegram did not get to their rooms at the Metropolitan Hotel until early evening. While waiting, Kautz had time to read some recent local newspapers. He was surprised to read in the *New York Times* of April 3 an order for him to report to Governor's Island in order to go with recruits over the Rocky Mountains by way of Fort Benton and Fort Walla Walla.

12. By Steamer to the Mullan Road

When Brevet Second Lieutenant John Mullan arrived in San Francisco with his West Point classmates in December 1852, he was assigned to the First Artillery Regiment. Transfer to the Second Artillery coincided with an appointment as topographical engineer to an expedition commanded by Isaac Stevens to map a potential rail route to the Pacific Northwest.[1] Mullan, Stevens and part of the team worked from May to November 1853 on the eastern end of the route while a team led by Captain George McClellan worked from the west. When Stevens left to take over as governor of Washington Territory, Mullen's team completed the exploration in the summer of 1854.

Mullan then went to Washington City to lobby for funds to complete a military road to the Pacific Northwest. Through his and Stevens's lobbying efforts, $30,000 was appropriated, but legislation for use of the funds was not passed because the War Department saw little use for a road to the peaceful Northwest.

The outbreak of the Indian war of 1855–1858 provided the impetus to resurrect the project and Stevens finally got approval. Mullan was Stevens's choice to head the military road project and the War Department consented. The road was to be built from Fort Benton in Montana to Fort Walla Walla in Washington Territory. The very war which provided the incentive for the road-building effort was the thing which prevented its accomplishment. The area around Fort Walla Walla was too dangerous for the exploratory work to proceed. Mullan disbanded his team and served as topographical engineer in Colonel George Wright's successful campaign in eastern Washington. In the winter of 1858–59, Mullan returned east to ask for additional money for the project. He was so convincing that, in March 1859, $100,000 was added to the $30,000 which had already been appropriated.

Work on the road began at Fort Walla Walla on July 1, 1859, with about 100 laborers and an escort of 100 artillerymen. If you are going to have a military road, you need to have some military to travel the road. This is where August Kautz comes in.

As we have seen, when Kautz returned to the States from his European tour in March 1860, he found orders awaiting him to report to Fort Columbus on Governor's Island, and proceed to Jefferson Barracks, Missouri, by the first of May with a company of recruits enlisted at Governor's Island. The recruits were to be transported from St. Louis to Fort Benton via steamship and thence to Fort Walla Walla via the Mullan Road.

Learning that about half of the recruits were to be raised at Newport Barracks, Kentucky, Kautz called on General Winfield Scott to request that he be assigned to men at Newport Barracks rather than Fort Columbus. General Scott was absent, but Colonel George Thomas, his old tactics instructor, "was very kind and attentive and was kind enough to have me ordered to Port Columbus instead of Newport Barracks [this reversal was Kautz's error]."[2]

On April 11, Kautz and Pegram took the night train for Washington, where Kautz went to the adjutant general's office to get information about the expedition, but learned nothing. He had a brief visit with Joseph Lane before catching the evening train for Ohio. He regretted not having an opportunity to bid Pegram goodbye.

After a four-day visit home, Kautz, along with Lieutenant George W. Carr of the Ninth Infantry, assembled the 150 recruits for the train trip to Jefferson Barracks near St. Louis.

Major George Blake[3] of the First Dragoons, the commander of the expedition, did not arrive until April 29. Kautz had met Blake twice while in Europe. On both occasions, Blake had suggested that they travel together, but Kautz declined, saying in his journal, "I don't think he would make a pleasant companion. His manners are not agreeable.... I shall avoid going with him if possible." Now Kautz was going to travel with Blake and there was no possibility of avoiding it.

The dual purpose of the expedition was to test the possibility of transcontinental travel over Mullan's new road and also to supply recruits for the Ninth Infantry. The Ninth had suffered from the double attrition caused by the Indian war and by desertions of men wishing to strike it rich in the western gold fields. More importantly, the Ninth had been organized in 1855 and all of the men's enlistments would be expiring in 1860.

The 300 men were divided into four companies of about seventy-five men each. The company commanders were Captain DeLancey Floyd-Jones, Captain John H. Lendrum of the Third Artillery, First Lieutenant George W. Carr of the Ninth Infantry and First Lieutenant August V. Kautz. Each company had a second lieutenant as adjutant, one of whom was Martin D. Hardin, who wrote an account of the expedition for the *United Service Magazine* in 1882. Also along was Pierre Chouteau of the American Fur Company, who had contracted to supply the transportation to Fort Benton.

Chouteau provided three steamers, the *Spread Eagle*, a 400-ton side-wheeler, and the *Key West* and *Chippewa*, stern-wheelers of 175 tons each. The American Fur Company was to be paid $100 for each officer, $50 for each of the recruits and $10 for each 100 pounds of supplies, which included wagons, oxen and subsistence for the men during the trip. The *Key West* and *Chippewa* drew only thirty-two inches of water and were expected to make it all the way to Fort Benton, while the *Spread Eagle* drew forty-eight inches. It was anticipated that the *Spread Eagle* would not make the entire journey and would have to be unloaded at some point prior to reaching Fort Benton.

The Blake Recruit Expedition, as it was known, got off on its 2700-mile voyage up the Missouri on May 3, 1860. Kautz's company and that of Floyd-Jones were aboard the *Spread Eagle*, Carr's on the *Key West* and Lendrum's on the *Chippewa*.

Travel on the uncharted Missouri River was safe only in the daylight hours. The ships tied up the first night at the confluence of the Mississippi and Missouri Rivers. During the first ten days, progress was slowed by the exceedingly low condition of the river. The anticipated spring thaw in the far-off Rockies had not yet reached the lower Missouri. On May 21, all three ships had to be unloaded and hauled across a bar below Sioux City where the water was only 28 inches deep. This operation took the better part of two days and Kautz noted in his journal on May 22, "We are authorized to return to [Fort] Randall if we cannot reach Fort Benton, by instructions received today. The river is reported as exceedingly low, and some doubt of further progress exists."[4]

To this point, the tone of Kautz's journal entries suggests a gloomy atmosphere on the three ships. Besides the low water level, there were other troubles. One of the officers was intermittently drunk and several were sick with boils and fevers. Another received a gunshot wound in the shoulder in an altercation with one of the crew of the *Key West*. Desertions of the recruits occurred on an almost daily basis and others were stealing away at night to the towns. As we read Kautz's journals, we can feel the exasperation he felt. The mood suddenly changes with the following notation on May 25, "We went along today without any interruptions. We met a considerable rise in the river this afternoon, and it is hoped it is the long expected June rise."[5]

As though to reflect the elation felt on board, when the three steamers arrived at Fort Randall, South Dakota, the following day, they were treated to "four or five hours entertaining and being entertained.... The landing of three steamers at one time is an event witnessed for the first time. Some of the officers became quite merry.... The Adjutant, who under the influence of wine became exceedingly agreeable, ordered out the band, which entertained us for an hour just before leaving."[6]

Although many more difficulties presented themselves in the succeeding six weeks, they seem to have been met with greater optimism. There would yet be numerous bars to pull the ships over. The small fleet was forced to stop several times each day to cut wood for the boilers, and wood was becoming scarce as they passed into the prairies beyond Fort Randall. These heavy labors, however, served more to break the monotony than to break the men.

The last town passed was Sioux City. Beyond that point there was nothing but wildlife and scenery and a few forts occupied by the army or by fur-trading companies. The first buffalo was sighted on June 14, but great herds were seen later. On June 22, Kautz noted, "We have not been out of sight of them [buffalo] for several days."[7] Firing from the ship at buffalo relieved the monotony of the voyage as well as the monotony of the dinner menu.

As had been planned, the *Spread Eagle*, because of her greater draught, did not go all the way to Fort Benton. The two companies aboard were transferred to the *Key West* and the *Chippewa* just above the mouth of the Milk River. Both of the stern-wheelers had been much lightened by the discharge of freight at Indian reservations and at various military posts along the route, so there was room to spare on the two smaller ships.

Fort Benton was reached on July 2 and, the next day, "a very pretty encampment made of Sibly tents, new and clean"[8] had sprung up on the plain near the fort. On July 4, the officers were treated to a few bottles of champagne courtesy of Pierre Chouteau prior to his departure with the *Key West* and the *Chippewa*. Next day, the steamers were off amid the firing of cannons.

Having made it this far, the expedition was forced to wait almost a month before proceeding. Mullan had experienced delays, not the least of which was the need to blast a six-mile long cut through the Bitterroot Canyon, which occupied 150 men for a period of six weeks. Kautz attempted to stay busy through the wait. He fished almost daily to supplement the officers' mess. On July 19, he and several other officers began a three-day excursion to the Great Falls of the Missouri. On July 13, he had noted that Mullan and his assistant, W.F. Raynolds, had arrived at a camp about ten miles distant, but that the working crews were far behind. On July 29, he complained to his journal that the activities of the officers had deteriorated to lounging , gossiping and sleeping during the day, but was quick to add that he had never been able to do the last of these.

Twice during this period, Kautz commented on the dyspepsia which had bothered him off and on since 1857. On July 12 he "had an unpleasant cholic, having had no dinner," and, on August 7, he attributed a "derangement of the stomach" to "being so long during the day without anything to eat." From the distance of 150 years, these symptoms strongly suggest peptic ulcer disease.

Mullan arrived at Fort Benton on the first day of August. He had not yet come down to earth after learning that he had been allocated an additional $100,000 to repair and refine his road. Kautz had not seen Mullan since 1852 and he wrote in his journal that he "had a long talk with Mullan about his road and his troubles. He is decidedly more monomaniacal in his demonstrations than I ever knew him. He imagines everybody who is not in favor of his road to be against it."[9] It is not clear whether Kautz was being critical of his friend or merely stating a fact as he saw it. Certainly a man who has spent eight years of his life working on such an ambitious project from its inception to its completion is entitled to some degree of monomania.

The Blake Recruit Expedition was finally on the road on August 7. The road, some portions of which are still in existence today, followed approximately the route of Montana State Road 200 from present-day Great Falls to Missoula, then Interstate 90 to near Spokane before dropping south along the branches of the Snake River to Walla Walla. It crossed the Continental Divide at Rogers Pass and the Bitterroot Range at Lookout Pass. It was the most ambitious engineering project ever attempted by the frontier army. The going was slow, the oxen often unable to move over the rough road at more than one mile per hour. The expedition crossed the Sun River on August 9 and camped at the Blackfoot Indian Agency on August 10. The Dearborn River was reached on August 12. They crossed the Continental Divide at Rogers Pass on August 18. That evening, Kautz wrote, "We got an early start, and often assisting the wagons up the hill to the Divide, we pushed on."[10] He failed to note that Mullan's crew had placed a marker at the summit indicating a distance to Fort Benton of 150 miles.

On August 21, the expedition reached the first white settlement to be passed, the house of a trader named John Grant, who lived beside the Hell Gate River. By August 27 and 28, settlers and traders became more numerous near where the Hell Gate joins the Bitterroot River.

On September 1, Kautz noted, "Our road lay over high, steep hillside cuttings, dangerous in many places, for six miles." He was no doubt describing the section of road just west of the present-day town of Alberton which had set Mullan's schedule back six weeks. Two days later, Kautz noted that they had passed a large band of Coeur d'Alene Indians who were on their way across the mountains to the "buffalo country."

The St. Regis Borgia River was crossed twenty-six times between September 6 and September 10 on the climb to the summit of the Bitterroot Mountains. They crossed the Bitterroots at Lookout Pass on September 11.

The expedition fought through mud and forty-eight crossings of the Coeur d'Alene River over the next three days and arrived at the Coeur d'Alene Mission on September 15. Captain Floyd-Jones expressed the relief of the entire command when, in his report, he said, "The sight of a church and dwelling house, surrounded by cultivated and enclosed fields was highly grateful to all — a sight we had not witnessed since our departure from Fort Randall on the Missouri."[11]

The expedition met a party of Mullan's road-builders at their camp on September 14. Mullan was with them and he carried with him bundles of mail for the expedition. There were orders for Kautz to proceed from Coeur d'Alene to Fort Colville in northeastern Washington Territory with 149 of the recruits.[12] After delivering the recruits to Fort Colville, he was to proceed to Fort Chehalis on Gray's Harbor on the Washington coast. Fort Chehalis was home to Company A of Kautz's 4th Infantry Regiment under the command of Captain Maurice Maloney. In Kautz's mail was also a letter from Maloney with directions to Fort Chehalis.

On September 17, it was decided that Lieutenant Martin Hardin, Lieutenant Caleb H. Carlton of the Seventh Infantry and Dr. George Cooper would accompany Kautz and the 149 recruits on the march to Fort Colville. Since Major Blake felt it necessary to take the entire baggage train with the remainder of the recruits to Walla Walla, the party detailed to Fort Colville was required to await the arrival of an empty train from that fort.

They were finally on the way on September 23. Although the going was difficult, Kautz was impressed by the magnificent scenery they passed. They made the 120-mile march in eight days.

After clearing the paperwork required to transfer the recruits and their baggage, Kautz, Hardin, Carlton and Cooper left Colville on October 4. Now traveling without the recruits, they made better time, averaging close to thirty miles per day. The little party crossed the Snake River on October 9 and arrived at Walla Walla two days later in time to see the departure of an expedition for the Emigrant Road which was leaving "on account of a massacre that is said to have occurred of an entire train of immigrants."[13] At Walla Walla, Kautz met Captain A.J. Smith, whom he had fought beside in the Battle of Hungry Hill in Oregon. If Smith had heard of Kautz's correspondence with Lieutenant Horatio Gibson, it wasn't mentioned. Although Kautz was concerned that Smith might be upset by remarks made about Smith's performance at Hungry Hill, he found Smith to be cordial.

When Kautz arrived at the town of The Dalles on October 13, he did not comment on the comfort of the bed at the Umatilla House, the first he had lain in in five months, but he did say that he went to bed early.

The next leg of Kautz's journey was a boat ride down the Columbia River to Vancouver Barracks. From there, he proceeded to Fort Steilacoom on horseback.

Kautz had not seen Kitty, Lugie and Augustus for eighteen months. Their reunion was surprisingly brief and seemingly unemotional as his journal entry of October 25 relates, "Did not get away from Olympia this morning until near noon, I found my horse considerably broken down.... I went by the reservation and stopped an hour. They were glad to see me and seemed in the most perfect health. I find that they have conducted themselves very well and remained on the reservation since I went away. I did not reach Steilacoom until after eight o'clock."[14]

13. Fort Chehalis

When Dutch Kautz arrived back at Fort Steilacoom in October 1860, he received a letter from Captain Lewis Hunt requesting that he take part in Hunt's wedding at the fort to Colonel Casey's daughter, Bernice, the following month. The letter had been mailed from Fort Steilacoom and it had followed him back to its point of origin. He was anxious to get on to Fort Chehalis but, not wanting to disappoint Hunt, he delayed his departure until after the wedding.

Kautz was disappointed with the social life at the post. A number of officers' wives were now present and he complained that the women controlled the social calendar. "The post is much more disagreeable for bachelors as they have less freedom and ease."[1] Perhaps he was referring in part to the freedom to cohabit with Indian women. He did not elaborate.

Lewis Hunt and Bernice Casey were married on November 28 and Kautz got away the following day, saying, "I left Steilacoom with few regrets. My stay has not been very pleasant."[2]

He stayed at Aunt Becky's Hotel in Olympia that night, noting that it cost $40 to have his baggage carried the twenty-five miles from Fort Steilacoom compared to the $64 it had cost to ship it from New York. Kautz, Kitty and the boys, aided by some Indians, made the trip down the Chehalis River in three days, staying at Indian camps the nights of December 3 and 4. He noted at the Satsop River stop that they "supped on dried salmon and potatoes."[3] They arrived at Fort Chehalis about midnight of December 5.

According to Kautz, "Fort Chehalis was situated on the endspit called Peterson's Point south of the entrance to the bay and between the southern arc of the bay and the ocean beach, partially concealed by the stunted pines that nearly surround it."[4]

"I found a set of quarters just completed and ready to be taken."[5] The house was also occupied by his friend from happier days at Fort Steilacoom, Dr. Horace Wirtz.

Kautz enjoyed, as always, the company of Mrs. Maloney. Although he still complained of Captain Maloney's command style, there were no confrontations. Perhaps Kautz deserves much of the credit. He said, "It is utterly out of the question to reason with him about anything, he persists in his opinions against all reason."[6]

He busied himself with hobbies to occupy his spare time. He built a workbench in the attic of his quarters and spent many hours there and in the post carpenter's shop, where he completed much of the furnishings for his new quarters. He sketched a bit and read everything he could get his hands on, including Dumas's *Three Musketeers* (then known as *The Three Guardsmen*) and the lesser-known sequel *Twenty Years Later* in the original French language version.

The isolated post offered little in the way of social amusements. The only other officer present besides Kautz and Maloney was Lieutenant Edward Conner.[7] The only white women at the post were Mrs. Maloney, the wife of the post sutler, named McKee, and his two unmarried daughters, Anna and Helen. Kautz described the girls as "quite pretty but exceedingly shy and not at all interesting."[8] Kautz either misjudged the McKee girls or they got over their shyness rather quickly. He described a private theatrical performance put on by the girls "under the protection of Mrs. Maloney" and "strictly concealed from McKee whose religious notions would be shocked by such impropriety.... The girls dressed in short dresses and went through fairy dances and song, very boldly it is true and very improperly also I should say."[9]

Kitty had the companionship of a woman named Anna, who was living with Horace Wirtz, and we can only assume that the two women were a comfort to each other.

Both Nugen and Doctin suffered significant injuries in March. On March 11, Kautz wrote, "Lugie has been in bed all day. He fell on his abdomen and cut a wound just below the navel with a broken bottle that gave us much alarm when he was first brought in by a soldier bleeding very profusely. The wound proved light but still a narrow escape."[10]

Two weeks later, Doctin was scalded. "An exceedingly painful accident occurred to Doctin this morning. He ran against a bucket of hot water which his mother was carrying and severely seared his face, breast and right arm. The Doctor came to his relief immediately, covered the wounds with sweet oil and lint and afterwards prepared a compound of sweet oil and lime water which seems to relieve him much." The following day he added, "Doctin bears up with his misfortune exceedingly well and will recover without anything worse than a marked face."[11]

Kautz, like all officers in the remote Pacific Northwest in 1861, had a very personal interest in the national news. Depending on the weather and other factors, it took three to four weeks for news from the East to reach posts such as Fort Chehalis, but even that was far quicker than it had been prior to the inception of the Pony Express the previous year. Kautz complained, "We received our letters and papers quite regularly, but long after the rest of the world had forgotten what they contained."[12]

So the men waited, sometimes patiently, often not, to learn of events back east which would profoundly effect their lives.

The news of Abraham Lincoln's election arrived before Kautz left Fort Steilacoom, but it was not until January 17, when Lieutenant Conner arrived back from a trip to Fort Steilacoom with rumors of the possible secession of South Carolina, that Kautz's journal begins to reflect his growing anxiety. According to Kautz, Conner said that "great excitement prevails everywhere. People are so much excited that they will not even take U.S. Treasury drafts and the general impression is that our commissions have expired by limitation, there being no government to sustain them." Kautz was skeptical, however, adding, "It is another evidence of what people's excitement will do."[13] Despite this early rumor, the news of South Carolina's actual secession arrived on February 5 along with additional rumors that blood had already been shed.

By the end of March, Kautz had learned of Lincoln's arrival in Washington and that General David Twiggs had surrendered the Department of Texas to that seceding state.[14] He concluded, based on newspaper accounts, "that unmistakably there will be a Southern Confederacy."[15] He read Lincoln's first inaugural address one month to the day after it was given, but failed to comment on it, and, when he wrote in his journal on April 11 that Fort Sumter was to be abandoned by the Union and that "there will probably be no fighting,"[16] he had no way of knowing that the South Carolina fort would be fired upon the following day, thus starting the U.S. Civil War.

The first week of May ended months of uncertainty for Kautz, but not until he was forced to make a difficult decision. On May 1, he received an order from regimental headquarters detailing him for the government recruiting service in the East. On the same day Captain Maloney received a leave of absence[17] and three days later Doctor Wirtz departed Fort Chehalis for the East.

Kautz was not required to accept the recruiting assignment. With Captain Maloney's departure the command of Fort Chehalis would fall to him. With the title of post commander would come a $46 per month pay raise. Kautz deliberated briefly, but decided to accept the recruiting duty and leave command of the fort to Lieutenant Conner. Thinking of his relationship with Kitty, he reasoned, "I may as well break up now as a year hence. It will be less difficult now than then.[18]

The day before Maloney's departure, Kautz wrote, "Those who remain are disappointed and those who go away are much excited about the prospect."[19] Nonetheless he seemed to have been procrastinating about leaving until mail arrived on May 8 with news from the East containing full particulars of the fall of Fort Sumter. His comment was, "Matters look exceedingly warlike. I shall get ready to leave immediately."[20] The following day, after seeing the Maloneys off, he started packing.

Because Kitty and the boys were going with him, he planned to return via the Chehalis River, then overland to Steilacoom and seek passage to San Francisco from there, leaving his Indian family at the Nisqually Reservation. He could find no Indians to transport them and their belongings up the river, so he paid a Mr. Berg and three other white men twenty dollars to do the job.

They were off on May 12 in two canoes. It had rained heavily and the river current was so swift that the men could make little progress. Kautz noted in his journal the second night out, "The white men we have are not very expert at working canoes. I have found it impossible to get Indians."[21]

On the fourth day, in order to reduce the labor of the men, all of their belongings were transferred to one large canoe, leaving little room. Kautz decided to walk on ahead and wait. As Kautz tells it

> About two o'clock Mr. Berg came up and reported that the canoe had been wrecked and one of my trunks and many loose things in the canoe were lost. It was a wonderful escape for those in the canoe. In ascending a rapid ... they lost command of the canoe and the current forced it upon a snag where it split and went to pieces leaving the squaw and two children ... clinging to the wreck with two white men. The other two men were washed off and were able to get ashore, one of them after three hours delay was able to bring up one of the other canoes and take them off. How they all clung to such a frail support for so long is incomprehensible and that none were drowned is miraculous.... Of course Berg has lost his wages and I have lost my trunk containing many valuable things and two previous volumes of my journal.... I congratulate myself that no lives were lost. Kate is much worried and annoyed at her losses.[22]

When efforts to recover their belongings from the muddy water failed, Kautz offered a reward of fifty dollars for recovery of the trunk and moved on. They arrived at Olympia on May 20. Kautz went on to Fort Steilacoom and Kitty, Nugen and Doctin went to the reservation.

Having heard that the steamship *Pacific* was due at Victoria and would be heading to San Francisco, he left Steilacoom for Victoria on June 3, but not before spending the previous night with Kitty, Nugen and Doctin. As luck would have it, he missed the *Pacific*, giving him an opportunity to have a final visit with the Tolmies at their home at Cloverdale before returning up the Sound.

The steamer stopped off briefly at Port Townsend on the way, allowing Kautz to bid farewell to George Pickett. The one-hour visit with Pickett was revealing. "Pickett was very much concerned at the course things have taken. He says if his state secedes he must resign. He condemned South Carolina in very strong terms. I advised him to hold on, that his Regt. [Ninth Infantry] would not be ordered east and he probably would not be called on to participate in the war."[23]

Pickett did not take Kautz's advice.

Kautz arrived at Olympia early in the morning of June 7 and found, once again, that no steamship was due to leave for San Francisco in the foreseeable future. There was, however, a sailing vessel, the bark *Ork*, Captain Frank commanding, which was about to depart Steilacoom for San Francisco with a load of lumber. Kautz decided to take a cabin on the *Ork*.

He spent the night with Kitty and the boys and "bid them goodbye at the reservation" once again. He boarded the *Ork* and was underway the following morning. He wrote, "It will be a new experience to me to take so long a voyage on a sail vessel."[24]

After his departure, Kautz feared that Kitty was neither financially or emotionally able to care for the two boys. Even before he left, he arranged with Edward Huggins, who had replaced William Tolmie as chief factor at Fort Nisqually, to have Nugen placed in the home of Wesley and Catherine Gosnell. Gosnell at the time was Indian agent at the Nisqually Reservation and later farmed a few miles to the south in Lewis County. In 1867, Huggins was able to arrange for Doctin to be placed with Warren Gove, the government-paid carpentry instructor at the Puyallup Reservation. For many years, Kautz sent bi-annual payments to Huggins, or directly to Gosnell and Gove, to cover expenses for the care of the boys. Payments mentioned in his journal alone total more than $2000. Apparently, he determined to discontinue his support of the boys when they reached the age of fourteen. The last payment which he mentioned was $70 sent to Mr. Gove in July 1873. He maintained contact with the boys through Huggins and their foster parents and, later, directly with them.

There is no indication that he ever wrote to Kitty or heard from her directly, but Huggins mentioned her often in his letters, usually negatively. She was remarried on July 3, 1875, to a man named William Diggins. That marriage ended in divorce and she married again on February 15, 1884, to Henry Walker. She had no more children. She died in 1891.

14. The Sixth U.S. Cavalry

The bark *Ork*, with its load of lumber and only two passengers, reached the Straits of Juan de Fuca twenty-four hours after leaving Steilacoom, but it took another week for it to emerge into the Pacific Ocean, fighting fierce headwinds and flood tides.

When the *Ork* sailed into San Francisco on June 27, Kautz took a room at the Metropolitan Hotel and reported to headquarters. After drawing his pay and taking an oath of allegiance,[1] he bought a "Chinese trunk," filled it with blankets, clothing and other supplies for Kitty and the boys, enclosed seventy-five dollars and dispatched it to Edward Huggins at Fort Nisqually.

On June 30, he was again annoyed by a note from Lieutenant Horatio Gibson asking an explanation of the statements he had made about Gibson's part in the Hungry Hill fight. He finally put the matter behind him by accepting Gibson's statement that he was not drunk and retracting his own statement to the contrary.

His old friend Rodney Glison and Captain Frank of the *Ork* were the only well-wishers to see Kautz off when he boarded the steamer bound for Panama on July 1. When the ship put in overnight at Acapulco on July 9, the passengers, anxious to learn of the progress of the war, clamored to read the papers. Kautz found his name in the papers. He wrote, "We seized on the papers to get the news. The army has been increased by the addition of nine new regiments of infantry and one of cavalry and one of artillery. I see my name down as captain of the (Sixth) 3rd Cavalry."[2] He would, therefore, not be going on recruit duty.

Kautz arrived in New York on August 2 to the news of the Battle of Manassas (also known as First Bull Run), "in which," as Kautz erroneously reported, "the Southern forces have been disgracefully repulsed."[3]

Kautz reported to Colonel A.J. Smith, commander of the recruiting service. Since he was no longer assigned to recruit duty there, he was granted permission by Smith to travel to Washington. There, he stayed with Dr. George Suckley and met James Denver, who had recently been appointed brigadier general of volunteers. When he reported to the adjutant general's office the day after arriving, he learned that he was to report to his regiment at Pittsburgh.

On August 7, Kautz visited the Washington Navy Yard to learn whether his brother Albert, who had graduated from the Naval Academy the previous summer, was stationed there. He learned instead that Albert had been taken prisoner by the Confederates. Unable to learn more in Washington, he took the morning train on August 9 to Philadelphia, where he boarded Albert's ship, the USS *Flag*. A midshipman from Cincinnati named Dexter was able to give him additional details.

Albert had been assigned in May to the USS *Flag* of Admiral Louis Goldsborough's North Atlantic Blocking Squadron. On June 20, the *Flag*, commanded by Lieutenant Louis Sartori, took as a prize the brig *Hannah Balch* off Savannah, Georgia. On the same day, Albert was ordered by Sartori to take command of the *Hannah Balch* and proceed with her to Philadelphia where she was to be turned over to the District Court for determination of her status as a prize of war.

Albert sailed the *Hannah Balch* into the Gulf Stream and was proceeding northward when, on June 25, she was overtaken and captured off Cape Hattaras by the armed steamer *Coffee*, commanded by the privateer Thomas M. Crossan. The six men under Albert's command were imprisoned at Fort Macon, North Carolina, and Albert was sent to Raleigh, North Carolina, but was paroled with permission to live in Warren County, North Carolina.

After speaking with Dexter, Kautz returned to New York, where he found his orders to report to headquarters of the Third Cavalry at Camp South, two miles east of Pittsburgh. Suffering again from malaria, he took the early train on August 15 for Cincinnati, intending to spend a few days at home before reporting to his regiment.

When the train reached Pittsburgh, it was learned that it could proceed no farther because floods had washed out bridges between Pittsburgh and Cincinnati. Kautz took a room at the Monongahela House. At the hotel, he met the commander of his regiment, Lieutenant Colonel William H. Emory,[4] who, because the regiment was short of officers, pleaded with Kautz to forego his planned trip home and remain in Pittsburgh. Kautz wrote, "I determined to stay and in the evening went out to camp and went to duty."[5]

On April 15, 1861, the day after the surrender of Fort Sumter, Abraham Lincoln had issued a proclamation declaring that a state of insurrection existed and calling for 75,000 militia to be raised by the states for a period of three months. On May 3, when it became apparent that hostilities could not possibly end in three months, Lincoln issued a call for an additional 42,000 volunteers, these to serve for three years or the duration of the war if it should end sooner. At the same time, he ordered the regular Army to be increased by eight regiments of infantry, one of cavalry and one of artillery, thus raising the total strength of the regulars from about 16,000 to more than 23,000 and the size of the entire army, regulars and volunteers, to approximately 155,000.[6]

A further restructuring of the army involved the cavalry wing. In an effort to modernize the mounted branch of the service, the two regiments of dragoons and one of mounted rifles of the old army were designated simply as cavalry. This change became effective August 3, 1861, two weeks before Kautz arrived in Pittsburgh. As a consequence, Kautz's newly-formed Third Cavalry became the Sixth Cavalry.

When Kautz reported to duty on August 16, he was given command of about eighty recruits, mostly from western Pennsylvania and northern Ohio, "with instructions to organize them into Company B." He later wrote, "It was no easy task to take charge of so many men without a single noncommissioned officer or man among them that knew anything of a soldier's life or had any clear idea of duty or subordination. I had to do first sergeant's duty, keep the books, and attend to all the details usually performed by the noncommissioned officers."[7]

Kautz gives us but a brief overview of the difficulties he encountered in these first few days. These included obtaining and distributing uniforms, cooking gear and other personal equipment for the men, and arranging for army rations (the men had, up to then, been fed by a civilian contractor). He purchased furniture and other equipment for the camp, much of which he paid for from his own pocket with the hope of being reimbursed from the company fund.

At least two other companies of the Sixth Cavalry were at Camp South but, by August 28, all had been moved to a camp near Bladensburg, Maryland, thirty miles north of Washington. As new recruits continued to arrive, the regiment was made up of about 1000 men in three battalions of four companies each. If any of the other company commanders had less difficulty in getting their companies organized, Kautz's journal fails to tell us so. Among the company commanders were Captains Joseph H. Taylor, John Savage, James S. Brisbin, William S. Abert, George C. Cram, Andrew W. Evans (a classmate of Kautz at West Point), Charles R. Lowell, William P. Sanders, John Irvin Gregg and his cousin, David M. Gregg.

Immediately after arriving at Bladensburg, Kautz took the train into Washington to report and to procure rations and various regimental properties and equipment, but he was able to do little more than procure the rations. The following day he tried again, this time accompanied by Captain Taylor. Once again, their efforts were less than successful. Kautz commented, ... "There is considerable delay in procuring anything here.... All is confusion and excitement," and in a wonderful description of the old army run-around, "The circumlocution of the various officers is extraordinary."[8] On the latter occasion, Taylor took Kautz to dinner at the home of his father, Colonel Joseph P. Taylor, Commissary General of Subsistence for the army. Major General Irvin McDowell was also present and Kautz greatly enjoyed the company of the two older men, although he said of McDowell, "[He] was very sleepy and dull, whether from fatigue or not, I could not tell."[9]

Kautz was still very concerned about his brother Albert, and, on September 7, accompanied by General Denver, he met with Major General Benjamin Butler, recently arrived from a successful campaign at Cape Hattaras. It was hoped that Butler might shed some light on Albert's whereabouts. Butler could offer no information, but was kind enough to offer to send a letter, quickly written, through the lines to Albert.

On September 8, Kautz managed to get a ten-day leave of absence for the visit home he had anticipated the previous month. After a pleasant visit with his family, he returned on September 18 and was "exceedingly disgusted" to learn that Major Lawrence A. Williams had been transferred to the regiment during his absence. Williams, a classmate of Kautz at West Point, was a distant relative of Robert E. Lee and, as a result, he had gained favor with some of the high-ranking officers of the old army, including Lee's close friend, Winfield Scott. Kautz was of the opinion that, because of these connections, Williams had been promoted beyond his ability. Kautz was not alone in his low opinion of Williams. On the day Williams reported for duty, he wrote in his journal, "He was received very cooly by the officers. His appointment is very unpopular with all."[10]

At Kautz's request, two veteran noncommissioned officers, Sergeant Nolan and Private Murphy of Company K of the Second Cavalry, were transferred to his company. Sergeant Nolan would serve as first sergeant of Company B and Murphy would be its clerk, easing the burden of administrative duties which Kautz had complained of earlier.

By the first week of October, most of the regiment had been supplied with horses, and training began in earnest with daily drills in evolution of the line. It was said at the time that infantry soldiers could be thoroughly trained in as little as three months, but satisfactory training of cavalry troopers required one to two years, so progress was slow.

The campsite at Bladensburg proved to be unsatisfactory and, after searching for some time, Colonel Emory found a suitable site on the outskirts of Washington adjacent to the Congressional Cemetery. The move to the city took place on October 12.

On October 26, Second Lieutenant Christian Balder, a German-born officer who had worked his way up through the ranks, reported for duty in Kautz's Company B. Having acquired a thorough knowledge of cavalry tactics, Balder proved an able assistant.[11]

Meanwhile, Kautz continued to seek information about his brother and learned that Albert had been confined at Libby Prison in Richmond. On November 2, he wrote in his journal, "It stormed very hard most of the day and I remained in my tent most of the day. I was much taken about by Albert who popped his head through the closely tied tent front this afternoon. At first I thought it was Fred. I was completely taken by surprise to find that it was Albert. He was accompanied by Genl. Denver. He left Richmond three days since and has been released with parole for fifty days with permission to procure an exchange. I went to the city with him and remained until after dark."[12]

He learned that the order for Albert's imprisonment was given August 15 by Confederate President Jefferson Davis and signed by Secretary of the Navy Stephen R. Mallory. It was in retaliation for the confinement of Confederate Naval Midshipman Albert G. Hudgins in the Tombs at New York City. Hudgins was being held as a criminal rather than as a prisoner of war. The order stated that Albert and a Lieutenant Seldon should be placed in "two cells as nearly the size as that in which Mr. Hudgins is confined," and that the prisoners "may be informed that the cruel treatment of Mr. Hudgins has constrained us to subject them to this severity."[13]

It was Albert himself who set in motion a series of events which would lead to his own release and to that of many thousands of Union and Confederate officers and enlisted men through the course of the war. Only twenty-two years of age and just out of the Naval Academy, he devised a plan which he felt would provide for an equitable exchange of prisoners of war held by the two governments. The plan had such merit that the prison commandant arranged for Albert to meet with Confederate Secretary of War Judah P. Benjamin to discuss it. So impressed were Confederate officials with the plan that, on October 29, Albert was given a parole of fifty days for the purpose of arranging an exchange of prisoners then being held. According to Albert's own report to U.S. Secretary of the Navy Gideon Welles, "I pledged myself to call upon the President and urge an exchange of prisoners now held in Richmond for those held by the U.S. Government."[14]

Two days after popping his head into his brother's tent, Albert met with Secretary Welles, Secretary of State William H. Seward and President Lincoln. According to August Kautz's journal, "The question of exchange was fully discussed. Albert is not satisfied with the result.... Mr. Seward objects to exchange generally and to the privateers in particular."[15]

Albert left Washington for home the following day. His meetings with officials of the two governments did have the desired effect. Guidelines for the exchange of prisoners were set and, as a result, many thousands of prisoners were subsequently exchanged.

Albert's own exchange took a different course. In mid–November, Albert's former commander, Flag Officer Louis Goldsborough and Confederate Major General Benjamin Huger, commander of the Department of Norfolk, acting independently of their governments, arranged an exchange of eight officers, including Albert.

On the day that Albert departed for Ohio, August Kautz noted in his journal, "My rheumatism [which had been bothering him for weeks] has become so bad that I have great difficulty in getting on a horse and I did not attend drill in consequence today."[16] The regimental surgeon advised him that a change of climate might be helpful and suggested that he leave the city for a few days. He subsequently left for New York on November 12 and returned nine days later. By the time he returned to Washington, the stables at the camp were completed and work was well under way on completion of the barracks. Through a long winter, the regiment continued with daily drills, often in deep mud and snow.

Albert Kautz in his Navy uniform, circa 1870. He would later reach the rank of rear admiral. From August Kautz's photograph album, courtesy Virginia (Kautz) Borkenhagen.

Although the men made steady progress, it was not always rapid enough to satisfy either Colonel Emory or Captain Kautz.

According to Kautz, "The winter passed gaily and pleasantly enough with a pleasant intermixture of duty and the gaiety that prevailed in the winter of 1861 & 62 in the Capital owing to the immense floating population the war had brought to the city."[17] In that floating population was the Fourth U.S. Infantry, who were encamped adjacent to the Capitol, and Kautz had ample time to socialize with his former comrades. After one trip into the city, he wrote, "I made quite a number of visits with various officers living in the city, and hanged in that great gossiping place of the city, Willard's."[18] He met often with the Casey family (Silas Casey had been appointed brigadier-general of volunteers in August), including the eighteenth birthday party of Miss Bessie Casey on February 17. He also spent time with General Denver and with George Suckley and George Gibbs, both of whom were friends form Washington Territory.

The "duty" which Kautz referred to included occasional patrolling of the streets of the city. Drilling of the troops continued in company, squadron and regimental formations. The Sixth Cavalry was brigaded with the Fifth Cavalry under the command of Brigadier General Philip Cooke and, as the winter wore on, drilling of the entire brigade became more frequent.

It had been expected for some time that Colonel Emory might be promoted and, on March 6, it was learned that he had received an appointment as brigadier general and would command the brigade. Emory's successful evacuation of his troops from Indian Territory the previous spring ahead of pursuing Confederates, must have been a factor in the promotion.

On March 7, Kautz was saddened to learn from Lewis Hunt that Hunt's mother-in-law, Abby Casey, whom Kautz greatly admired, had suffered a stroke while attending a concert at Willard's Concert Hall the night before and was not expected to live more than a few hours. If there was a funeral for Mrs. Casey in Washington, Kautz either failed uncharacteristically to mention it in his journal or, possibly, missed it because he and the Sixth Cavalry received their marching orders while at breakfast on the morning of March 10.

15. The Peninsula

After its humiliation in the First Battle of Bull Run in July 1861, a battle which Kautz had initially perceived as a victory, the Army of the Potomac fell back to the Washington defenses, regrouped and grew to a formidable force of more than 100,000 men under the leadership of Major General George B. McClellan. The Rebel army, soon to acquire the title Army of Northern Virginia and commanded by General Joseph E. Johnston, had also been severely mauled at Bull Run and was content to remain near the Bull Run battlefield and stare menacingly toward Washington from behind a line of fortifications set up at Centerville, thirty miles from the capital.

So things remained through the winter which Kautz considered so gay and pleasant. News of minor Union victories in the West and along the Atlantic Coast produced optimism in the Federal camps around Washington that the war would soon end.

President Lincoln knew that would not happen until the major Federal armies got moving. Deeply troubled by the lack of action, on January 27, 1862, he issued General War Order No. 1, specifying a general offensive on all fronts to commence on Washington's birthday, February 22.

In the West, things got started even sooner. By mid–February, the small command of Ulysses Grant had forced the capitulation of Forts Henry and Donelson on the Tennessee and Cumberland Rivers. The result of these relatively minor engagements was remarkable. The Confederates were forced to fall back to southern Tennessee and northern Alabama and Mississippi.

Back east, Washington's birthday came and went and the Army of the Potomac failed to move. McClellan did, however, wage a sporadic war of words with Lincoln and with Secretary of War, Edwin M. Stanton, claiming their failure to support him or his army. Having used his impressive organizational and administrative skills to build his army from the ground up, McClellan seemed reticent to risk using it up in battle. McClellan did have a grand strategy which had been formulated as early as January, but he had endless excuses for not putting it into action. His plan included a move around Johnston's right flank by sea to the vicinity of Urbana near the mouth of the Rappahannock River, followed by a quick thrust inland, thus cutting Johnston's army off from the Confederate capital at Richmond.

The outlook for the South appeared bleak at this point. Having lost so much in the West, Confederate strategists, fearing for the safety of the Army of Northern Virginia, ordered Johnston to withdraw from his exposed position outside Washington to a safer line behind the Rappahannock River and its tributary, the Rapidan.

If President Lincoln couldn't get McClellan to move, it seems Joe Johnston could. Johnston commenced his movement to the Rappahannock on March 7 and had his entire army, less a small rear guard, out of the Centerville area by March 9. McClellan had no choice but to move his army into the void left by the departure of Johnston. McClellan later explained that he made the move "to take advantage of any opportunity to strike the enemy, to break up the permanent

[Rebel] camps, give the troops a little experience on the march and in bivouac, get rid of extra baggage and test the working of staff-departments."[1]

While they were at breakfast on March 10, the Sixth Cavalry received orders to march toward Centerville by 11 A.M. with three days' provisions and forage. The regiment, now 1000 strong and brigaded with the Fifth U.S. Cavalry under the command of Brigadier General Philip St. George Cooke, got off on time. Despite a drizzling rain which lasted all afternoon, they were met by crowds of men waving their hats and women waving their handkerchiefs as they marched down Pennsylvania Avenue and across Long Bridge. It was after dark when they went into camp near Fairfax Court House amid considerable confusion and surrounded by the entire Army of the Potomac.

The following morning, Cooke's Cavalry Brigade left the infantry behind and made a reconnaissance past the abandoned Confederate entrenchments at Centerville to Manassas Junction. There they found the public buildings, torched by the Confederate rear guard, still smoldering. Later in the day, the Sixth Cavalry served as escort as General McClellan toured the Bull Run battlefield. Fatigued by a full twelve hours in the saddle, the regiment went into camp near Centerville and were thankful to remain undisturbed the following day.

Additional reconnaissance on March 13 failed to turn up any sign of the enemy. Cooke's Cavalry Brigade, along with part of Brigadier General William French's Brigade of infantry, all under the command of Brigadier General George Stoneman, moved out the next day to reconnoiter along the line of the Orange and Alexandria Railroad. The Fifth Cavalry had two men wounded as they drove in Rebel pickets at Cedar Creek, but Kautz saw no enemy as he moved along the rail line in command of the First Squadron of the Sixth Cavalry.

The cavalry stood to horse all that night in a drizzling rain. The following morning, they found the enemy in force guarding the railroad and retired to the Bull Run battlefield. As the rain had continued all day, they were fortunate to find shelter in huts occupied by a North Carolina regiment the previous winter. Finding Bull Run swollen by persistent rain, they were forced to return to the huts for a second night before retiring to Fairfax Court House on March 17.

Kautz later described the two-day reconnaissance with a bit of self-deprecating humor.

> When I recall this, my first experience of the war, I cannot help but smile at our inexperience. It was regarded as a very dangerous reconnaissance, although I saw no enemy and no one was killed, but the absurdity of it was in the management of the march which was conducted with all the caution and slowness consequent upon marching in close column with flankers and being instantly prepared to form line of battle. Later in the war after we had more experience, a patrol of ten men and a good sergeant or lieutenant could have ascertained all that we did in far less time and with much less trouble and fatigue.[2]

Johnston's withdrawal resulted in a change in McClellan's plan. A movement to Urbana would no longer place his army between that of Johnston and Richmond, so he would have to debark the Army of the Potomac farther south. The point chosen was Fortress Monroe at the tip of the Virginia Peninsula. Fortress Monroe had never fallen into Confederate hands and was well garrisoned and easily able to be defended either by land or sea.

McClellan assembled his army around Alexandria, Virginia, preparatory to embarkation to Fortress Monroe. The Sixth Cavalry went into camp at Alexandria on March 18 and remained idle for the next ten days.

During these days at Alexandria, it was learned that Colonel Emory had been promoted to brigadier general and been placed in command of the Cavalry Brigade in place of Cooke. Major Williams took command of the regiment.

The Sixth Cavalry embarked at Alexandria on March 27 and 28. Kautz's company was aboard two small schooners which were placed in tow behind the steamer *Long Branch* and, after passing through a severe snowstorm at sea, arrived in the harbor at Hampton Roads "that presented an immense front of masts and smokestacks."[3]

Kautz had not felt completely well for several weeks prior to the voyage and, on arrival at Fortress Monroe, he was immediately hospitalized with a high fever at what had formerly been the Aqueia Hotel. When the regiment marched inland on April 4, Kautz was too sick to join them. He tells us, "For the first time in all my service, I was left behind because I was unable to travel."[4] He remained hospitalized until April 27, nearly a full month, at which time McClellan's army was besieging the city of Yorktown, twenty miles up the peninsula.

When the Army of the Potomac reached the outskirts of Yorktown early in April, they had been opposed by only about 15,000 Confederates under the command of Major General John B. Magruder. Magruder had managed to deceive McClellan into thinking his Confederate force at Yorktown was much larger than it actually was, allowing time for reinforcements to arrive from Joe Johnston's Army of Northern Virginia. By the end of April, Johnston, now in command, had about 50,000 men in the Yorktown defenses. Johnston, however, seeing that he was still outnumbered, saw the futility of defending Yorktown and fell back through Williamsburg to positions closer to Richmond.

When news arrived on May 4 that Johnston had abandoned Yorktown, the Sixth Cavalry was on the march again but, once again, Kautz was too sick to march and was forced to remain behind with the regiment's baggage trains near Yorktown. In an unusual disclosure of his feelings, he wrote, "I am full of anxiety, disappointment and chagrin and can barely refrain from mounting my horse and riding to the front. The certainty that I should be permanently laid up without achieving any useful result deters me."[5]

Kautz finally felt strong enough to join his regiment on May 10. He loaded his mess kit and a few supplies on a spare horse that morning and reached "deserted and dreary" Williamsburg in the evening, noting in his journal, "I took a walk through the town in the evening. The buildings are occupied as hospitals and are full of wounded and sick of our troops and the enemy."[6] He caught up with his regiment near Cumberland on the Pamunkey River, a branch of the York, twenty miles upstream from Williamsburg.

In Kautz's absence, Emory's Cavalry Brigade, part of the advance directed by Stoneman, had led the Army of the Potomac's march from Yorktown to Cumberland with Kautz's Squadron, composed of Companies B and H, the only ones armed with repeating rifles, invariably in the advance. Captain John Savage of Company H had taken over the squadron in Kautz's absence.

General McClellan had been undecided whether to approach Richmond from north of the Chickahominy River, with his base of supply on the Pamunkey River, or south of the Chickahominy, with his base on the James.

The position of the Chickahominy River is of critical importance to a full understanding of the Peninsular Campaign. This small river flows from just above Richmond to empty into the James not far from the tip of the peninsula. Heavy spring rains had caused it to overflow its banks and flood the low country on either side. None of the fords of the river were serviceable and the bridges across the river had been washed away or destroyed by the armies.

McClellan favored the southern approach, but he was hoping to be reinforced by Major General Irvin McDowell's Corps, which was at the time encamped near Fredericksburg. If McDowell's Corps could be brought south as promised, McClellan must remain north of the Chickahominy in order to form a junction with McDowell.

As a result of McClellan's decision, when Kautz arrived at Cumberland on May 11, he found that the bulk of the Army of the Potomac was arriving there also.

On the morning of May 12, General Stoneman ordered Kautz to move the Sixth Cavalry three miles farther up the Pamunkey to the White House, the baronial manor owned by Robert E. Lee's son, William Henry Fitzhugh Lee. White House was strategically important because it lay near where the Richmond & York River Railroad crossed the Pamunkey. Major Williams was already at the White House with one squadron of the regiment. General Stoneman would follow later in the day with the remainder of the "advanced Guard ... a mixed command of several thousand men, Artillery, Cavalry and Infantry."[7]

For the next two weeks, McClellan moved his army slowly up the peninsula with portions of the advanced guard skirmishing almost daily with rear guard elements of Johnston's army. During this period Kautz, usually in command of the First Squadron of the regiment, moved his Company B forward through sleepy little villages whose names would become famous in the succeeding months and years.

On May 27, McClellan, still hoping to be reinforced by McDowell's Corps, sent an expedition commanded by Brigadier General Fitz John Porter toward Hanover Court House, twenty miles north of Richmond. The purpose was to drive off a force of Confederates defending the two railroads which ran north out of Richmond, the Virginia Central and the Richmond, Fredericksburg & Potomac. Porter's command consisted of the infantry division of Brigadier General George W. Morell, the brigade of Colonel Gouverneur Warren and Emory's Cavalry Brigade. Occupying Hanover Court House was a force of about 8000 Confederates composed of four North Carolina regiments of Brigadier General Lawrence Branch's Brigade supplemented by cavalry and artillery.

The weather had been rainy for weeks and a torrential downpour began during the night and continued all morning, turning the already muddy roads into wallows. Kautz's Squadron got moving about 7 A.M. and took the lead in the twenty-mile march. By noon, they had driven enemy pickets for about five miles to the farmhouse of a Mr. Winslow about two miles south of Hanover Court House and just east of the Virginia Central line. Here they met the advance of Branch's force, made up of at least one regiment of infantry, supported by artillery, drawn up in line of battle.

For about an hour the cavalry were in support of Captain Henry Benson's light horse artillery while Benson dueled with Rebel artillery.[8] When the enemy's artillery were finally silenced, Emory's Brigade drove in behind the Rebel regiment, cutting it off from the main body of Branch's force, driving it two miles past the courthouse and capturing about 500 prisoners.[9] This maneuver left the cavalry open to fire from its left flank and rear from Branch's main line, forcing them to retire.

By shortly after noon, Morell's entire division was in action and Warren, having been delayed by the need to repair several bridges, was arriving. The battle was fiercely contested all afternoon. Eventually, Branch was forced to fall back about ten miles to the village of Ashland on the Richmond, Fredericksburg & Potomac Railroad.

Emory's Brigade camped on the battlefield that night. Losses in the battle were high considering the small numbers engaged. The Union forces had 62 killed, 223 wounded and 70 missing or captured. The cavalry losses were only two killed and one wounded.[10] General Porter estimated Confederate losses at about 200 killed and 730 captured.[11]

The following March, Kautz received a brevet promotion to major in the regular Army for his part in the Battle of Hanover Court House, the first of six brevets he would receive in the war. Lieutenant Christian Balder of Kautz's Company was breveted to first lieutenant and Captain William Abert was breveted to major.[12] In his report of the battle, General Emory singled out Kautz and Captain John Savage for their part in the battle as well as the entire campaign by saying, "The first squadron of the Sixth U.S. Cavalry, composed of Companies B and H, commanded by Captains Kautz and Savage, led the advance, which they have done most of the way from Yorktown, in the most gallant style."[13]

No sooner had McClellan ordered Porter's move to Hanover Court House than he learned from Washington that McDowell's 20,000-man Corps had been ordered to the Shenandoah Valley, where Confederate Major General Thomas "Stonewall" Jackson was marching up and down the valley to the embarrassment of Union Major General Nathaniel Banks. With reinforcements from McDowell out of the question, McClellan decided to move his army south of the Chickahominy and move his supply base from the White House on the Pamunkey to Harrison's Landing on the James. Although the Chickahominy was in flood and most of its bridges destroyed, Erasmus Keyes and Samuel Heintzelman had their two corps across in short order, leaving the two corps of Fitz John Porter and Edwin Sumner temporarily north of the river guarding the vital supply route while the move was taking place.

As a result, Porter's expedition to Hanover Court House, instead of being one to clear a route for the arrival of McDowell, became one to block any attempt by Stonewall Jackson to reinforce Joseph Johnston. For several days after the Battle of Hanover Court House, Porter's command was busy burning rail depots and other public buildings and destroying rail and road bridges and ferries across the Pamunkey and South Anna Rivers, with Emory's Cavalry Brigade doing much of the heavy work. On Kautz's part, on May 29, he took a portion of his squadron up the Fredericksburg Road to screen for Captain Abert's Squadron while they burned the rail bridge over the South Anna. At the same time, one platoon of Kautz's squadron was burning some nearby road bridges.

Porter then fell back to the Chickahominy and the Sixth Cavalry went into camp at Walnut Grove Church about two miles from the Chickahominy midway between Cold Harbor and Mechanicsville.

General Johnston, with almost all of his army south of the Chickahominy, saw an opportunity to attack McClellan while his forces were astraddle the swollen river. On May 31, he launched a vicious, if somewhat uncoordinated, attack on the Union entrenchments near Fair Oaks. The Battle of Fair Oaks (also known as Seven Pines) raged for two days with heavy casualties in both armies, but no decisive victor. One important outcome of the battle was the serious wounding of Johnston. Johnston was replaced by Robert E. Lee.

Kautz, at his camp a mere five miles north of the battlefield, could hear the sounds of the battle. He noted in his journal that the brunt of the Rebel assault had fallen on General Silas Casey's Division. He failed to mention that Casey's Division was part of IV Corps, commanded by his one-time friend, Erasmus Keyes, nor did he learn at the time that Casey's son-in-law, Lewis Hunt, who had just been appointed colonel of the 92nd New York Infantry, was seriously wounded.

For the next two days, Kautz was in command of his own squadron and two squadrons of the Sixth Pennsylvania Cavalry in a move to destroy what ferries might still be in working order on the Pamunkey and to arrest a Dr. Wormley, operator of one of the ferries. A canoe was found to cross the river and Wormley was arrested. The ferry boat, eight yawls, a 25-ton sloop (*Golden Gate II*) and a metallic lifeboat were found hidden among some felled trees and destroyed.

Over the next weeks, Emory's Cavalry Brigade occupied itself with picket duty and various details on the right flank of the Army of the Potomac. On June 13, a squadron of the Fifth Cavalry was overrun at their camp at Old Church by the 1500-man cavalry force of Confederate Brigadier General J.E.B. Stuart on his celebrated ride around McClellan's army. Stuart had ridden north out of Richmond on June 12, passed to the west of Ashland, then turned east through Hanover Court House to Old Church. Kautz felt at the time that all of the Federal cavalry should have moved after Stuart immediately. In fact, General Cooke[14] did assemble the entire Reserve Cavalry Division near Old Church, but then did nothing. By the time Cooke got moving, Stuart had a twenty-four-hour head start. Further pursuit would be futile. The actual physical damage by Stuart's raid was insignificant; the damage to the morale of the Union army was, however, great. Kautz was quick to recognize, in observing Stuart's raid, that the two armies were using their cavalry in different ways. The Union cavalry were, for the most part, being used in small detachments as pickets or advanced guards or in minor details such as messenger service. Although the Confederate cavalry performed these duties, their most effective service was in raids such as Stuart's or in quick offensive thrusts using large numbers of horsemen. The Union would eventually learn to use their cavalry in this way.

Through June 28, Emory's Cavalry Brigade continued to picket on the right flank of Porter's Corps, the only corps still north of the Chickahominy, near the village of Mechanicsville. The duty seemed pleasant enough to Kautz at the time and he commented in his journal while picketing near the village of Hanover (not Hanover Court House) on the Pamunkey River, "The position is a pleasant one. We get plenty of cherries, berries and vegetables from the inhabitants."[15] The following day he noted that he had come down with diarrhea and blamed it, no doubt correctly, on the water rather than on the fruits and vegetables. The camp diarrhea had spread through the regiment and Major Williams was one of those most seriously effected.

Despite McClellan's desire to keep Stonewall Jackson out of his hair during the campaign against Richmond, Jackson managed to evade his pursuers in the Shenandoah Valley and, by June 24, the first units of his command were approaching the South Anna River. Robert E. Lee saw Jackson's approach as a means of destroying Porter's Corps while it was isolated on the north bank of the Chickahominy. Lee ordered the divisions of Generals A.P. Hill, D.H. Hill and James Longstreet to move due north from Richmond and cross the Chickahominy well upstream at Meadow Bridge and, on June 26, fall on the unsuspecting Porter in his defensive positions at Mechanicsville. Had Jackson arrived on time, he would have pushed Emory's cavalry aside without difficulty, driven in Porter's right flank and, no doubt, annihilated Porter's Corps.

For reasons still not entirely clear, however, Jackson was a no-show at the Battle of Mechanicsville. The attacking Rebels suffered heavy casualties, but hit Porter hard enough to force his withdrawal to already prepared fortifications around the town of Gaines' Mill, with his back to the only bridges across this stretch of the Chickahominy.

The following day, the Army of Northern Virginia struck at Porter's Corps again at Gaines' Mill, but could do little more than dent Porter's lines, with Kautz's friend, George Pickett, and his division making the largest dent. Porter was able to withdraw across the Chickahominy and join the rest of the Army of the Potomac. Over the next five days of the "Seven Days Battle," McClellan withdrew to his new supply depot at Harrison's Landing on the James River, his army driven from the gates of Richmond, but still intact.

Meanwhile, it had been learned in the cavalry camp as early as June 22 that there was increased activity by the Confederates around Meadow Bridge. As a result, the Sixth Cavalry was ordered to "stand to horse" all day on the Old Church Road. Kautz was now commanding the regiment because Major Williams was laid up with the prevailing complaint. When Kautz returned to camp with the regiment at nine o'clock that night, he was of the opinion that Stuart's exploit of a few days before had produced overcautiousness in the army, saying in his journal, "There seems to me that now there is an unnecessary vigilance exercised after the enemy have done this work."[16]

On June 25, Kautz received orders to march with the regiment to Haw's (Machine) Shop and, again, they were required to stand to horse all day before falling back behind Totopotomoy Creek (a small branch of the Pamunkey), where they went into camp that night without food for the men nor forage for their horses. When Kautz rode out from camp that morning, Major Williams remained behind in camp incapacitated by the diarrhea. Kautz later wrote, "As I never saw him again during the war, I will here gladly take leave of him."[17] Kautz would remain in command of the regiment for the remainder of its time on the peninsula.

Kautz received more orders on June 26 than he could successfully carry out. Most dealt with the burning of bridges and the blocking of roads. It was obvious that the cavalry were retreating, but he was unable to understand why. There were no enemy to be seen. It wasn't until mid-afternoon, when heavy cannonading was heard from the direction of Mechanicsville, ten or twelve miles distant, that he learned of Lee's move against Porter. After that time, Emory's Brigade continued to fall back accompanied by a brigade of infantry commanded by Colonel Robert Buchanan, the whole force commanded by General Stoneman.

More cannonading was heard from the direction of Gaines' Mill on June 27, even louder than that of the day before. Stoneman's force reached the old supply base at White House, found it nearly deserted, and attempted to burn or otherwise destroy anything there which might be of use to the enemy. As they rode away shortly after dark, the White House itself, Rooney Lee's beautiful home, was in flames.

There was a rest of only a few hours that night near New Kent Court House before the retreat was continued. Kautz commented that he saw no reason for so hasty a retreat. In fact, he saw no reason at all to be moving away from the Army of the Potomac for, "If McClellan was hard pressed he needed our assistance, if he was not hard pressed we ran no risk in returning to him."[18]

In fact, J.E.B. Stuart's Cavalry had followed them as far as the White House,[19] but he turned away to the south on June 9 to rejoin Lee's Army of Northern Virginia. Nevertheless, Stoneman's mixed force continued to fall back through Williamsburg and Yorktown, reaching the relative safety of Fortress Monroe on the first day of July. They were, however, far from the rest of McClellan's Army of the Potomac.

On July 3, Kautz rode into the fort for supplies for the regiment, including tents and cooking utensils. He also sent one of the lieutenants of the regiment to Harrison's Landing in order to retrieve the personal baggage of the officers. When General Emory, who was rankled because he did not have the comforts to be derived from his own personal baggage, learned what Kautz had done, he called for Kautz and asked upon what authority he had sent for the baggage. When Kautz replied that it was on his own authority as regimental commander, Emory declared, according to Kautz, "I am very sorry, sir! But I consider it a conspiracy against my authority; go to your quarters under arrest."

Kautz immediately penned a letter of complaint in which he mentioned, besides his own unfair arrest, a host of other irregularities in Emory's command technique, including what he called "a tendency to alarm in the vicinity of the enemy which was harrowing in the extreme to all."

Emory confronted Kautz about his letter and Kautz was kind enough to add the phrase "by exaggerating the danger" to somewhat soften the above sentence. Emory, still not mollified, polled some of the other officers of the regiment for their opinions. When he learned that they, too, were "similarly disposed in their views of his service," the arrest order was lifted.[20] Three days later, Emory was transferred to command of an infantry brigade. The transfer, no doubt, had nothing to do with Kautz's letter of complaint and, in fact, Kautz was convinced that Emory did not pass the letter up through the chain of command as required.

In the change of command, George Stoneman was given command of all of the cavalry of the Army of the Potomac, both regulars and volunteers. Kautz's Sixth Cavalry was brigaded with the Fifth Cavalry and David M. Gregg's Eighth Pennsylvania Cavalry. Gregg was given command of the brigade at his volunteer rank of colonel, although he was outranked by Kautz in the regular Army. Kautz admired Gregg and the two men remained good friends, but Kautz was bothered by being required to serve under an officer who was junior to him.

Meanwhile, on July 7, the cavalry brigade was transported by water to Harrison's Landing. For the greater part of a month, the Army of the Potomac lay idle at Harrison's Landing. The "Seven Days" had exacted a heavy toll on both armies. Despite their losses, both felt they had achieved a limited victory. According to Kautz, "We have been defeated in our entry into Richmond, but the enemy has been defeated in his attempt to wreck us. McClellan has saved his army and will soon be able to act on the offensive again."[21] He later added, "It looks as though we are going to remain here some time. No troops arriving and nothing going on. Our principal duty will be to watch the enemy until an opportunity occurs to do something."[22]

If the bulk of McClellan's army was idle, the cavalry remained busy with the "principal duty" of watching the enemy to which Kautz had referred. From their camp near Westover Plantation, the cavalry manned the picket lines in front of the army's entrenchments and sent out occasional reconnaissance patrols.

In mid–July, when the Sixth Cavalry received unwarranted criticism regarding the cleanliness of their camp by General Porter, Kautz wrote, "It is not a pleasant duty to command a regiment, especially when you moved temporarily to the command."[23] Kautz objected through channels to Porter's criticism. Further inspection showed that police of the camp was, in fact, exemplary.

It was extremely difficult for the entire army to maintain even a minimal level of cleanliness. The ground for some distance away from Harrison's Landing, although very fertile, was elevated just enough to prevent it from being a swamp. Even in the driest of times, this giant camp would have been muddy, but the persistent rains of the summer of 1862 produced a ten-square-mile mud puddle. When latrines were dug they filled with water and the accumulated waste from 100,000 men and almost as many horses filled the air with a most disagreeable odor. Mosquitoes, flies, fleas and "red bugs" tortured men and horses alike.

As the hot, sticky month of July oozed uncomfortably by, McClellan found himself under increasing pressure from President Lincoln and Secretary of War Stanton to take the offensive. Lincoln came down from Washington twice to confer with McClellan in person, but came away with no clear idea of the general's plans. McClellan, who had no respect for the "country bumpkin" who lived in the White House, paid little attention to the president's pleading but, as he became increasingly aware that public opinion was beginning to turn against him, he decided to take some action.

At the time, Robert E. Lee's Army of Northern Virginia occupied a line of entrenchments along Bailey's Run about twelve miles to the west of Harrison's Landing with its flanks well covered by the James River on the right and White Oak Swamp on the left. Lee had thrown a sizeable force forward to Malvern Hill, no more than four miles from McClellan's headquarters.

On August 2, McClellan ordered Major General Joseph Hooker to move to Malvern Hill with a force of about 10,000 men of his and another division, supported by the cavalry brigade, now commanded by newly-promoted Brigadier General Alfred Pleasonton, who had replaced David Gregg as brigade commander on August 1. The supposed purpose of the movement was to determine the strength of the Rebel force on Malvern Hill and, if possible, to drive them off and occupy the high ground.

Kautz had met Hooker but once before and that had been in the previous September, when Kautz and Captain Joseph Taylor had visited Hooker at his camp near Washington. Kautz wrote that Hooker received them very kindly, but added, "The Genl. indulged very freely in liquor, too much so, I think, for a man of his rank."[24]

The expedition to Malvern Hill got started on the evening of August 3 but, by some error of Hooker or someone on his staff, they moved out on the wrong road and the whole movement had to be postponed. Kautz later commented, "The troops did not seem to fancy the move as it was understood to be simply a demonstration inaugurated by Genl. Marcy for the purpose of giving the Northern people an idea that we were not altogether idle."[25]

The movement was attempted once more on the night of August 5. Kautz was mildly censured by Hooker for arriving at the latter's headquarters an hour late, but the Sixth Cavalry was able to get off on time on Long Bridge Road along with the rest of Pleasonton's Brigade, then crossed over to the Quaker Road in advance of Hooker's infantry. Kautz marched his men until 11 P.M. when they met the first of the enemy's pickets and rested for the night.

Before dawn on August 6, Kautz's Regiment continued northwest on the Quaker Road well past Malvern Hill to Quaker Church, pushing the Confederate pickets ahead of them. They then turned left on a country lane toward New Market Road. As they approached New Market Road, they came under fire from a battery of Confederate artillery. Kautz ordered his regiment to take shelter behind a low, wooded hill and they suffered no casualties. Finally, a battery of Union artillery was brought up and opened on the Confederate battery, forcing it to withdraw.

Meanwhile, Hooker's force had moved left from the Quaker Road and assaulted the flank of the Rebel position on Malvern Hill, forcing a retreat with minimal casualties on either side. A few hundred of the Rebels were captured, but most managed to extricate themselves and retreat down New Market Road towards the safety of the entrenchments at Bailey's Run.

As Kautz and his regiment reached New Market Road, they came upon a squadron of the Eighth Illinois Cavalry under the command of Colonel William Gamble. Gamble had been in contact with retreating Rebels; his squadron had been repulsed and Gamble himself severely wounded in the chest. Kautz was appalled that Hooker had failed to put a larger force forward to New Market Road to cut off the escape of the Confederates. His regiment and the Fifth Cavalry picketed New Market Road for the rest of the day, but found that the bulk of the Confederates had escaped.

Hooker continued to occupy Malvern Hill through most of the day of August 7 while Pleasonton's Cavalry Brigade patrolled New Market Road all the way to Bailey's Run. About noon, Kautz rode over to Curl's Neck on the James River and observed that the enemy's entrenchments behind Bailey's Run were easily visible from the river. He got Hooker's permission to approach the Union gunboat *Port Royal*, which was lying idle in the river, to shell the Rebel entrenchments and, in so doing, make it difficult for Lee's army to move out against Hooker's men on Malvern Hill. The captain of the gunboat declined to do so, saying that a flag of truce was in effect on the river and that he was under orders not to fire.

Disappointed in his attempt to get help from the navy, Kautz started back to his regiment's camp near New Market Road. By that time, it was dark and, being unable to locate the orderly who had been holding his horse, he started out on foot. He soon was met by "a tremendous volley at the point where I had left the reserve of my pickets and between me and the camp and took refuge on the *Port Royal*."[26]

What had happened in Kautz's absence was that Lee had sent Major General James Longstreet and his entire corps forward to retake Malvern Hill. Longstreet had driven back Kautz's pickets and the volley which had so startled Kautz was an entire brigade of Longstreet's Corps firing at a company of the Sixth Cavalry commanded by Lieutenant Joseph Kerin. Longstreet had no difficulty occupying Malvern Hill without firing another shot because McClellan had ordered Hooker to withdraw to Harrison's Landing earlier in the day.

The *Port Royal* moved down to Haxall's Landing (midway between Harrison's Landing and Malvern Hill) during the night and Kautz rejoined his regiment there.

Kautz summed up the Second Battle of Malvern Hill in a short paragraph. He wrote, "Thus ended this reconnaissance which I learned from Col. Gregg was conceived by Genl. Marcy and carried into execution to furnish an item for the Northern papers to quiet the complaints against McClellan's inactivity. Had Genl. Hooker been equal to the occasion, we would have captured a four-gun battery and about fifteen hundred prisoners which would have been a very satisfactory item to send north and would have made the point that Genl. Marcy desired."[27]

On August 9, Kautz learned from his friend, Captain John Savage, who was returning from a leave of absence, that the president had finally given up on McClellan's Peninsular Campaign and ordered him to abandon the peninsula and move his army north. The point of embarkation would be Fortress Monroe.

The move from Harrison's Landing to Fortress Monroe got under way on August 14. Kautz's pickets were the very last troops to depart from Harrison's Landing on August 17 and they took casualties as advance units of the Army of Northern Virginia rushed in to take possession of the camps. As rear guard, Kautz's Regiment was the last to cross the Chickahominy River on a pontoon bridge before the bridge was taken up by the engineers. Pleasonton's command went into camp near Yorktown on August 20 awaiting transportation north.

In the short time that Kautz had been under General Pleasonton, he had made entries in his journal concerning Pleasonton's assignment of officers of his regiment to a variety of extra details. He even wrote a letter of complaint to the general on the subject. A short journal entry of August 23 seems to be no more than another expression of Kautz's mild resentment of the general's actions, but proved later to be of much more importance. Kautz wrote, "Genl. Pleasonton amused himself by tieing [*sic*] up one of Capt. Brisbin's noncommissioned officers."[28] This seemingly innocuous notation of a seemingly unimportant incident would have serious repercussions for Kautz, costing him command of the regiment and almost leading to court-martial.

It seems that Captain Brisbin had ordered a Corporal Michael Molkay to put a standing martingale on an unruly horse to attempt to correct the horse from rearing up. As a result of Molkay's efforts, the horse was bleeding from the mouth just as Pleasonton came by. Without investigating, Pleasonton ordered Molkay tied to a wagon wheel as punishment. Several hours later, Captain Calvert W. Cowan of Pleasonton's staff came into Kautz's tent and told Kautz that the general wanted Molkay broken. Kautz paid little attention to the indefinite verbal order. Several days later, Molkay sent in a complaint about his treatment, endorsed favorably by Captain Brisbin. Kautz passed it along to Pleasonton's headquarters.

Immediately afterwards, Kautz received a note from Cowan asking if he had broken Molkay. Kautz answered by endorsing the note, saying that there were only two ways to break a man, by court-martial or at the recommendation of his company commander, and that neither course had been pursued. Immediately afterwards, Cowan appeared in Kautz's tent with his side arm on and placed Kautz under arrest for "Disobedience of an order and Highly insubordinate conduct in forwarding a complaint from a noncommissioned officer." Kautz was flabbergasted and later wrote, "It seems hardly credible that an officer of the Regular Army who had been able to get a commission as Brig. Genl. of Volunteers would perpetrate such a set of charges in good faith. Capt. Sanders succeeded to the command and received an order to reduce Cpl. Molkay. He did so but issued another order at the same time making him a Sergt. He had the benefit of my experience."[29]

The last of the Army of the Potomac got off on August 24, leaving only Keyes's Corps at Fortress Monroe. The cavalry finally sailed for Alexandria on August 30 aboard the steamer *Knickerbocker*, arriving on September 2, too late to be involved in the Second Battle of Bull Run.

Two days after their arrival at Alexandria, the Sixth Cavalry moved out to the vicinity of Falls Church, Virginia, where they made contact with J.E.B. Stuart's Cavalry. Stuart was screening the right flank of Lee's army as he marched it into Maryland. Portions of Pleasonton's Brigade remained in contact with Stuart as he crossed the Potomac on September 6. Kautz noted how different it was to be marching through an area where the natives were friendly and the towns had not been touched by the war, but added that there was not time to stop, but only to look through the windows and doors at the lighted interiors of the houses. The Sixth Cavalry crossed the Potomac at Georgetown and moved along the River Road to Poolsville and then to Barnesville. There was a sharp engagement with Stuart's men near Sugarloaf Mountain on September 7 as the cavalry continued to protect the left flank of the Army of the Potomac. At the time, that army was strung out from Washington to beyond Rockville with McClellan's headquarters at Rockville.

Kautz remained under arrest through this time, but rather than being held at the regiment's camp, he was kept in the advance by General Pleasonton, "liable to be engaged any time, yet not permitted to carry the means even of self defense."[30]

In this unhappy state of affairs, Kautz got to bed late on September 9 after a long evening march only to be awakened at 2 A.M. with news which would change the course of his career. The next evening he wrote in his journal, "I was waked up last night by Lieut. [Leroy S.] Elbert, the Genl's aid, and informed that Genl. Marcy wished to know whether I could accept the command of the 2nd Ohio Cavalry now stationed at Fort Scott, Kansas. I said I could and this morning Genl. Pleasonton released me from arrest with orders to report to Genl. Marcy."[31] Kautz departed for Rockville the next morning.

16. The Second Ohio Cavalry: Fort Scott, Camp Chase

From the time he learned, at Acapulco, Mexico, that he had been promoted to captain, August Kautz was well aware that the approaching war could lead to significant elevation in rank for officers of the regular Army. He later wrote, "From a Lieutenant near the foot of the list, I had been promoted to senior Captain of the 6th Cavalry; Captains had been made Colonels, and Politicians had been made Generals."[1]

One route to higher rank was via the volunteer service. Although a few officers were able to take leaves of absence from the regular Army to join the volunteers at higher rank, such action was taken in the face of opposition by General Winfield Scott, who felt that it would lead to the diminution of the effectiveness of his regular Army.

In October 1861, Kautz met with Governor William Dennison of Ohio, who was visiting in Washington, "and had a talk with him about the chance of getting an Ohio regiment. He said there would be no difficulty about it except the objection of the War Department." Kautz seemed a little less enthusiastic when he added, "He has been succeeded by Gov. Todd [sic]."[2]

He seems to have put the idea of joining the volunteer service out of his mind until July when, in a shuffling of officers and of regiments, the Fifth and Sixth U.S. Cavalry were brigaded with David Gregg's Eighth Pennsylvania. Gregg was placed in command of the brigade at his volunteer rank of colonel, although he was outranked by Kautz in the regular Army. Kautz was understandably indignant when he wrote, "I received an order detailing the 6th to report to Col. Gregg. This is the most unpleasant stroke of all. After having adhered to the regular service so long, to be made a volunteer of in spite of myself."[3]

The next day he added, "I wrote a letter to the governor of Ohio offering my services. I have made up my mind to enter the volunteer service and push up as high as I can and, so long as I don't get beyond my capacity, I shall still retain my self respect. I find men whom I feel to be my inferiors high in command doing great harm to the country by occupying these positions."[4]

It seems that Kautz had given up the idea when he wrote in his journal on July 28, "I have not yet heard from Gov. Todd [sic]. I fear that he still has no commission for me. That office is too much in demand to give me a chance."[5] We can only imagine his surprise when he was awakened early in the morning of September 10 with the offer to take command of the Second Ohio Cavalry.

There was little time for goodbyes to the officers with whom he had shared the dangers of the previous summer. He tried later to explain his feelings: "I was leaving a gallant Regiment which could have done me credit. I had no enemies in it and was always served with cheerfulness and good will by the officers and men." He then went on to describe his lack of confidence in General Pleasonton and concluded, "Being satisfied of his incompetency, I turned my back on his command with a light heart."[6]

Three days before Kautz left the Sixth Cavalry, he received a letter from his father written from Philadelphia informing him that his brother Albert was in the Pennsylvania Hospital for the Insane. After he concluded his business in Washington, Kautz was officially on leave, so he determined to visit Albert himself. He reached Philadelphia on September 15 and stayed with the family of Captain John Savage, who was home on sick leave.[7] He then went to the hospital to see his brother.

After Albert had been exchanged the previous November, he was assigned to the flagship *Hartford* of Admiral David Farragut's Gulf Squadron. Farragut and his fleet had been almost continuously engaged in combat operations through the spring and summer of 1862 leading to the surrender of New Orleans in April and the passage of Vicksburg in June. At New Orleans, Albert had taken an active part in negotiations with Mayor John T. Monroe leading to the surrender of the city and had personally raised the American flag over the U.S. Customs House.

On August 11, at the termination of Farragut's successful campaign, he wrote to Secretary of the Navy Gideon Welles asking for replacements of both officers and ships, saying, "The Department must be aware that I am getting short of officers as well as ships. They are going home daily from much the same cause — used up."[8] Later in the same letter he mentioned that Lieutenant Albert Kautz had been sent home on medical leave the previous day.

When Albert reached Philadelphia on his way home, he took a room at the Continental Hotel. He was so sick with fever, however, that he became delirious. William Nason, the hotel manager, assuming that Albert was mentally ill, sent a telegram to Ohio requesting that someone come immediately to Albert's aid and had him admitted to the Hospital for the Insane. George Kautz went to Philadelphia as requested and wrote the letter, which Kautz received September 7.

Kautz visited his brother on September 15 and 16 and, determining that Albert was beginning to improve, continued his journey via New York to Columbus, Ohio.

When Kautz arrived in Columbus on September 19, he took a room at the recently completed Neal House, and, next morning, walked to Governor Tod's office at the Capitol. He said of the governor, "I was fascinated by his appearance and manners. He had a remarkably fine face and head, fine brown eyes, an exquisite mouth and a youthful appearance for a man so near sixty years of age. His figure was full, of medium height and with shoulders rounded; he was deliberate in his motions, and his bearing was dignified and self-possessed."[9]

While the governor was out of the room preparing Kautz's commission as colonel (which he dated September 10, the day Kautz left the Sixth Cavalry), the governor's aide, Judge Benjamin F. Hoffman, filled Kautz in on the history of the Second Ohio. The regiment had been mustered into service in October 1861 under the patronage of Senator Benjamin F. Wade and Congressman John Hutchins. It was commanded by Colonel Charles W. Doubleday. After a period of instruction at Camp Dennison, the regiment, 1200 strong, was sent to western Missouri, where it campaigned against Confederate guerrillas under William Quantrill. From May to July 1862, it operated in Indian Territory, including a successful expedition against Cherokee Indians under Chief Stand Watie. Due partly to Doubleday's mismanagement, most of the regiment's horses had died or were unserviceable. The regiment then returned to Fort Scott, Kansas Territory, disorganized and demoralized. Colonel Doubleday, frustrated in his hope of being appointed brigadier, resigned his commission and returned to civilian pursuits. The regiment was subsequently broken into detachments. Lieutenant Colonel Robert W. Ratliff, was so confident of his promotion to colonel that he had written to Hoffman in June 1862 to suggest which of the majors of the regiment should be advanced to the lieutenant colonelcy when he took over. When Doubleday resigned, Governor Tod saw that Ratliff, whom he had known since childhood, was not up to command of the regiment. He sought an officer of the regular Army to straighten the regiment out and wrote to the Secretary of War for the recommendation of an officer from Ohio.

The governor's message was passed down to Major Thomas Vincent, who made a list of eligible officers and, putting Kautz's name at the top of the list, recommended him.[10]

After meeting with Governor Tod, Kautz spent a few days at home. His brother Albert returned home also, apparently recovered, and the two met briefly. Kautz then headed west, reaching Department of Missouri headquarters at Saint Louis on October 3. Strangely, no one at headquarters, including Department Commander Major General Samuel R. Curtis, could tell him where the Second Ohio was with any certainty.

Armed with the previous suggestion that his regiment was at Fort Scott, Kautz determined to go there. He took the train to Fort Leavenworth, where he met Drs. Taylor and Ortalia, two surgeons assigned to his regiment, who were planning to rejoin the regiment at Fort Scott. He spoke with the commissary and quartermaster officers at Fort Leavenworth about acquiring horses and learned that there were none in the entire department. He then accompanied the two doctors to Fort Scott in their ambulance, arriving on October 12.

His arrival at Fort Scott is described by one of his troopers, Isaac Gause:

> The Second Ohio was treated to a surprise. When the stage rolled up to the Bourbon House, among the passengers was an unpretentious-looking officer, who, with others, walked in and registered as a guest.... No one noticed the newcomer as he mingled with the other guests. He wore the cavalry uniform with captain's bar. Next day he walked leisurely up the hill to the camp of the Second. The first one that took any notice of him was the camp guard, who saluted him and was saluted in return.
> "What are you doing here?" was the question of the officer.
> "On guard," was the prompt reply.
> "I see nothing here to guard," said the officer. "You can go to your quarters."
> "But I am on camp guard, and can't go until released by the corporal."
> "Go to your quarters," said the officer, "and if anyone says anything to you, tell him Colonel Kautz relieved you."
> It was soon known that the Second Ohio had a new colonel. The camp was then moved to a shady place by the river, and many other noticeable changes took place for the better.[11]

Kautz stayed in town for more than a week waiting for his baggage to catch up. While there, he learned what more he could of the Second Ohio. At the regiment's camp a mile from town were about 100 men of the regiment, about ten men per company, and 100 more were serving as a provost guard in town. A detachment of about 200 who still had serviceable horses were with Brigadier General James Blunt in his campaign in northern Arkansas. Another 125 had been formed into a light artillery battery and were with Blunt also. Another one hundred had been assigned to duty with the quartermaster and ordnance departments and about 50 to 100 were in south-central Kansas helping to guard the border with Indian Territory. The company-based structure of the regiment had been completely upset. Kautz almost despaired of being able to bring the regiment together and strongly considered turning down the colonelcy and returning to the Sixth Cavalry.

> Whilst waiting for my baggage and thus hesitating about taking command, I learned something of the character and feeling of the officers and men. When they heard that an officer of the Regular Army had been appointed Colonel, they were all quite outraged and declared they would have no whippersnapper West Pointer about them. What they proposed to do I don't know, but they had some exaggerated idea on the subject and fancied their new Colonel would lead them a terrible life with his martinettish notions. I must, however, have turned out very different from what their fancy painted me, for when they found that I did not take command and sometimes talked of giving up the Regt., the officers hoped I would not think of it, and even the men, when they met me singly and alone, would stop and tell me they hoped I would take command, and very soon. I found they wanted someone who understood military duty and had experience. I found the privates exceedingly intelligent and perfectly aware of the ignorance of their officers. This state of things gave me some hope. Moreover a rumor reached us that the Governor of Ohio had procured an order for the Regt. to proceed to Camp Chase, Ohio to remount and refit. With these prospects I took command on the 20th of October and, my baggage having arrived, I moved up to camp.[12]

One of the first things Kautz did, as Isaac Gause said, was to move the camp. The encampment had been placed on a high hill during the heat of summer to take advantage of cooling breezes and to avoid mosquitoes. With winter coming on, those gentle breezes had become bitingly cold as they blew across the prairie. In addition, the need to carry both firewood and water to the hilltop had become a most disagreeable chore for the men. Kautz chose a location in a grove of trees near the creek which provided protection from the weather and a ready supply of wood and water. The men were understandably pleased with the move.

Kautz next turned to administrative matters. He quickly learned that all the various returns, reports, rosters and rolls prepared by the companies of the regiment were being sent in either totally incorrect or not at all. One of the regiment's officers, Major George G. Miner, had served in the Mexican War and had given his assurance that he knew the army's system of record-keeping and taught it within the regiment — unfortunately completely wrong. Kautz noted that the morning reports were especially defective. To correct the situation, he "issued a circular containing instructions how the morning reports should be made out. To my surprise the following morning they came in, and were remarkably correct." With that success, he prepared additional circulars covering other items of paperwork, and: "In a few weeks I had the Administration duties running as smoothly as they could possibly run in a Regular Regt."[13]

Kautz, however, did not have a "Regular Regt.," but only fragments of a volunteer one. Over a period of several weeks, he managed to get all of the various detachments reassembled at Fort Scott except those two detachments serving with General Blunt in Arkansas. At the same time, he evaluated the officers of the regiment and found among them a number of very competent men, including Lieutenant Colonel Ratliff and Majors Henry L. Burnett, George A. Purington and Dudley Seward.

Despite the rumor that the Second Ohio had been ordered back to Ohio to remount and refit, no order came to that effect. Kautz became certain that such an order had been written, but that it had somehow been suppressed by someone in the department. He strongly suspected that it was General Blunt, who was reluctant to release the men serving under him in Arkansas. In fact, Kautz was correct. The order, written at the War Department, had arrived at department headquarters in St. Louis and had been forwarded through General Blunt's headquarters. Blunt had simply not forwarded it.

On November 17, Lieutenant Collier of the Second Ohio, who was serving on General Blunt's staff, arrived at Fort Scott carrying dispatches to department headquarters and to Governor Tod. Although Collier could not, or would not, disclose the contents of the dispatches, Kautz concluded, again correctly, that they were requests to have his order to return to Ohio countermanded. In order to try to counteract the effect of Collier's mission, Kautz sent Major Burnett to Saint Louis to consult with General Curtis and, if necessary, to Columbus to meet with Governor Tod.

Burnett left for Saint Louis on November 18 and returned nine days later with the order for the Second Ohio to move to Camp Chase in his pocket.

The regiment left Fort Scott on December 2, marched to Fort Leavenworth and took the cars to Columbus, arriving late on December 16. They marched out to Camp Chase the following day.

Located on the National Road four miles west of the state capitol, Camp Chase, named for Treasury Secretary Salmon P. Chase, was opened in 1861 as a camp of instruction for newly recruited volunteer regiments. Late in 1861, a few Confederate prisoners of war were impounded there, but after the surrender of Forts Henry and Donelson in the spring of 1862, the number of prisoners rose to almost 2000.[14] The prison function of the camp is remembered today, but history has forgotten that almost 150,000 Union soldiers received part of their training there.

When the Second Ohio arrived on December 17, 1862, August Kautz estimated that, in addition to the prisoners, there were approximately 5000 Union soldiers, captured and paroled, but not yet exchanged. The camp also housed one other full regiment (the Ninety-Fifth Ohio

Infantry), detachments of at least five others and a constantly changing number of new recruits. The only unit permanently assigned to the camp was the Governor's Guard, commanded by Major Peter Zinn, the camp commander.

Always a stickler for proper military protocol, Kautz declined to report to Major Zinn, an officer he ranked by two grades, and sent his reports directly to General James Cooper, commander of the Columbus District. Kautz felt that Cooper should command Camp Chase, but the general was in such poor health that he declined to take the duty and left it to Zinn. According to Kautz, Zinn was "surprised and affronted"[15] by Kautz's action. Perhaps, had he been a regular Army officer rather than a Cincinnati lawyer, he would have been less surprised. General Cooper wisely ended the standoff by naming Kautz camp commander in Zinn's place.

Kautz was not pleased to have the extra responsibility, although he had brought it on himself. The most troublesome aspect of camp command was dealing with the paroled Union soldiers. Serving under officers whom they neither knew nor trusted and anxious to get either home or back to their regiments, discipline among them was nonexistent. Fortunately, by the beginning of January, all were gone.

On December 19, Governor Tod held a dinner and reception for the officers of the regiment. It was at this reception that Kautz first met General Cooper. The governor's family was also at the affair and Kautz said of the governor's three daughters, "The daughters are pleasant enough, one of them is pretty."[16]

On December 23, Major George Purington arrived with the detachment from Arkansas and a group of recruits came in from Cleveland, bringing the strength of the regiment to about 700 men. Over the next few weeks, Kautz reorganized these men into two battalions, allowing him the luxury of dismissing the least effective officers. In order to fill out the regiment, a battalion of cavalry which had been recruited as part of the Eighth Ohio Cavalry was added to the Second Ohio to bring it up to strength. This Third Battalion, however, was in the field near Mount Sterling, Kentucky, and would not join the regiment until April. Kautz sent Major Purington to Kentucky to take command of the Third Battalion.

At the same time that the reorganization of the regiment was taking place, Kautz earned the approval of the men by ensuring that each man had an extended furlough. He was gratified that almost all of the men returned from furlough on time. As winter gave way to spring, the men were armed with Burnside breechloading carbines and remounted on serviceable horses.

Governor Tod was most attentive to the needs of the regiment and aided Kautz as much as possible. The two men became friends and Kautz often visited the governor's family at their home on Town Street in Columbus and at their Brier Hill estate near Youngstown. Kautz learned much of the governor's history and character. He was the son of George Tod, an early justice of the Ohio Supreme Court. He studied and practiced law and was elected to the Ohio Senate in 1838. He made a fortune as a pioneer in the coal and steel industries in Ohio and was a founder and president of the Cleveland & Mahoning Valley Railroad. In 1844 and 1846, he ran unsuccessfully for governor on the Democratic ticket and, from 1847 to 1851, was minister to Brazil. In 1860, Tod was a delegate to the Democratic Party's national convention in Charleston and was elected vice-president of the convention. When all the southern delegates walked out over the issue of slavery, Tod reconvened the convention in Baltimore, where Steven A. Douglas was nominated for the presidency. When the Civil War began, Tod became discouraged at the pro–Southern leanings of many in the Democratic Party and joined the fledgling Union Party. He ran for governor and was elected by a wide margin. In his two years in office, he strongly supported the war effort and President Lincoln is quoted as having said, "Governor Tod has aided me more and troubled me less than any other Governor."[17]

Tod performed many charitable acts for Ohio soldiers and for their families. His kindness did not confine itself to the Union soldiers. He often aided the families of men in the prisoner camp as well. During the winter of 1862–63, a smallpox epidemic struck the prison camp, killing more than 400 in February alone. At first, the Confederate dead were buried in the Columbus City Cemetery, but as their numbers grew, Kautz and Governor Tod initiated a move to provide a separate cemetery for the Confederate soldiers. Before the war ended, more than 2200 men would be buried there.[18]

On the night of March 9, 1863, about seventy-five men of the Second Ohio marched into downtown Columbus and systematically ransacked the High Street offices of the *Crisis*, a Copperhead newspaper which was in the habit of printing the speeches of Clement Vallandingham, a well-known Southern sympathizer. A year before, the *Crisis* had printed a vitriolic article critical of the Second Ohio while they were in Kansas and this raid on the *Crisis* office was the means the men chose of gaining revenge for the insult. In addition to destroying the newspaper's presses and furnishings, some of the men made off with souvenirs from the office. By mere coincidence, one of these items was a meerschaum pipe which Kautz had entrusted to a friend who worked at the newspaper to deliver to a mutual friend serving in the navy. Although he was somewhat in sympathy with the actions of the raiders, he considered resigning his colonelcy at the thought that men under his command would demonstrate such scandalous behavior.

The following day, Kautz had the enlisted men's quarters searched, but no stolen items were found. He surreptitiously let it be known that if he got his pipe back no more effort would be made to implicate the men of the regiment. Isaac Gause, who, no doubt, was one of the ringleaders, tells of a meeting of the men afterwards. Some of the men

> denounced our Colonel as a Copperhead and in sympathy with the *Crisis* people, and no one appeared to know anything about the pipe. Gold pens, fine inkstands and other trophies were plentiful. I ... defended the Colonel, as did the majority. He had inaugurated many reforms, and had, in fact, been our benefactor. We decided that he was loyal, and that the connection of the pipe with the *Crisis* office, as he said, was only a coincidence. We then dispersed, and a man six foot three ... stepped up to me and drew from a side pocket a morocco case, with the gilt letters A.V.K. on one side. He opened the case and displayed a fine meerschaum.... As a result the pipe was wrapped up and addressed to A.V. Kautz, and entrusted to me. I strolled leisurely up to the officers' quarters and ... slipped the pipe through the slot into the mail box at headquarters."[19]

Kautz, in his *Reminiscences*, tells the story of the raid, but fails altogether to mention the pipe. Always interested in proper discipline, he showed a hint of pride in his men by finishing with, "The men came to town and went back in a perfectly orderly manner otherwise."[20]

Twice in the month of March, Kautz received orders from Brigadier General Horatio Wright's Department of Ohio headquarters in Cincinnati to move into Kentucky, but both times Kautz wired headquarters that he wasn't ready. Finally, at the end of March, he concluded that the Second Ohio was ready for field service. Before he moved, however, he had one piece of personal business to attend to.

During a short visit in December 1862, his brother Fred had informed him that their sixteen-year-old sister, Sophie, was living in a boarding house in Cincinnati and had voiced a desire to stay with him in Columbus. Kautz arranged for Sophie to come to Columbus. He wrote, "I had my sister visit me during the winter, she boarded in town and I enjoyed the first opportunity I had ever had of her society since she had reached maturity. I took great pleasure in introducing her into the best society and to bring her out. I took her with me on my visit to Philadelphia and gave her an opportunity to see the great eastern cities."[21] On March 23, Kautz took a leave in order to take Sophie home. By the time he returned on March 31, General Cooper had died and General Wright had been replaced by Major General Ambrose Burnside as commander of the Department of Ohio. Kautz immediately notified Burnside that the Second Ohio was ready for the field.

17. Operating in Kentucky

In the spring of 1863, three separate Union armies were operating in Kentucky and Tennessee. The huge Army of the Cumberland, under the command of Major General William S. Rosecrans, was concentrated at Murfreesboro, planning to move toward Chattanooga. Farther west, Ulysses Grant's Army of the Tennessee was preparing to move down the Mississippi River toward Vicksburg.

The smallest and least well-organized of the three Union armies, Ambrose Burnside's Army of the Ohio, was spread out across southeastern Kentucky, serving more as a defense against Rebel incursions into Kentucky than as an offensive weapon.

It was on April 1 that Kautz wired General Burnside that his Second Ohio was ready for duty. On April 4, he received a telegram directing him to have the regiment in Cincinnati the following day. Kautz later wrote, "This was practically impossible, but it was not an unusual thing ... for the Genl. to issue orders that could not be executed."[1] To Kautz's credit, the regiment was in Cincinnati on the morning of April 7.

Kautz met with General Burnside and learned that the Second Ohio was to be assigned to Brigadier General Samuel D. Sturgis's Division of the XXIII Corps and was ordered to leave immediately for Mount Sterling, Kentucky.[2] The first part of the trip was by boat to Maysville, followed by an overland march to Mount Sterling, which was reached on April 11. Over the next four days, Kautz received, and seemed bewildered by, conflicting orders which caused the regiment to march from Mount Sterling to Winchester, to Lexington and eventually to Stanford, Kentucky, where they should have been ordered in the first place, without benefit of their baggage.

When Kautz reported to Brigadier General Samuel Carter's[3] headquarters in Stanford about midnight of April 15 after marching all day in a driving rain, he was "immensely disgusted"[4] to learn that he was not expected, that there was no reason for the rapid march in the first place and, since the wagons were far behind, that his weary men would have to rest that rainy night without benefit of blankets or tents. It seems that Carter was apologetic for the way the Second Ohio had been treated, but that did not prevent him from ordering them, after one day's rest, to move again, this time to Somerset, Kentucky. Again lacking baggage wagons, the men were not only blanketless and tentless, but supperless when they arrived at Somerset on the evening of April 17 after a march of thirty-five miles.

The remainder of Carter's Brigade followed to Somerset a few days later.

Somerset lay ten miles north of the meandering Cumberland River. Various Confederate units were south of the river. The river had no bridges, but there was a ferry at Mill Springs consisting of two small boats useful only when the current was not too swift. There were also several fords above and below Somerset useful only when the water was low. Since the area south of Somerset was sparsely settled and heavily forested, there was little forage available for the horses of Carter's predominantly cavalry force. Kautz later said that "the principal occupation [of his regiment was to] hunt for food for our animals, which was not an easy task."[5]

On May 1, Carter managed to get most of his brigade across on the Mill Springs ferry. Kautz never learned with certainty what Confederate forces were present south of the river, but they offered little resistance.[6] Carter occupied the town of Monticello, twenty miles past the river, for several days and sent Kautz's regiment on a reconnaissance as far as Travisville beyond the Tennessee border. Kautz found the Confederates in force at that place, and Carter crossed back over the river on May 5 and 6 and went into camp at Somerset.[7]

In one of the reorganizations of XXIII Corps on May 11, Kautz was given command of the Third Brigade, First Division, XXIII Corps, a brigade consisting of his Second Ohio Cavalry and the Seventh Ohio Cavalry. The Seventh was called the "River Regiment" because it had been recruited in the counties along the Ohio River. Although Kautz had never met the regiment's colonel, Israel Garrard, a Cincinnatian, he was well acquainted with Garrard's brother, Kenner, who had graduated from the Academy in 1851. Kautz did not comment on the fact that the Seventh Ohio's lieutenant colonel was George Miner, whose mistaken ideas about military paperwork had given him so much trouble the previous September. With Kautz's elevation to brigade command, George Purington took command of the Second Ohio.

On June 4, Kautz's Brigade was diminished by the temporary transfer of 150 "picked men" from each of his two regiments for an expedition into East Tennessee led by Colonel William P. Sanders. Kautz's former comrade from the Sixth U.S. Cavalry would lead a very successful raid against the railroads around Knoxville.[8]

Through this period, Kautz developed a profound respect for General Carter based primarily on Carter's method of dealing with the men under his command. He was also under the impression, probably correctly, that the general favored him by giving him the most important assignments.

On May 8, based on intelligence that a large Rebel force, probably that of John Pegram,[9] had occupied Monticello, Kautz was ordered to demonstrate in that direction with a force of 800 men consisting of about 400 of his own brigade, about 70 men of the Forty-Fifth Ohio Mounted Infantry, and a four-gun battery of Lieutenant Jesse Law's Mountain Howitzer Battery, all of whom would cross the Cumberland at the ford on the main road from Somerset to Monticello. They would be joined by about 300 men of the Second Tennessee Cavalry and the Forty-Fifth Ohio Mounted Infantry under Lieutenant-Colonel Silas Adams of the First Kentucky Cavalry, who were to cross the river at the Mill Springs ferry. The major purpose of Kautz's move was to keep Pegram's Brigade occupied and prevent it from moving against Sanders's raid into East Tennessee.

Kautz got under way at about 4 P.M. on June 8, crossed the Cumberland and went into camp about three miles from the crossing. Colonel Adams joined him the following morning at the farm of a man named West near where the road from Mill Springs meets the main road. Kautz learned from West that Pegram occupied Monticello with his brigade of cavalry, probably about 1800 men. West cautioned Kautz not to attempt an assault because of Pegram's superior numbers. Kautz moved forward nonetheless, attempting to give the appearance of the vanguard of a much larger force.

Pegram's pickets retired and, as Kautz's command moved toward Monticello, they met the enemy's main force drawn up in line of battle four miles beyond West's farm. A sharp skirmish developed, but the enemy retreated when Law's Battery opened on them. The Rebels were pursued through Monticello to Beaver Creek, four miles beyond the town. Rather than attempt a crossing of the creek in the face of heavy odds, Kautz retired to Monticello and appropriated or destroyed what military stores could be found.

About 1 P.M., Kautz retired to West's farm to go into camp with his own brigade and sent the force under Colonel Adams back across the Cumberland via the ferry at Mill Springs. He left Major Dudley Seward at Monticello with three companies of the Second Ohio to act as rear guard. About midafternoon, Seward was attacked by what was probably the majority of Pegram's Brigade and was driven from the town. Seward failed to notify Kautz of the enemy's movement and he had been driven almost to West's before Kautz was aware of the danger. Kautz said in his report,

> I had made arrangements to go into camp, and a single company of the Second Tennessee only was available, which I marched a half mile to the rear, and met the rear guard retiring in some confusion. I had only time to put this company in position before the enemy appeared through the woods, and the advance not [being] immediately checked, the rear guard was rallied, and with only 200 men the enemy was driven back over a mile through the dense timber, where they took up a position behind a stone wall, compelling us to fall back a few hundred yards out of range. The enemy rallied, and sought in turn to drive us back. By this time reinforcements of the Seventh Ohio Cavalry and Second Tennessee and a section of howitzers arrived, and the enemy again were severely checked and fell back. Night was now interposed, and, gathering up the dead and wounded that could be found in the darkness, we fell back to West's.[10]

In his reminiscences, Kautz describes his part in the affair. "This little affair ... was very sharp and destructive. During the whole war I was never so exposed as on this occasion for the time it lasted. I was obliged to remain on horseback and had to keep up with the front line, as my personal presence was necessary to make the men hold their ground until arrival of the rest of the command. I was surprised and gratified to think that I had escaped without injury. I was, however, still more gratified to think how narrowly I had escaped disaster.... The enemy, although outnumbering us, was fairly repulsed."[11]

The next morning, Kautz had his men up at 2 A.M. and was back in Somerset by sunup. Casualties in Kautz's command were seven killed and about thirty wounded. Confederate casualties totaled about sixty, including twenty captured. Several of Kautz's wounded troopers were left at Mr. West's farm and cared for by Dr. Smith, one of Kautz's regimental surgeons. About five Confederate wounded were cared for by Smith as well. According to Kautz, Pegram's men "were much gratified at the Dr. being left to take care of their wounded, and they were equally considerate in permitting him to come and go from Somerset."[12]

The affair at Monticello was a minor one in a remote and relatively unimportant field of the war, but it succeeded in keeping Pegram's Brigade occupied long enough to allow Sanders to enter East Tennessee with little resistance. The fact that Kautz's small force had succeeded against heavy odds earned high compliments from General Carter as well as General Hartsuff. Late on June 9, General Burnside wired General Sturgis, "Telegraph General Carter to thank Colonel Kautz's command for their gallant behavior today."[13] As a result of Kautz's part in the affair, he received a brevet promotion to major in the regular Army "for gallantry and meritorious service," the second of six brevets he would receive in the course of the war. Perhaps Kautz was most pleased by the praise his troopers received from the enemy, as related to him by Dr. Smith, when they "spoke of having met men worthy of their steel."[14]

A reconnaissance on June 16 found that Pegram did go in pursuit of Sanders, but he was too late to offer significant resistance to the raiders.

On June 20, Kautz was directed to make a demonstration in the direction of Jamestown, Tennessee, forty miles south of Monticello, with a force of 1000 men, cavalry and infantry. The purpose of the move was to be on hand to reinforce Colonel Sanders if he should return north in that direction or to make a demonstration in his favor in case he did not. When Kautz's advance reached Jamestown, he found no forage available for his animals and, with the knowledge that Sanders had already returned by a route far to the east, he marched his command back to Somerset.

The next day, General Carter was directed by General Burnside to place Kautz under arrest for disobeying a direct order in not supporting Sanders. Carter, however, did not arrest Kautz and the arrest order was countermanded the same day. Kautz seems never to have learned why his arrest was not carried out. In his reminiscences, written many years later, he still pondered the circumstances. He apparently never found out that Carter had informed Burnside that he had ordered Kautz back, thus taking responsibility for Kautz's return on himself.

On the day that Kautz returned from Jamestown (June 23), General William Rosecrans telegraphed General Burnside from Murfreesboro that Confederate General John Hunt Morgan had crossed to the north side of the Caney River (Caney Fork) about fifty miles east of Murfreesboro with his force of about 2400 cavalry. Burnside in turn wired General Hartsuff, "Communicate this to Carter at once, and tell him to send word to Kautz, and also try to communicate with Sanders."[15] Both Kautz and Sanders would be busy for the next few weeks.

18. Chasing Morgan

Captain John Hunt Morgan's name first appeared in newspapers, both North and South, after his squadron of cavalry destroyed a trestle on the Louisville & Nashville line near Bacon Creek Station, Kentucky. From that time forward, Morgan's command would always be referred to as Morgan's Raiders.

Born in Alabama, John Morgan spent most of his childhood in Lexington, Kentucky, where he was educated at Transylvania College. In 1857, he took over the captaincy of a colorfully-clad militia company called the Lexington Rifles. In 1861, after Kentucky declared its neutrality, most of the company opted for the Confederacy. Acquiring horses, their numbers grew until Morgan commanded a full squadron of cavalry.

Promoted to colonel on April 4, 1862, Morgan was given command of the Second Kentucky Cavalry Regiment, of which his squadron became a part. Through much of 1862, his command, first a regiment, then a brigade and, finally, a division of cavalry, raided through Kentucky in support of the Confederate offensive which terminated in the Battle of Perryville in October. On September 27, 1862, one brigade of Morgan's Division attacked and partially burned the town of Augusta, Kentucky, located almost directly across the Ohio River from the Kautz homestead in Ohio. The Ripley (Ohio) Home Guard, in which Kautz's brother, Louis, was a lieutenant, were called on to aid in the defense of Augusta. As they were preparing to cross the river, they asked August Kautz, then home on leave, to command them. Kautz declined the invitation, writing, "It would be impossible for me to accomplish anything with such troops."[1]

Morgan was promoted to brigadier general in December 1862 and, by the spring of 1863, he was in command of a division of cavalry in Major General Joseph Wheeler's Cavalry Corps of Braxton Bragg's Army of Tennessee. The two brigades of his division were commanded by his brother-in-law Colonel Basil Duke and Colonel Adam R. Johnson.

Bragg, at his headquarters at Tullahoma, was contemplating falling back to Chattanooga. He knew that his Army of Tennessee would be especially vulnerable to attack by Rosecrans's Union Army of the Tennessee during the move. Morgan suggested to Bragg that he could take his cavalry division north into Indiana and Ohio, forcing Rosecrans to send troops after him, thus making it unlikely that Bragg would be molested during his move. Bragg reluctantly assented, but gave permission for Morgan to take only 1500 men, just over half his division, and specifically ordered Morgan to limit his raid to Kentucky. Morgan negotiated with his immediate superior, General Wheeler, and, convincing Wheeler that he could not safely complete the mission with fewer than 2000 men, was permitted to take 2000.

Morgan marched out of Alexandria, Tennessee, on June 11, 1863, with more than 2400 troopers. He crossed the Cumberland River near Carthage, Tennessee, and was about to assault that town when he was recalled by Bragg and ordered to East Tennessee to intercept William Sanders, who, as we learned in the previous chapter, was on a raid of his own.

Morgan, like John Pegram, was unable to make contact with Sanders. Forced to resupply, it was almost two weeks before he could get his raiders moving north again. As he approached the Cumberland River for the second time, he found the river swollen out of its banks.

On June 26, General Samuel Carter heard that part of Morgan's command was at Monticello, and he sent Kautz's Brigade and that of Colonel Frank Wolford[2] to Jamestown, Kentucky, thirty-five miles southwest of Somerset, in anticipation of Morgan's possible crossing near that point. When Kautz's reconnaissance units found small parties and individual troopers from Morgan's Division on the north side of the river, it became obvious that Morgan was looking for a place to cross. Kautz later wrote, "The rains prevailed and the Cumberland was quite swollen and I had little faith that Morgan would attempt to cross in such a stage of water."[3]

Kautz became convinced that Morgan's crossing would be farther downstream. He urged Wolford, who, by seniority, was in command at Jamestown, to move twenty miles further west to Columbia, a town which Morgan would have to pass through if he could effect a crossing, but Wolford did not consider himself authorized to leave Jamestown. On June 30, Kautz sent a report to General Carter stating his opinion that he and Wolford "were not properly posted" and "urging a change to Columbia."[4]

Forty miles to the west near Marrowbone, Kentucky, Brigadier General Henry M. Judah's Third Division of XXIII Corps was also on the lookout for Morgan. The three brigades under Judah were commanded by Brigadier Generals Mahlon D. Manson, Edward H. Hobson and James M. Shackelford.

In the last days of June, Morgan seemed to the Federal commanders to have disappeared from the area, giving the impression that he had returned to the Army of Tennessee. Morgan's disappearance was not, however, designed to deceive. He had his men busy constructing flatboats to be used in crossing the Cumberland near the town of Burkesville, about midway between Jamestown and Marrowbone. On July 1, he sent an advanced guard of one regiment across the river at Burkesville. They fought a brief engagement with a small detachment of Hobson's Brigade, then fell back to the river.

Late in the day of July 1, General Shackelford learned of the engagement near Burkesville and rushed his entire brigade to that place, arriving about 10 P.M. As he was setting out to greet Morgan's main force the following morning, he received an order from General Judah to return to Marrowbone. As a result of Judah's order, Shackelford's advanced cavalry regiments, already in contact with Morgan, broke off contact and returned to Marrowbone.[5]

Back at Jamestown on July 1, Wolford, hearing that Morgan was crossing at Burkesville, sent a patrol under Lieutenant Keen of the First Kentucky to reconnoiter. Keen returned on July 2 with the intelligence that one of Morgan's regiments had already crossed.

As soon as Keen returned, Wolford sent Major Dudley Seward with a squadron of Kautz's Second Ohio north to the town of Liberty and a squadron of his own First Kentucky under Captain Jesse M. Carter west to Columbia in an effort to try to determine Morgan's route. Carter ran headlong into Morgan's main body, now across the river, at Columbia on the morning of July 3. A stiff engagement followed which lasted several hours. Carter was mortally wounded and his small force routed. Lieutenant Colonel Silas Adams with the remainder of the First Kentucky had followed in support of Captain Carter and also skirmished with Morgan's main force. Adams, finding himself outnumbered, withdrew his own and Carter's troopers and returned to Jamestown on the morning of July 4.

A small Independence Day celebration had been scheduled at noon for the troops at Jamestown. A heavy thunderstorm occurred at midday and the festivities were rescheduled for late in the afternoon. Before it could begin, however, Wolford and Kautz received orders to join in the pursuit of Morgan and, as Kautz tells it, "As night set in we moved out on the road to Liberty and the great chase after Genl. Morgan commenced."[6]

Morgan's Raiders rushed north out of Columbia more intent on making time than in making contact with Union forces. When, however, they reached the bridge over the Green River at Tebb's Bend twenty miles north of Columbia on the morning of July 4, they found five companies of Colonel Orlando H. Moore's Twenty-Fifth Michigan Infantry posted in excellent defensive positions blocking the crossing. At first Morgan sent a message under a flag of truce to Moore demanding that he surrender, but Moore answered that he felt it would be unpatriotic to consider doing so on such an important national holiday. When repeated assaults failed to dislodge Moore's Michiganders, Morgan found a ford several miles downstream and crossed there, but not until he had lost half a day's march on his pursuers.

In addition to the fight at Green River, Morgan's forces experienced surprisingly strong resistance from the small garrisons at Lebanon on July 5 and at Bardstown on July 6.

The brigades of Hobson and Shackelford and of Wolford and Kautz reached Lebanon on July 6. There General Hobson was placed in command of all forces pursuing Morgan. Orders, issued at 4:30 P.M. July 6, read in part, "You will combine the commands of General Shackelford and Colonel Wolford, and, after ascertaining as near as possible the direction of General Morgan's route, you will endeavor to overtake him or cut him off."[7] With portions of nine regiments under his command, Hobson's force was of almost equal strength to that of Morgan.

The acrid smell of burnt gunpowder still hung in the air over Lebanon from the fight the day before. It had taken the better part of the day for Morgan's main force to subdue the 400 men of the Twentieth Kentucky Infantry under Lieutenant Colonel Charles S. Hanson who held the town. The reward for Morgan's Raiders was a large supply of rations and a small arsenal of weapons. It had come at the cost of nine men killed, including John Morgan's brother, Tom. Six of Hanson's men were killed and all the rest captured.

Despite the delays, Morgan's advance rode into the Ohio River town of Brandenburg on the afternoon of July 7, still about a day ahead of his pursuers.

Kautz's Brigade had marched out of Lebanon on the afternoon of July 6 and went into camp at 10 P.M. five miles past Springfield. They were in the saddle again at 2 A.M. and reached the main line of the Louisville & Nashville Railroad at Bardstown Junction about five o'clock in the afternoon. There they received a much-needed supply of forage and rations from a supply train. The train also brought newspapers "with the news of the defeat of Lee at Gettysburg and the capture of Vicksburg by Grant. These victories cheered the men greatly."[8] Morgan's men had met a northbound train at this same point the day before, but the train was a passenger train and offered no food or forage, just jewelry, cash and a lot of mail.

Kautz could not account for the fact that he did not receive orders from General Hobson to march until 7 A.M. on July 8. With his men's saddlebags full and their spirits buoyed by the news of the Union victories, he felt they should have been on Morgan's trail much earlier. During the march, it was learned that Morgan's advance had commandeered two steam river packets, the *John T. McCombs* and the *Alice Dean*, and that Morgan's command was using them to ferry across the Ohio at Brandenburg.

That evening, Hobson ordered his command into camp at Garnettsville, less than ten miles from Brandenburg. Kautz was disappointed, saying, "We halted at sundown at Garnettsville.... The delay was unaccountable to me. It seemed to me that if he was really crossing, that his forces must be divided by the river and no better place for an attack could be desired."[9]

Morgan's crossing was interrupted twice by fire from Federal gunboats and from a small band of militia on the Indiana shore. Required to make many trips in the two small packets in order to shuttle all of the men, horses, artillery and wagons across, the last of Morgan's Division did not reach the north shore until almost dawn on July 9. In view of this, it seems likely that a determined march by Hobson's command on the afternoon of July 8, as Kautz had suggested, might have done considerable damage to that portion of Morgan's command still on the Kentucky side.

When Hobson reached Brandenburg the following morning only a few stragglers were left to be rounded up. As Kautz tells it, "On the morning of the 9th we went into Brandenburg and found the enemy all across the Ohio. The remains of a steamboat [the *Alice Dean*] that had been used in ferrying Morgan over were smoking on the Indiana shore having been burned to the waters-edge.[10] The enemy finished crossing about daylight. Crowds of boats arrived to aid in our crossing and by night we were nearly all across."[11]

Morgan moved his command due north from the river to the town of Corydon, where he found the local Home Guard ready and quite willing to impede his progress into the town. The 450 men of the Home Guard put up a spirited defense, but, seriously outnumbered, were forced to surrender.

Morgan then headed east. Much has been written about the suffering of Morgan's men and of their horses as they sped across southern Indiana. A bit has also been written about the suffering of the inhabitants and of their horses as well. That Morgan's men committed depredations during the march is a fact. The reality is that they could have done worse, but did not.

Kautz described his march across Indiana, always about a day behind Morgan:

On the morning of the 10th we took the road to Corydon where we arrived early in the afternoon and found that the militia had undertaken to oppose Morgan at the entrance to town, but were overpowered and compelled to surrender. We continued on towards Salem until 10 P.M. when we bivouacked about five miles from Salem. Morgan took possession of Salem and burned the depot. The men robbed the stores. We reached the town on the morning of the 11th and the inhabitants gave us breakfast, they turned out liberally for us. Thus far it was difficult to see the aim of this raid. A few houses and some mills were burned and other mills and factories were obliged to pay to save their property from being burned. We continued the pursuit through Canton, New Philadelphia and Lexington. Near the last place we camped. The day was warm and the road very dusty. The inhabitants flocked to the roadside with baskets of provisions and water and we ate and drank as we rode along on horseback. This was a different welcome from what we had in Kentucky; there, if we got a meal, it was a poor one and had to be liberally paid for. Even this was difficult for the officers, the privates had nothing if they could not draw their rations. The liberality north of the Ohio was a matter of surprise to the Ky. Regts. who supposed that Ky. could not be excelled in anything. They were astonished at the thrifty character of the country and the greater population, the neat villages and the number of them, and I heard many of them say they would never live in a slave state again. The people were in every respect superior to those we left in Ky. The girls were gaily and costly dressed and cheered us and sang "Rally the Flag, Boys" as we passed, that took away much of the fatigue of that long chase and has left a pleasant remembrance that has greatly outlasted the dust and fatigue and other discomforts of that famous pursuit.

We moved on the 12th through Paris, and Dupont to Versailles, where we camped. The enemy tried to pass through Athens, but were confronted by the militia, whom they declined to attack, after having demanded a surrender which they declined. Our average daily march was about fifty miles.... On the morning of the 13th I was in a sorry plight in more ways than one. I caught a severe cold during the night and did not rest well; my horse had given out and could travel no further. I took another one of Morgan's abandoned horses, blind of an eye, that had one day's rest and might possibly go until I could secure another. I left my horse with an old acquaintance that resided in Versailles and never saw him again. After getting breakfast we continued the pursuit through Milton, New Alsace and Dover to Harrison.[12]

Kautz and his men were in their home state of Ohio.

Morgan's column had arrived at Harrison late in the morning of July 13. This being the largest towns they had seen for a while, the division, reduced by casualties, desertions and straggling to fewer than 2000 effectives, spent several hours relieving the homes and stores of useful items before burning the bridge over the Whitewater River and moving on. Straight ahead lay the city of Cincinnati, at more than 200,000, the eighth largest city in the nation. The city, if given time, was capable of mustering many thousands of militia to make life miserable for Morgan's 2000.

Morgan wisely moved past Cincinnati as quickly as possible. Marching all the night of July 13–14 and sticking to major roadways, he crossed the Great Miami River at Miamitown, then turned north and east. Keeping a respectable distance between himself and the Queen City, various portions of his command passed through the towns of Bevis, New Burlington, Glendale, Reading, Sharonville, Deer Park and Montgomery. Hoping to acquire a fresh supply of horses, one brigade moved toward Camp Dennison, which lay beside the Little Miami River near the village of Miamiville. Arriving near the camp in the early morning of July 14, they were driven off by a detachment of "convalescents" from the camp's hospital. Turning north from Miamiville, they derailed a train on the Little Miami Railroad south of Loveland.

Continuing the march all day on July 14, Morgan's men passed through the town of Batavia and came wearily into camp at Williamsburg, more than thirty miles east of Cincinnati.

Kautz's Brigade was busy on July 14 also. He wrote,

> We were again on the road on the morning of the 14th. We marched through New Baltimore where a fine bridge had been burned by the enemy. We passed through Glendale and Miamiville. At this last place Morgan captured a train of cars on the Little Miami Railroad. Troops from Camp Dennison repulsed an attempt to burn the R. R. Bridge. The enemy also captured some wagons at a depot not far from where we camped[13] which was about seven miles from Batavia. This days march took us round Cincinnati, within a few miles of the city and the enemy was evidently apprehensive of forces coming out of the city for he made the circuit round the city very rapidly.[14]

Isaac Gause described his day with a little more detail:

> As this day's march was a record breaker, I will endeavor to give a more accurate description of it. It was near the middle of July, and the sun shone down intensely hot. Most of those that had tenaciously held to their blankets and cooking utensils discarded them during the day. We passed through a fertile and thickly settled part of the country, and the towns and villages were occupied by wealthy people. The most noted was Glendale ... the residence of business and professional people who received their supplies from the city.... The streets were crowded with ladies carrying buckets of water and lemonade, pies, cake, bread and butter, ham sandwiches, and in fact everything one could wish for. Many of the ladies were extravagantly dressed, but they worked hard and paid no attention to the dripping water or flying dust that covered them from head to foot. They felt jubilant to know that they were permitted to help us on our journey, which they thought would result in the capture of the raiders before night, as they had passed but three hours before us.... During the twenty-four hours we covered a distance of seventy-five miles, and at 7 A.M. the next day went into camp for a little rest. I took a bath in a running brook, put on the clean underclothes, and threw away those I had worn from Somerset. It was the first time I had taken off my boots since leaving Jim Town.[15]

At Williamsburg on the night of July 14–15, Morgan's Raiders also had a good night's rest, the best they had since crossing the Cumberland.

Satisfied that he had made it safely past Cincinnati, Morgan split his force at Williamsburg. After burning the bridge across the East Fork of the Little Miami River, he, with the main body and most of the trains and artillery, followed a route due east roughly paralleling the present Appalachian Highway through Mount Orab, Sardinia and Winchester.

About 300 men of his Second Brigade under his brother, Colonel Richard C. Morgan, took a more southerly course through Bethel to Kautz's boyhood home town of Georgetown. Arriving about 9 A.M., they cleaned out the grocery and clothing stores. Henry Brunner, a local shoemaker, claimed that the troopers got away with fifty dollars' worth of boots. There is no indication that the Rebels learned that Brunner's shop was just around the corner from the home where Ulysses Grant spent most of his childhood.

Colonel Morgan moved on to Ripley on the Ohio River looking for a potential crossing, where, according to Lieutenant Commander Leroy Fitch of the navy, he drove in the Home Guard's pickets, but did not enter the town. Dick Morgan found no boats to use in crossing at Ripley except a Union gunboat (perhaps Fitch's) and the river too deep to ford.[16] He then moved northeast and camped at West Union before rejoining his brother at Locust Grove the next morning.

All along, John Morgan had been considering crossing the Ohio River at the ford at Buffington Island near Portland and he decided to move toward that place, 120 miles away, as quickly as possible. Despite their haste, his men managed to burn the long bridge over the Scioto River at Jasper and to destroy railroad depots and public buildings in most of the towns they passed. Having covered almost ninety of those 120 miles by the evening of July 17, he hoped to reach the crossing at Buffington Island the following day. Morgan could see that his men were wearing out. More importantly, so were their horses. Subsisting off the land, they were constantly remounting themselves on horses taken from barns and stables as they passed.

Meanwhile, Hobson was having problems similar to those of Morgan. Although the towns-people at each stop were more willing to give up their bread, hams and pies to Hobson's troopers than to Morgan's raiders, the only horses easily acquired along the route were those jaded mounts which Morgan's men had discarded. Despite his best efforts, Hobson continued to remain a full day behind Morgan.

Early on the morning of July 15, Kautz rode with his advanced guard into Batavia and had breakfast. He had to wait two hours for the main force, which had been led astray by a guide who Kautz suspected was one of Morgan's men masquerading as a local. Kautz described the day, "The command was breakfasted by the inhabitants of Batavia, after which we moved on through Williamsburg where the enemy had camped the night before and they burned the bridge before leaving early that morning. Passing through Mt. Orab we reached Sardinia and camped. I was kindly entertained by Maj. McIntyre, whose home was in Sardinia. He was Major of the 7th and made an unexpected visit to his home."[17]

Kautz, noting the slow progress of the column, partly due to a sizeable train of wagons, had urged General Hobson to permit him to detach his two regiments from the main body and move ahead with the hope of overtaking Morgan's column and forcing them to do battle. At Winchester, Hobson finally consented. Kautz said,

> On the morning of the 16th my Brigade took the advance. Genl. Hobson had observed that when I had the advance we gained on the enemy, and when Wolford or Shackelford had it we lost ground again. He authorized me to take the advance at Winchester and keep it and pursue the enemy as I thought best. I pushed steadily on until evening without gaining materially on the main column. Passed through Jacksboro leaving Locust Grove on our left and reached Jasper on the Scioto about eleven P.M. Here the bridge over the canal was burned and also several buildings. We rested until daybreak.

In an effort to slow Morgan down in the hilly country through which he was now passing, Kautz "despatched Lt. Long of the 7th to go to Chillicothe and take the cars and get in advance of Morgan and have the people obstruct the roads."[18] Subsequently this tactic worked. Although Morgan's horsemen would have no trouble riding around felled trees and barricades, the roads had to be cleared to allow passage of his artillery and trains.

On the next day, according to Kautz,

> We were delayed an hour or two building a bridge over the canal and went to Piketon where we got breakfast. As there was a telegraph station there I telegraphed General Burnside the progress of the command and the route of Morgan, and pushed on towards Jackson.[19] I was overtaken by a response from Genl. B. who stated that Morgan ought to be caught; a view in which I agreed with him entirely. We reached Jackson about dark. The inhabitants turned out liberally for us and gave us a good supper in the Market House.[20] I was joined here by Col. Sanders with two pieces of artillery.[21] My horse with the blind eye failed me here; again I changed for another of Morgan's abandoned horses. The old horse came near injuring me. He shied with his good eye in crossing a rickety little bridge and went over the end of the bridge on the blind side. Fortunately I was not hurt, notwithstanding — it was quite a fall.[22]

Kautz goes on:

> On the 18th we marched before daylight and passed through Keystone Furnace and Vinton to Rutland where we arrived early in the evening and learned that the enemy had tried to advance through Pomeroy but he found the road obstructed and was compelled to take the road to Chester. I also was informed that he contemplated fording the Ohio at Buffington Island. I therefore pushed on determined to travel all night. We halted for an hour and fed at Rutland and stopped to get supper and let the column close up at Chester. The Chester Mill was still burning when we reached there showing that we were gaining on the enemy rapidly. Hobson's force was left a long distance in the rear.[23]

At 4:30 P.M. on July 18, Kautz sent the following telegram to General Hobson from Rutland:

> The Rebels tried to force an entrance into Pomeroy, and have been repulsed. Captain Higley, Seventh Ohio Cavalry, left Morgan's rear an hour ago on Chester road, between 7 and 10 miles from here. They are supposed to be marching for Buffington Island, about 25 miles from here, where they will try to ford the river. It is too high, however, and the gunboats are on the alert. General Scammon commanded at Pomeroy. No serious damage done. I have stopped to feed and rest, and shall push on tonight. An intelligent lady, at whose house Morgan was this afternoon, thinks they consider their case hopeless unless they can cross at Buffington Island tonight.

He added a PS: "I have had no communication with General Judah, but the country people saw him to-day marching on Pomeroy. He could have been in Morgan's front to-day (this morning) by marching about 25 miles last night. The Rebels are bent on crossing to-night, but they cannot do it."[24]

July 18 was a hard day for Morgan's men. Leaving Wilkesville before dawn, the bulk of the division moved toward the river in the vain hope of finding either of the ferries at Middleport or Pomeroy operational. During the march, they were intermittently harassed by fire from local militia companies. At Pomeroy the enemy was no longer militia but two regiments of volunteer infantry which included two future presidents of the United States. They were veterans of campaigning in western Virginia under the command of Brigadier General E. Parker Scammon, whom Kautz had mentioned in his telegram. Colonel Rutherford B. Hayes of the Twenty-Third Ohio Infantry had urged Scammon to allow his regiment and the Thirteenth West Virginia to go to Ohio to attempt to head Morgan off. Scammon agreed, and, in fact, took over the expedition personally. They traveled from near Charleston to Pomeroy by steamer and, on July 18, stood between Morgan and Buffington Island, backed up by a large number of militia.

As Morgan moved along the river between Cheshire and Middleport, Hayes's Twenty-Third Ohio, which included another future president, Lieutenant William McKinley of Company D, skirmished briefly with Morgan's advanced guard, then withdrew to the bluff above Pomeroy to take pot shots at Morgan's column as it passed.

After Morgan was past, Scammon moved across the river to the West Virginia side to intercept any of Morgan's command who might succeed in crossing. He had the foresight to send several hundred militia to man the small earthen fort which overlooked the ford at Buffington Island.

The Ohio River makes a sharp bend to the south between Portland and Pomeroy. At the time, the best road across the fifteen-mile-wide "boot" between the two river towns passed through the village of Chester and, as we have seen, the rear guard of Morgan's column left Chester only a few hours before the arrival of the first of Kautz's troopers. Knowing that the Yankees were so close was an extra incentive to spur their tired horses, but it was well past nightfall when the last of Morgan's men reached Portland, a mile upstream from the Buffington Island ford.

Before the series of navigational and flood-control dams on the Ohio River were built, the depth of water at the ford in midsummer was usually no greater than two to three feet, but heavy rain had fallen in the mountains of West Virginia so that, on July 18, John Morgan found the water flowing swiftly more than six feet deep. Despairing of sending his men across at night in such conditions, he determined to wait until morning to attempt a crossing. Instead he went into camp at Portland with his men deployed in a mile-wide half-circle around the sleeping little river town with Basil Duke's Brigade on the left and Adam Johnson's on the right. If the townspeople were sleeping, Morgan's men were not. Pickets were thrown out on the two roads leading into town. Through the night, many were busy building rafts and caulking leaky old rowboats. They also located the small ferry boat which served the town. As part of the preparation, two of Basil Duke's regiments were sent from the town in the pre-dawn hours to clear the militia from the small fort which guarded the ford at Buffington Island.

The low, flat land by the river was encased in fog as Kautz's brigade, now numbering fewer than 300 effectives, approached on the road from Chester. Isaac Gause was part of the four-man point of Kautz's column moving along the bluff, about 200 feet above and two or three miles from the river, as the first gray hint of dawn made its appearance in the eastern sky. They were just ahead of the advanced guard consisting of Company E of the Second Ohio. Gause and his companions were fortunate to capture the horse of one of Morgan's scouts and Gause noted that the saddle pockets were filled with "dress-patterns, women's shoes, boxes with pocket knives, silver spoons, needles and thread, with many other things too numerous to mention."

Gause said,

> As we were making our examination, the company arrived. The lieutenant said "Gause, take the horse to Colonel Kautz. He asked me to get one for him, and this is the first opportunity I have had...." The column had halted for a rest. On arriving at the head of it, I inquired for Colonel Kautz. On hearing his name pronounced, he raised up and answered "Here." After the customary salute I said "Lieutenant Newton sends his compliments, with a fresh horse." He apparently paid no attention to what was said, but inquired:
>
> "How far is it to the river?"
>
> "About three miles."
>
> "Where did you get your information?"
>
> "From a woman at the cabin and a man we met on the road."
>
> "How long since Morgan passed?"
>
> "The rear guard left the cabin since daylight."
>
> "He sprang to his feet and exclaimed, "We've got them, we've got them! Saddle my horse, sound assembly!"[25]

As Kautz later told it,

> On Sunday morning, the 19th, we came upon the enemy's pickets about two miles from Portland. We had marched all night in consequence of the enemy having taken the road leading directly to the river and supposed that he would attempt to cross this morning. Hobson, with the main force, I knew to be half a day behind. Sanders was behind with his two pieces of artillery and escort, about an hour. I paraded my command at once for an attack and could only muster about two hundred men of both Regts. about a hundred of each. I formed them in two lines of skirmishers, and ordered an advance. At this point several of my officers came to me and asked if I intended to attack. I answered, "Undoubtedly." "Do you expect to whip three thousand men with two hundred?" asked the Lieut. Col. (Purington). I replied that I did not expect to whip that number, but we must attack or else we had made our extraordinary march for nothing. Morgan was on the bank of the river and would be across in three hours if not prevented, and we could annoy him if we could not whip him. Seeing that I was in earnest, the officers took their places with a will, and we soon had the pickets driven in to the edge of the timber that borders the fertile plain back of Portland. My force was too small to reveal by pushing it farther than the edge of the timber. I was impatient for Sanders to arrive with his guns and had not long to wait. I calculated that opening with Artillery would make Morgan think that Hobson's entire forces had arrived. I realized my most sanguine expectation. The first shot, I learned subsequently, passed a few feet in front and along the entire line of Basil Duke's Regt. It turned and fled up the plain and was followed by the rest of Morgan's command in the wildest and complete rout. Not an

effort was made to find out our strength.... As soon as this precipitate flight set in I directed Col. Sanders to pursue with his two squadrons of Michigan Cavalry."[26]

Isaac Gause was one of the men detailed to hold the horses as Kautz's dismounted cavalry charged down the hill into the Rebel position below. From his position on the high ground, he had an excellent view of the action as Kautz's skirmishers moved down the hill and drove Morgan's pickets, part of Colonel Adam Johnson's Brigade, from the woods into the corn and wheat fields adjacent to the town. He described Kautz's actions: "The Colonel sat on his horse as if there was nothing unusual going on, and when the men were all dismounted, said to the men holding the horses, 'If I send a messenger for you, come quickly. Tie the horses to trees, turn them loose, or anything to get there quick.' He then rode away following the column."[27] Kautz obviously knew that he was taking a dangerous gamble and might need every man available in case help did not arrive soon.

Just as the two guns of the Eleventh Michigan Artilley opened fire, Kautz heard the sound of gunfire well to his right along the river. He had no clear idea at the time what the noise represented, but he was encouraged by it nonetheless.

Even before Kautz had deployed his small command as skirmishers, two regiments of Basil Duke's Brigade had moved out of Portland to attack the militia holding the small fortification at the ford. They found that the militia had abandoned the fort during the night. Morgan then ordered one of the regiments to move down the river road to picket the road while the crossing planned for just after sunrise took place. The regiment, the Sixth Kentucky Cavalry (CSA), had only gone about 500 yards when it ran headlong in the fog into the advance of General Henry Judah's forces marching up the river road from the direction of Pomeroy.

Judah had been taken out of the chase for Morgan almost two weeks before. When it was learned that Morgan had crossed into Indiana, Judah took command of Mahlon Manson's Brigade and headed north to Louisville. He traveled to Cincinnati by steamship and was in Cincinnati while Morgan was passing there. He then moved to Portsmouth by steamship and arrived there July 16. His five fresh regiments had marched for two days along the Ohio River parallel to Morgan's Raiders and was moving cautiously toward Buffington Island when they met the regiment sent out by Morgan at about 5:30 A.M. on July 19.

In the dense fog along the river, the two forces were within 100 yards of each other before either was aware of the other's presence. Judah was marching with the advance of his column, which had not even taken the precaution of loading its weapons. The Rebels opened fire immediately and charged into Judah's advanced guard, capturing most of them. Judah escaped and was able to get back to the rest of his command safely. It was almost two hours before he could organize his force, the largest on the field, and get them back into the fray.

Lieutenant Commander Leroy Fitch of the navy had been patrolling the Ohio River with a number of gunboats under his command. He had ships in position to harass any potential attempt to cross at the various fords and ferries along the river. He had been in contact with both Scammon and Judah and, on the morning of July 19, he had his flagship, the USS *Moose*, anchored in the river just opposite Buffington Island. As soon as Fitch heard the sounds of battle, he moved the *Moose* to the Ohio shore near the upper end of the island and began throwing shells from the Dahlgren guns aboard the *Moose*. Although Fitch was firing blindly, some of his shells found their marks and contributed to growing panic within Morgan's ranks.

Almost simultaneously with the opening of Fitch's huge guns and Colonel Sanders's little ones, Sanders was ordered by Kautz to charge with his two Michigan regiments into the Rebel lines behind Portland. As Sanders and his men charged past Kautz's line of skirmishers, the Confederates broke to the rear, completely disorganized.

When Judah finally got moving, his five regiments also moved toward Portland, sweeping

Morgan's men before them. The artillery under Judah's command joined with those of Fitch and Sanders. There were no roads leading out of Portland up the river to the north and, with enemy forces closing in on them from the west and south, many of Morgan's men took to the forested hills above Portland. From his vantage point on the hill overlooking Morgan's camps, Isaac Gause described the scene as he saw it:

> Everything in Morgan's camp was broke; many of the teams were hitched and others partly hitched. So many of the horses having been recently taken from farms were fresh and strong, and not used to the sound of artillery, so they tore away, breaking the lines, one end of which would fly up in the air and then recoil.... Wagons were turned over, scattering the goods they had taken from stores on the route. The ground being loose, the air was soon full of smoke, dust, corn-stalks, sheaves of wheat, silk, cloth, muslin and calico, one bolt of which was more attractive than the others, for one end caught to a horse and unwrapped as he ran and the other end flew in the air for a moment like a streamer from a mast.... The firing at the head of the column served to cut the fleeing raiders in two parts. Those having passed the junction of the ravines made good their escape, but all the others were compelled to surrender, about two thousand in number, with every wheel they had in possession.[28]

Gause had exaggerated the numbers, but it was indeed a rout. Despite his best efforts, Morgan could not organize a defense. Individual Confederate soldiers and small detachments made a stand and fought bravely, but it only delayed the inevitable. Outnumbered at least three-to-one, the raiders abandoned all of their wagons and artillery[29] and either surrendered or moved into the hills to the north.

General Hobson arrived near the scene late in the morning. He sent Shackelford's Brigade to the left of Sanders and Wolford's small brigade even farther to the left to cut off the Confederate retreat. Only about half of Morgan's force was able to escape up the river. After passing beyond the Union lines two miles north of Portland, about 360 of them, along with Colonel Adam Johnson, were able to cross the river later that day at a ford at Reedsville, fifteen miles north of Portland. Quick work by Leroy Fitch, who followed Morgan's escaping raiders up the river on the *Moose*, prevented the crossing of the remaining 700 of Morgan's men there.

Another contingent of almost 200 men doubled back around Hobson's forces to the west, passed through Rutland and eventually reached Cheshire where they hoped to cross the river. On the afternoon of July 19, after having a short rest and some food, Kautz was ordered to report to General Shackelford to help in running down these Rebels. He had difficulty assembling his brigade as many of his men were moving with the Michigan regiments north of town, and others, exhausted from the march of the last two days, were resting in town or among the captured wagon train. It was not until the following morning that he joined in the pursuit once again. On July 20, these Confederates surrendered to some of Colonel Wolford's Brigade near Cheshire. There is no indication that Kautz took part in the capture.

General Morgan himself, with about 600 men, continued to move in a northeasterly direction for another week before being captured near New Lisbon, Ohio, not far from the Pennsylvania border. He was imprisoned in the Ohio State Penitentiary at Columbus, but later escaped and returned to the South. He was given command of the Department of Southwestern Virginia and was able to conduct other raids before being killed at Greeneville, Tennessee, on September 3, 1864.

Casualties at the Battle of Buffington Island were relatively light considering the numbers involved. This is probably, as Sanders stated in his report, because "very little actual fighting took place."[30] Morgan probably had fifty-seven men killed and the Union forces probably lost no more than six killed. One man under Kautz's command died as a result of a gunshot wound inflicted by an inexperienced militiaman who was accompanying Kautz's Brigade. It is impossible at this late date to get an exact number of raiders captured in the battle. If we include those captured at Cheshire on July 20, the total number is more than 900.

It is interesting to read the official reports of the various general officers who took part in the Battle of Buffington Island, each attempting to take as much credit for the victory as possible. Especially self-serving is that of General Judah, who either ignores or excuses the several blunders he committed in the chase and capture of the raiders at the same time that he gives almost full credit for the victory to himself and the troops under his command. The Fiction Award, however, must go to Leroy Fitch, who rushed off to Cincinnati after the battle to make sure the newspapers were aware that he had defeated Morgan almost singlehandedly and in a telegram to Rear Admiral David Porter dated July 19 said, "After chasing Morgan nearly 500 miles, I at last met him on the river at this point [Buffington]. I engaged and drove him back, capturing two pieces of his artillery. He abandoned rest to General Judah. His forces broke in confusion from the banks, and left his wagon train, many horses and small arms in my possession. General Judah is now in pursuit of the remnant of his forces."[31]

The surviving reports of the various subordinate officers who took part in the battle are, for the most part, much more modest. Historians today tend to give the greatest credit to Hobson, but fail to mention that Hobson's success was based largely on his bowing to the wishes of an impetuous young cavalry officer to ride a day ahead of Hobson's main force with his undermanned brigade. Kautz's report gives a matter-of-fact description of his movements and gives credit to Colonel Sanders and others. Near the end of his report, he gives an honest statement of what credit should be due him: ...The particular work accomplished by my command in this affair was the continuous march from Jackson to Portland, a distance of nearly 70 miles, in less than thirty hours, and coming upon the enemy in time to prevent his orderly retreat from the river if molested by other forces, and the spirited attack of the men that induced the enemy to believe that General Hobson's entire force was at hand, thus causing in a great measure their disorderly retreat....[32]

Kautz would not learn the manly art of beating his own drum for years to come and would not use it to his advantage until the eve of his retirement from the service.

19. East Tennessee

Three days after the Battle of Buffington Island, Colonel Kautz received an order from General Judah's headquarters to form a temporary brigade, including his own regiments and those of Colonel Sanders, to gather up all of the Confederate prisoners, including any stragglers he might round up, and ship them to Cincinnati, along with all captured horses and equipment. So Kautz was to be in charge of mopping up while General Shackelford's forces moved out after the remnants of Morgan's Raiders. Kautz wryly noted, "Shackelford followed for a week longer and then telegraphed, 'By the help of Almighty God I have captured John Morgan.' I was struck by this acknowledgment of superior aid. He ought to have been caught several weeks before without such aid."[1]

The move satisfied Kautz well enough as he had already declared his brigade unfit for further combat service. Leaving the work to junior officers, Kautz himself went to Cincinnati by boat, taking time to visit his family in Levanna on the way. Arriving in Cincinnati on July 28 and finding the horse herd still days away, he went to Columbus on regimental business and also visited Governor Tod's family at their home in Cleveland and his cousin Lou in Wilmington.

He finally got away from Cincinnati on August 10 and met General George Hartsuff that night at the Phoenix Hotel in Lexington. Although Kautz had been under Hartsuff's command for several months, this was their first meeting since leaving the Academy eleven years before. Kautz learned that XXIII Corps had again been reorganized and that the Second and Seventh Cavalry had been assigned to General Shackelford's Brigade, leaving Kautz without a command.

General Burnside arrived in Lexington the following day and informed Kautz that he would probably go to General Rosecrans's Army of the Cumberland, then in the vicinity of Chattanooga. Burnside said that Rosecrans had been telegraphing him weekly all summer to have Kautz transferred. Kautz later wrote, "Hartsuff, who was opposed to the arrangement, managed to have me detailed on his staff as Chief of Cavalry of the 23rd Corps.[2] This was a piece of favoritism on the part of Genl. Hartsuff, who was a classmate at West Point with me."[3]

Burnside had been planning for some time to move into East Tennessee with his Army of the Ohio. When the raid by Colonel Sanders into the area in mid–June demonstrated that the eight or ten thousand Confederates at Knoxville under Major General Simon Buckner would offer little resistance, he was ready to move. Morgan's raid had set Burnside's schedule back but, with Morgan out of the way, he started issuing orders for the move. The reorganization of XXIII Corps was in anticipation of the move.

Kautz soon learned that his assignment as Chief of Cavalry was not all he had hoped. General Shackelford was given command of the cavalry division of the corps and, as the army moved south from Lexington into Tennessee, it became apparent that both Burnside and Hartsuff were issuing orders directly through Shackelford to the cavalry and leaving Kautz to serve as a high-ranking messenger. Assessing his assignment as Chief of Cavalry later, Kautz said, "I presumed I would have something more to do than sport the title."[4]

The move south was slowed by rough roads in mountainous country for the 24,000-man army and its supply train. The movement commenced on August 14 and the army reached Knoxville where headquarters were established on September 4.

So far in the war, East Tennessee had been an embarrassment to the federal government and to the Union army. In no other part of the South was pro–Union sentiment so strong as in East Tennessee, yet the army had failed to establish a military presence in the area. If there were political and psychological reasons to bring East Tennessee into the Union fold, there was one very important military reason. There were but two rail lines linking the eastern states of the Confederacy with those in the west and one of those ran through the "Great Valley" to Knoxville and on to Chattanooga. The blockage of traffic on that line would present a severe threat to logistics for the South.

Burnside's Army met with minimal resistance entering East Tennessee and, within several days, learned that Buckner had been called to join Braxton Bragg's Army of Tennessee near Chattanooga. On September 19, they would take part in the Battle of Chickamauga. Burnside had also been ordered to the Chattanooga area to reinforce Rosecrans's Army of the Cumberland, but chose to remain in East Tennessee. Kautz's comments on the subject are of interest:

> Burnside's orders were positive to join Rosecrans, but he decided to go towards Knoxville and on the 4th we occupied that city without opposition.... We were, therefore, a detriment to Rosecrans instead of a benefit. We reinforced the enemy opposed to Rosecrans instead of reinforcing the latter and no doubt Rosecrans was sacrificed in consequence.... Had we found an army in the country to oppose us we would have been justified in remaining. Our plainest duty was to reinforce that army since the enemy had abandoned the country to reinforce Bragg. Genl. Hartsuff urged it. Genl. Burnside offered as a reason ... that he was senior to Rosecrans and would embarrass him. To which Hartsuff replied that he could send him and his corps, and Genl. B. to return to his command, the Army of [the] Ohio.[5]

On September 5, Kautz found himself carrying orders to various cavalry regiments around Knoxville in anticipation of a proposed movement to occupy Cumberland Gap. The cavalry expedition got off on time and Burnside returned a week later with the news that Cumberland Gap had been taken and 2600 prisoners captured without a shot being fired. Kautz commented, "There was quite a noise made over this capture and much capital was made out of it in favor of Burnside. It probably saved him from the consequences of his failing to join Rosecrans."[6]

While maintaining his headquarters at Knoxville, Burnside posted cavalry units as far east as Greeneville, sixty miles to the east, and Sweetwater, fifty miles to the southwest. Defensive works were laid out around the city. The chief engineer of XXIII Corps was Captain Orlando Poe, with whom Kautz shared quarters.

Toward the end of September, General Hartsuff took a medical leave because the wound he had received at Sharpsburg the previous year was giving him trouble. He was relieved of command of XXIII Corps and was replaced by General Manson. Kautz was distressed to see one of the few friends he had at headquarters leave. At the same time that Manson took over the corps, William Sanders was promoted to brigadier general and given command of the cavalry division of XXIII Corps in place of Shackelford, making Kautz's title of Chief of Cavalry even more distasteful to him.

Meanwhile General Rosecrans and his Army of the Cumberland had been soundly whipped at the Battle of Chickamauga and was settling into Chattanooga, besieged by Bragg's Army of Tennessee. Satisfied that he had Rosecrans pinned down and immobile, Bragg sent General James Longstreet's Corps, supplemented by four brigades of Wheeler's Cavalry, in the direction of Knoxville in an attempt to reopen the rail communications with the east. After assembling his command near Sweetwater, Longstreet proceeded to push Burnside's advance units back toward Knoxville.

General Sanders, with his cavalry, fought a masterful delaying action to allow further work on the city's fortifications until, on November 18, he was mortally wounded and died the following day. Kautz said of Sanders, "We buried him in a churchyard at ten o'clock on the night of the 19th. All the officers of rank attended, but there was no ceremony. He was a gallant, generous gentleman, careless and devoid of method; but always ready when there was anything to do."[7]

The cavalry continued to fall back slowly into Knoxville, giving Captain Poe time to finish the defensive works around the city almost to his satisfaction. On November 29, Longstreet's Corps launched an assault on the fortifications, but were repulsed, the heaviest fighting taking place at a salient named Fort Sanders in honor of the fallen general. Unable to take Knoxville by force, Longstreet laid siege to the city.

Meanwhile, on November 23, Burnside sent a message to Ulysses Grant, now in command at Chattanooga in place of Rosecrans, stating that his men were running out of food and ammunition and, if not relieved within ten days, he would have to either surrender or try to fight his way out of the city. Grant immediately sent a large force, consisting of Major General William T. Sherman's Corps along with Major General Jefferson C. Davis's Second Division of XIV Corps and Brigadier General Charles R. Woods's Division of IV Corps, from Chattanooga to relieve Knoxville. At the same time, Grant sent an order, carried by Col. James H. Wilson of his staff and Charles A. Dana of the War Department, for Burnside to hold out at all cost as help was on the way.

On December 5, learning of the approach of Sherman's forces, Longstreet lifted the siege and moved east up the valley of the Holston River, where he was in position to move either east or west as conditions might dictate. The next day, Kautz noted that Generals Sherman and Sheridan had arrived in the city and said of his old friend Sheridan, "[He] became my guest overnight and entertained me with his account of the part he took in the defeat of Bragg."[8]

A week after their arrival at Knoxville, Sherman began a movement in pursuit of Longstreet, but, finding little food or forage present in the country and assuming that Longstreet was returning east to join the Army of Northern Virginia, he gave up the pursuit at Strawberry Plains, only twenty-five miles from Knoxville. Kautz was with the Union forces at Strawberry Plains and had an opportunity to visit several times with his brother Fred, whose Fifty-Ninth Ohio was a part of Woods's Division. Sherman's forces, in their haste to relieve Burnside, had marched from their camps near Chattanooga expecting to fight a brief battle, then return immediately. As a consequence, they had left most of their transportation behind and carried only two days' rations; few if any of the men had tents, blankets or overcoats. When the weather turned bitterly cold on the first of the year, many of the men had worn out their shoes and it is said that the paths through the snow in the camps were marked by bloody footprints. Kautz describes a meal he had with Fred which consisted only of cornbread in which much of the corn had not been sufficiently ground, leaving whole kernels of corn in the bread.

At about this time, Major General John G. Foster arrived at Knoxville, having come down from Kentucky through Cumberland Gap with about 2000 troops. Foster had orders relieving Burnside as commander of the Army of the Ohio. Foster in turn gave command of all of the cavalry in East Tennessee to General Samuel Sturgis and also named him Chief of Cavalry of the army, leaving Kautz with no command and not even a title. With no job and seeing that the campaign in East Tennessee was over until spring, Kautz applied to General Foster for a leave of absence on December 20. According to Kautz, Foster was of the opinion that the campaign was just beginning. He later wrote that Foster treated him "very discourteously" and threatened to place him under arrest. Kautz added, "He [Foster] said that he was very much astonished that I should ask for a leave at a time when the troops were in the face of the enemy."[9] When Kautz attempted to explain that he was without a job, Foster abruptly interrupted him and closed the interview. Not satisfied, Kautz forwarded his application for a leave, marked with Foster's denial, to General Grant along with a letter of explanation.

Grant himself arrived at Knoxville on December 31 to assess the situation in East Tennessee. Kautz called on Grant the evening after his arrival and Kautz was quite pleased with the meeting. Noting that the two had not met since 1853 at Vancouver Barracks,[10] Kautz wrote, "He met me in the most cordial way, addressed me by my Christian name, and gave me an hour's conversation, during which he made all necessary inquiries about old friends and acquaintances. His treatment of me made a decided impression on Genl. Foster, who seemed quite willing to forget his rough treatment a few days before."[11] Kautz asked Grant whether he had received his letter and the general answered that he had. When Grant made no further comment on the subject, Kautz let it drop. Grant remained at Knoxville until January 5.

On January 5, Kautz was called into General Foster's headquarters. Grant was present in the office as Foster detailed a plan in which Kautz was to take charge of about 4000 men, recruits and refugees from East Tennessee who were at Camp Nelson in Kentucky, and organize them into a brigade. Once organized, they were to cooperate with the rest of Foster's Army of the Ohio in an offensive to drive Longstreet's Corps out of East Tennessee.

Kautz left Knoxville two days later.

20. The Cavalry Bureau

Before Ulysses Grant left Knoxville in January 1864, he ordered General John G. Foster to prepare to move his Army of the Ohio up the valley of the Holston River to dislodge Longstreet's Corps from East Tennessee. In a subsequent order to Foster, Grant wrote: "In conjunction with your move against Longstreet ... I think it will be advisable to send a cavalry expedition against Abingdon and Saltville.... The Tennessee troops now organizing in Kentucky I think will be sufficient for the move.... Kautz will be a most excellent officer to intrust this expedition to, and if selected had better begin at once organizing it."[1]

Having learned only a few days before that Kautz and Grant were personal friends, Foster bowed to the wishes of the soon-to-be-named Commander in Chief and named Kautz to take charge of the Tennessee brigade. He even suggested to Kautz, at a meeting attended by Grant, that there might be an appointment as brigadier in it for him.

Kautz left Knoxville on January 7, 1864, and met with Governor Andrew Johnson on January 14 in Nashville. Kautz got the impression that the governor "did not fancy my taking charge of his people as I was not from his state."[2] The following day Kautz met again with General Grant, who had arrived from Knoxville also, and learned that the Tennessee troops were being moved from Camp Nelson in Kentucky to Nashville at the governor's request. As the move would take some time, Kautz applied to Grant for a ten-day leave to go home and Grant generously granted it.

Ice on the Ohio River preventing his getting to Levanna so he opted to visit Governor Tod and his family in Columbus. On the train, he met Brigadier General James H. Wilson, who was on his way to Washington to take over as chief of the Cavalry Bureau. According to Kautz, Wilson "says he intends to have me ordered to assist him as he confesses his ignorance of the administrative duties that will be required."[3] He knew Wilson's reputation for stretching the truth when it was to his advantage and made no further comment in his journal.

On January 29, he received a telegram from Wilson informing him that he had, indeed, been ordered to Washington for duty in the Cavalry Bureau. Wilson requested that he not delay. Kautz reported to the Cavalry Bureau at the Chain Building on H Street in Washington on January 31.

The Cavalry Bureau had been established in July 1863 to oversee the procurement and inspection of horses and arms for the cavalry, functions which had previously been under the jurisdiction of the Quartermaster and Ordnance Departments. One of the major problems to be overcome was the fraudulent practices of some civilian contractors with whom the War Department dealt. Other difficulties included the inconsistent inspection of horses and matters related to their care, such as transportation and the provision of adequate forage.

George Stoneman, the bureau's first chief, had done a creditable job of organizing the bureau, but neither he nor his successor, Brigadier General Kenner Garrard, had been able to institute sufficient reforms to greatly improve the situation. Wilson was tapped to succeed Garrard at the

This portrait was made in 1864. Note that Kautz has the stars of a major general on his shoulder, but is still wearing the uniform of a colonel (one row of buttons). From August Kautz's photograph album, courtesy Virginia (Kautz) Borkenhagen.

recommendation of Assistant Secretary of War Charles Dana. Wilson accepted the post with two major conditions. First, he required of Grant that the assignment be only temporary and that afterwards he be given command of troops in the field. Second, he demanded that he be given full rein to hire qualified officers to serve under him in the bureau. His choice to serve as his right-hand man was August Kautz.

With little prior knowledge of the bureau, it took Kautz little time to learn that "the most serious troubles that had embarrassed its operations were the jealousies of other bureaux with which it, to some extent, conflicted." Noting that the "Quartermaster Dept. was fully able to supply the wants of the service," he added, "The objectionable feature was that it had been made a bureau of supply when all that was needed was a bureau of inspection."[4]

Despite Kautz's opinion that the function of the bureau should be limited to inspection and care of horses, leaving procurement of new animals to the Quartermaster Department, the bureau continued to serve in both capacities during his and Wilson's tenures there. Kautz and Wilson worked well together. Kautz said of his boss, "Genl. Wilson was an officer of unusual activity of thought and action. He could keep everybody under him constantly occupied and employed. The trait he needed most was fixedness of purpose." If Wilson, indeed, lacked "fixedness of purpose," that was one of Kautz's major traits. As Kautz put it: "As I was some years older in service, he deferred greatly to my judgement and my service with him was very pleasant and satisfying."[5]

Wilson appointed three-man teams of inspectors, hand-picked by him for their honesty. He refused to meet socially with contract suppliers, honest or dishonest, and had a number of them arrested and imprisoned for defrauding the government. Wilson, Kautz and Lieutenant Colonel James Ekin, the bureau's quartermaster, visited procurement depots to ascertain whether they were functioning up to the standards set.

Kautz inspected the depots in Columbus, Indianapolis and Chicago between February 11 and February 29. He then stopped off to see his family in Levanna before returning to Washington. On the way, he found his sister Sophie living in Cincinnati and picked her up, bag and baggage, and moved her back home where he thought she belonged.

Much of Kautz's time was devoted to the care of horses already in service rather than to procurement of new horses. He worked with Charles Dana at the War Department and they often went together on inspection tours to the depot for the recuperation of horses at Giesboro Point.[6] Much time was spent at his desk writing or conferring with cavalry officers about conditions within their units. Among his writings was a paper which gave him great pride because of the amount of research required for its completion. It was entitled *Instructions for the Care and Transportation of Cavalry Horses*. It was used by the army for many years after the Civil War.

As time went by, Kautz was able to convince Wilson that the procurement function of the Cavalry Bureau should be returned to the Quartermaster Department and that the bureau should concentrate its efforts on resupplying those regiments already in the field. On April 4, 1864, Wilson wrote a long report to Secretary Stanton which largely discussed which cavalry regiments in the Western Theater were in need of horses. He specifically stated that those regiments should receive replacement mounts before any new regiments were placed in the field.[7] General Grant, after having seen Wilson's report, concluded that Wilson's work at the Cavalry Bureau had reached a successful conclusion and kept the promise he had made to Wilson of a field command. On April 7, Wilson was ordered to report to General Sheridan as commander of the Third Division of Sheridan's Cavalry Corps of the Army of the Potomac.

On the same day that Wilson was relieved of command of the Cavalry Bureau, Lieutenant Colonel Ekin was placed in command. Kautz was a bit confused by this turn of events because he had been assured by General Wilson that he would be ordered to take over the bureau.

Besides, he was the ranking officer in the bureau and, based on rank alone, he should have taken over. On April 8, Kautz wrote in his journal, "I was sent for by the Secretary [of War, Edwin Stanton] this morning. He asked me if I thought I could take charge of the Bureau. I told him I thought I could, I never had failed at any duty to which I had been assigned. He told me to go on and perform the duty and I am, therefore, for the present in charge."[8]

Of course this caused a problem. Stanton's verbal order could in no way supercede the written order placing Ekin in charge. Finally on April 14, Kautz had a meeting with Stanton and General Henry Halleck, Army Chief of Staff which lasted the greater part of the day. Kautz was able to convince Stanton, and Halleck concurred, that the supply and inspection functions of the Cavalry Bureau should be separated. At the conclusion of the meeting, he was informed that the bureau would be placed under General Halleck's office and split into two departments, Ekin to command the supply department and Kautz to command the inspection department.

That evening, Kautz made a social call on General Grant and his wife Julia at Willard's Hotel. Kautz brought Grant up to date on news from Brown County and, in the course of the visit, Grant asked him how he would like to take the field. When Kautz replied that he was willing to do whatever the General in Chief directed, Grant told him that there was an opening as Chief of Cavalry in General Benjamin Butler's Army of the James. Grant added that Kautz did not have enough rank, but that Secretary Stanton said that could be arranged. Kautz added in his *Reminiscences*, "He said this in such a quiet, undecided way that I did not attach much importance to it."[9]

Two days later, Kautz went to the Adjutant General's office to learn whether the orders regarding the changes at the Cavalry Bureau had been printed. Colonel Edward D. Townsend, the Adjutant General, brought in a pile of General Orders No. 162, dated April 14, which named Kautz chief of the inspection branch of the Cavalry Bureau and Colonel Ekin chief of the procurement branch. Colonel Townsend then went to Secretary Stanton's office and returned saying, with a "peculiar smile on his face,"[10] that the General Order could not be issued as written.

The following day, Kautz learned what Townsend's "peculiar smile" meant when he received an order promoting him to brigadier general of volunteers and directing him to report to Benjamin Butler's Army of the James.

When General Order No. 162 was issued, the paragraph containing Kautz's name had been removed.

21. The Cavalry Division, Army of the James

Ulysses Grant was named commander in chief of all Union armies on March 9, 1864. With the title came a promotion to the rank of lieutenant general. Grant's first order of business was a reorganization of the army's chain of command.

Grant brought all nineteen of the former army departments together into three armies, or wings as he called them: the Army of the Potomac, commanded by Major General George G. Meade (Grant considered this the army's center); the Army of the West, commanded by Major General William T. Sherman (Grant's West Wing); and the Army of the James, commanded by Major General Benjamin F. Butler (the East Wing).

Grant's plan, which he called his Grand Campaign, was to put the three wings in motion simultaneously as soon as weather permitted. Each was given a distinct role in Grant's mind. The primary role of Meade's Army of the Potomac in the Grand Campaign was the destruction of Robert E. Lee's Army of Northern Virginia; that of Sherman's Army of the West was the destruction of the Confederacy's Army of Tennessee, then commanded by General Joseph E. Johnston. Secondary goals were the capture of the cities of Richmond and Atlanta respectively.

By far the smallest of the three wings was Butler's Army of the James. In Grant's mind, its goal was commensurate to its size, to threaten Richmond from the south in order to force Lee to maintain a significant force south of the capital — soldiers who would otherwise be part of Lee's Army of Northern Virginia.

When General Butler took over the Department of Virginia and North Carolina and its army (known as the Army of the James) in November 1863, he commanded a few regiments clinging to the Virginia peninsula and a number of forts and other footholds along the Atlantic Coast from Maryland to South Carolina. Grant stripped these scattered garrisons, leaving most with little more than a custodial staff. The troops acquired formed a sizeable corps (XVIII Corps), which he placed under the command of Major General William F. "Baldy" Smith. From the Department of the South, Grant pulled enough troops to form another corps (X Corps), commanded by Major General Quincy A. Gillmore. Added to these, Grant found four regiments of cavalry and enough artillery and engineers to transform Butler's Army of the James into a potentially formidable fighting force of more than 35,000 men.

Ben Butler was beaming. A little man of more than average intelligence and unlimited ambition, Butler had been the first volunteer major general appointed by President Lincoln in 1861. He had served satisfactorily, but not brilliantly, on the Virginia peninsula in 1861 and, later, along the North Carolina Coast. Appointed Military Governor of New Orleans, his dictatorial administration earned the hatred of the Confederates and his tendency to nepotism and graft earned the condemnation of the North. Relieved from the governorship in December 1862, Butler remained idle until his appointment to command of the Department of Virginia and

North Carolina. He set about with his usual vigor to organize the army which Grant had provided him.

On April 13, 1864, Butler wired Grant, "I have no cavalry officer. It is of the last importance that I have one at once."[1]

Grant replied the same day, "I can send you Colonel Kautz. He is a good cavalry officer. Do you want him sent?"[2]

Butler recalled meeting Kautz in Washington in 1861, but had reservations because of Kautz's rank. He answered the following day, "Colonel Kautz is a most excellent officer, but all my cavalry colonels rank him."[3]

On April 15, Grant sent a wire to General Halleck: "Please ask the Secretary of War to give Colonel Kautz certificate of appointment as brigadier-general, and order him to report to Major-General Butler to command his cavalry."[4]

Halleck was quick to respond. He passed Grant's request on to Secretary of War Stanton who, on the same day (April 15), wired Grant, "I will give Colonel Kautz the brigadier's commission, and send him to Fortress Monroe immediately."[5]

Halleck, however, must have had reservations based on his and Stanton's interview with Kautz on April 14 because, at 12:30 P.M. on April 16, he wired Grant, "Colonel Kautz will be sent to General Butler, if you deem him more useful there than here in charge of the Cavalry Bureau. There is no competent person here to take his place, and the difficulty of getting horses is daily increasing."[6]

Grant answered at 6 P.M. the same day, "General Butler is absolutely without a cavalry commander, and I can think of no one available equal to Kautz. Cannot General J.W. Davidson, or some officer of lesser rank, now that the duties of the Cavalry Bureau have been changed, do the duties as well?"[7]

Halleck must have given in because, on April 17, Special Order No. 150 was issued by the adjutant general's office, stating in part, "Brig. Gen. August V. Kautz, U.S. Volunteers, will immediately repair to Fort Monroe, Va., and report for duty to Major-General Butler, U.S. Volunteers, commanding the Department of Virginia and North Carolina."[8]

April 18 was a remarkably busy day for the new brigadier. He closed out his business at the bureau amid the congratulations of his friends, arranged transportation for himself and for his horse, which he had left in Columbus, Ohio, packed his belongings for shipment to Fortress Monroe and hired a personal servant, an African-American named George Washington Lee.[9]

Still busy packing, Kautz missed the morning train to Baltimore on April 19, but made it to the afternoon train. He then boarded the Fortress Monroe boat and arrived on the morning of April 20. He met with General Butler at 10 A.M. and, immediately afterwards, Butler issued the following General Order No. 47: "Brig. Gen. August V. Kautz, U.S. Volunteers, is hereby announced as chief of cavalry for this department, and will be obeyed and respected accordingly."[10]

Also on the twentieth, Kautz received the following order, signed by Butler's chief-of-staff: "General: You have been by general orders assigned to duty as chief of cavalry in this department, it is the desire of the commanding general that you make your headquarters at or near Portsmouth, Va., and take immediate command of all the cavalry in the district, organize and discipline it, that it may be made as effective as possible, with a view to active operations."[11]

After a brief discussion with Butler of the plans for the Army of the James, Kautz crossed Hampton Roads to Portsmouth, where his cavalry division was located. They had been screening the bases at Portsmouth and Norfolk from Confederates who held the line of the Blackwater River, twenty-five miles to the west.

On April 28, Kautz wrote his first general order. He named the Third New York Cavalry, commanded by Major Ferris Jacobs, and the First District of Columbia Cavalry, commanded by Major Stannard Baker, to the First Brigade. The Second Brigade would be composed of the Eleventh Pennsylvania Cavalry, commanded by Lieutenant Colonel George Stetzel, and the Fifth Pennsylvania Cavalry, commanded by Lieutenant Colonel Christopher Kleinz. Colonel Simon Mix was named to command the First Brigade and Colonel Samuel Spear to command the Second Brigade. The order also named Captain Myer Asch as division adjutant.

Kautz quickly learned that many of the men of his division had no horses. In fact, six companies of the First D.C. had never had horses or saddles and were serving as infantry.[12] Although all of the men of the First D.C. were armed with the new .44 caliber Henry repeating rifles,[13] most of the men of the division had breechloading rifles. A few, however, had only pistols and sabers. Kautz made an effort to correct the deficiencies, with limited success.

The day set for the commencement of Grant's Grand Campaign was May 5.

In the West, Sherman massed his combined armies, numbering about 98,000 men, south of Chattanooga for a movement against General Joseph Johnston's 60,000-man Army of Tennessee, which was entrenched on steep ridges north of Dalton, Georgia. Meade, under the watchful eye of Grant, began his part of the Grand Campaign on the night of May 3–4 when he moved the bulk of his 122,000-man Army of the Potomac across the Rapidan River. After some minor skirmishing, he came face-to-face with the 66,000 men of Lee's Army of Northern Virginia in the Battle of the Wilderness.

In a move which took the Confederates entirely by surprise, Butler's Army of the James boarded transports at Hampton Roads on May 4 and was carried up the James River the following day to Bermuda Hundred, the narrow neck of land above the confluence of the James and Appomattox Rivers. One division of colored infantry commanded by Brigadier General Edward Hincks encamped across the Appomattox at City Point. Butler then proposed a night march to Fort Darling near Drewry's Bluff on the line of the Richmond & Petersburg Railroad on the night of May 5–6. Although essentially unopposed by any Rebel army, Butler allowed his subordinate officers to dissuade him.

On May 6, Butler moved forward and occupied a line about three miles in length anchored on the south on the Appomattox at a place called Point of Rocks and on the north on a sharp bend in the James River. Here, they dug in. Butler's 35,000-man army was now safe from harassment by the few Confederates in their front. From their positions Butler's soldiers were able to see the spires of the Petersburg churches seven miles to the southwest. Richmond lay but fifteen miles away to the north. The Richmond & Petersburg Railroad, the major lifeline for the Confederate capital city, was less than three miles in front of them. Major General George Pickett was in command of the Confederate forces at Butler's front, but the fewer than ten thousand men of Pickett's command were scattered over an area of more than 400 square miles, unable to oppose any move Butler might choose to make.

Over the next ten days, Butler sent increasingly larger forces forward in an effort to occupy the Richmond & Petersburg Railroad. A first attempt on May 7 was unsuccessful because General Gillmore failed to move. A second, on May 9 near Chester Station, was initially successful, but Butler pulled back to Bermuda Hundred to plan a more aggressive attack on the defenses south of Richmond. In this last move, the three-day Battle of Drewry's Bluff, in which Kautz's Cavalry Division was marginally involved, about half of Butler's Army of the James was soundly defeated by a Confederate force composed of ten makeshift brigades pulled together by Pickett and his superior, General P.G.T. Beauregard.[14]

As additional Rebel reinforcements arrived, the threat to Richmond was over. Grant, in his report of the campaign of 1864–65, described Butler's position after these attempts as follows: "He was forced back, or drew back, into his entrenchments between the forks of the James and Appomattox Rivers, the enemy intrenching strongly in his front, thus covering his railroads, the city, and all that was valuable to him. His army, therefore, though in a position of great security, was as completely shut off from further operations directly against Richmond as if it had been in a bottle strongly corked. It required but a comparatively small force of the enemy to hold it there."[15]

22. Raiding Railroads in Virginia

While Ben Butler was demonstrating toward Richmond, Kautz's Division had not been idle. On May 4, Kautz issued orders to his two brigades to be ready to march at daylight the following day carrying three days' rations for themselves and two days' forage for their horses, with no transportation except ambulances. One section of the Eighth New York Artillery Battalion under Lieutenant Peter Morton was to go along. Notably absent would be the six unmounted companies of the First D.C. Cavalry.

Butler had suggested a raid toward Hicksford on the Meherrin River, but Kautz felt it would be impossible to cross the heavily guarded bridges and fords of the Blackwater that far south. He suggested a raid farther north and Butler agreed.[1]

The division assembled near Suffolk about noon. With Spear's Second Brigade in the lead, the division marched due west to the hamlet of Andrews Corner near the Blackwater in order to give the impression that they planned to attempt a crossing of the lower Blackwater. After a 38-mile march, they rested about 9 P.M. in the woods near Andrews Corner.

On the road again by 1 A.M., Kautz hurried north to Isle-of-Wight Court House, then turned west again to Fernsville on the Blackwater, where he feigned a crossing of the bridge which carries the Norfolk and Petersburg Railroad across the Blackwater. Once past the big bend of the Blackwater, the column turned southwest to cross the river at Birch Island Bridge.[2] Colonel Spear's Second Brigade drove off a crew who were busily attempting to dismantle the bridge. The woodsmen of the First D.C. Cavalry quickly rebuilt the two spans which had been destroyed[3] and the entire column continued on to the village of Wakefield on the Norfolk & Petersburg Railroad, where Spear's men burned the railroad station and some rolling stock, tore up some track and cut the telegraph lines. When the last of Colonel Mix's Brigade reached Wakefield at 9 P.M., the entire division rested until 2 A.M. Colonel Mix estimated the distance traveled the second day as 47 miles.[4]

On the third day, Kautz had the Third New York of Mix's Brigade in the lead. Passing through the village of Littleton, a small Confederate wagon train of commissary supplies was surprised and one officer and seven men were captured. The Union troopers made good use of the hams, corn and hardtack in the wagons. By this time, about forty of the horses had already failed due to the unusually warm weather, requiring that time be spent scouring the countryside for replacements as Kautz had seen Morgan's men do in Ohio.

Beyond Littleton, the road crossed to the south side of the Nottoway River, passed through the village of Sussex Court House, then recrossed to the north of the Nottoway on Bolling's Bridge as the river made a wide swing to the north. A small detachment of Confederates was caught attempting to destroy Bolling's Bridge, but they were easily brushed aside. Just beyond Bolling's Bridge, the Petersburg & Weldon Railroad was reached at Stony Creek Station where the rail line crossed Stony Creek on a 110-foot span.

Kautz was aware that General P.G.T. Beauregard at Weldon, North Carolina, and his

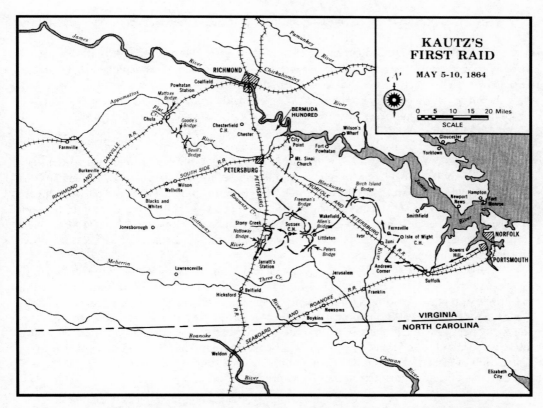

The route of Kautz's first railroad raid. From Robertson, William G., ***Back Door to Richmond*** (Newark: University of Delaware Press, 1987).

subordinate, General George Pickett at Petersburg, were attempting to hurry reinforcements north from South Carolina. Pickett, on May 7, knowing Kautz personally as well as by reputation, was worried that Kautz's goal was Petersburg itself, and he rushed the few artillery pieces available south of the city to block Kautz's suspected attack. Beauregard, however, suspected that Kautz was aiming toward the railroad bridge over the Meherrin River, so he was attempting to fortify that area as the first troops from South Carolina began to arrive at Weldon. Kautz knew that, if he was going to do much damage to the railroad, he was going to have to hurry. He sent Colonel Spear with one regiment five miles to the south to the railroad bridge over the Nottoway River while he had Colonel Mix attack the Stony Creek bridge with the Third New York.

Since the men from South Carolina had not yet arrived, the Stony Creek bridge was defended by a small detachment of Holcombe's South Carolina Legion commanded by Major M.G. Ziegler. Ziegler's men were posted on the south side of the bridge. Mix dismounted his men and deployed the majority of one regiment facing the bridge from the north while he sent two companies in a flanking movement across the creek to the right. A few rifle shots were fired from both sides, but, when Mix opened up with artillery, Major Ziegler sent up the white flag, surrendering forty-seven men, including himself. In the engagement, which lasted little more than a quarter of an hour, one of Mix's men was killed and two were wounded. Kautz's Division then burned the Stony Creek Station, two wood-storage racks, two water tanks, three freight cars filled with lumber and a large stockpile of spare bridge timbers. They also destroyed a railroad turntable and burned the 110-foot bridge that carried the Petersburg & Weldon Railroad over Stony Creek. Afterwards, they feasted on corn and bacon they had acquired at the station, then rested near Bolling's Bridge.

Meanwhile, Spear had ridden to the Nottoway River bridge with the Eleventh Pennsylvania and arrived about sunset. Finding a large number of Confederates deployed at the bridge, he decided wisely to return to Stony Creek for additional help. The Confederates at the bridge were the Fifty-Ninth Virginia of Henry A. Wise's Brigade, commanded by Colonel William B. Tabb, the first of the reinforcements to arrive from South Carolina. With them were two companies of the Twenty-Sixth Virginia and one company of Holcombe's South Carolina Legion.[5] The Fifty-Ninth had arrived by train at Hicksford on the Meherrin River only hours before, then been ordered by Beauregard to march to Stony Creek. Tabb and his men had gotten as far as the Nottoway River bridge from the south minutes before the Eleventh Pennsylvania.

Kautz planned an attack on the Nottoway Bridge on the morning of May 8. He sent Spear's Brigade by road at 3 A.M. to pass the bridge, then move on the bridge from the south. Mix was to move down the Petersburg & Weldon Railroad line later, destroying track as he went. Spear and Mix should arrive at the Nottoway Bridge at about the same time and attack it from two directions.

Meanwhile, Kautz himself made a reconnaissance northward with two companies of the First D.C. Cavalry to the bridge over Rowanty Creek to see if it was well-defended. According to his official report, "Finding a force defending the Rowanty bridge ... I withdrew to Bolling's Bridge, and, to my great disappointment, found Colonel Mix had not moved. Deeming it too late to cooperate with Colonel Spear, I recrossed Bolling's Bridge and moved directly on Nottoway bridge, and found that Colonel Spear with his command had devoted the morning to the destruction of Jarratt's Station, where my orders reached him."[6]

Colonel Spear's report describes the morning's work:

> The brigade took up the line of march about daylight, and went toward Jarratt's Station, on the Petersburg and Weldon Railroad, the Eleventh Pennsylvania being in the advance. Arriving at the station we were met by a portion of Holcombe's Legion; the carbineers of the Eleventh Pennsylvania Cavalry dismounted, and, after a desperate conflict (taking into consideration the number engaged), were repulsed. The Fifth Pennsylvania Cavalry was then ordered forward (they all carry carbines), were dismounted and ordered to charge the enemy. After a short fight the place was carried; 37 prisoners were taken, among whom were several line officers. Previous to this time about 2 miles of railroad and telegraph line had been destroyed near the station and at it; the office, depot, and a number of public buildings, together with a large amount of Confederate Government stores, were destroyed. My brigade was then countermarched and moved toward Nottoway River bridge, the Fifth Pennsylvania marching by file on the railroad, the Eleventh going by the road.[7]

Spear's Second Brigade arrived at the Nottoway Bridge by midafternoon. Kautz with Mix's Brigade was already present and Mix had already commenced an assault. Since his arrival the previous day, Colonel Tabb had time to set up positions on both sides of the bridge with a redoubt on the north bank. He had sent one company of the Fifty-Ninth to a position about one mile to the southeast with a line of skirmishers between that point and the bridge. When Spear arrived, Mix's Brigade was driving the skirmishers back toward the bridge. A portion of the First D.C. was pushing in on Tabb's right flank. Spear sent both his regiments in on the left while the artillery of the Eighth New York were firing from behind him. Tabb's Virginians put up stiff resistance before falling back across the bridge. The 210-foot bridge was set afire and fell into the river after about twenty minutes. Seeing the bridge fall, the raiders pulled back out of rifle range and rested. Kautz had expected a more difficult fight at Nottoway Bridge. He was of the opinion that, had Tabb maintained his position in the redoubt and not exposed his men in the open ground around the bridge, the loss on the Union side would have been extreme.

Kautz added in his report: "I should not neglect to mention that I effected, through a flag of truce, an exchange of 3 or 4 prisoners of my command that had fallen into the hands of Colonel Tabb, some of them wounded. I could, no doubt, have captured Colonel Tabb's command, but reflecting that the loss of ammunition probably necessary to do it, and the increased number of prisoners and the time lost, might seriously interfere if it did not altogether defeat my return to City Point, I reluctantly left him to guard where the bridge had been." In assessing his situation, he added, "I now found myself hampered by about 130 prisoners and about 30 wounded, among them several officers.[8] A large portion of Beauregard's forces was on the way from Weldon, and it was reasonable to expect difficulties in the direction of Petersburg."[9] With the majority of his mission accomplished, it would be wise to get back to Union lines as quickly as possible.

After a brief rest, the division moved to Sussex Court House and bivouacked from about midnight to 3 A.M. on the 9th. They crossed the Nottoway on Allen's bridge, then moved north on the Jerusalem Plank Road to within eight miles of Petersburg. Turning east, the entire command arrived at City Point by noon on May 10.

In a telegram to Secretary of War Stanton, Butler summarized briefly the work which Kautz's men had done in the raid. Stanton replied, "General Kautz was confirmed [by Congress] as brigadier on Saturday, and I am rejoiced he is so well vindicating the merit of the appointment. His commission will be forwarded immediately."[10]

If the men of Kautz's division thought they deserved to rest after their six-day ride, they were disappointed. Butler had plans for them. An hour after his return, Kautz received a telegram from Butler's chief of staff directing him to move to Bermuda Landing and report to headquarters. Apparently Kautz didn't report soon enough. He received another telegram sent at noon and signed by Butler himself. It was short and to the point, "Report in person."

The reason for Butler's insistence was the need to discuss plans for his upcoming move toward Drewry's Bluff on May 12. Butler felt that the success of the offensive would be guaranteed if the left wing of his army were protected by a screen of cavalry. In addition, Butler wanted Kautz's Division to commence a move on the Richmond & Danville Railroad at the same time. That movement would be masked by the movement of the rest of Butler's army. He needed Kautz and his troopers. Kautz protested mildly, saying that his troops were exhausted, but Butler insisted. He had already postponed the demonstration against Richmond for one day waiting for Kautz to return from his raid. Any further delay would permit additional reinforcement by Beauregard or by Lee.

Kautz's order to his men, as quoted by Colonel Baker of the First D.C., said in part, "Prepare to march at once leaving all wagons, pack-mules, baggage, led horses, and sick behind."[11]

May 11 was a day of preparation for the cavalry division. In addition to the move across the pontoon bridge from City Point to Bermuda Hundred, rations, forage and ammunition were prepared and distributed. Those men (and horses) deemed unfit to march were culled from the ranks. Lost and damaged equipment was replaced or repaired. The work went on well into the night of May 11–12. According to Kautz's report, "The night of May 11th it rained hard and materially interfered with this duty, and the command was under the necessity of moving before I could satisfy myself that it was fully equipped."[12]

With both the Richmond & Petersburg and the Petersburg & Weldon Railroads cut, the only rail link connecting Richmond (and Lee's army) to the rest of the Confederacy was the Richmond & Danville Railroad. If Kautz could do significant damage to the R & D, Richmond would be completely, although temporarily, isolated.

As Kautz's Division rode out past the Federal entrenchments at Bermuda Hundred on May 12, the torrential downpour of the night before had moderated to a steady rain which would continue off and on for the next three days. The rain, on top of the short notice, had delayed the cavalry's departure until 9 A.M., but Godfrey Weitzel's Division of Smith's Corps, whose left flank they were to screen, was moving slowly as well.

Just before reaching Chester Station on the Richmond & Petersburg Railroad, Kautz and his men passed the battlefield where Alfred H. Terry's Division had fought on May 9 and 10. Unburied corpses of men and horses were decomposing on the damp earth and many of the battle-hardened cavalrymen were sickened by the sights and smells of this little piece of Virginia real estate.

The march continued through the rain to the village of Chesterfield, where a few government supplies were destroyed and several Union sympathizers who had refused to serve in the Confederate army were liberated from the county jail.

The Richmond & Danville Railroad was reached at the town of Coalfield, ten miles west of Richmond, at about 11 P.M. Kautz would not let his troopers rest until the telegraph office, the railroad station, the water tank, some stores of lumber and a tannery were burned. After watching in awe as six freight cars loaded with munitions were torched and subsequently exploded, they set about tearing up track, using heavy tools commandeered from the nearby coal pits. Colonel Spear wanted to set the coal in the mines on fire, but Lieutenant Colonel George Stetzel of the Eleventh Pennsylvania, who knew something about coal mining, cautioned that, once ablaze, the mines might burn for decades. Kautz ordered the mines protected.

The division marched several miles southwest on Buckingham Pike before Kautz allowed them to get a few hours rest in the rain-soaked fields.

Up before dawn, the men continued the march, with the Second Brigade in the lead, to Powhatan Station, which was reached about 9 A.M. After destroying the telegraph office and cutting the wires, the men set about burning the railroad station and the freight warehouse. Finding

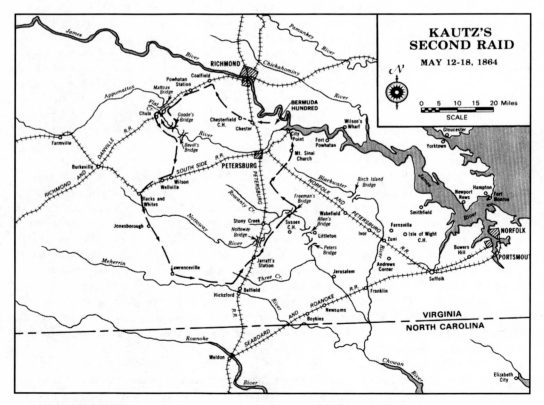

The route of Kautz's second railroad raid. From William G. Robertson, *Back Door to Richmond* (Newark: University of Delaware Press, 1987).

a large hoard of foodstuffs and fifteen freight cars loaded with hay, they gathered enough corn and hams to feed themselves and enough hay for their horses, then set the cars and the remaining food ablaze.

Continuing the march in a southwesterly direction, it was another seven miles to the Mattoax bridge where the railroad crossed the Appomattox River. The Fifth Pennsylvania was the first to reach the high iron bridge on the Mattoax and they began deploying on the right (east) bank of the river. When Kautz arrived, he and Spear surveyed the scene. Across the river were seen a line of entrenchments with artillery in place. It appeared that a large force occupied the fortifications. Had the bridge been of wood construction, Kautz would have asked his men to attempt to burn it while under fire from the opposite bank. As it was, however, it would have required considerable time to dismantle the steel bridge — no doubt at a considerable loss of life — even if proper tools for the job were at hand.

Reluctantly, Kautz ordered his men toward Goode's bridge, five miles to the east, where the road crossed the Appomattox. That bridge had been partially dismantled by some local people, but it was rebuilt quickly enough to afford a crossing soon after dark. Moving west again on the opposite bank of the Appomattox, the railroad was struck again at Chula Station. Here Kautz was disappointed to learn that the defenders he had seen at Mattoax bridge numbered fewer than 200, but that they had now been reinforced by a full regiment, the Thirtieth Virginia, which had arrived from Petersburg via the Southside Railroad to Burkeville, then back eastwardly on the Richmond & Danville. Two of the trains which had carried the Confederate regiment to Mattoax bridge had already returned empty. A trap was set for the third by blocking the switch near the station. When the empty train arrived, it derailed amid the cheers of the cavalrymen, who later destroyed it.

At the break of day on May 14, Kautz sent both his brigade commanders, Samuel Spear and Ferris Jacobs, who had temporarily replaced Mix, north a short distance with the Eleventh Pennsylvania and three companies of the Third New York to reconnoiter the small bridge where the railroad crossed Flat Creek with specific orders not to attack if the bridge appeared well defended. The Flat Creek bridge, like the Mattoax bridge, was defended by a full regiment, the Seventeenth Virginia, which had arrived the day before with the Thirtieth Virginia. The timbers of the Flat Creek bridge had been covered by metal and were so wet from the incessant rain that the bridge could not have burned. Despite that and the fact that the bridge was heavily guarded, Spear, who was in command, ignored Kautz's admonition and charged the bridge. After at least three abortive assaults, Spear was ordered by Kautz to desist, but not until about thirty casualties had occurred, mostly in the Third New York.

While the unfortunate assault was taking place at Flat Creek, the balance of the division busied themselves doing what damage they could at Chula Station. Some of the men moved along the rail line ripping up track while those left at the station destroyed the telegraph office, the station, a water tank, several warehouses and several empty rail cars.

After Spear returned to Chula Station, the entire command headed south and, after about twenty miles, reached the Southside Railroad at Wellville. There and at nearby Wilson's Station the depots, a large amount of firewood, several rail cars and about two miles of track were destroyed. Moving west on the Southside near dark, the troops found that the pickings were better at Black's and White's Station. An abundance of forage for the horses and food for the men were found. After eating, the men burned the station, several warehouses, thirteen freight cars, wood storage facilities, water tanks and another mile of track. After the work was completed, Kautz ordered his men to continue their southward movement, not allowing a halt until 2 A.M., when they slept in an open field in a heavy rain. It had been a busy day.

May 15 was far less eventful. A twenty-mile march southward took the column to the village of Lawrenceville. There was no railroad at Lawrenceville to damage, but a few Confederate soldiers were captured and a small supply of commissary stores was destroyed. A quiet night was spent near Lawrenceville and, thankfully, the rain ended.

The road east from Lawrenceville ran parallel to the Meherrin River toward Hicksford and Belfield, where the Petersburg & Weldon Railroad crossed the river. Kautz, learning that the bridge over the Meherrin was again heavily guarded, stopped his advance four miles from the bridge and turned toward Jarratt's Station ten miles to the north. The feint toward the Meherrin River bridge was about all the division's dwindling ammunition supply could support.

Jarratt's Station was a disappointment. Kautz found the rail line which his men had broken eight days before completely restored. Construction of a new station was well underway. A newly-built water tank was operative. Men of the Fifth Pennsylvania, some of whose comrades had died here, were discouraged, but set about to repeat the work of a week before with some energy. As the column was marching out of Jarratt's Station, a pontoon train was found and destroyed. These were the pontoons which had been thrown across the Nottoway River after Kautz's raiders had destroyed the railroad bridge there the week before. The fact that the pontoons were no longer needed was an unwelcome signal that the Nottoway bridge had already been repaired.

The weary column moved north roughly parallel to the Nottoway River. A brief reconnaissance to the Nottoway bridge was made. Kautz found "a structure sufficient to permit trains to cross over the Nottoway, replacing the bridge we had destroyed on the 8th. It was guarded, and late in the evening, and would have delayed us another day to destroy it."[13] The next crossing of the Nottoway was at Freeman's bridge. The head of the column reached Freeman's bridge near midnight and found a party of Confederates working to destroy the bridge, two-thirds of the task already completed. It fell to Baker's First D.C. to drive the Confederates off and make the necessary repairs while the rest of the division rested. According to the chaplain of the First District of Columbia Cavalry,

> When the advance reached Freeman's bridge ... it was discovered that the whole command was in a trap. The river for a considerable distance was unfordable.... The enemy was gathering in force in the rear.... The river must be crossed, or a battle must be fought on the enemy's chosen ground.... A major of a New York regiment, commanding the advance, declared that the bridge could not be made passable before the afternoon of the next day.... Company D [of the First D.C. Cavalry] was ordered up and told what was wanted. In a short time tall pines in the neighboring woods had fallen before the axes of one party, and stalwart men, by means of the drag ropes of a battery, had drawn them out. Another party had in the meantime crossed the river on a little float they had fortunately found, and stood on the remaining part of the bridge on the other side. The ropes were thrown to them, and the stringers were drawn across the chasm and placed in position. To cover them with rails was but the work of a few moments and in less than three hours ... the column passed in safety.[14]

The work on the bridge was completed about 3 A.M. of May 17, allowing Baker's men about two hours sleep before they fell in behind the other three regiments. As in the previous raid the division moved north on the Jerusalem Plank Road, then east to City Point, which was reached late in the afternoon. They once again removed some track from the Norfolk & Petersburg Railroad on the way.

In the thirteen days of marching and fighting, Kautz's Division lost fourteen men killed, sixty wounded and twenty-seven missing or captured. Almost a third of the loss was during the battle at Flat Creek bridge. Kautz's Division had marched more than 400 miles, not considering frequent countermarches. In addition to the several engagements mentioned here, they were harassed almost constantly by small detachments of regulars and militia as they were moving through enemy territory. Speaking only of the second raid, Kautz, in his official report, added, "We marched from 30 to 40 miles daily for six days, during which a great deal of rain had fallen, and the roads in some places very heavy. Considering the work done, comparatively few of the horses have failed. We captured about as many horses as we lost on the marches, and brought in besides several hundred mule and a large number of negroes; many more of the latter would have followed if we had had transportation for them."[15]

At a time when the huge armies of Generals Grant and Lee were slugging it out north of Richmond, Kautz's little cavalry division was getting a surprising amount of press in the Northern newspapers, much of it positive. At the same time, Kautz and his men were castigated in the Southern press which — drawing on the accidental burning of several private dwellings, Kautz's need to feed his men off the land, and a few isolated episodes of true wrongdoing — described Kautz's two raids as orgies of rape and pillage, comparing Kautz to Attila the Hun.

Kautz, although he knew the accusations to be gross exaggerations, took the charges personally. In his official report of the raid submitted on June 3, he wrote, "I have, however, to deplore a disposition to pillage and plunder on the part of some of the men and a want of proper officering on the part of some of the officers to check this tendency. There seems to be a looseness of sentiment (not unusual to cavalry) in this respect in the command that is to be regretted, as it adds no luster to our cause, but rather mars the splendor of their military achievements."[16]

The following day, he issued his General Order No. 4, a remarkable 495-word document on the subject of pillaging which would be to the credit of any commander in time of war. It begins by stating that some pillaging on the recent raids had been brought to his attention, then admonishes his officers to make every effort to prevent it and his men to avoid it in the future. After warning that pillaging leaves the men open to punishment by their own officers and to retaliation by their enemies, it concludes: "The general commanding warns offenders that he will use every effort to bring them to punishment. He is satisfied that there in no unusual tendency to steal and rob (for such are the names of these offenses in times of peace) in the command, but he is anxious to have it entirely free from such imputations, and to make it so will be the object of his labors, and he trusts to the hearty co–operation of the officers and men to accomplish this end."[17]

23. The First Petersburg Assault

General Grant apologized for using the phrase "as if it [the Army of the James] had been in a bottle strongly corked" to describe Benjamin Butler's situation at Bermuda Hundred, saying that the idea had originated with a member of his staff. Despite Grant's apology, the analogy fits so well that Grant's words will not go away. In the same report where the above phrase appeared, Grant went on, "I determined, therefore, to bring from it all available forces, leaving enough only to secure what had been gained."[1] On May 22, he ordered Baldy Smith's XVIII Corps to join the Army of the Potomac north of Richmond.

The day before Grant ordered Smith north, he wired Chief of Staff Henry Halleck, "I fear there is some difficulty with the forces at City Point which prevents their effective use. The fault may be with the commander, and it may be with his subordinates. General Smith, whilst a very able officer, is obstinate, and is likely to condemn whatever is not suggested by himself." Grant appears to have read Smith well, but much of the "difficulty" which Grant feared was between Butler and Gillmore rather than Smith. Grant went on in his telegram to Halleck, to ask that "a competent officer" be sent "to inspect and report ... what is being done and what ... it is advisable to do."[2] He didn't wait to find out.

The departure of XVIII Corps thinned the ranks of the Army of the James considerably. In order to strengthen the defensive position at Bermuda Hundred, Butler ordered, "General Kautz will dismount his men, leave his horses in the most convenient places, in charge of as few men as possible.... General Kautz will be in command of the line now occupied by General Smith."[3]

So Kautz's Cavalry would be serving as infantry. Supplemented by some ninety-day volunteers from Ohio and some of the men of XVIII Corps who had been deemed unfit for the march north, Kautz's command now amounted to a division of infantry numbering about 6000 men, occupying the left side of the Bermuda Hundred line. That line saw little activity for the next ten days. Picks and shovels were the weapons of choice as both armies strengthened their fortifications. What little skirmishing took place was hardly more heated than the constant bickering between Butler and Gillmore.

The relationship between Butler and Gillmore deteriorated even further when Butler got wind of the fact that Gillmore, ignoring the chain of command, had written directly to General Halleck about the situation at Bermuda Hundred. Butler learned of Gillmore's letter, but would have blown his top had he known the details, including a denunciation of Butler's recent offensive and a denial of any part in its failure. The letter, marked "Private," ended, "There is a long story to be told of operations here, but I cannot act the part of historian now."[4]

Although Kautz was aware of the Butler-Gillmore controversy, he did not speak of it publicly, nor did he seem to take sides at the time. His journal contains but a single terse comment, "I fear that there is not a great deal of harmony among our commanders."[5]

The interval on line at Bermuda Hundred provided a welcome rest for the horses of the cavalry division and, to a lesser extent, for the men. Kautz noted that at least 400 men of his command were still armed with swords and pistols. He found rifles for the majority. However, these were muzzleloading rifles, suitable for their present role, but nearly useless as cavalry weapons.

On June 8, he was called to General Butler's headquarters. The summons sounded important.

Benjamin Butler had received intelligence from escaped slaves, Confederate prisoners and deserters—even from the Richmond papers—that Petersburg was essentially undefended. As early as June 1, Brigadier General Edward Hincks, who commanded the division of colored troops at City Point, had suggested an attack on Petersburg, stating in part, "It seems to me to be entirely practicable to ... enter the place with about 6,000 men."[6] If Butler could mount a quick and decisive movement against the city, capture it and destroy the bridges, Hinks felt he could hold the city against any force the Rebels could throw against him. The speed of the movement was critical.

On June 8, Butler was meeting with General Hincks to plan such a move, to include about 3500 of Hincks's colored infantry and 1400 of Kautz's Cavalry. General Gillmore arrived at Butler's headquarters while the meeting was taking place, and afterwards requested permission to lead the expedition. Butler agreed. As finally drawn up, the movement would send four regiments, totaling about 2000 men drawn from Gillmore's forces at Bermuda Hundred, under the command of Colonel Joseph Hawley, along the City Point Road toward Petersburg. General Hincks, with about 1200 men, would move along the Jordan's Point Road parallel to and about a mile south of Hawley. Kautz, with his 1400 cavalry, would move in a wide arc to the south, then move north toward Petersburg on the Jerusalem Plank Road.[7]

Reports on June 8 from the signal station on Spring Hill indicated that there was movement of Rebel troops toward Richmond, but none were seen passing in the other direction.[8] Petersburg would still be lightly defended.

Kautz met the next day with Butler and, separately, with Gillmore and issued orders to his brigade commanders to be ready to move at midnight. "Three days rations in the haversack and 20 quarts of oats on the horse will be supplied each man. No vehicles of any description will be allowed excepting ambulances."[9]

Gillmore's orders to Hawley directed "that you have your command in readiness to march this P.M. at dark, with one day's rations and 60 rounds of ammunition."[10] He also sent a message to Butler suggesting that he should take along a full battery of artillery.

Butler replied that he should take along but two sections of a battery. "This is not to be artillery work, but a quick decisive push."[11]

Kautz's part of the "push" toward Petersburg got started around midnight. He had with him 640 men of the Eleventh Pennsylvania, 450 of the Fifth Pennsylvania and the six mounted companies of the First D.C., a total of 1400 men. The Third New York and the remainder of the First D.C. were left behind to man the trenches at Bermuda Hundred. There was some delay in getting across the pontoon bridge over the Appomattox to City Point because some of Gillmore's infantry, whom the calvary were supposed to follow, took the wrong road and wound up marching through a swamp.

The movement from City Point began at 4:30 A.M. With the Eleventh Pennsylvania in the advance, Kautz's small division marched several miles on the City Point Road, then turned in a southwesterly direction toward the Jerusalem Plank Road, which was reached about six miles south of Petersburg. At one point near their crossing of the Prince George Court House Road, the Fifth and Eleventh Pennsylvania were attacked by a regiment of cavalry estimated at 300 to 400 men supported by artillery.

Turning north on the Jerusalem Plank Road, the lead regiment reached a line of entrenchments less than two miles from the heart of the city at 11:30 A.M.

Meanwhile, the two columns of infantry under Gillmore had moved from City Point just after Kautz. Having but four or five miles to travel compared to Kautz's twenty, they arrived at the entrenchments in their front at least two hours earlier. Both Gillmore, who moved with Hawley's Brigade on the Jordan's Point Road, and Hincks, on the City Point Road, surveyed the enemy's works from a distance. Without hazarding so much as a reconnaissance in force, they decided that the enemy's position was too strong to attempt an attack. Despite the fact that Gillmore had been ordered by Butler to assault the works, neither he nor Hincks even drove the Confederate pickets into their entrenchments. About 1 P.M., Gillmore gave the order to withdraw. His men fell back two miles, stopped for lunch, then marched back to Bermuda Hundred, arriving before dark. It is difficult to determine at this late date exactly how many Confederates manned the entrenchments in front of Gillmore. Confederate Brigadier General Raleigh Colston said that there were no more than 150 around the City Point Road.[12] It was certainly no more than two regiments of infantry and, perhaps, a portion of the regiment of cavalry which had hampered Kautz's march. They were, however, strongly supported by artillery.

Kautz, not aware what had happened east of him, sent a mounted squadron of the Eleventh Pennsylvania toward the entrenchments to determine his enemy's strength. Although the cavalry charge was driven back by a volley from the men in the trenches, it was easy to see that the line was not heavily defended. Kautz estimated their strength at about 200.

Had Kautz been there three hours earlier, he would have found the entrenchments at his front completely deserted. Around 9 A.M., the church bells and fire bells in the city had sounded, calling out the militia. A courier had ridden into the city from the south with the news that a large force of cavalry was approaching from that direction. Brigadier General Henry Wise, who was in command at Petersburg, ordered the bells rung while he rode across the Appomattox to gather his brigade of infantry from in front of the Bermuda Hundred lines. The call for militia was answered by about 150 men, mostly young boys and old men known as Archer's Battalion and commanded by Major Fletcher Archer. Archer's small force had arrived on the Jerusalem Plank Road less than an hour before Kautz's Cavalry. Also, shortly after the initial saber charge of the Pennsylvanians, General Colston, who had been living in Petersburg awaiting assignment, arrived on the scene with a single howitzer taken from the line about a mile to the east. As the senior officer present, Colston took over command from Archer.

Kautz next ordered the Eleventh Pennsylvania to dismount and charge the Confederate works. As the assault began, the Pennsylvanians were surprised by fire from the late-arriving howitzer and they fell back. Finally, the order was given for the majority of the division to dismount and make an assault. Formed in a line which stretched well beyond both flanks of the defenders, the attackers carried the works without difficulty. Colston later estimated the loss to his militia as fourteen killed, twenty wounded and thirty captured, plus the loss of the howitzer.[13]

The entire battle had taken less than an hour, but Kautz knew that any further delays would put his command in jeopardy. As soon as arrangements could be made for care of the wounded Confederates, he moved his men forward toward the city. The Jerusalem Plank Road descended into a deep ravine formed by Lieutenant Creek, which emptied into the Appomattox just below the city. Beyond the ravine was Reservoir Hill, which overlooked the city. As the advance reached the ravine, they were met by a hail of artillery fire, which fortunately, due to the declination, passed harmlessly over their heads. These were artillery which had arrived from north of the river. According to Colston, "The moments gained at such fearful cost [at the entrenchments] barely gave time for Graham's battery to cross the bridge. They came up Sycamore Street at full gallop and unlimbered on the summit of Reservoir Hill just as the head of the Federal column was coming down the opposite slope into the hollow."[14] The artillery were followed by a full regiment of cavalry who had come from across the river and another battery of artillery which had been released from the eastern entrenchments by Gillmore's inaction. Supported by the fire of the two batteries, the cavalry drove Kautz's advance, the Eleventh Pennsylvania, back onto the opposite hill, where they regrouped.

According to Kautz's official report, "The prospect of entering the city was here suddenly defeated, for while I thought it possible that the enemy at that moment was not very strong, it was strong enough to delay me an hour or two in the commanding position they held. By that time they could be reinforced. I could hear nothing of General Gillmore's command; no firing could be heard in the direction of City Point, and I felt certainly that his forces had retired. I therefore ordered the command to fall back.... Before leaving the intrenchments the enemy's camp of forty or fifty tents and some huts were burned, and also a large house with some stores and ammunition.... We captured altogether 42 prisoners."[15] Kautz reported his losses as four killed, twenty-six wounded and six missing. The division was back in the lines at Bermuda Hundred by 11 P.M.

About the same time that Kautz and his men were marching across the pontoon bridge to Bermuda Hundred, General Gillmore wrote to General Butler offering to go with his fifty-man personal escort to rescue Kautz's supposedly lost division. Butler, of course, refused: "I have ordered your escort back. General Kautz is at my quarters, having come from the inner line of intrenchments of Petersburg, having carried the outer and only line of intrenchments."[16]

The next morning, June 10, Kautz questioned some of the prisoners his men had captured. One, Anthony M. Keiley, a Petersburg lawyer who had been with the militia at the Petersburg entrenchments, later wrote about the interview,

> I ... found myself in the presence of the celebrated raider. Kautz is a man of about five feet ten inches in height.... [He] has a swarthy complexion, a square massive German head, wears his hair and beard cut close, speaks slowly and thoughtfully, and has the breeding of a gentleman. He desired me to take a seat, offered a cigar, and we were soon engaged in a free conversation, which protracted for a couple of hours.
>   I did not hesitate to tell him how insignificant the force opposed to him in his attack of the previous day was, and asked him, with as innocent an expression as I could assume, why he did not enter Petersburg after passing us? He very frankly replied:
>   "Only because I did not know how I could get out again. The failure of the expedition on the river roads, which was relied upon to support me, made it necessary to be cautious, and while I might have dashed into town and burned some property, I might have lost my command."
>   ...I learned he was a West Pointer.... He was, by education, an infantry man, and observed that he thought the Government had spoiled a good infantry soldier by giving him a cavalry command. I discovered also that the general was somewhat piqued at his failure to receive credit with the Southern people for what he had done. He claimed to have planned and lead [sic] the expedition that resulted in Morgan's capture on the Ohio the year before, and yet had hardly been mentioned in connection with it. But what surprised him most was, that in the raid which he had made around the south of Petersburg, his name had escaped notice except in one or two instances, where *it was misspelled*, while the credit or discredit of the expedition was divided between Colonel Spears [sic], who served under him, and General Custer, who was not present.

Keiley concluded with, "On the whole, I was favorably impressed with this officer, and regard my interview with him as among the most pleasant episodes of my sojourn *in partibus infidelium*."[17]

Shortly after his interview with Kautz, Keiley was questioned by General Butler. Butler was also told that there had been no Confederate soldiers in Petersburg on the morning of June 9. Keiley's opinion of Butler was, by the way, as negative as his opinion of Kautz was positive.[18]

Butler questioned other prisoners and, again, was told that the Confederate works in front of Gillmore and Hincks were lightly manned. At 1:20 P.M., he sent a note to Gillmore demanding a report of his part in the expedition by 5 that afternoon.

The following day, armed with Gillmore's report and that of Kautz, Butler penned a letter to Gillmore, as caustic as any written by one general officer to another could be, outlining a host of charges of his dereliction of duty. Butler in his letter claimed, with much more detail than can be offered here, that (1) his original verbal order was to attack the enemy's lines at a point some distance from the roads which Gillmore and Hincks followed, rather than right at the roads where the lines were much more strongly constructed, (2) Gillmore took one more regiment with him than originally proposed, (3) he got started late, (4) he kept General Hincks "waiting in the saddle 2½ hours," (5) he allowed his regiments to get lost within their own lines and march through a swamp, (6) he erred in reporting the times at which different events took place, (7) he failed to get close enough to the enemy's entrenchments in front of Petersburg to know how weakly they were manned, (8) he disobeyed the order to attack the works, (9) he failed to support Kautz or even to communicate with him,[19] and (10) he failed in seven or eight other matters, including some which were direct orders.

At the end of Butler's letter, he called Gillmore's attention to his request on the evening of June 9 to go to Kautz's aid with his personal escort, adding, "It would seem that if when you were within 5 miles of him with 3,500 men you were not able to open communication with him, it was hardly worth while to try with a body guard of 50."

The letter ended, "To probe anew the acute wounds of hopes blasted when so much was expected, to be obliged to comment even with deserved severity upon the actions of an officer whose personal relations have been as pleasant as mine with you, has been a most painful task, to which nothing but a conviction of the stern necessity of a duty to the country to be done could have compelled me."[20]

On June 14, Butler forwarded the official reports submitted by Kautz, Gillmore and Hincks to General Grant. To Gillmore's report he added the endorsement, "Report of the expedition of which General Gillmore volunteered to take command is entirely unsatisfactory; it fails to comply with the order requiring it in many particulars; it states times, orders, and occurrences with much inaccuracy. The conduct of the expedition, as disclosed by it, and in fact, was dilatory and ill-judged; the demonstration upon the enemy too feeble to be called an attack — was in direct disobedience of orders. The whole affair, in view of the forces known to be opposed, was disgraceful to the Union arms."[21]

In a letter to Grant accompanying the reports, Butler wrote, "A more disastrous defeat has not been sustained by the American arms.... Had the movement been a success, as it easily might have been, Petersburg would have been in our possession, ... the whole railroad destroyed effectually, the line of the Appomattox secured, and the enemy's defensive works in our front rendered useless.

"I also inclose a copy of the Richmond Sentinel with the account of the Petersburg Express of the affair. It will be seen by that account that the enemy never discovered that Generals Gillmore and Hincks with the real attacking column came against them at all. They describe the movements of the real column of attack simply 'as feints to deceive our forces' while the real movement for the surprise and capture of the city was on the Jerusalem plank road coming to Petersburg from a southerly direction."[22]

Butler ordered Gillmore relieved of command of X Corps, but General Grant softened the blow somewhat by requesting Butler to rescind the order and then relieving him of command "at his own request."

Kautz, for his part in the first Petersburg assault, was breveted to the rank of lieutenant colonel in the regular Army.

24. The Second Petersburg Assault

According to the strategy of General Grant's Grand Campaign, in the event that Lee's Army of Northern Virginia were to withdraw into the Richmond defenses, General George G. Meade's Army of the Potomac was to move south of the James River and join the Army of the James in operations against Richmond. It was probably the failure of Gillmore's move against Petersburg which induced Grant to put the plan into effect. Grant said in his official report written one year later, "Attaching great importance to the possession of Petersburg, I sent back to Bermuda Hundred and City Point General [William F.] Smith's command by water ... to reach there in advance of the Army of the Potomac. This was for the express purpose of securing Petersburg before the enemy ... could re-enforce the place."[1]

As early as June 11, Grant wrote to Butler that the move south would begin the following night and that the 15,300 men of Smith's XVIII Corps would be the vanguard of the movement. Grant concluded his letter to Butler, "If you deem it practicable ... to seize and hold Petersburg, you may prepare to start.... I do not want Petersburg visited, however, unless it is held, nor an attempt to take it, unless you feel a reasonable degree of confidence of success."[2]

Whether Grant intended the last sentence as a rebuke for the failure of the June 9 assault, or if Butler read it as such, Butler accepted the challenge to move, and to move quickly.

Some of Smith's XVIII Corps had already arrived by June 13. As the remainder of the corps was disembarking on June 14, Grant visited Butler at Bermuda Hundred and they put together plans for another movement against Petersburg to commence the following day. It would again involve Kautz's Division.

On his part, Kautz issued an order to his brigade commanders, Spear and Mix (and to Lieutenant Colonel Patton of the First New York Mounted Rifle Regiment, now assigned to the Cavalry Division), to have their commands "in readiness to move on a moment's notice."[3]

That "moment's notice" came at midnight of June 14 when the cavalry division departed Bermuda Hundred by way of the pontoon bridge to City Point. By 5 A.M. they were on the march along City Point Road toward Petersburg in the lead of Smith's Corps. Kautz's Cavalry made up 2500 of Smith's 18,000-man attacking force.[4] Following were Edward Hinck's colored division and the divisions of Brigadier General William Brooks and Brigadier General John H. Martindale.

Kautz's advance met a line of entrenched skirmishers near the house of a man named Baylor. The enemy was well dug in and supported by a battery of artillery. These were men of Brigadier General James Dearing's[5] small brigade of cavalry, whom Kautz had met on June 9. Deeming the charging of such works the work of infantry, Kautz requested General Hincks to deal with the enemy line and moved on. XVIII Corps were in position to assault the Rebel lines by early afternoon. Smith then halted, reconnoitered the Rebel lines, and adjusted and readjusted his forces preparatory to an assault. In a message to General Butler at 1:30 P.M., he complained, "The fight at Baylor's house broke up my arrangements, so that I have not been able to straighten my line; but this, however, will be done at once."[6]

The Confederate defenders were arrayed in a ten-mile line of entrenchments about two to three miles from the city, extending from the Appomattox River below the town to the Appomattox above the town. At regular intervals along the line were small fortifications called lunettes sufficient to hold artillery. These were numbered from one to about fifty from east to west. Beauregard had his forces evenly distributed along the eastern half of the line from Lunette #1 near the river to #26 near the Jerusalem Plank Road. The entire line west of the Jerusalem Plank Road was unmanned.

Kautz marched his division in a southwesterly direction. Upon reaching the line of the Norfolk & Petersburg Railroad, he moved north along the railroad to the enemy's entrenchments, arriving between noon and 1 P.M.

Beauregard, thinking that Kautz's approaching cavalrymen represented the main thrust of the Federal offensive, pulled two whole regiments from other parts of his line to support the meager forces deployed there. There were already at least five artillery pieces present in the lunettes which commanded the approaches along the rail line, so Beauregard was confident that he would be able to hold off a strong assault.

Beauregard had learned from spies and captured Yankees as early as June 13 that Smith's Corps and at least a portion of Major General Winfield Scott Hancock's II Corps were arriving at Bermuda Hundred and City Point.[7] He wired General Lee repeatedly to rush reinforcements to Petersburg. Lee, thinking that Beauregard was mistaken, didn't even bother to answer. Beauregard's position was not one to be envied. He had stripped the left of his line in order to meet Kautz's small division, while, entirely unknown to him, Smith's entire XVIII Corp was poised to strike and another corps, Hancock's II Corps, was moving up to support Smith.

The Third New York Regiment, which had marched at the head of Kautz's column from City Point, drove in the pickets in front of the Rebel works near the railroad. Kautz then ordered his artillery, only two guns from Captain George B. Easterly's Fourth Wisconsin Light Artillery Battery, to unlimber and open on the enemy works.

Kautz's official report describes the afternoon's work well enough:

> Several hours were occupied in reconnoitering the enemy's works and bringing up the column. Several miles of intrenchments were in view, the ground in front was comparatively level and afforded little or no cover from the enemy's artillery to approach the works. The enemy opened with artillery from five redoubts as soon as we appeared in view, and subsequently two more redoubts were developed on our extreme right. The works were not strongly manned with infantry, and I decided to make a demonstration, and, if possible, to get through the line. About 3 o'clock all the carbineers were brought forward, except the First New York Mounted Rifles, which were held in reserve, the First Brigade on the right and the Second on the left. A general advance was ordered and the skirmishers pushed forward to within 500 yards of the intrenchments. As only a portion of the men are armed with carbines, and so many men are required to take care of the horses, our line was really weaker than the enemy's in men, and the skirmishers could not be advanced any farther. We held on until about 5:30 P.M., hoping to see more indications that General Smith had carried the enemy's line on our right, but for several hours no firing had been heard in that direction, the skirmishers were getting short of ammunition, and on the right they were already falling back. I, therefore, ordered the left to retire also, as I had observed indications that the enemy were re-enforcing in that direction. My impression proved correct, as Colonel Spear reported that he could not have held his position any longer. I withdrew my entire command to the Jordan Point Road and bivouacked. It was a fatiguing day's work, and the men having had no rest the night before, preparing for the march and fighting and skirmishing all morning, they were in no condition to assault intrenchments, even if they had been the proper arm for such service. I had but two pieces of artillery, which were served to the extent of their capacity in drawing the enemy's artillery fire, but were entirely inadequate to the artillery of the enemy, which at one time amounted to twelve pieces.
>
> Our loss was small, as the enemy's artillery was very badly served. Had it been well served we never could have made the advance we did. I regret to announce the loss of Colonel Mix.... He was left mortally wounded in front of the enemy's works on our right.[8]

Kautz didn't mention in his report that, on the way back to Jordan Point Road, his division met Major General David Birney's Third Division of II Corps. Birney's Division was attempting to move up to support Smith, but were hampered in their effort by conflicting orders. Kautz gave Birney directions to the Norfolk Road and, according to Birney, "reported the enemy in great force and that he had been 'hanging all day by the eyelids.'"[9]

Meanwhile, the entire XVIII Corps stood off from the eastern defenses of Petersburg all afternoon. It was not until 7 P.M. that Smith finally ordered an all-out assault. Within an hour, nine of the lunettes were occupied and fifteen guns and more than 300 prisoners were captured.

Had Smith pressed on, his entire corps might have walked into town unopposed. Instead he halted. As he put it, "It is impossible for me to go farther tonight, but, unless I misapprehend the topography, I hold the key to Petersburg."[10] He apparently failed to turn the key.

Smith's actions on June 15 have never been adequately explained. General Grant, in his official report, said, "General Smith got off as directed, and confronted the enemy's pickets near Petersburg before daylight ... but, for some reason that I have never been able to satisfactorily understand, did not get ready to assault his main lines until near sundown.... Between the line thus captured and Petersburg there were no other works.... The night was clear, the moon shining brightly, and favorable to further operations."[11]

Beauregard had difficulty explaining Smith's inaction as well: "Strange to say, General Smith contented himself with breaking into our lines, and attempting nothing further that night. All the more strange was this inaction on his part, since General Hancock ... was actually there ... on the evening of the 15th."[12]

Interestingly, one of the last orders which Smith sent to Hincks prior to his final order to attack at 7 P.M. concluded, "Should General Kautz by any chance get into the town, you will take every precaution not to fire into him as he sweeps down the enemy's lines."[13] By this time Kautz and his division were well on their way to their bivouac on the Jordan Point Road.

The following day, Kautz's cavalry picketed the left of the Federal forces as Major General Ambrose Burnside's IX Corps and Major General Gouverneur Warren's V Corps moved up to join Smith and Hancock. Early in the day, Kautz suggested to Warren (and Grant so ordered at 10:15 A.M.[14]) that V Corps take a position on the Jerusalem Plank Road where the Confederate lines were thought by Kautz to be weakest. Lieutenant Colonel Cyrus Comstock, an engineer on Grant's staff, however, countermanded the order. Comstock said that Grant would not have sent the order if he knew that, in so doing, Warren would be separated from the rest of the army by a swamp and a "considerable interval." He sent Warren to the vicinity of the Norfolk & Petersburg Railroad instead, where Kautz had been the day before.[15]

As the huge Army of the Potomac continued to pour down across the James, Beauregard was able to get some meager reinforcements also. Major General Robert Hoke's depleted division arrived from the vicinity of Drewry's Bluff after dark on June 15. Early on the sixteenth, Beauregard, faced with the decision of defending either Petersburg or the Bermuda Hundred line, but not both, chose Petersburg. He pulled Bushrod Johnson's entire division from Bermuda Hundred at dawn, leaving nearly empty trenches to face the Union X Corps, commanded by Alfred Terry, who had replaced Gillmore. Between them, the men of Hoke's and Johnson's commands constructed a new line of defenses about half a mile to the rear of those which were lost on June 15. The Union forces at Petersburg on June 16 numbered about 53,000 and were opposed by but 10,000 Rebels.[16] If Lee didn't come to their aid, they could not hold out much longer.

Meanwhile General Terry at Bermuda Hundred discovered the lack of an enemy at his front and moved forward unopposed to Port Walthall Junction on the Richmond & Petersburg Railroad, destroying two or three miles of track and all the public buildings. Butler, feeling the need for a force of cavalry to screen Terry's forward movement, sent an urgent message to Kautz: "You will, immediately upon receipt of this order, move with your command to the old lines, leaving one regiment with General Smith. Your cavalry are of the utmost importance on this line."[17]

Butler's order passed through General Meade's headquarters and, at 5:45 P.M., Meade added the following endorsement: "I have read the within order, and under the instructions of Lieutenant-General Grant have suspended the order until after dark, or the arrival of the Fifth Corps, as General Kautz's cavalry is required in the position assigned him by General Grant, to protect the left flank of this army until more infantry arrives." At 9:30 P.M., Meade sent a message to Kautz, "As General Warren has arrived, I no longer desire to suspend the order you received from General Butler, and you can obey it, if you think proper."[18]

So Kautz was free to go to Butler's aid, but it was too late. The first of Lee's Army of Northern Virginia were finally coming through Richmond on their way to Petersburg. Lieutenant General James Longstreet's Corps (probably men of George Pickett's Division) had arrived on the flank of Terry's men at Port Walthall Junction early in the afternoon and drove them back to the Bermuda Hundred lines. Terry had at least delayed the arrival of Lee's army at Petersburg for twelve and, perhaps, as much as twenty-four hours.

Kautz's Cavalry Division returned to Bermuda Hundred some time after 3 A.M. on June 17 and moved into the trenches. Major General Horatio Wright's VI Corps, the last of the Army of the Potomac to arrive from north of Richmond, was also sent to Bermuda Hundred with two divisions of his corps. On June 17, Terry's X Corps, supported by Wright's VI Corps, made a disorganized attempt to break out of the Bermuda Hundred "corked bottle," but were unsuccessful. There is no indication that Kautz's Cavalry were asked to take part. In fact, Kautz slept through most of the morning and spent the afternoon looking for a suitable camp for his tired command.

Back on the south side of the Appomattox River, Hancock's Corps assaulted the Confederate entrenchments to the east of Petersburg late in the afternoon of June 16 with capture of several more of the lunettes, but was not able to advance farther. For the next three days, the Army of the Potomac and Smith's Corps of the Army of the James continued to pound up against the Petersburg defenses, but were repulsed by Lee's Army of Northern Virginia, which had arrived in its entirety by the 19th.

The siege of Petersburg had begun.

25. The Wilson-Kautz Raid

After the of Army of the Potomac's failure at Petersburg, Ulysses Grant determined to block the railroad lines leading into Richmond from the south, hoping to force Robert E. Lee to abandon Richmond and move into open country. Grant set in motion a plan for Major General George Meade to move against the Petersburg & Weldon Railroad at Reams' Station on June 23. If the move were successful, it would leave only the Richmond & Danville Railroad and the connecting Southside Railroad still open. Grant decided to send a cavalry raid toward those railroads to cut them temporarily at least.

Grant ordered Meade to use James H. Wilson's Third Division of Philip Sheridan's Cavalry Corps for the raid. Wilson asked that a portion of Kautz's Division accompany his division on the raid. Since this would be the first time that Grant's former staffer was to operate independently, Grant thought it would be helpful if the experienced Kautz went along. Grant asked Benjamin Butler for the use of a portion of Kautz's Division to join Wilson's movement. Butler, in an uncharacteristically generous gesture, offered Kautz's entire division. On June 20, he ordered Kautz to report to Wilson near Petersburg.[1]

Since June 16, Wilson's Division, seven regiments divided into two brigades under Colonels John B. McIntosh and George H. Chapman, had been in camp near Prince George Court House.

One of the regiments of McIntosh's Brigade was Kautz's old Second Ohio Cavalry. After completing their three-year enlistments in the western theater in the spring, most of the regiment had reenlisted and was assigned to Wilson's Division. Not comfortable with the more rigid adherence to army protocols in their new surroundings, the men were also not happy with their new division commander. Wilson had issued a number of unpopular orders which, if not well accepted by his men, had the effect of improving the division's organization, appearance and performance.

June 20 was another busy day of preparation, especially for the First D.C. "At four o'clock in the afternoon of the twentieth, an order was received to be ready to march at an hour's notice. At nine o'clock the horse equipments arrived from Washington ... and so unacquainted were the men with horse gear, that many of them were unable to adjust the various parts ... and yet, three hours later, they started on the celebrated Wilson's raid."[2]

Late in the afternoon, Kautz's Division crossed the Appomattox and bivouacked at Mount Sinai Church near Prince George Court House. The men of the Second Ohio were happy to see their old colonel. Understandably, Kautz was pleased to see them as well and to renew old acquaintances. The following night, he wrote, "I visited with the 2nd Ohio and took dinner with the officers."[3]

Wilson received his final orders from Meade on June 21 and discussed the plan with Kautz. The ambitious Wilson had reservations. He feared that failure in this, his first independent command, might destroy his reputation and slow the meteoric rise of his career. He voiced concern about the location of Major General Wade Hampton's Cavalry Division and, wanting to

August Kautz (1864). From August Kautz's photograph album, courtesy Virginia (Kautz) Borkenhagen.

assure an escape route if difficulties should arise, asked Meade to be certain to occupy Reams' Station. He was somewhat relieved when told that Hampton was tied up fighting the other two divisions of Sheridan's Cavalry near White House. Meade, who himself was not enthusiastic about the raid, assured him that Reams' Station was to be attacked on June 23.

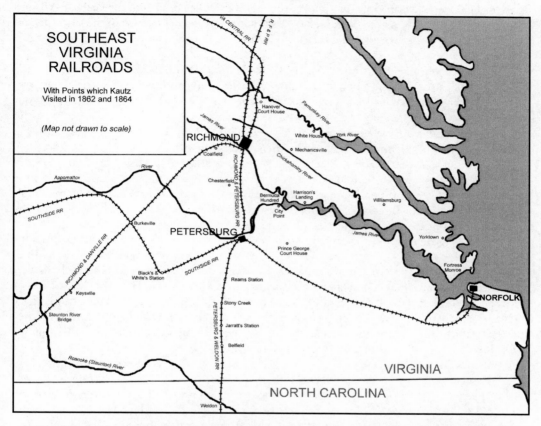

Rough map of southeast Virginia showing the railroads entering Petersburg and Richmond.

In a message to Grant on the morning of June 21, Meade wrote, "Wilson will be ordered to leave at 2 A.M. tomorrow.... Hampton being yesterday at White House will relieve Wilson of any apprehension of being disturbed, and I trust Sheridan will keep Hampton occupied." Later in the message, Meade added, "If Sheridan were here there would be no doubt, I think, of he and Wilson going to Lynchburg."[4]

The movement got under way at 2 A.M. on June 22. Kautz reported that he had 2414 officers and men of his division on the march. Wilson had about 3300. Despite Wilson's later opinion that Kautz's Division was "the wildest rag-tag and bob-tail cavalry I ever saw"[5] and "poorly organized,"[6] he appears to have had sufficient confidence in them at the time to allow them to take the lead on the march toward Burkeville.

Colonel Spear's Second Brigade arrived at Reams' Station by 7:30, drove in the few pickets there, tore up a few hundred feet of track and destroyed the depot and a train of thirteen freight cars.[7] Kautz learned from captured pickets "that two brigades of cavalry, under W.H.F. Lee, were stationed at the Six-Mile House guarding the railroad. In order to place this force in our rear, I directed the head of the column south, crossing the railroad to the Boynton pike, along which we marched for four or five miles, and then turning westward reached Dinwiddie

Court-House about noon."[8] After an hour's rest, Kautz's Division pushed on to the Southside Railroad at Sutherland's Station, then followed the railroad to Ford's Station, which was reached about 5:30 P.M.

Meanwhile, Rooney Lee had learned of the movement. Seeing that his small cavalry force of about 1500 was incapable of stopping Wilson and Kautz, Lee nipped at the heels of Wilson's Division, harassing him all day. Wilson had Chapman's Brigade, which was in the rear, turn on Lee. A brief fight occurred, allowing the rest of Wilson's column to continue on in the wake of Kautz's Division.

The last of Wilson's Division arrived at Ford's Station about 11 P.M. By that time, Kautz's troopers had destroyed the station, water tanks and wood piles and two trains with their locomotives. Spear's report says that the trains were composed of "eighteen platform and other cars."[9] The work of destroying track continued past midnight.

At 2 A.M. (the 23rd), Wilson sent Kautz's Division on to Burkeville, where the Southside Railroad crossed the Richmond & Danville line. With Spear's Brigade again in the lead, they passed through Wilson's Station, Black's and White's Station and Nottoway Court House, destroying rail cars and track as they went. They reached Burkeville at 3 P.M. The last time Kautz's men had been in the neighborhood, it had rained incessantly. This time, there hadn't been a drop of rain for three weeks and it was extremely hot, making the heavy labor of tearing up and burning ties and bending track over the fires almost unbearable. At Burkeville, Kautz sent Spear's Brigade north in the direction of Richmond and Robert M. West's Brigade[10] south toward Danville to destroy more track. Again they worked until midnight. The Richmond & Danville rail line was constructed of strap rails. Instead of having solid metal rails, each rail was composed of a strap of metal attached to the surface of a wooden rail. Here the destruction of the track could be accomplished by piling fence posts or other wood on either side of the track and setting them afire. The wooden portion of the rails was consumed along with the crossties and the heat of the fire bent and warped the metal "strap." About five miles of the Richmond and Danville was destroyed in each direction.

Wilson's Division had left Ford's Station shortly after Kautz's. At Black's and White's Station, Wilson took the wrong road and was forced to retrace his steps. The time thus lost allowed Rooney Lee to interpose his division between those of Wilson and Kautz. Chapman's Brigade ran into Lee near Nottoway Court House. In the extreme heat of the afternoon, Lee and Chapman fought a battle which lasted almost until dark. Equally matched, neither side was able to gain an advantage. Thus delayed even further, Wilson withdrew and, after conferring with Kautz by messenger, decided to bypass Lee. After bivouacking on the night of the 23rd near Black's and White's, he marched his division via Hungarytown to Meherrin Station on the Richmond & Danville Railroad about twelve miles south of Burkeville.

Once united, the two divisions spent the entire hot day of the 24th completing the total destruction of the railroad between Burkeville and Keysville, where they bivouacked at midnight.

The united commands got started at first light on the 25th. Again Spear's Brigade was in the lead. By afternoon, both men and horses were giving out in the blistering heat. Destroying track as they went, the two divisions made slow progress through Drake's Branch Station, Mossing Ford and Carrington Station. As horses failed, parties were sent out in an attempt to "recruit" new mounts from the countryside, previously untouched by the war. Near Mossing Ford, West's Brigade burned a large steam sawmill and two smaller mills, thought to be the only local source of replacement crossties.

Spear's Second Brigade reached Roanoke Station about 5 P.M. Just beyond the station, the railroad crossed the Staunton River on a long, covered, wooden trestle. As Spear's advance approached the bridge, they were met by rifle fire from skirmishers and artillery fire from across the bridge.

A quick reconnaissance by Kautz and Spear showed that the approach to the bridge was across a half-mile-wide wheat field which provided no cover except a wide ditch which ran parallel to the river about 150 yards from the bridge. The Confederate defenders occupied a row of well-concealed rifle pits on the near side of the bridge. Beyond the river, the ground rose sharply to a low ridge. Another row of rifle pits could be seen at the base of the ridge, and nearer the summit were two small fortifications occupied by artillery. What Kautz and Spear saw was a 938-man contingent supported by six artillery pieces under the command of Captain Benjamin Farinholt, formerly of the 53rd Virginia Infantry. Farinholt had 296 regular reserves posted in the rifle pits on the near side of the bridge. The remainder of his force was made up of Home Guards from the surrounding counties, all on the far side.

Kautz advised Wilson that he felt an assault impracticable. Wilson, however, feared that his reputation would suffer if he failed to at least make a try. According to his official report, "The day was very hot, and the approach to the head of the bridge through a bottom field of growing grain. I posted the batteries on the hill, nearly three-quarters of a mile from the bridge, and directed General Kautz to dismount his division and endeavor to push close enough to the end of the bridge to set fire to it. After a most gallant and exhausting effort he was compelled to give up the task. Many of the men fainted from exhaustion, thirst, and heat. They had been hard at work from daybreak in the heat of the sun, made more hot from the burning railroads and buildings, and were in no condition to overcome the natural defenses of the bridge, under a heavy fire of artillery and musketry."[11]

Kautz's report was a bit more specific: "General Wilson directed me to make the attempt to burn the bridge. About 6 P.M. the First Brigade advanced on the right of the embankment leading toward the bridge, and the Second Brigade on the left. The attack was maintained for two or three hours, but failed, with the loss of about 60 killed and wounded, among them a large proportion of officers.... Our forces had to advance on a double bottom land, commanded at every point by the enemy, and no shelter for the men. The heat was intense, a number of officers and men fell from sunstroke; the burning of the bridge was, therefore, reluctantly abandoned."[12]

The reports of Kautz's brigade commanders give us even a bit more detail. According to Colonel Robert West of the First Brigade,

> I was ordered to dismount my brigade and advance on the right of the bridge; I was also ordered to have a detail provided with light combustible material, to be carried along, with which to fire the bridge.... Our advance was not opposed, except by artillery fire, for some distance, nor until we were within musket-range of the bridge, where a sharp fire was opened upon us, both from the bridge and from the opposite side of the stream. As the Second Brigade advanced on the opposite side of the railroad, and as soon as artillerists got the range of the bridge, the enemy at the end of the bridge nearest us grew very unsteady, and I thought a direct and rapid charge down the railroad would frighten them away. This I tried with two companies of the Third New York, but found the fire of artillery and musketry so well directed ... that I was forced to come down and join the main body on the flat below. We worked our way, skirmishing to within about 200 yards of the main bridge, where we came to a small bridge, underneath which the lines of the two brigades (First and Second) became united. Under cover of this bridge I formed an assaulting party and directed it up the embankment, in the hope that by a quick move we might obtain possession of the main bridge sufficiently long to fire it. The men tried repeatedly to gain a foothold on the railroad, and to advance along the side of the embankment, but could not. The height of the railroad embankment enabled the enemy from their position down by the water's edge, across the stream, to sweep the sides and track with a terrible fire while they were in a position of complete security.[13]

Chaplain Samuel H. Merrill of the First D.C. of Spear's Brigade, speaking of his own regiment, was able to summarize the major problem facing all of Kautz's men: "The regiment did but little actual fighting here, for the simple reason that they could not get at the enemy."[14]

By this time, Rooney Lee's cavalry had arrived on the scene. Lee made contact with Chapman's Brigade, which was acting as rear guard, skirmished for a while, then retired soon after dark.

Wilson finally realized what Kautz had known from the start. In his report, he states, "Having convinced myself by personal inspection of the great difficulty and loss we should necessarily experience in again endeavoring to carry the bridge, I determined to withdraw to the eastward and march back to the James River."[15]

In retrospect, it is easy to see that the attempt on the Staunton River bridge should not have been made. Wilson, already unpopular with the enlisted men who served under him, was condemned for the loss of life in what they considered a useless adventure. Roger Hannaford of the Second Ohio felt that "any general of good judgement would never ... have ordered the second attack; many a brave man's life was uselessly lost here, and our ambulances and wagons crowded with wounded, all of whom were afterward abandoned to the enemy."[16]

If Wilson felt any remorse, it did not appear in his report. "Having thus completed the work assigned me, under cover of the night I withdrew my command to Wylliesburg and halted about daylight, fed, and rested."[17]

The next morning, Captain Farinholt, the hero of what the Confederacy dubbed "the Battle of Old Men and Young Boys," advanced his skirmishers a half mile and "discovered that the enemy had left quite a number of their dead on the field. In this advance 8 prisoners were captured.... Of the dead left on the field I buried 42, among them several officers. My loss, 10 killed and 24 wounded."[18]

The return march began before midnight of the 25th with Wilson's Division in the lead. The weather grew even warmer and great clouds of dust marked the progress of the column as it passed through Christiansburg late on the afternoon of the 26th. George Purington noted "the thermometer standing at 105° Fahrenheit in the shade at 2:30 P.M."[19] The war had not previously come to this part of Virginia and, as horses gave out in the extreme heat, foraging parties were able to find replacements for some in barns and stables along the route. A large body of runaway slaves began to follow in the wake of Spear's Brigade. Wilson halted the column about 1 P.M. and they were again on the road early enough on the 27th that the last of Spear's troopers were across the Meherrin River on Saffolds's Bridge by 8:45.

Hannaford wrote in his diary that "the heat was so terrible that we had to move very slowly, yet fast enough to keep out of the way of the enemy.... If it had not been that we were continually capturing horses fully half the command would have been dismounted; as it was a number were now footing it." Hannaford added, "The slaves began gathering ... in droves, men, women & children; many of them had appropriated horses and wagons; some few had carriages, some carts, &c., in which they had their families.... The Negro Brigade [was] swollen to about 1200 and hourly increasing."[20]

Having crossed the Meherrin River, Wilson was faced with an important decision. Should he proceed in an easterly direction and arrive well to the rear of the Union army or turn north to Reams' Station, which he had been assured would be occupied by Federal forces? The first, and longer, route would take him well away from contact with any sizeable number of Confederates. The latter carried the probability of once again coming into contact with Lee's cavalry or, perhaps, other Rebel units. Kautz advised the more southerly route. Wilson, with his command tiring rapidly and seemingly confident that he could handle Lee's small division, chose the latter route.

A severe thunderstorm broke on the night of the 27th, providing some relief from the extreme heat. This was possibly the first rain that had fallen in southside Virginia since Kautz's men were in the neighborhood in mid–May. Following the main road which crosses the Petersburg & Weldon Railroad just north of Jarratt's Station, Wilson's lead division reached the road bridge across the Nottoway River about 2 P.M., then halted for two hours while the wagons, ambulances, artillery, Negroes and, finally the rear guard (Spear's Brigade) were across. From there, Wilson anticipated overcoming the small detachment of Lee's cavalry reported to be defending the bridge at Stony Creek, then march all night to Prince George Court House and safety.

As Wilson had anticipated, McIntosh's advance guard ran into pickets just before reaching Stony Creek Station. Unanticipated, however, was the large force of cavalry which attacked and drove McIntosh's advance back into Wilson's main column. Wilson ordered McIntosh's Brigade to dismount and counterattack. They did so with "great spirit," driving the Rebels back to a line of poorly constructed breastworks near Sappony Church. Wilson learned that he was facing not only Lee's small cavalry division, but also the larger division of Wade Hampton, which he had been told was well north of Richmond.

Wilson attempted to break through the Confederate line in a series of assaults using one regiment at a time. All were repulsed by Brigadier General John R. Chambliss's Brigade of Lee's Division.

By the time Kautz's Division arrived on the scene it was well past dark, but the firing had not yet died down.

Wilson determined to move around the right flank of the enemy and march to Reams' Station, which he believed was being held by General Meade's Army of the Potomac. Meade had, indeed, attempted to occupy Reams' Station. As part of General Grant's effort to block the rail line, Meade had sent the II Corps and VI Corps toward Reams' Station on June 23. They had gotten as far as the Jerusalem Plank Road before being outmaneuvered and defeated by Confederate Lieutenant General A.P. Hill's Corps.

Kautz felt it would be safer to backtrack to Jarratt's Station and head east toward the rear of the Union army. Hannaford recorded a rumor which passed among the men of his brigade that Kautz urged Wilson "to destroy our wagon trains, spike the guns, take only ambulances enough to convey ... wounded and then he offered to safely lead the column in the hours of darkness to the east of the R. R., but ... General Wilson would not [listen].... Whether these rumors were true or not I cannot say, but they were extensively circulated among the men and generally rec'd as Gospel truth, heightening the men's admiration of Kautz and their dislike of ... Wilson."[21]

Wilson ordered Chapman to dismount his brigade to support McIntosh while Kautz moved north toward Reams' Station on the Stage Road, which parallels the railroad. Kautz's movement began shortly after midnight with Spear's Second Brigade in the lead. Three companies of the Third New York were detailed to guard the bridge over Stony Creek until the trains were safely across.

Spear's Brigade turned off the Stage Road onto a side road leading toward Ream's Station at about 6 A.M. of the 29th. When the Eleventh Pennsylvania advanced to within a half-mile of the station, they were fired upon by artillery and driven back. Spear dismounted his two regiments and formed a line of skirmishers while the two batteries of artillery which accompanied him (Batteries A and K, First U.S. Artillery) unlimbered and began returning the enemy's fire. Just as Spear got his men in position they were attacked by a brigade of infantry. This was Brigadier General John Sanders' Brigade of Brigadier General William Mahone's Division, five regiments of well-rested, battle-hardened Alabamians.[22] Spear's men rose up, met the charge and drove the Alabamians back to the woods from which they had emerged, capturing about fifty of their number.

Spear's two regiments managed to hold their position until one of the Alabama regiments got around their left flank, forcing them to fall back about 500 yards to a position near the artillery. Spear said later in his report, "The command was so much exhausted that it was almost an impossibility to keep them from falling asleep while on the skirmish line."[23] At this point, Kautz ordered West's First Brigade to take a position to the right of Spear.

Captain Edward W. Whitaker of General Wilson's staff volunteered to ride the eight or ten miles east to General Meade's headquarters in order to plead for relief. Kautz assigned Lieutenant Ford's G Company of the Third New York as an escort for the captain. Whitaker managed to get through, arriving early in the afternoon, although half his escort were killed or wounded. Kautz said in his report, "Considering the enemy too strong to assault, there seemed no other course left except to intrench and hold onto our position until relieved by the Army of the Potomac. I accordingly ordered such defenses to be made as our means afforded."[24]

Meanwhile Wilson's Third Division had difficulty disengaging from Hampton's and Lee's Divisions at Stony Creek. Most of Chapman's dismounted troopers were separated from their horses. Chapman was able to ride away with only about 300 of his brigade. Many of the remainder were captured, although some were later able to rejoin the brigade. Wilson, with the first of his damaged division, arrived near Reams' Station about 9 A.M., although the last of Chapman's Brigade didn't get through until about noon. Lee and Hampton were in hot pursuit. Hannaford describes the Third Division's movement: "Evidences of a regular panic began to be noticeable.... The road was filled with stragglers.... Nearing Reams' the appearance became worse and worse.... The panic visibly increased among the disorganized mass, and the fright of many of the negroes was nearly painful to witness.... I plainly saw that the whole Division was disorganized, one great and principal cause being the want of confidence felt in our Commanding General.... The feeling against him was bitter in the extreme."[25]

Upon arrival at Reams' Station, Hannaford and the rest of McIntosh's Brigade was placed in line to the left of Spear's Brigade. Wilson considered the possibility of attempting to force his way through but, after conferring with McIntosh, saw it to be impossible. Wilson was surrounded on three sides and outnumbered almost two to one. His thoughts at that time show clearly in his report: "It was evident from the deliberate movements of the rebel infantry that they fully expected to capture my command. The situation was critical.... It was plain nothing but great celerity of motion could extricate the command."[26] Kautz quoted Wilson as having said that cavalry must fight or run away, and "about one o'clock he gave the order to retreat by the route we had come, directing me to follow him with my Division."[27]

The only route open to Wilson was in the direction from which he had come. Rather than moving straight south, however, he wisely ordered his command, with Chapman in the lead, to head west to the stage road, then turn south, thus bypassing Hampton's Division of cavalry. At the same time, he ordered the guns of the artillery spiked and the entire wagon train, except for the ambulances, burned. The wounded were to be left behind with the ambulances in the care of the surgeons. The retreating raiders would be traveling light.

Just as the movement was getting started and Kautz's Division was attempting to disengage from the enemy at his front, a brigade of the Confederate infantry, supported by Lee's cavalry, managed to get around the left of the Federals. They drove a small detachment of the Eleventh Pennsylvania in confusion through McIntosh's Brigade, splitting it in half. McIntosh's Second Ohio and Fifth New York Cavalry Regiments remained to the north with Kautz's Division while his First Connecticut and Second New York Regiments were able to fall in line behind Chapman's Brigade.

Now it was early afternoon and Wilson's raiders had essentially become two separate detachments with a strong Confederate force in between. On the north, closest to Reams' Station, was Kautz's Division supplemented by two regiments and several small fragments of McIntosh's Brigade. Moving in full retreat to the south and west was the remainder of Wilson's Division along with portions of Kautz's Eleventh Pennsylvania and some of Kautz's command which previously had been attached to the wagon train.[28]

Wilson moved as quickly as possible. Many of the men were on foot. All were exhausted from two days of hard fighting with no sleep and a week in the saddle. None had eaten in two days. Some few were wounded. Their horses, as badly off as the men on their backs, were staggering and falling, some not to rise again. Hampered at first by the press of escaping slaves, by stragglers trying to find their way to their units and by Confederate sharpshooters, they pushed on. It was about dark by the time they crossed Stony Creek. Having had no communication with Kautz and having heard heavy firing to his rear, Wilson assumed that Kautz's Division had either escaped or had been captured. In neither case could he be of any assistance to Kautz, so he continued south. He reached Jarratt's Station at dawn of June 30 and, turning east on the road which Kautz had suggested two days before, he did not stop to rest his command until they had crossed the Nottoway River at a ford near the destroyed Peter's Bridge.

It had been about 2 P.M. when Kautz received Wilson's order to bring up the rear in the retreat from Reams' Station. He passed the order along to his brigade commanders, Colonels West and Spear: "Prepare to cut loose from everything and save, if possible, the men and horses."[29] In an example of almost unbelievable understatement, Kautz's report says, "Finding that I could not get to the stage road, I immediately determined to turn the enemy's left flank and thus seek to reach our lines. This was done without opposition."[30]

According to the historian of the First D.C., "Gen. Kautz had marched but a short distance when he found himself in a triangle, two sides of which, including his rear and left front, were held by the enemy in overwhelming numbers. Extending along his right front was the railroad, running through a cut from ten to twelve feet in depth, and beyond that an extensive swamp, supposed to be impassable."[31]

At about 3 P.M., Colonel Spear received Kautz's order to "take the advance and cut my way through to the [Jerusalem] plank road, which was accomplished by taking a southeasterly course through an almost impenetrable woods and swamp, passing the enemy on either flank, enforcing a passage."[32]

Colonel West gives a little more detail in his report. He was ordered to bring up the rear behind Spear. "This I attempted to obey, but the artillery got between my brigade and Spear's, and I held back my men to let the artillery pass.[33] [We came] up to a swamp stream, after having passed through a pine timber.... The enemy held the stream not 200 yards to our right, and were advancing (not an imaginary enemy, but a real enemy) in force, in line of battle upon our rear."[34]

Colonel George Purington of McIntosh's Brigade said in his report that his Second Ohio Regiment, finding no way of rejoining Wilson's Division, "reported to General Kautz, finding him and his command under a terrible fire of shot and shell and falling back in disorder. He advised me to rely upon my own judgement and get out the best way I could."[35]

Roger Hannaford witnessed the meeting between Kautz and Purington and described the sequence of events which followed, "General Kautz took command.... The side on which the enemy had not attacked us was very swampy, and any person looking at it would judge it impossible for the cavalry to push themselves through such a tangled, swampy jungle. But it was our only chance.... As first we entered it, there sat our old Colonel, and not one of our regiment but felt infinitely better when they understood he was in command; he was sitting leg thrown over his horse's neck, and seemingly as cool as though the situation was perfectly agreeable. He had a pocket map of Virginia spread over his knee, while in his left hand he was holding a mariners compass, and was looking at the sun ... then ... he pointed out the course."[36]

Chaplain Samuel Merrill added, "Under the circumstances, almost any other man would have surrendered. Not so the indomitable Kautz. It was a wild and exciting scene to see those mounted men slide down the steep embankment to the railroad track, scramble up the opposite bank, dash down the next declivity into the stream, and wallow through mire and water, the horses in some instances rolling over and the men going under, amid the thunder of artillery, and with solid shot plunging, shells exploding, grape and cannister raining, and musket balls whistling around them, till they reached the opposite shore and disappeared in the swamp, which had been made passable by a drought of great severity."[37]

Kautz added in his report, "As we pursued no road, but marched by compass,[38] passing most of the way through timber and heavy undergrowth, the artillery could not be brought through. It was hauled off the field and finally abandoned in a swamp, where the carriages mired, and could not be extricated."[39] So close was the pursuit of the enemy that thirty-two of the seventy-two members of Lieutenant Michael Leahy's artillery battery were captured while attempting (successfully) to spike the guns.

Colonel Purington gives us some idea how narrow the escape was. He said, "It is my opinion that had we remained fifteen minutes longer in line the enemy would have so far carried out their plans for our capture that few, if any, of us would have succeeded in escaping."[40]

After they "disappeared" into the swamp, Kautz's Division was unable to get into any semblance of marching order until they had reached the Jerusalem Plank Road about 5:30 P.M. Here, they met the Union army's advance pickets. They were back within Union lines by 8:30 that evening. Within an hour, Kautz reported to General Meade, "My division, and a portion of General Wilson's division, has just arrived here. Our expedition was very successful until this afternoon, when we were surrounded and overpowered and had to abandon our transportation, wounded and prisoners. I escaped with my division by taking it through the woods and charging across the railroad. General Wilson has probably gone back to go around by way of Jarratt's Station. The fight occurred near Reams' Station on the Halifax Road."[41]

Meade already knew that Wilson was in trouble from the message delivered by Captain Whitaker. That afternoon he had sent an order to General Sheridan to come with his First and Second Divisions to Wilson's aid and also sent VI Corps west toward Reams' Station. By the time Sheridan's cavalry and the VI Corps infantry were able to respond, Wilson had already arrived within Union lines.

After its brief rest just beyond Peter's Bridge over the Nottoway, Wilson's command had taken to the road again and were back in Union lines by the afternoon of July 1.

Kautz's men, meanwhile, were up surprisingly early on the morning of June 30 and were on their way to their old position at Bermuda Hundred when Kautz received an order to join Sheridan in the relief of Wilson. Kautz begged off, however, saying in a message to General Grant, "My command is in no condition to do anything; the main cause of our rout was the worn-out condition of the men. Men and horses have had nothing to eat for forty-eight hours, and they are exhausted from loss of sleep. If Wilson cannot extricate himself we can do nothing more for him.... I hope the order will be rescinded."[42]

The following day, Kautz wrote in his journal, "In the afternoon I went over to City Point and reported to Liss Grant what we had done and what had been the cause of our route [sic] by the enemy."[43] As a result of the meeting with Grant, the order to march was, indeed, rescinded. When Wilson learned later that Kautz had chosen not to come to his relief, he was highly critical of Kautz.

Sheridan did eventually arrive at Reams' Station with his two divisions of cavalry. General Horatio Wright's VI Corps, also sent by Meade, had arrived even before Sheridan, but it was much too late, "Wilson having already disappeared, followed by the enemy."[44]

Although he was a lifelong friend of Kautz and was not particularly fond of Wilson, Sheridan was careful not to be overly critical of Wilson, stating that "the only criticism that can hold against him is that he placed too much reliance on meeting our infantry at Ream's Station.... He ought to have marched on the 28th by Jarrett's Station ... to the rear of the Army of the Potomac." Although Sheridan conceded that the destruction of railroads by Wilson's expedition had caused "serious embarrassment to the Confederate Government," he doubted that "this compensated for the artillery and prisoners that fell into the hands of the enemy."[45]

Public opinion in the North at the time was mixed. Many thought, as did Sheridan, that the mission was too costly of both men and equipment. Others, including General Grant, disagreed. Even a year later, Grant said, "The damage to the enemy in the expedition more than compensated for the losses we sustained."[46]

Even General Meade, who had been opposed to the raid at its onset, felt it to be a success. His report echoed Grant's, stating, "Although regretting the disaster at the termination of the expedition, the brilliant success of the operation and the heavy injuries inflicted on the enemy were deemed ample compensation for the losses we sustained."[47]

Assistant Secretary of War Charles A. Dana had arrived from Washington at Grant's headquarters on July 1. His reports to Secretary of War Stanton concerning the Wilson raid were generally positive. Also, in a message to President Lincoln on July 1, he said, "Grant thinks all the railroads are well broken up."[48] The opinions expressed by Grant and Dana were reported in the Northern press and, for a while, both Wilson and Kautz became minor heroes at a time when the nation seriously needed heroes.

The Southern press, as can be expected, carried little information about the destruction of military property, but was filled with reports, real or imagined, of atrocities committed by Wilson's raiders against private citizens. Dana's correspondence with Stanton gives us an idea of the Southern viewpoint. On July 4, he wrote, "The Richmond Examiner of Saturday claims that they have taken 500 prisoners from Wilson's command, including 250 wounded, 16 cannon, and between 500 and 700 negroes of all sizes and sexes.... Many of the Negroes were dressed in the finery of their masters and mistresses.[49] The captured soldiers were loaded, according to the Examiner, with stolen watches, silverware, and ladies' and children's clothing. That paper argues,

This 1866 print entitled "The Return of Kautz's Cavalry" appeared *in Harper's Pictorial History of the Civil War* (1868). It clearly portrays the condition of Kautz's troopers and of some of the slaves they liberated.

in a bitter article two columns long, that they ought not to be treated as prisoners of war, but as bandits and assassins."[50]

Casualty figures for the Confederates were negligible compared to those of the raiders. Kautz's report set the figures in his division at 29 killed, 78 wounded and 462 missing.[51]

The amount of damage done to the railroads in the raid is impressive. More than sixty miles of track and a large amount of rolling stock and other public property were destroyed. Although the resourceful Confederates were able to employ wagon trains to bypass the damaged track within a few days, it was three months before both lines were fully operational. According to one of Charles Dana's messages to Edwin Stanton, the *Petersburg Express* suggested "that the Yankee prisoners should be fed on bread and water only, rather than starve the Confederate soldiers and people in the two cities."[52]

Despite what others might have said, Kautz himself considered his part in the raid, especially his actions on June 29, the highlight of his Civil War career.

26. First Deep Bottom
and the Beefsteak Raid

After the fatigues of the last two weeks of June, Kautz's Cavalry Division enjoyed a month-long respite at a camp on a high bluff behind the Bermuda Hundred lines overlooking the James River. Kautz noted, "The Rebel papers still continue to abuse me ... which is the best evidence of the damage we have done."[1] As the number of Confederate deserters coming into Union lines increased, Kautz attributed it to the cavalry raids, saying, "The cutting of the Railroads caused the cutting down of rations to the troops in Richmond and Petersburg,"[2]

On July 3, he wrote, "In the afternoon, I visited General Butler's H.Q. where I had to sit for my photograph for Brady with Genl. Weitzel."[3] On July 16, Generals Sheridan, Gregg, Torbert, Merritt and Reno and Colonel Forsyth hopped a tugboat up the James to make a surprise visit to Kautz's tent. Kautz entertained them with the limited means at his command: "Claret punch was the best I could offer and it seemed to be appreciated for the party remained until after dark and went away in great good humor on the tug that brought them."[4]

If Kautz and his troopers were taking it easy that July, some of the men of General Ambrose Burnside's IX Corps were hard at work digging a mine under the Rebel lines near where "Baldy" Smith had spent the greater portion of June 15 reconnoitering. The mine was to be filled with explosives to blow a hole in the Rebel line sufficiently wide to allow the whole of Burnside's Corps to drive through to Petersburg. General Grant was skeptical, saying, "The advantages reaped from the work would be but small if it were exploded without any coöperative movement."[5] Accordingly, he ordered General Hancock's II Corps to cross north of the James to demonstrate against Richmond in hopes that enough Rebels could be drawn from the Petersburg defenses to ensure the success of the mine operation. General Sheridan, with the cavalry divisions of Gregg, Torbert and Kautz, was to move in support of Hancock, giving him a force of 24,000 men. If the opportunity presented itself, the cavalry were to move to the right of Hancock's infantry and attempt to destroy as much of the Virginia Central Railroad and its bridges as possible.

Hancock got started across the pontoon bridge at Jones Neck on July 26, but his corps moved so slowly that it was noon on the 27th before the last of Kautz's Division, which was bringing up the rear, got across. Kautz was disappointed by the slowness of the movement, noting on the night of July 27, "We camped on the plain of Curl's Neck in sight of the camp I had been occupying for a month."[6]

Actually, Hancock's Corps had gotten a good start on July 27. His initial advance along the New Market Road captured a four-gun battery of heavy artillery and hundreds of prisoners, but he failed to follow up on the advantage thus gained. He then sent Torbert's and Gregg's Divisions to the right to Darbytown Road hoping to move around the Confederate flank, but the cavalry found the Rebel lines extended much farther in that direction than had been supposed and nothing more was done. The following day, Gregg and Torbert moved around to the right again, but they were repulsed by four infantry brigades. Skirmishing continued through most of the day between Hancock's men and Rebel reinforcements sent, as hoped, from Petersburg.

Having succeeded in drawing large numbers of reinforcements from Petersburg, Hancock began to withdraw during the night of July 28 so as to be in position to take part in the Federal offensive which was to commence after the explosion of the mine on July 30. Late on July 29, Kautz's men, who were serving as rear guard, skirmished briefly with pursuing Rebels near Malvern Hill, losing two men wounded, before crossing the bridge. Kautz arrived back at his camp at Bermuda Hundred at 6 A.M. on July 30, about an hour after the explosion of the Petersburg mine.

Owing to a number of monumental blunders and miscalculations, Burnside's mine offensive, known today as the Battle of the Crater, was a total disaster for the Federal forces engaged. In his writings, Kautz did not have time to dwell upon it (nor do we), as he had other things to do.

On the day that the Petersburg mine exploded, Phil Sheridan was ordered with his First and Third Divisions to the Shenandoah Valley, where Confederate General Jubal Early was moving up the valley and threatening Washington. This left only David Gregg's Second Division to picket the rear of the Army of the Potomac and Kautz's Division was ordered across the Appomattox to assist Gregg. Kautz's Division was to remain on assignment with the Army of the Potomac until ordered otherwise. This left General Butler with no cavalry. He was furious. Butler was mollified, however, when he was told that the arrangement would be temporary.

Kautz wasn't happy either, but for different reasons. He felt that the major function of cavalry was to operate on the offensive when a quick thrust was required. Picket duty should be left to infantry. "This misuse of the Cavalry," he wrote, "was the practice in the Army of the Potomac and resulted in a great expense to the government without corresponding benefit."[7] In addition, he was convinced that his undermanned division was too small to perform the job well. His effective mounted force had been reduced to about half its nominal strength over the previous three months, the major problem being a lack of serviceable horses. His "dismounted camp" behind the Bermuda Hundred lines now held 1000 troopers waiting to be supplied with mounts.[8]

At first, Kautz placed two regiments on picket to attempt to cover the fifteen miles assigned to him. His other two regiments were kept in reserve and the regiments were rotated daily. On August 12, however, Gregg's Division was called away to support Hancock's II Corps and X Corps (now commanded by Major General David B. Birney) in a move north of the Appomattox, known as the Second Battle of Deep Bottom, another attempt to cut the Virginia Central Railroad. Next, Gregg's Division and portions of Kautz's were ordered to offer support to two minimally successful corps-sized attempts to occupy the Petersburg & Weldon Railroad.

Through this period of activity on the flanks of the army, Kautz was left to protect the thirty-mile-wide rear with four, then two and, finally, one understaffed regiment. Because he had marched his division through the area repeatedly, he knew that it would be impossible for his small force to do so alone. In a series of messages on August 13 and 14 to General Meade's Chief of Staff, Major-General Andrew A. Humphreys, Kautz made certain that Meade knew it as well. He warned which portions of the picket line were most vulnerable and specifically mentioned that the army's huge beef herd was grazing in an exposed position and should be moved to a safer location nearer City Point.[9]

Humphreys' reply on August 16 may have lessened Kautz's anxiety: "The commanding general [Meade] ... has requested Lieutenant-General Grant to have the cattle herd drawn in nearer to City Point. You must make the best disposition you can of your force, keeping it as much concentrated as possible.... The enemy have but one division of cavalry on this side of the Appomattox."[10] On August 26, Kautz was relieved even further when Gregg's Division returned to picket the army's rear from Reams' Station to the Jerusalem Plank Road, leaving Kautz, with his command now intact, to cover the line from the plank road to the James River.

By August 28, Kautz wrote in his journal, "Active operations seem suddenly to have been suspended again."[11] These words reflect a feeling which was growing throughout Grant's army that the war was not going well. A great loss of life had occurred in recent months with so little gained. In addition Kautz, himself, was troubled by the limited role he was being called upon to play in his present assignment. He later wrote, "I looked upon the month of August, 1864 as the darkest period of the war, and remember the despondency of many officers about this time."[12]

Kautz had little time to dwell on his own despondency. On August 1, he was ordered, along with Gregg, to march west in support of G.K. Warren's Corps to see what could be done to block the wagon traffic between Stony Creek Station and Petersburg. Kautz was skeptical of the success of the mission, writing, "They never consult those interested as to how such expeditions are to be executed."[13]

The expedition moved out the next day with one of Gregg's brigades in the lead. As Kautz described it: "As I anticipated, we went over in great force to Warren's camp and stood there all day as a brigade dashed out and found the [Jerusalem] Plank Road fortified and defended. As they did not wish to bring on a fight outside of the trenches, they had to come back again without doing anything. In the evening we marched back again to camp."[14] Some of the force which was met on the Plank Road were from Wade Hampton's Cavalry Division, which had recently returned from north of Richmond. Kautz would soon hear more from Hampton.

The following day, Kautz learned that one of his regiments, the First District of Columbia Cavalry, was ordered disbanded by the War Department and the men transferred to the First Maine Cavalry, a regiment in Gregg's Division. As Kautz said in a message to Gregg, "There is great dissatisfaction in the regiment.... It virtually breaks up and destroys one of the most efficient regiments in the service. They are much discouraged by the order, as they have heretofore felt great pride in their regiment on account of being armed with a peculiar and effective weapon."[15] This was another blow to Kautz's ego as it would bring the strength of his division down to three undermanned regiments, hardly a decent sized brigade. He wrote, "I rode down to City Point this afternoon to get the order suspended. I met Genl. Grant and staid to dinner. He cannot rescind the order but directed me to make a statement in writing."[16]

If there was despondency within the Union army, that emotion pervaded the camps of the Confederates to an even greater extent. A shortage of horses was but one of many problems. They were almost surrounded, their communication lines were under attack, supplies of weapons, ammunition and clothing were limited and the food supply was so endangered that the men were on reduced rations. The Weldon Railroad was functioning at a fraction of its usual capacity. The Virginia Central was still connected to the Shenandoah Valley, often called the "Breadbasket of the Confederacy," but thanks to Phil Sheridan, the fertile valley was rapidly coming under Federal control.

In this setting, Confederate Major General Wade Hampton approached Lee with a plan to capture the Federal beef herd, which was again in an exposed position east of Sycamore Church. Lee assented.

Hampton started on September 11 with the 2000-man division of Rooney Lee and the smaller divisions of Brigadier Generals James Dearing and Thomas Rosser. In all he had 4500 cavalrymen, supplemented by a battery of artillery, a band of certified Texas cowboys and some sheep dogs to aid in the herding. They moved south from Petersburg, then east, staying far from Federal forces. They then turned north, crossing the Blackwater River at Cook's Bridge late on September 15.

At 5 A.M. on September 16, Hampton sent his three brigades against Kautz's pickets by three different roads. Lee's Brigade struck a portion of the line held by the Eleventh Pennsylvania and drove them northwest to Prince George Court House, where the Third New York was encamped. Colonel Ferris Jacobs of the Third New York responded quickly and he was able to push Lee back. Lee, however, was not interested in bringing on a fight. He only wished to hold on long enough for Rosser and Dearing to complete their work. When Rosser's and Dearing's Brigades struck the portion of the picket line held by the First D.C. at 5 A.M., they swept along the line, capturing more than 200 members of the regiment, most of its officers and all the regiment's records. While Lee held off Jacobs, Dearing and Rosser rounded up the cattle and, by eight o'clock, were driving them off in the direction of the Blackwater River.

After wiring Brigadier General Henry Davies, who was temporarily in command of Gregg's Division, for his aid, Kautz got the Third New York and part of the Eleventh Pennsylvania, about 700 men, mounted and on Hampton's trail shortly after 10 A.M. The advance of Kautz's small force made contact with Hampton's rear near the Jerusalem Plank Road shortly after dark and exchanged a few shots. Outnumbered almost ten to one, Kautz fell back and waited for morning. Kautz had been hopeful that General Davies would be able to move south on the Jerusalem Plank Road in time to head Hampton off. Davies had, indeed, moved down the plank road with about 2000 men and met Rosser's pickets. Realizing that he was outnumbered, he also withdrew.

In the morning Hampton was gone.

Hampton's raid, now known as the "Beefsteak Raid," was one of the most effective cavalry raids of the Civil War. At a cost of sixty-one men killed, wounded or captured, he liberated 2486 beef cattle from Union captivity, enough to provide about twenty pounds of beef to every man in the Army of Northern Virginia. Kautz's loss was four men killed, four wounded and 214 missing, almost all from the First D.C. In addition to improving their diet, the success of the raid provided a much-needed morale boost to the men in gray. Both armies were able to see some humor in the affair. Later, when asked by a reporter when he would push Lee out of Petersburg, General Grant replied, "Never if our armies continue to supply him with beef cattle."

Although officially exonerated from any blame in the affair, Kautz could see that he was the butt of much of the humor. In a long message to General Gregg's headquarters on September 19, he once again described in detail the inadequacies of his picket line and the difficulty of holding such a line with cavalry rather than infantry. He finished with, "I do not submit these suggestions in a spirit of complaint ... but I consider it my duty to represent my command as it is, in order to relieve myself from the responsibility of any consequences that may result from conditions that may possibly not be altogether unavoidable."[17] It seems Kautz was excusing himself in advance for any future incursions on his line.

Although Kautz made no note of it, he derived one benefit from Hampton's raid. The loss of all of the records of the First District of Columbia Cavalry delayed the transfer of the men of the regiment to the First Maine. Kautz would have the use of the regiment for a little while longer. He was careful to note, however, that on September 20, he was finally reinforced by a small brigade of infantry.

In the days following Hampton's raid, Kautz suffered another flare-up of malaria, but he was bothered even more by the fact that he was not receiving much mail. Commenting in his journal about a three-week-old letter from his father, he wrote, "Fred [whose regiment had completed its three-year service] had not reached home yet. His little boy had died aged seventeen months. He never saw him."[18]

Kautz was finally roused from his depression by the following order on September 27 marked "Confidential": "The major-general commanding [Meade] directs that when your division is concentrated to-day at Prince George Court House you report in person to Major-General Butler." Kautz and his division were finally back in the Army of the James.

27. Chaffin's Farm and Johnson's Farm

When General Kautz reported to General Butler's headquarters on the morning of September 27, 1864, he learned that his division was to take part in another two-pronged offensive planned by Grant. The main thrust was to be against the Weldon and Southside Railroads. With Phil Sheridan now occupying a position on the Shenandoah Valley end of the Virginia Central Railroad, the proposed movement would leave only one rail line, the Richmond & Danville, connecting Richmond to the rest of the Confederacy. According to Grant, "The great object, however, is to prevent the enemy sending re-enforcements to [Jubal] Early."[1] Butler's Army of the James was to cross the James River as a diversionary movement intended to threaten Richmond and draw Rebel troops from the Petersburg trenches, thus easing the work of the Union forces attacking the rail lines.

Surprise was to be a major aspect of Butler's movement, which explains why Kautz's order to report to Butler was marked "Confidential." In fact, Butler was so secretive that he left Major General David Birney, who was to command X Corps, with the impression that he was being sent to Wilmington, North Carolina.

On the evening of September 28, Butler, Kautz, Birney and Major General Edward O.C. Ord, who now commanded Butler's XVIII Corps, met at Butler's headquarters and Butler distributed written orders for the movement which covered sixteen pages of letter paper. Kautz seemed greatly impressed by the document, saying later, "It evinced great thought and much labor and unusual knowledge of the situation and what was essential to success. It was the only instance, in the whole war, that I experienced, where the course of each officer was so clearly and minutely laid down, and the success that resulted from it proved the merits of the principle."[2]

Although laid out in great detail, Butler's plan was relatively simple. Birney's X Corps was to cross the James River from Jones Neck to Deep Bottom on the existing pontoon bridge while Ord and his XVIII Corps were crossing farther up the James at a point called Aiken's Landing on a pontoon bridge to be constructed by the engineers on the night of September 28–29. The object of the two corps, totaling more than 20,000 men, was to break through the complex lines of Rebel fortifications with sufficient speed to prevent reinforcements from arriving from the Petersburg front or from in front of the Bermuda Hundred lines. So important was celerity in Butler's mind that his orders definitely stated that no artillery were to take part in the initial assault.

The first objective of X Corps was the fortified position, part of the outer defensive line, at New Market Heights, only a mile from the Deep Bottom crossing, while XVIII Corps was to assault the more complex intermediate line where the Varina Road (the road from Aiken's Landing to Richmond) crossed that line. If successful, the two corps would link up near the intersection of the Varina and New Market Roads and move toward Richmond.[3] In addition, Ord would send a small force to destroy the pontoon bridges across the James over which reinforcements might come.

Kautz's Cavalry Division, even though supplemented by the addition of Colonel Edwin Vose Sumner's First New York Mounted Rifle Regiment and eight pieces of "horse artillery" from Battery B of the First U.S. Artillery and the Fourth Wisconsin Artillery Battery,[4] numbered fewer than 2200 effectives. He was directed to cross the James as the assaults of the two corps were taking place and march "with celerity" to the Darbytown Road and turn toward Richmond. If opposed on the Darbytown Road, he was to continue on to the Charles City Road and move toward Richmond.[5]

In his plan, General Butler had estimated the strength of the Confederate forces on the peninsula as no more than 3500 men. He was essentially correct except that he had neglected to include about 2500 Rebels manning an array of artillery posted in the works. The guns would make the work of the expedition, armed with no artillery at all, considerably more difficult than anticipated, especially in XVIII Corps's sector.

Ord's Corps suffered heavy casualties in assaulting the salient on the intermediate line known as Fort Harrison and, as a consequence of their success in carrying the works, were too disorganized to move any farther.

Birney's Corps, although it had suffered fewer casualties in carrying its first objective, New Market Heights, was worn out from marching all night and fighting half the morning. Half his men were straggling far behind. When Birney assaulted the salient on the intermediate line known as Fort Gilmer, he learned that his men had little fight left. The Confederate artillery massed at Fort Gilmer, reinforced by infantry and militia, cut his assaulting units to pieces. He could move no farther that day.

Ord was able to gather a few of his units in an attempt to move on the James River bridges but, unfortunately, a minor bullet wound of the leg took him out of action. Had he been able to remain in command or if he had had an opportunity to fully inform his replacement, General Charles Heckman, of the situation, XVIII Corps, having already broken through the enemy's principal defensive line, might have regained its organization sufficiently to move on to the city.

General Grant came to the scene late in the morning. He met with Birney, but failed to find the wounded Ord. Seemingly satisfied that the offensive was going well, Grant returned to his headquarters to make preparations for the movement south of Petersburg planned to commence the following day. Before he left he suggested to Butler an all-out, coordinated assault by both X and XVIII Corps. Both he and Butler were concerned at this point, however, about the fate of Kautz's Cavalry Division.

The cavalry had gotten started across the bridge to Deep Bottom shortly after dawn. Kautz halted his troopers there and waited, as ordered, for Birney's Corps to clear the way. It was between eight and nine before Kautz proceeded up the New Market Road, but found that stragglers from Birney's command impeded his progress. By the time the division reached the intermediate line of entrenchments on the Darbytown Road, it was past eleven o'clock.

Kautz had Colonel Robert West's First Brigade dismount and assault the Rebel line with the Fifth Pennsylvania in the lead. West's men were met by heavy artillery fire from the entrenchments and, after suffering about twenty casualties, retired into the woods a mile or so from the entrenchments. Neither West nor Kautz was aware that the only defenders in the trenches to their front were the artillerymen working the dozen guns which had driven West back. There was absolutely no infantry force present. Had Kautz ordered his command to ride into the Rebel line on horseback, it is likely that they would have overrun the defenders and had a clear road into the Confederate capital. But Kautz turned cautious and, having been specifically ordered to avoid a fight, he regrouped his command and moved farther north, as ordered, to the Charles City Road near where it joined the Williamsburg Road.

Once again Kautz dismounted his men, this time the entire division, and again ordered an assault. By this time, Confederate reinforcements had arrived and, as Colonel Samuel Spear's

Second Brigade moved forward, they met both artillery and small arms fire. The Wisconsin Battery assisted in the attack, but they were no match for the heavy guns in the trenches. The assault was called off by midafternoon.

Butler's "celerity of movement" was no longer an issue, but Kautz was determined to continue to circle the city looking for an opening in compliance with Butler's directive. After conferring with his brigade commanders, he continued the move north in an attempt to get around the enemy's flank. He sent Spear's Second Brigade on toward the Williamsburg Road, following himself with West's Brigade. When Kautz arrived at the Williamsburg Road about 4:30, he found that Spear had failed to stop there. Before Spear could be halted, it was almost dark and he was more than three miles past the Williamsburg Road at a narrow country lane leading to the farm of a Mrs. Christian. Rather than countermarch to the Williamsburg Road, Kautz attempted to enter the city on the Christian Road. By the time he got his command dismounted and in line of battle, night had fallen. According to Kautz, "The night was cloudy and so dark that the column became lost in the abatis and the hope of doing anything was given up." He went on to explain, "Had not Col. Spear taken the wrong road or had he moved in on the Charles City, Long Bridge [Kautz no doubt meant to say Nine Mile] or Williamsburg Road, we would have had ample daylight to have decided the feasibility of getting in.... Had I remained with the head of the column, I think I would have had the satisfaction of getting into the streets of Richmond from which, however, I should have been as speedily driven as I would have entered, because the necessary support would not have been at hand."[6]

Kautz was only partially correct on this last point, as he learned the following day. At least one brigade of Alfred Terry's Division of X Corps had been sent up the Darbytown Road in search of, if not actually in support of, Kautz. By the time they were in position to be helpful, however, it was late afternoon and the cavalry were miles to the north.

The long day was followed by a long night groping over unfamiliar roads to the safety of friendly lines. Not until about 9 A.M. on September 30 did Kautz report back to Butler's headquarters on the New Market Road.

Robert E. Lee had been slow to recognize the threat to his meager forces north of the James but, by the morning of September 30, the Confederate forces in the Richmond defenses had been almost tripled by reinforcements from the Bermuda Hundred line, from Petersburg and from the militia of Richmond itself. Lee, in a characteristic move, ordered a counterstrike on Fort Harrison. Multiple uncoordinated assaults were repulsed with heavy casualties in the Confederate ranks. Kautz's Cavalry were picketing the right of the army and saw no action that day.

On the afternoon of October 1, Kautz's Division was in support of a portion of Terry's Division in a reconnaissance in force against the Rebels' intermediate line. Terry sent his Second Brigade forward on the Darbytown Road with West's Brigade on his left and Spear's Brigade on the Williamsburg Road to his right. Confederate skirmishers were pushed back into the intermediate line. Finding that line well-manned by both infantry and artillery, Terry withdrew. During the three-hour engagement, called the Battle of Roper's Farm, casualties were light on both sides. The dismounted advance of Spear's Brigade came closer to the heart of Richmond than that of any Federal force until the evacuation of the city in April 1865.

Meanwhile, the Army of the Potomac's movement on the railroads south of Petersburg, as ordered by Grant and carried out by V and IX Corps, supported by Gregg's Cavalry Division, got started well on September 29, but it subsequently turned into a disaster. Fortunately, casualties in killed and wounded were relatively light, although more than 1800 of Meade's men were missing or captured.

North of the James, casualties in killed and wounded had been somewhat higher, totaling almost 400 killed, 2300 wounded and 650 missing. Kautz's Cavalry had but two men killed, twenty-five wounded and ten missing.

No accurate count of Confederate casualties is available, but various estimates place the numbers at about half the Union losses both north of the James and south of the Appomattox.

As of October 2, Butler wanted to continue the attempt to enter Richmond, but Grant wanted nothing more than for the Army of the James to hold onto the real estate which it had fought so hard to occupy. The battle, known as the Battle of Chaffin's Farm, was over. A formidable fortified line about ten miles long started to take shape on the peninsula. Fort Harrison was the keystone of that line and XVIII Corps, now under command of General Godfrey Weitzel, held that fort and dug in from there south to Chaffin's Bluff overlooking the James River. Birney's X Corps constructed a line of entrenchments from Fort Harrison to New Market Road, where the line bent sharply to the right to face almost due north with Alfred Terry's Division anchoring the flank. When the new line was formed, Kautz was ordered to place his cavalry division along the Darbytown Road about a mile in advance of Terry's Division on the right flank of X Corps.

On the morning of October 3, Butler again informed Grant that he thought he could break through the Confederate line, asking once more, "Can we not have the other corps here?"[7]

Grant responded, telling Butler that he would be going to Washington the following day and reiterating, "As much of present foothold north of the James as can be held I want held."[8]

Kautz was not pleased with the position he was asked to hold. He later wrote, "An examination of my position revealed the fact that it was dangerous in the extreme and that if I was attacked in force I could not possibly save my artillery." What he was referring to was the fact that directly behind his position was a branch of Four Mile Creek and for some distance on either side of the creek "was a dense thicket and swamp and quite an obstacle for infantry and nearly impassable for cavalry." The only road through the swamp was a narrow country lane which was no less swampy than the ground around it. At the same time, the area to Kautz's front was open and elevated with an excellent road over which an attacking force might approach. Kautz tried to explain the situation to both Birney and Butler, but was told by Butler that he must stay. On October 5, he rode to Butler's headquarters and "requested entrenching tools that," as he put it, "I might strengthen the position as much as possible. He replied that the 18th and 10th Corps had all the entrenching tools and he had no more to give us. I asked him what he expected his cavalry to do when his infantry found it necessary to intrench in rear of it. He answered that 'Cavalry has legs and could run away.' I returned to my camp and gave orders for the different reserves and the two batteries to make themselves as strong as possible with such tools as they had in their camp."[9] Using bayonets, cook pots and other improvised tools, Kautz's men managed to dig a row of shallow rifle pits, woefully inadequate for the form of defensive warfare which had become the norm by 1864.

Before he left for Washington, Grant wired Butler, "Send me a list of all the promotions by brevet or otherwise that you would like made from your command, stating the particular services for which brevets are asked, and I will take pleasure in recommending them."[10]

Butler answered on October 5 with a list of ten deserving officers, among them Kautz. Butler, in his telegraph, wrote of Kautz, "I would recommend Brigadier-General Kautz, commanding Cavalry Division of this army, as brevet major-general, for gallant and meritorious service in conducting the cavalry expedition and cutting the Weldon railroad on the 5th of May, 1864, and again cutting the Danville and Richmond road on the 16th of May; again for gallant service in the expedition under General Wilson, bringing in his cavalry safe from the attack of the enemy; and, lastly, for his vigilant and successful movements in the late advance on the north side of the James."[11]

Just after dark on October 6, two refugees came into the cavalry's lines. On questioning them, Kautz learned that they had left Richmond just after noon and had seen at least three brigades of Confederate Major General Charles Field's Division marching north toward the

York River Railroad a mile or two west of Kautz's position. Assuming that this movement of the enemy could be for no other purpose than to attack either his or General Terry's position, Kautz sent the refugees to General Birney's headquarters along with messages to both Birney and General Butler cautioning them to be on the alert.

Kautz had his 1700 troopers up early on October 7. The horses were sent to the rear with "horse-holders," thus reducing his available manpower by one-fourth. By sunup, the remainder of his men were in their unfinished entrenchments waiting for an attack which Kautz felt was inevitable. His pickets on the Charles City Road were equally on the alert.

It was just after dawn when Field's Division struck Kautz's picket line. The pickets fell back in good order, delaying the Confederate advance. As the attackers neared Kautz's main line, they came under fire from the four-gun Battery B of the First U.S. Artillery, who were posted behind Robert West's Brigade west of Johnson's house, and the four guns of the Fourth Wisconsin, which were with Spear's Brigade east of Johnson's. The cannon fire was especially effective on Colonel West's front and the Rebel charge became disorganized as it neared the Union line about 7 A.M. The Rebels halted to regroup, causing Kautz to be uncertain whether this was merely a reconnaissance in force or an all-out assault.

After a pause of about thirty minutes, the Confederates came rushing on again, now supported by three or four artillery batteries. Kautz counted four regimental battle flags on his left and four more on his right as the Rebels moved forward.

Spear's Second Brigade, composed of hardly more than 400 men of the Eleventh Pennsylvania and the remnants of the First D.C., was the first to give way. The withdrawal was orderly at first, but, when Spear's men reached the swampy thicket to their rear, their formations were broken up, as much by the terrain as by the Confederate advance.

On West's front, the charge of the enemy broke through the line between the Fifth Pennsylvania and the Third New York. The Fifth Pennsylvania was able to change front temporarily to face the Confederate regiment which had broken through, but were soon forced to fall back.

This left the artillery of Kautz's command exposed. Both batteries continued to work their guns for a period of ten or fifteen minutes more before they were forced to limber up and head for that one narrow country lane which led through the swamp to the rear. Unfortunately, they got only a few hundred yards down the road when the lead gun of the Fourth Wisconsin became hopelessly mired and could move no farther.

Meanwhile, Confederate Brigadier General Martin Gary's Cavalry Brigade had moved around Kautz's right flank and gotten between Spear's Brigade and the X Corps trenches on the New Market Road. By this time, Kautz had left his headquarters at the Johnson house and was attempting to rally his troopers while, at the same time, seeing what could be done to get the artillery pieces moving again. Kautz found the men of Colonel Alexander Haskell's Seventh South Carolina Cavalry Regiment of Gary's Brigade systematically shooting at the artillery's horses to ensure that they could move no farther. Colonel Haskell is said to have personally shot and wounded two of the officers of Kautz's Division before he himself was shot in the face and left on the field for dead.[12] One of those officers was Captain Kerr of the Fifth Pennsylvania, who was knocked from his horse while standing right next to Kautz.[13] At the same time, Kautz's horse was shot in the knee and Kautz commandeered one of the artillery horses.[14]

Able to rally enough of his fleeing forces to save them and himself from capture, Kautz ordered the artillery pieces spiked and abandoned. The disorderly retreat through the swamp continued.

It was not until Kautz's Division approached the New Market Road that sufficient order was restored to turn and slow the Confederate advance before being forced to fall back behind the well-prepared entrenchments of General Terry's Division. They saw no more action that day.

The grey-clad infantrymen of Field's Division emerged on the southern end of the Four Mile Creek swamp about 11 A.M. They, too, regrouped and attempted an assault on Terry's entrenchments on the New Market Road. They found the Union lines well-manned by artillery and infantry armed with Spencer repeating rifles and were repulsed. Now the roles were reversed and it was the Rebel forces who were driven in confusion through the swamp. Terry's men advanced and drove the Confederates back beyond the Darbytown Road. By 1 p.m. the Battle of Johnson's Farm was over. The outcome of the battle might have been decidedly different if the Confederate division of Major General Robert Hoke, which had been ordered to support Field's Division, had gotten involved. Hoke, however, failed to move in Field's support and his men stood at arms miles from the scene of the battle.

In his report of the battle, Kautz summarized by saying, "The loss of the two batteries (eight guns and caissons) is serious; but I do not attach any blame to the officers and men. It was the natural result to be anticipated from a spirited attack in superior force, and to the defect of position, which was unavoidable, as the necessary tools to make a road and to finish the intrenching could not be had. The real defect consisted in the advanced position of the cavalry with nothing to rest upon, and a serious obstacle in rear, with avenues of approach from every other direction. This defect was of course fully known to the rebel commander, as he took every possible advantage of it. Had there been any surprise about the attack the entire command must have been sacrificed."

He continued, "My loss ... is not so serious as was at first supposed.[15] By far the largest is in prisoners, which is due to the fact that the Seventh South Carolina Cavalry (Colonel Haskell) succeeded in turning our right and getting in our rear."[16]

The following day, Kautz's Division returned to their positions on the Darbytown Road armed with a large supply of shovels and axes.

Kautz later noted that some of the Northern papers carried articles critical of his cavalry division's part in this affair. He said, "I bore with these attacks and made no defense. My defense would have been the imperative orders of Genl. Butler and his neglect to regard my suggestions. When discussing the subject with Genl. Butler the following day and reminding him of my warnings, he spoke of my loss.... The General appreciated my silence in regard to the Darbytown affair and several weeks after handed me a Commission of Brevet Major-General in the U.S. Volunteer Service for gallant conduct on the 7th of October, 1864."[17] This was the fourth brevet promotion received by Kautz in the course of the war.

28. Through the Long Winter

After the Battle of Johnson's Farm, Kautz put his men to work strengthening their line. At the same time, the Confederates of Major General Robert Hoke's Division occupied and began work on the old exterior line which had been started during McClellan's Peninsular Campaign.

While Kautz's line was being improved, so was his cavalry division. Sumner's First New York Mounted Rifle Regiment was permanently assigned to his division on October 10 along with the First Maryland Cavalry, commanded by Kautz's classmate and comrade from the Sixth U.S. Cavalry, Colonel Andrew Evans. Kautz formed the two new regiments into a third brigade and placed Evans in command. With six regiments, Kautz was able to say with some satisfaction, "The Div. will be a very comfortable command."[1]

On October 12, General Butler ordered a reconnaissance by Terry's Division, supported by Kautz's enlarged division of cavalry. On the night of October 12, Kautz wrote in his journal, "I do not like the proposed movement as it is not made in sufficient force and may prove disastrous."[2] In his later writings, he said that the movement "was begun ... with a feeling on the part of nearly every officer and soldier in the command that we were simply marching out to lose several hundred men and be repulsed."[3]

And so it was. On the morning of October 13, Terry's Division attacked on the Darbytown Road and the cavalry took the Charles City Road. Terry lost several hundred men in the ill-conceived movement, which is known as the Battle of Darbytown Road.

On the day of the battle, Kautz felt the beginnings of a relapse of malaria, which was not controlled by large doses of quinine. On October 21, saying, "I fear I shall not be fit for duty if I stay,"[4] he asked General Butler about the possibility of a leave. Butler suggested that Kautz speak with General Grant. On hearing of Kautz's illness, Grant approved his application.

Kautz turned his division over to Robert West and left for Ohio. Among the relatives he met was his father's first cousin, Jacob Kautz. The old man, totally blind, was brought to Levanna to ask if Kautz knew anything of his three sons, Philip, David and Jacob, all of whom were in the army. Kautz, of course, could offer no information about his sons.[5]

On November 8, Kautz rode up to Ripley and voted in the presidential election. His vote, like those of the majority in the army, went to Lincoln.

On his return to Virginia, Kautz met General Butler in Washington and boarded the steamer *Greyhound* with him for the trip back. Butler had been ordered to New York City to aid in the suppression of riots which were anticipated at the time of the election. On his way south, Butler was entertaining a group of dignitaries, including Senator Henry Wilson, Chairman of the Senate Committee on Military Affairs. Kautz tagged along and enjoyed the opportunity to express his views on military topics to Senator Wilson.

When Kautz arrived back with the Army of the James on November 18, he learned the details of Grant's latest two-pronged offensive, which had occurred on October 27. II, V and IX Corps of Meade's Army of the Potomac had been sent southwest of Petersburg in another attempt to cut the rail lines. In the resultant indecisive battle, known as the Battle of Boydton Plank Road or Hatcher's Run, Kautz's second cousin, Jacob Kautz, was one of 166 Union soldiers who lost their lives.

In support of this movement, the Army of the James had been ordered to make a demonstration against the Confederate left near the Williamsburg Road. Little was expected from this diversionary movement and little was accomplished.

In his *Personal Memoirs*, Ulysses Grant wrote, "This closed active operations around Richmond for the winter.... It would prolong this work to give a detailed account of all that took place from day to day."

And so it was with Kautz and his division. Through the long winter they anchored the right flank of the Army of the James. On New Year's Eve, Kautz wrote in his journal, "I hoped before this to see the end of the war, but it still continues and there seems little doubt but what it will last another year."[6]

Only once, on December 10, was the position which Kautz's Cavalry occupied challenged by the enemy. Kautz was quite satisfied with the defense that his men put up and was able to write in his journal, "Genl. Ord is highly pleased with the conduct of the cavalry on the 10th."[7]

At the time, Ord was temporarily in command of the Army of the James. General Butler was preparing an expedition to attempt the capture of Fort Fisher at the entrance to the harbor of Wilmington, North Carolina. Butler took with him two divisions of infantry under the command of Godfrey Weitzel and was backed by a flotilla of sixty warships commanded by Admiral David Porter. After two days of heavy bombardment by the 600 guns of the fleet, on Christmas Day, Butler landed his force of 6000 men north of the fort, which held a garrison of no more than 500. Deeming an assault on the fort too costly of lives, Butler withdrew and returned to Virginia without a fight.

On December 29, Dutch Kautz rode down to headquarters for a talk with Butler. In his journal, he wrote, "I heard his explanation of his failure to capture Fort Fisher. He threw the blame on the Navy, that they were so long getting ready."[8]

Although Kautz remained a supporter of Benjamin Butler, he had become personally somewhat critical of the major general. In an interview with Butler early in December, Kautz had questioned the loss of the Third New York Cavalry from his command and its replacement by the Twentieth New York. According to Kautz, "He was evidently out of humor and abused the cavalry," implying that the cavalry was adept at "running away." "The reproach was uncalled for and unjust. When he saw my displeasure, his manner changed and he tried to smooth matters over and invited me to dinner."[9] On another occasion while they were at dinner with some visiting dignitaries, Kautz was disgusted with Butler's comments on obtaining political support in exchange for political favors.[10]

There had long been pressure to have Butler removed from department command, especially from the Democratic Party in Washington.[11] President Lincoln had considered his removal several times. Butler, however, had many influential friends, or, at least, political cronies whom he called friends, both in Washington and in his home state of Massachusetts. Add to that the fact that he was the ranking major general in the Union army and it can be seen that it would take some doing to get rid of him. His dismal failure at Fort Fisher offered an excellent excuse and on January 7, 1865, he was removed from command and ordered home to Lowell, Massachusetts, to await orders.

Kautz, despite his occasional criticism of Butler's personality, remained appreciative of the support which Butler had provided him. Butler had been responsible for Kautz's promotion to brigadier general. Although Quincy Gilmore and Baldy Smith had been sacked by Butler for their parts in the Petersburg assaults, Butler had praised Kautz for his role in those failed expeditions. Butler had twice recommended Kautz for brevet promotions. Kautz would later write,

"I visited much at Genl. Butler's headquarters.... I had occasion to remember my experiences with pleasure.... He was always entertaining when he chose to be and with me he was rarely otherwise."[12]

Kautz's relationship with Butler's successor, Edward O.C. Ord, would not be so cordial.

Unlike Butler, Ord was a West Pointer, graduating in 1839. He had taken command of XVIII Corps in July 1864 and, as we have seen, was wounded near Fort Harrison. He was appointed commander of the Army of the James on January 8, 1865.

On January 9, Kautz rode to Department Headquarters to pay his respects to his new commander but, as he wrote later, "I was a 'little taken down' by Genl Ord when he informed me that in riding through the Cav. he had discovered that two-thirds of the horses should be condemned and that four-fifths of the men should be dismounted and turned into the Infantry."[13]

Kautz must have been more than a "little taken down" by Ord's statement. He later explained, "I never have been able to understand Genl. Ord's antagonism, for the statement he made to me had no foundation in fact. He had that day ridden along the picket line. The 20th New York was on post. This Regt. was in a bad condition and had only a few days before been exchanged for the 3rd New York, one of my best Regts ... with the object that I should improve its character. I informed Genl. Ord of the fact, but he made no admission that he might have done the other Regiments in my command an injustice by his observations of one. Subsequent events showed that he ... had no intention of changing his opinion."[14] In support of Kautz in this difference of opinion, Major Samuel Starr of the Cavalry Bureau arrived to inspect Kautz's command on the same day that Kautz was "taken down" by Ord. Starr departed four days later with a very positive opinion of the division.

It seems likely that Ord's antagonism toward Kautz grew, at least, in part, from his intense hatred of Benjamin Butler. Butler's favoritism toward Kautz seems to have rankled Ord, thus leading to Ord's petty dislike of Kautz.

As the winter of 1864–65 wore on, the forest of second-growth pine that covered much of the landscape gradually disappeared. Although the supply of wood seemed adequate, the quartermaster department had difficulty supplying the army with other essentials, especially forage for the horses. Rations of forage were drastically reduced and Kautz noted, "We are in great want of forage. The horses have not had any for several days."[15]

Later, the quartermasters were able to meet the demand but Kautz did not learn of it. His cavalry horses continued on half rations. On January 19, while having dinner at Ord's headquarters, he learned that supplies had been adequate for some time. He noted in his journal, "The Genl. thought it a good joke that the order removing the restriction on forage had failed to reach me through the carelessness in his office."[16]

Because his horses were underfed, Kautz thought it wise to limit their activity in case they were needed for some important work. Ord, however, insisted on keeping the cavalry busy. Kautz wrote in his journal, "The Genl. thinks we are not doing much and desires to give us employment.... Genl. Ord pretends that he has information of movements of the enemy on Williamsburg."[17]

Although Kautz was reasonably certain that the Confederates were not moving on Williamsburg, he obeyed General Ord's order and sent Colonel Evans on a reconnaissance toward the Chickahominy River with a force of 1000 men. When Evans returned two days later, Kautz wrote, "He saw nothing but a few pickets."[18] Kautz was amazed several days later when he received a communication from Ord stating, according to Kautz, that "information has been received that Col. Evans could have gone into Richmond if he had attempted it. That I think is very erroneous information as he did not go towards Richmond or as near to it as we are now. On the contrary he went farther and farther away."[19]

Despite Kautz's seeming preoccupation with his relationship with his two commanding officers, he remained busy with other matters during that long winter of relative inactivity. He took a great interest in the sad plight of the few civilians who remained in their homes within and between the lines of the two armies. On February 8, he noted with sadness the death of his close friend and respected enemy, John Pegram, who had been shot through the heart by a rifle ball near Hatcher's Run two days before.

Feeling a need to get away before spring would bring about renewed fighting, on March 1, Kautz applied in writing to General Ord for a short leave of absence, but it was denied. On March 8, he spoke with Ord and again asked for a leave. Ord replied that he had no objection, but that General Grant objected to the absence of officers from his command. Kautz obtained Ord's reluctant permission to speak with Grant. The following day, Kautz took the boat to Grant's headquarters at City Point and was pleased to meet Julia Grant, who was visiting her husband. Grant had no objection to Kautz's taking ten days off. On the way back to his quarters, Kautz stopped at Ord's headquarters to obtain the written order for his leave from the grumbling Ord and two days later he was on the boat north. Immediately upon his return on March 23, he learned that Brigadier General Ranald Mackenzie had been placed in command of the Cavalry Division of the Army of the James, which he had led for almost a year, and that Kautz had been ordered to take command of the First Division of XXV Corps.[20]

Early the previous December the Army of the James had undergone a complete reorganization. XVIII Corps had been deactivated, and X Corps was broken up and portions of it moved to North Carolina. In the reorganization, most of the white regiments of the two corps became the new XXIV Corps while all of the Negro regiments (32 in all) were assigned to the new XXV Corps, which was commanded by Godfrey Weitzel.

On the morning of March 24, Kautz reported to General Weitzel "in obedience to orders received" and later visited General Ord. He wrote, "That interview satisfies me that Genl. Ord ... expects me to refuse the command."[21]

Of course, refusal of command would result in being shelved or, worse yet, being forced to resign, which was Ord's intention in the first place. Kautz later explained his position in greater detail: "The assignment of Genl. Ord of myself to the 1st Div., 25th Corps, was no doubt made with the expectation that I would decline the command on account of race prejudice, of which I, however, had less than he supposed.... I think the General was disappointed that I ... expressed no dissatisfaction at the change. I felt really much aggrieved and was apprehensive that some misrepresentations had been made against me by Genl. Ord to Genl. Grant. On this account I asked permission to visit City Point to which reluctant consent was given."[22]

Kautz's trip to City Point proved far more eventful than he anticipated. He arrived at Grant's headquarters on the same day as President Lincoln. Kautz joined Lincoln's entourage as it reviewed troops. Kautz described his encounter with Lincoln in a long entry in his *Reminiscences*, which began, "I renewed my acquaintance with the President," and ended, "He also perpetrated some joke over the capture of the beef cattle by Wade Hampton the previous fall ... which I had to vindicate as well as I could."

Later that evening, Kautz had a private interview with General Grant.

> I sought an opportunity to vindicate myself with Genl. Grant. I told him that Genl. Ord was unjust to me in the condemnation of my Cavalry command. Genl. Ord had said it was the worst Cavalry in the service and I considered it the best. I told the Genl. that ... he could call for the report of the Special Inspector of the Cavalry Bureau who recently inspected it, or he could call for the opinion of Genl. Mackenzie, who relieved me, or he could send his own inspector. I told the Genl. he had selected me for that Cavalry command, and I wished to assure him that I had done my duty in regard to it. I think my statements surprised the Genl. a little. I also told him that the only objection I had to the change was that I could not, I feared, have time to familiarize myself with my new command and that Genl. Mackenzie felt as I did in regard to taking command of Cavalry, his previous experience being entirely with Infantry.[23]

When Kautz returned across the James the following day, March 26, he again joined Lincoln's party as it reviewed the Second Division of XXV Corps and a division of XXIV Corps. It was during this time that Kautz learned of Grant's plans for the spring campaign.

Kautz officially took command of the First Division of XXV Corps on March 28. That same day, his old Cavalry Division, now under Ranald Mackenzie, whom Kautz thought was "a very gracious officer,"[24] moved south of the James River. They joined Phil Sheridan's Cavalry Corps for another movement by the Army of the Potomac against the railroads southwest of Petersburg. Unlike Grant's efforts the previous fall, there was to be no diversionary movement by the Army of the James against the Richmond defenses. Instead Grant ordered almost all of the Army of the James to move south of the James River and cooperate with the Army of the Potomac in the campaign. Only Kautz's First Division of XXV Corps and the Third Division of XXIV Corps under Brigadier General Charles Devens were left behind north of the James. This skeleton force was placed under the command of Godfrey Weitzel.

On March 30, Kautz noted in his journal that he was able to hear the sounds of battle coming from the direction of Petersburg, but there was no news until late on the night of April 1, when Grant telegraphed that Phil Sheridan's Cavalry Corps had broken through the Confederate lines at a place called Five Forks and had captured three brigades of infantry. Grant sent several more telegrams on April 2 of continued Federal successes and, by the end of the day, it was learned that 12,000 Confederates had been captured and that the remainder of Lee's Army of Northern Virginia had abandoned Petersburg and were moving west.

Grant ordered Weitzel to be ready to assault the Confederate capital. His last telegram, however, late on April 2, informed Weitzel that Lee was evacuating the city. During the night of April 2–3, the sounds of loud explosions were heard coming from the city as the fleeing Confederates destroyed ammunition and other supplies they were unable to carry with them.

Early in the morning of April 3, the colored troops under Kautz and the white troops under Devens moved forward. They met no opposition and soon it was a race to the Confederate capital. Kautz was on the River Road and Devens on the New Market Road. As Kautz, at the head of his command, approached the intersection of the two roads, he was ordered to halt his colored division to allow the white division to pass.

Kautz tells us that his troops were "annoyed," thinking that whoever marched the fastest should have the honor of getting into the city first. Kautz himself must have been terribly disappointed at not being the first Union general officer to ride into Richmond, the spires of which he had first seen in 1862 and had viewed expectantly from afar for almost a year. Neither his journal nor his later writings tell us so. He said simply, "By eight o'clock we were all in the city."[25]

29. *The Company Clerk* and *Customs of Service*

General Edward Ord was not the first of August Kautz's commanding officers whose methods he questioned. When Kautz was stationed at Fort Steilacoom in 1857 and 1858, he and Captain Maurice Maloney had a dispute over the relative duties of the post commander (Maloney) and the post's quartermaster (Kautz). Despite their differences, the two men remained friends. Again, at Semiahmoo Bay in 1859, Quartermaster Kautz had similar disagreements with post commander Captain Dickinson Woodruff. The only point of agreement between them was that there was nothing in army regulations which clearly and concisely spelled out the duties of each.

It was in April 1861, when Kautz was stationed at Fort Chehalis, again under Maloney, that he "got the idea of writing a small guide for young officers" which would explain those duties and many others. He suggested the idea to Dr. Horace Wirtz, the post surgeon, and, according to Kautz, Wirtz "approved of the idea so highly that I determined to act upon it and wrote a page on the availability of property."[1]

Kautz was a prolific writer. It would seem a little manual would be no trouble at all. No manual, however, was forthcoming.

The next mention in Kautz's journal of writing a book came in November 1861, when he was camped near Washington with the Sixth Cavalry. Perhaps it was his recent exposure to Colonel William Emory and Major Lawrence Williams that got him started again. He wrote, "I have in mind to undertake a manual for officers, but the plan of the work is not well defined."[2]

This time he must have been more determined to get started, but he was having trouble envisioning the outline of the book, saying, "I hope my work will take shape and form some day. At present, I have no definite plan."[3] He was, however, now in earnest because, over the next several months, he purchased a gazetteer, a large Webster's Dictionary and "some other books to assist me in preparing my notes on military duties."[4]

Unfortunately, the Peninsular Campaign got in the way. His notes remained in storage until they caught up with him at Harrison's Landing at the end of July when he wrote, "I commenced to overhaul my notes and I will try to resume them again if I can get up the energy during this hot weather."[5] Again no book was forthcoming.

At Fort Scott in1862, he found the paperwork of his new regiment, the Second Ohio Cavalry, in bad shape. The reports, rolls and rosters of the companies were being filled out improperly or not at all. In response, he wrote a brief circular which he distributed to the company clerks explaining how to prepare a morning report. To his surprise the next morning, all the morning reports came in perfectly done. He then wrote additional circulars explaining how to prepare each of the company records and, within a few weeks, all were being completed properly. Pleased with his success, he wrote, "I came to the conclusion if that kind of instruction worked well with one regiment it would work well with others.... If the Regts. were all right, it will be easy for the Brigade to be right, and the Brigade being right, the Division was easily arranged; thus the whole army would be right if all the companies could only be started right."[6]

Kautz wrote to D. Van Nostrand & Co., a publishing company in New York. Although Van Nostrand was willing to publish his "circulars" in pamphlet form, it seems they were unwilling to do so in book form. At the suggestion of his West Point classmate George Mendell, who was on the faculty at West Point, Kautz contacted Joshua Lippincott of J.B. Lippincott & Co. in Philadelphia, who agreed to publish the book if Kautz would take some of the financial risk. The book was published in the spring of 1863. The 5 × 7-inch, 142-page book, entitled *The Company Clerk*, contained instructions, quite clear in most cases, for the preparation of more than forty different reports. The little book was successful far beyond Kautz's expectation. At $1 in cloth cover and $1.25 leather-bound, it sold more than 5000 copies in its first six months and another 3000 in the succeeding six-month period.

In January 1864, Kautz was assigned to the Cavalry Bureau in Washington and, on the trip east, he stopped in Philadelphia and met with Mr. Lippincott to arrange for the publication of another book, a guide for noncommissioned officers. He mentioned his pleasure at the success of *The Company Clerk* and, perhaps with a little surprise, wrote, "Lippincott treats me as a successful author.... This time he takes all the risk and gives me the same percentage."[7]

Kautz worked diligently and managed to rush through completion of the last few pages as he was packing to join the Army of the James in April 1864. When it came off the press in August, this 4 × 6-inch book of 300 pages, entitled *Customs of Service for Non-Commissioned Officers and Soldiers*, was an extremely detailed manual of duties and privileges of the common soldier covering everything from recruiting practices and pay scale to hints on maintaining one's health and cooking in the field. When Kautz received his first copies in early September, he chided himself for having made it so long. Sales were disappointing. Kautz attributed this in part to Lippincott's failure to market the book aggressively. It is more likely, however, that the common soldier in the Civil War, as would be the case today, did not feel the need for a book to explain his responsibilities. He had plenty of officers, both commissioned and non-commissioned, to do it for him.

One week after seeing his second book, Kautz began work on another manual, writing in his journal, "I have commenced a new book which I hope to finish this winter although it may take longer as it will require greater effort to write it as it is intended exclusively for officers."[8] So he was finally getting around to writing the "small guide" which he and Wirtz had discussed at Fort Chehalis. Over the next year and a half, Kautz's journal is filled with notations about his progress, or lack thereof. When he finally completed work on the book in January 1866, he noted in his journal, "It is a great relief to have it off my mind."[9] Entitled *Customs of Service for Officers of the Army*, the 3½ × 5-inch manual containing 380 pages was released in May 1866. It was extremely well written and received critical acclaim in both military and literary circles. Unfortunately, almost all of the tens of thousands of volunteer officers who had swelled the ranks of the army during the Civil War were back in civilian life. Nonetheless, sales were good.

All three of Kautz's little books remained in print and continued to sell reasonably well into the 1880s. Even after his retirement, he got Lippincott's agreement to publish revised editions, but was held up because army regulations were being rewritten at the time. All three of his books have been recently reprinted and are now available for the benefit of Civil War reenactors.

30. The Fall of Richmond

August Kautz's journal of April 3, 1865, tells us that, as he and his division marched into Richmond, "A terrible scene was transpiring."[1] The fires set by the Army of Northern Virginia had gotten out of control. Kautz later wrote, "It was an awe-inspiring sight. The lower portion of the city was in flames; clouds of smoke soon enveloped everything.... The heat caused currents of air to blow in all directions. The sidewalks were covered with cinders. The troops were called out to extinguish the flames, which was not accomplished until nearly night. The city ... had a deserted look. The buildings were mostly closed and few persons were to be seen upon the streets except our troops." With some pride in the soldiers, whom he had commanded for but a week, he added, "The conduct of the troops was orderly and no outrages were reported. It is remarkable that an army, which for four years had fought so determinedly to enter the Rebel Capital, should finally march in so quietly.... But for the exertion of the troops, the entire city would have been in ashes before night.... There was not a soldier in the command who did not feel the greatest possible pride over the event. The Armies of the Potomac and James, pursuing the Army of Northern Virginia, who were the real victors, did not have the same satisfaction that was vouchsafed our fraction of the Army of the James."[2]

After the fires were extinguished, Kautz posted two of his brigades in the redoubts which had been the western defenses of the city and had the third ferried across the James River to the town of Manchester. He set up his headquarters in the Powhatan Hotel. General Weitzel chose the Presidential Mansion, recently vacated by Jefferson Davis, as his headquarters.

In midafternoon of the following day, Kautz was drawn to the window by a commotion in the streets. To his surprise, he saw President Lincoln and his son Tad coming up from the river, escorted by Admiral David Porter and a small detachment of marines and surrounded by a large crowd of cheering Negroes.

Lincoln had come up from Fortress Monroe on Porter's gunboat, *Malvern*. Kautz directed Lincoln and his party to General Weitzel's headquarters, where an informal reception was held for the president of the United States in the former home of the president of the Confederacy. Afterwards, Lincoln, Weitzel, Porter and Kautz took a drive in an ambulance around the city, including a circuit of the capitol building. As the enthusiastic driver rounded the southeast corner of the building, "the President expressed some fears of the wagon upsetting."[3]

Although many Northern dignitaries visited Richmond over the next few days, Kautz's main interest was in the two armies as they moved in a westerly direction away from Petersburg and Richmond. Lee was intent on reaching Danville, where he hoped to resupply his army. Grant was in pursuit, hoping to head Lee off. Kautz was visiting at General Weitzel's headquarters on April 9 when a telegraphic message arrived from Grant announcing the surrender of Lee's Army of Northern Virginia at the sleepy little village of Appomattox Court House.

Although the troops occupying the city were well behaved generally, Kautz received occasional reports of offenses, both real and imagined, committed by his men against the citizens.

On April 8, he noted that Mrs. Christian, whose house he had visited the previous September, paid him a visit "concerning her servants, who have become insubordinate since the Yankees have arrived. I sent Lt. Brown out to quiet matters."[4]

After Lee's surrender, units of the Union army began to return to Richmond. As details of the final campaign toward Appomattox Court House became known, Kautz wrote in his journal with some satisfaction, "The Cav. Division has distinguished itself and Genl. Mackenzie takes special pains to give me credit for its good character."[5]

General Ord arrived back in Richmond with the bulk of the Army of the James on April 12 and immediately ordered XXV Corps to move to a camp south of Petersburg. This move, no doubt, had some racial undertones based on Ord's hearing reports that the colored troops were committing depredations against the citizens. The following evening, Kautz wrote in his journal, "Some of the gentlemen are disgusted at being ordered out of Richmond," but added, "Ord is very kind to order us away where he cannot interfere with us."[6]

On April 16, news arrived at camp that President Lincoln and Secretary of State William Seward and his son had been assassinated on the night of April 14. Apparently news traveled slowly to Kautz's camp because two days later he wrote, "We are all very anxious to hear further particulars from Washington about the President's death.... Genl. Ord we do not hear from in these matters as we should, but we do hear in some matters that we should not."[7]

The next several weeks were pleasant ones for Kautz. The leisure afforded by the end of hostilities allowed the officers to visit each other at their respective camps. On April 21, Kautz visited the camp of his old regiment, the Second Ohio Cavalry, now commanded by Lieutenant Colonel Alfred Nettleton. Kautz especially cherished time spent with his old friends, Phil Sheridan and George Crook, and both agreed to attend his upcoming marriage. (See Chapter 32.) On April 28, Kautz applied for a leave of absence to return to Ohio to finalize plans for that wedding.

On May 2, Kautz's leave was granted, but, later in the day, an order came for XXV Corps to move to City Point.[8] A separate order arrived from General Ord canceling his leave and requiring him to report to General Grant in Washington, for a "special assignment."

Since both he and his division were on their way to City Point, Kautz accompanied the division on the march. Kautz described the scene as the colored troops of his division marched through Petersburg, "I never shall forget the imposing effect of the Division marching in columns of platoons through Petersburg to the song of 'John Brown's body lies a mouldering in the ground.' The effect was thrilling, the ground seemed to shake with the tread of the command and the swell of seven thousand voices in accord was immense." He added, "When I took my leave of the officers of the division, it was not known that they were concentrating for the purpose of going to Texas. I never saw many of them again.... Most of their names and the memory of their faces soon passed out of my mind with the important events that crowded upon us."[9]

On May 4, 1865, Kautz left for Washington to take part in one of those "important events."

31. The Trial of the Lincoln Conspirators

When General Kautz arrived in Washington on the morning of May 5, 1865, he reported to Grant's headquarters immediately. Finding Grant absent, he was told nothing. While at headquarters, he met Henry Burnett, who had served under him in the Second Ohio Cavalry.[1] Burnett was strangely secretive, but suggested that Kautz might have been ordered to Washington to take part in a court-martial or commission of some sort.

Next day Kautz returned and met with Grant. The Lieutenant General knew that Kautz had been granted a leave a few days before and gave Kautz the option of going on leave or being detailed to the military commission which was to try those suspected of taking part in the assassination of Lincoln. Kautz chose to serve on the commission.

A massive manhunt had taken place after Lincoln's death. The investigation revealed a plot to kill Lincoln, Vice President Johnson, Secretary of State Seward and General Grant involving no fewer than ten persons. One of these, John Wilkes Booth, the murderer of the president, had been killed attempting to escape into Virginia. Another, John Surratt, had escaped to Canada. The other eight, Samuel Arnold, George Atzerodt, David Herold, Dr. Samuel Mudd, Micheal O'Laughlen, Lewis Paine (an alias used by Lewis Powell), Edman Spangler and John Surratt's mother, Mary Surratt, were to be tried by the commission.

President Andrew Johnson elected to have the conspirators tried by a military commission rather than in a civil court. Heated debate followed over the propriety, and even the constitutionality, of a military court. The debate followed party lines, with Radical Republicans favoring the military trial while most Democrats wanted a civil trial. One of the most vocal proponents of a civil trial was James Denver, now practicing law in Washington. The issue was settled in an opinion written by Attorney General James Speed showing that the plot was an act of treason occurring within the fortified city of Washington during a time of war and properly fell under the jurisdiction of the military.

The commission was to meet at 10 A.M. on Monday, May 8, only three days after Kautz's arrival. With Sunday free, Kautz spent most of the day with Phil Sheridan, who had just arrived in Washington from Petersburg, and the two went to Mathew Brady's studio to have their picture taken. Sheridan had been named commander of the Division of the Gulf with headquarters in New Orleans. He was detailed, however, to go to Texas, where a small Confederate army under the command of General Edmund Kirby Smith was still in the field. More importantly, Sheridan was to take command of a military buildup on the Texas-Mexico border in a show of force in support of Benito Juarez, whose revolutionary forces were attempting to overthrow Emperor Maximilian. Kautz's First Division of XXV Corps was one of the units which was on the way to Texas to serve under Sheridan.

When several members of the commission, including Kautz, were not notified of the location of the trial, it was postponed for a day. It got started on May 9 in a room on an upper floor of the Federal Penitentiary adjacent to the Armory. Besides Kautz, the members of the commission were Major General David Hunter, Major General Lew Wallace, Brigadier General Albion P. Howe, Brigadier General Robert S. Foster, Brevet Brigadier General James A. Ekin, Brigadier General Thomas M. Harris, Brevet Colonel Charles H. Tompkins and Lieutenant Colonel David R. Clendenin. Serving as prosecutor was the Judge Advocate General, Brigadier General Joseph Holt, aided by two Assistant Judge Advocates, John A. Bingham, who had recently taken a seat in the U.S. House of Representatives, and Henry Burnett, which explains why Burnett had acted so strangely when Kautz met him on May 5. The ranking member of the commission, General Hunter, was the presiding officer. Throughout the trial, he sat at the center of the bench, and General Wallace, who was second in rank, sat on his right. Kautz, third in rank, sat on Hunter's left.

The Military Commission which tried the conspirators in the assassination of Abraham Lincoln. *Left to right*: Col. Charles H. Tomkins, Maj. Gen. David Hunter, Maj. Gen. August V. Kautz, Brig. Gen. James Ekin, Maj. Gen. Lew Wallace, John A. Bingham, Brig. Gen. Albion Howe, Brig. Gen. Thomas Harris, Judge Advocate General Joseph Holt, Brig. Gen. Robert S. Foster, Col. Henry L. Burnett, Col. David R. Clendenin. Photograph by Mathew Brady.

On the first day, no real business was done. The prisoners were led in, chained and dressed in black with black hoods over their heads, and paraded before the commission behind a low railing. Kautz was appalled at their costume, saying at the time, "There seems to me to be unnecessary severity exercised in the control of them and great mystery in their arraignment,"[2] and adding later, "The mystery and apparent severity with which they were brought into the court room partook so much as my imagination pictured the Inquisition to have been that I was quite impressed with its impropriety."[3] The prisoners were never hooded again, although they remained in chains throughout the trial.

The commission finally got down to business on May 10. After swearing in, the charges and specifications were read and the prisoners were asked how they pleaded. All answered, "Not guilty."

Over the next seven weeks, the commission met six days a week from 10 A.M. to late in the evening with few exceptions. The room was usually crowded with spectators and, as summer

Mathew Brady photograph of Kautz (*center*) and Philip Sheridan taken May 7, 1865. Although not identified in the photograph, the junior officer on the left is, no doubt, Kautz's brother Fred.

approached, it became more and more uncomfortable. About 350 witnesses were examined and, by the time the prosecution closed its case on May 25, most of the details of the conspiracy were revealed.

According to the prosecution, as early as the summer of 1864, John Wilkes Booth had plotted to kidnap President Lincoln and hold him for ransom in exchange for the release of all

Confederate prisoners of war. Early on, Booth had recruited John Surratt and, later, Michael O'Laughlen, Samuel Arnold, Lewis Paine, David Herold and George Atzerodt to join in the conspiracy. Early in March 1865, a contemplated kidnapping of the president failed when he canceled plans to attend a play at Campbell Hospital outside Washington.

The prosecution claimed that Booth had become frustrated by the failure of this and other kidnaping attempts and, seeing that the Confederacy could not survive much longer, he altered his plan to one of murder. His now-desperate plot was to assassinate Lincoln, Vice President Andrew Johnson, Secretary of State William Seward[4] and Ulysses S. Grant, and in so doing, paralyze the federal government, rendering it incapable of continuing to prosecute the war.

The opportunity presented itself on April 14. Abraham and Mary Lincoln were to attend a play, *Our American Cousin*, at Ford's Theater, and Ulysses and Julia Grant were to be their guests in the presidential box. According to the prosecution's account, Lincoln and Grant were to be murdered at the theater and Seward and Johnson would be assaulted at their homes. As it turned out, the Grants declined the invitation to the theater at the last minute and that part of the plot failed.

The prosecution had little difficulty in establishing that Booth shot Lincoln and that he was aided in entering and leaving the theater by Edman Spangler, a stage hand at the theater. It was also easily established that Paine carried out the attack on Seward and that Herold aided Paine in finding Seward's home.

The prosecution was also able to show that, on April 14, George Atzerodt rented a room in the Kirkwood House directly above the room where Vice President Johnson had been staying since his inauguration, but could not present evidence that Atzerodt made any attempt to attack Johnson.

The prosecution attempted to show that O'Laughlen's part in the scheme was to murder Grant. O'Laughlen had left Washington in March, but returned on April 13. The case against O'Laughlen, however, was not convincing.

It was also established that Samuel Arnold and John Surratt were active participants in the kidnapping plot, but that both had left the city before the murder plot was initiated.

There was much evidence presented by the prosecution that Dr. Samuel Mudd was acquainted with several of the conspirators, but it could not be clearly established that Mudd took part in the conspiracy. It was shown, however, that Mudd treated Booth's broken leg the day after the murder of the president.

Evidence was also presented that Mary Surratt knew all of the conspirators, that several had stayed at her boarding house and that some of their meetings took place there. It was also shown that she carried messages back and forth between the conspirators both before and after the assassination. The most damning evidence against her, perhaps, was the fact that she was the mother of John Surratt.

Much time was spent by Judge Advocate Holt and his two assistants attempting to show that Confederate President Jefferson Davis and other Confederate officials in Richmond were involved in the conspiracy. It was shown that Davis and some of the others were aware of the plot to kidnap Lincoln (as well as other plots, such as one to blow up the White House), but took no part in the actual planning.

The case for the defense began on May 25 and continued until June 23. The prisoners were not permitted to speak in their own defense, but only through their counsel.[5] Kautz seems to have been impressed how smoothly the trial had progressed through the prosecution phase, but noted on several occasions that things heated up considerably in the defense phase: "There is much delay by the Judge Advocate Bingham who is constantly objecting to the questions asked by the counsel.... We do not make so much progress on the defense as we did on the prosecution. There is much more bickering now than before among the counsel."[6]

Despite brief notes such as these, Kautz's journal is remarkably quiet in regard to the testimony given throughout the trial. Occasionally he would give the name of a witness or mention that testimony was heard on behalf of one of the defendants, but the actual content of the testimony is never mentioned. Perhaps this was intentional, designed to prevent his own prejudging of the case. Whether that is the case or not, his *Reminiscences* gives us little additional information.

Early on, Kautz spent considerable time with Phil Sheridan and was present at the depot to bid him goodbye on May 21 amid a cheering crowd of onlookers. That same evening and on several other occasions, Kautz visited James Denver. He mentioned in his journal, "I am a little disgusted with his views. He is now taking a stand against the commission." Three weeks later he noted, "Genl. Denver paid me a visit this evening and talked a good bit about the commission and its irregularity and errors."[7]

Denver also wrote about these meetings. In a letter of June 18 to his wife, Denver wrote, "August has spent several evenings with us, and I have spent some time with him. He is strongly bent on carrying out his notions about the powers and authority of the Military Commission."[8] Another letter to Louise on July 2 added, "One of the worst signs of the times is that a man of as much good practical sense as August should get so bewildered about what is right and what is wrong.... He insists that the members were bound to meet and organize a Military Commission because their commanding officers ordered them to do so. Then, because there is no law authorizing such a tribunal ... he alleges there is no limit to its powers."[9]

On May 23 and 24, the city hosted the largest parade ever held in the country. An estimated 180,000 members of the Union Army marched down Pennsylvania Avenue and past a reviewing stand occupied by President Johnson and every important dignitary who could be rounded up. When the commission members arrived at the courtroom on May 23, there were no witnesses to be questioned. Everyone had gone to the parade. Kautz visited the reviewing stand for a while on the 23rd as units of the Armies of the Potomac and James passed in review. He noted, "It was a grand sight. Much excitement and enthusiasm prevailed.... There is a very large crowd of people in Washington."[10] The commission opted not to meet on May 24 and Kautz spent the entire day on the reviewing stand as Sherman's western armies marched by.

Business was back to usual on May 25 when Kautz wrote, "The crowd has disappeared from the city."[11] Unfortunately, the crowd in the courtroom remained.

After the defense closed its case, the commission took a long weekend off before returning to the courtroom on June 27 to hear two days of closing arguments. On June 29, the commission met at its usual 10 A.M., but now "with closed doors" and "proceeded to deliberate on the adduced evidence in the case of each of the accused."[12] Unlike civilian courts, only a two-thirds majority was sufficient to convict. Kautz's description of the prisoners, based on their appearance and actions during the trial, may give us a clue to how he voted:

> Mrs. Surratt was shown to have been active in the conspiracy to kidnap prior to the capture of Richmond. That she was a willing participant in his death was not clearly made out. My own impression was that she was involved in the final result against her will.
>
> Herold was a simpering, foolish young man, so short of stature that he appeared like a boy and never seemed impressed with the gravity of his position. He must have been simply a plastic tool in Booth's hands.
>
> Payne [sic] was a sullen character whose expression rarely changed. He seemed to be fully aware that he had taken a desperate chance and lost, and had the nerve to abide the result manfully. He was manly and strong in every respect, but how much moral character there was in his make up was not apparent on the surface.
>
> Atzerodt looked the hired assassin and the testimony went to show that he failed to perform his part of the compact, which was to kill Genl. Grant, either from want of courage or want of sufficient intelligence. He excited no sympathy from anyone.
>
> Dr. Mudd was the most intelligent looking and attracted most attention of all the prisoners.

There was more work done in his defense. His subsequent career showed him to be a man of more character and intelligence than anyone of the prisoners.

Spangler does not seem to have been a conspirator knowingly. He was simply a tool of Booth's and held his horse for him, and cut the stick with which Booth held the door to the box which Mr. Lincoln was in at the theater. His greatest crime was his ignorance, and that he did not see the ends to which he was being used.

Arnold was shown to have been associated with the conspirators, but what part he performed and to what extent he was implicated was not shown to the commission. He was a good looking, amiable young man, who seemed to have gotten into bad company. The same degree and character of guilt applied to O'Laughlen.[13]

By noon on June 30, the commission finished its deliberations and adjourned *sine die*. Their findings and sentences were delivered by Judge Advocate Holt to President Johnson. David Herold, George Atzerodt, Lewis Paine and Mary Surratt were found guilty of conspiring to murder and were sentenced to be hanged. Michael O'Laughlen, Samuel Arnold and Samuel Mudd were found guilty of slightly lesser charges and sentenced to be imprisoned at hard labor for life. Edman Spangler was found guilty only of aiding and abetting John Wilkes Booth in the murder of Lincoln and sentenced to be imprisoned at hard labor for six years.

It seems likely, based on his writings, that Kautz voted for the acquittal of Mudd and for a lesser sentence for Mrs. Surratt, although no evidence has been found to that effect. He was, however, one of five members of the commission who signed a letter addressed to President Johnson and recommending mercy for Mrs. Surratt based on the fact that no woman had ever been executed in the United States. The letter was given to Judge Advocate Holt to be delivered to Johnson along with the trial proceedings, findings and sentences. The letter failed in its intent. Johnson later claimed that he never saw the letter although a copy of it was printed in the newspapers several days after the conclusion of the trial. Joseph Holt insisted that the letter had been delivered. Whether the letter was suppressed by Johnson or by Holt or by the two men in collaboration has never been determined.

Arnold, O'Laughlen, Mudd and Spangler were imprisoned on Dry Tortuga Island in the Gulf of Mexico. In the summer of 1867, an epidemic of yellow fever spread through the prison. Dr. Mudd worked tirelessly throughout the epidemic to save the lives of many of the prisoners as well as some of the guards. One of those who was infected was Michael O'Laughlen. When O'Laughlen died on the night of September 23, Samuel Mudd was at his side. When news of Mudd's heroic efforts spread, public sentiment in his favor induced President Johnson to pardon him and he was released from prison in February 1868. Spangler and Arnold were pardoned the following month.

Mrs. Surratt, Herold, Atzerodt and Paine were, however, hanged in the yard of the Arsenal Penitentiary in Washington on July 7, 1865. By that time August Kautz had left the city. Immediately after the close of the trial, he was ordered to report to his home to await further orders. After hastily packing a valise and a small trunk, he took his leave of the city on July 2. His trusted servant, George Washington Lee, followed ten days later with Kautz's horse and the rest of his baggage.

32. Charlotte Tod

Shortly after Colonel August Kautz arrived at Columbus, Ohio, with the Second Ohio Cavalry in December 1862, he was invited to a dinner and reception at the home of Governor David Tod. Kautz noted that one of the governor's daughters was pretty.

We can only assume that the "pretty" daughter was Charlotte Tod. Kautz tells us later, "I ... managed to fall in love with Miss Tod and leisure to win her regard.... On the evening of our departure on the 5th of April [1863], I proposed marriage to Miss Charlotte and was accepted."[1] Although Kautz was anxious to be wed as soon as possible, it would prove to be a painfully long engagement.

Kautz and Governor Tod became good friends and the latter was willing to accept Kautz as a son-in-law but, despite the ease with which he imposed his will in business and governmental affairs, he left such family matters to his wife. For some reason, Maria Tod had developed a dislike of Kautz. She was not ready for her daughter to be married at all, but especially not to this bookish and boresome army officer, and she was able to convince Charlotte to put any thought of marriage off at least until fall.

Busy with matters in Kentucky and Tennessee, it was not until January 1864 that Kautz was able to obtain a leave of absence to return to Columbus and he arrived hopeful that he and Charlotte would be married immediately. His journal tells us, however, "I can make no progress in my relations with Miss Tod.... She will not consent to marry unless I can take her with me."[2] Knowing that to be impossible if he should be required to take the field, he "went to bed with a heavy heart"[3] the following night and returned to Washington a single man.

Kautz had two short but pleasant visits with Charlotte in Columbus in February while he was on an inspection tour for the Cavalry Bureau, but the following month he received a letter from her postponing their marriage again, this time until October. The following day he penned what he called "a decided letter ... that will undoubtedly either brake [*sic*] or heal all my hopes concerning her, but I intend it so, and shall await her answer with much anxiety."[4] In the answer Kautz received two weeks later, Charlotte said that she wished him to visit her at Brier Hill[5] so that they could make arrangements for the wedding.

It was, once again, not going to be that simple. On the day Kautz received orders to join the Army of the James, he wrote in his journal, "I wrote to Charlotte postponing our engagement indefinitely."[6] And so things stood for more than a year. Kautz did manage to get away for three short visits to Brier Hill, but the courtship was reduced to letter writing and the tone and content of Charlotte's letters often left Kautz in doubt as to her sincerity.

After Lee's surrender in April 1865, Kautz applied for a leave of absence to return to Ohio to get married. Now that things seemed settled, we can only imagine Kautz's chagrin when General Grant offered him the choice of going on leave or serving on the commission to try the Lincoln conspirators. His sense of duty prevailed and his matrimonial plans were put off again.

At the conclusion of the conspiracy trial, Kautz was disappointed when he arrived in Cleveland to learn that the Tods were vacationing at the small resort town of Bedford Springs,

Charlotte (Tod) Kautz. This postcard-type photograph was taken by Frederick Gutekunst in Philadelphia while the Kautzes were on their honeymoon. From August Kautz's photograph album, courtesy Virginia (Kautz) Borkenhagen.

Pennsylvania. He caught up with the Tods at a hotel in Bedford on July 12. He then went through the formality of asking Governor Tod for his daughter's hand in marriage. Kautz wrote, "He expressed no surprise and had no objections. Mrs. Tod he thought might object to Miss C. getting married to anyone, but he thought she would have no objections to me.... I was quite happy for the matter is at last settled. Mrs. Tod, opposed by her daughter and father, cannot object."[7]

Kautz then went home to Levanna and, a few days later, Charlotte returned to Cleveland to make arrangements for the wedding, which was set for September 14. Kautz spent most of the next two months at home. His servant George Lee had already arrived from Washington with his horse and heavy baggage and much time was spent "overhauling" his papers, arranging his library and, with George's help, packing those things he planned taking with him into married life. George found life in rural Ohio "irksome" and departed on the noon boat for Cincinnati on July 27.[8]

Kautz, too, was bored. Even his visits with relatives and old friends seemed unsatisfying. To break the monotony, he traveled to Christian County, Illinois, with his sister Sophie to visit his brother George and other relatives. On the return trip, he stopped at Brier Hill to present Charlotte with her wedding gift, a pearl pin and bracelet set which was made to order at Tiffany's in New York while he was there in July.

Kautz left Levanna for Cleveland on September 11,[9] accompanied by his brother Albert, who would serve as best man.[10]

The wedding took place at noon on September 14 "without any mishaps or contretemps" and, after "an elegant lunch" at which "the gentlemen indulged freely of the wine in honor of the occasion," the couple departed on the train for Niagara Falls.

The day after they returned to Cleveland, Kautz wrote a short note to his aide-de-camp, Lieutenant Sam Brown, who was at home in New Jersey, saying, "I shall await my orders here, and this will be my address hereafter.... I hope it will be some time before I receive orders, but I have not the slightest idea what or when it will be."[11] With this, Kautz seems to have put all thought of the army out of his mind (or, at least, out of his journal). He and Charlotte set up housekeeping in Governor Tod's spacious Cleveland home and enjoyed a full social life with Charlotte's friends and her extended family.

About the only military interest Kautz seems to have had was completion of his third book, *Customs of Service for Officers*, but he was having difficulty applying himself to that task. He, perhaps unfairly, put some of the blame on Charlotte, saying, "I spent the day ... in the society of my wife, who does not seem to have much taste or fondness for any kind of study and does not appreciate my taste for such pursuits. I, therefore, make very little progress with my book."[12]

On January 10, Kautz learned that the War Department had issued an order mustering out all volunteer officers and requiring all regular Army officers to vacate their volunteer commissions on January 18 and to report to their regiments by February 18. Kautz noted, "My regiment is in Texas, somewhere on the Rio Grande."[13]

A few days later, Phil Sheridan, noting that his old friend was ordered to his Division of the Gulf, arranged to have Kautz assigned as judge advocate at Division Headquarters in New Orleans at his brevet rank of major general. Although Governor Tod, desiring that his daughter remain close to home, wrote letters to Secretary of War Stanton and to General Grant to have Kautz's assignment changed, Kautz himself had no objection to the assignment and readily accepted, with Charlotte's reluctant approval.

They departed from Cleveland on February 16 and, joined by Charlotte's brother George, boarded the Steamer *Ruth* at Cairo, Illinois, on February 23. They arrived in New Orleans on the first day of March.

33. Reconstruction

In the years following the Civil War, the nation was groping its way into the peace, physically, financially and emotionally drained by the war. For officers of the regular Army, one area of uncertainty was the organization and eventual size of the peacetime army. Action by Congress was needed, but Congress was moving slowly. Legislation entitled "An Act to Increase and Fix the Military Peace Establishment of the United States" had been introduced in Congress by Henry Wilson,[1] whom Kautz had met briefly in 1864. The legislation, which Kautz called simply the "Army Bill," was being debated both in and out of the halls of Congress.

Kautz attempted to lobby for one or another feature of the Army Bill by writing articles for the *Army & Navy Journal*. On one occasion, however, recognizing that such efforts were futile, he wrote in his journal that he had prepared such an article, then added, "I must not send it even after I have written, as there is much doubt as to whether any good can be accomplished, since officers of the army are regarded as too interested in army matters to have anything to say about them."[2]

In the climate of uncertainty about the future of the army, Kautz was pleased by the degree of job security which his assignment as Phil Sheridan's judge advocate promised. Very few cases were handled in his office, most of which were claims against the government for damages incurred in the course of the war. On one occasion he confided to his journal, "I have nothing to do at the office now, but I go there for fear there should be."[3]

Sheridan's headquarters were located in the heart of New Orleans, and August and Charlotte Kautz enjoyed life in the city. The bachelor Sheridan, whom Kautz considered his best friend, was an almost constant companion, but Kautz also enjoyed the company of several of Sheridan's staffers and of Maurice Maloney, now a major in the First Infantry and stationed at nearby Jackson Barracks.

Many of the army wives returned north during the summer to escape the heat and avoid the tropical diseases so prevalent in the summer months. On April 7, Charlotte, along with her brother George, returned to Brier Hill with plans to return in October. Kautz was convinced that her reason for going north was related more to homesickness than to fear of disease, saying, "Charlotte expresses great regret in going, as well she may, for there is no great necessity for her to go."[4]

In Charlotte's absence, a friendship developed between Kautz and Major Marcus Reno of Sheridan's staff, based primarily on the fact that Reno's wife had also gone north for the summer. Kautz termed them "grass widowers ... who know how to sympathize with each other."[5]

During the first three weeks of May, Kautz was both pleased and saddened by a visit from his brother John, who had contracted tuberculosis and was advised to go south for his health. At Kautz's suggestion, he went on to Florida, where neither the climate nor a series of medical quacks offering miracle cures was able to arrest the progress of the disease. John then went home to Ohio. He died on January 4 of the following year.

Sheridan left for Texas on July 21 to demonstrate the determination of the United States to intervene on behalf of the Mexican revolutionaries if necessary. By coincidence, it was during Sheridan's absence that about twenty-five Radical Republicans, calling themselves the Association of 1864, met at Mechanic's Hall in New Orleans in an attempt to reconvene the state's constitutional convention of 1864 in order to provide for Negro suffrage. They hoped to gain the Negro vote, which would guarantee that the Republicans regain their domination of state politics. The radicals met on Friday, July 27, and adjourned until Monday. Kautz noted the meeting in his journal and, on Saturday and Sunday, wrote that apprehension was felt in the city because "the people expect a riot. Genl. Sheridan's absence is unfortunate at this time."[6]

The anticipated trouble did occur. In the afternoon of July 30 a group of Negroes marching in front of Mechanic's Hall was attacked by a mob of former Confederates and was driven into the convention hall. Apparently aided by the police, the mob followed and shot to death three of the Radicals and thirty-four of their black supporters and wounded more than 100 others.

At dinner that afternoon Kautz was interrupted by an order from Major General Absalom Baird,[7] who was commanding in place of Sheridan, which declared martial law in the city and appointed Major General Kautz military governor of the city.[8]

Kautz took to the job of military governor with a vigor he had not shown for more than a year. He took up his quarters in the office of Mayor John T. Monroe[9] and did not leave City Hall for three days. He took command of both the police force and troops from Jackson Barracks, imposed a curfew and ordered the saloons closed by 9 P.M. A degree of order was restored in the city by nightfall of July 30. The next day he noted, "The riot proves to have been nothing but a massacre of the Conventionists and Negroes by the police and their associates. The city, however, is as quiet as could be expected. I find the Mayor quite sulky, but the other officials all reported to me today and were instructed to continue their ordinary duties."[10]

Kautz did not sleep the first night and worked well into the night for more than a week as rumors of further disturbances continued to appear. Citizens, both black and white, were arming themselves. Weapons were being sold to such an extent that, on August 6, Kautz ordered the stores closed and prohibited the sale of firearms.

Sheridan had returned to the city on the day following the riot. As he approved of Kautz's actions, he allowed him to remain in command of the city. By August 15, things had quieted down sufficiently for Kautz to move from the mayor's office back to Sheridan's headquarters, but he continued as military governor.

Because of the tone of some of her letters, Kautz became concerned that his wife might postpone her return to New Orleans and asked Sheridan's permission to apply for an extended leave of absence to go north to fetch her. Sheridan preferred that Kautz remain longer, but agreed to allow him to leave on the first of September. Kautz boarded the train north that day "in no good humor," saying, "I feel ... that I ought not to leave the General just now when the work has just commenced. He promised if I would remain to give me the command of the sub-district of Louisiana."[11]

Kautz arrived in Cleveland in time to join former Governor Tod's family at a reception given for President Johnson and General Grant on September 3. He was surprised to meet George Crook, who had just arrived from his home in Cumberland, Maryland, to join the presidential party. Kautz wrote that Crook felt uneasy "for he is conscious he is concerning himself to get promotion."[12]

Kautz was concerned also. After going with the Tods to Brier Hill, he discussed his chances of being promoted with the ex-governor. After hearing of the passage of the Army Bill, Tod had made a trip to Washington especially to lobby for his son-in-law's promotion to the colonelcy of one of the new regiments. He had met with General Grant and with Secretary of War Stanton, but came away disappointed. The Army Bill provided that most of the vacancies would be filled by men who had served in the volunteer service during the war. This feature, of course, allowed for the distribution of political capital by members of Congress but, at the same time, was a slap in the face to the officers of the regular Army.

On September 22, Kautz finally received his appointment. He was named lieutenant colonel of the Thirty-Fourth Infantry, one of the new colored regiments, which was to be organized in Nashville, Tennessee. Although he had hoped for more, he seemed satisfied with the jump of two grades, saying, "I find that, with what they have to give, the department has been very favorable towards me and, but for the Governor's intercession, I should not have received anything. There were only 26 appointments made in the Infantry from the Regular Army, half Cols & half Lt. Cols."[13] After going to Chicago so he could take a proficiency test required for his promotion, Kautz and his wife were on the train to Nashville on October 23.

From the time that Kautz left New Orleans, he and Phil Sheridan had written to each other frequently, both desiring that Kautz should return to New Orleans. It seems likely that if he had done so, his appointment to lieutenant colonel would have been nullified. Kautz was unwilling to make the decision on his own. He wanted Sheridan to request his move to New Orleans, but it seems Sheridan was unwilling to ask his friend to give up his promotion. Kautz eventually asked Sheridan to "let it rest."[14]

When Lieutenant Colonel Kautz arrived in Nashville he was "disgusted to find that there was no need of my being hurried off so, as the 34th Infantry is not yet in existence."[15] Congress had not yet authorized funds to recruit the regiment. The next morning, Kautz went to the headquarters of the Department of Tennessee, also located in Nashville, and called on Department Commander Major General George Thomas. He had not seen the "Rock of Chickamauga" since he graduated from West Point and was pleased that his favorite instructor at the Academy still remembered him. Thomas had an order issued directing Kautz to wait in Nashville until his regiment should be designated.

The portion of Cumberland Barracks where the "not yet in existence" regiment was to be quartered was still under construction, so the Kautzes stayed at a hotel in town for more than a month. Finally Charlotte's severe homesickness forced Kautz to ask General Thomas's permission to return to Brier Hill. Hardly had he and Charlotte gotten back to Ohio when an order was received from Department Headquarters stating that War Department Order No. 92 had been issued designating the regiment and requiring that he return to Nashville. This time a young woman named Ellen Denelli came with them, ostensibly as a housekeeper, but more likely as a companion for Charlotte to aid in overcoming her homesickness. They were finally able to move into their quarters at Cumberland Barracks on Christmas Day.

The colonel of the Thirty-Fourth Infantry was Galusha Pennypacker,[16] one of the deserving volunteer officers appointed as a result of the Army Bill. Still suffering

Carte de visite of General Kautz made in 1865 and signed the following year, after he had been assigned to the 34th Infantry. From August Kautz's photograph album, courtesy Virginia (Kautz) Borkenhagen.

from a wound received at Fort Fisher in January 1865, Pennypacker was unable to report for service, leaving Kautz to command the regiment. As new recruits came in over the following weeks, they showed little enthusiasm for military life. Kautz had to deal with numerous complaints from Mayor William Brown, who represented the relationship between the troops and the local police as open warfare. A new guardhouse was under construction for the regiment and Kautz feared that it would not be large enough. On January 1, 1867, he instituted a "change of program,"[17] in which he came down heavily on the men and instructed the former volunteer officers of the regiment in proper military discipline. The new program seems to have had its desired effect.

On April 20, Kautz wrote, "We were all taken aback today by a telegram from Genl. Whipple announcing that the 34th Infantry had been ordered to Mississippi by Genl. Grant."[18] When the actual order arrived, it directed the regiment to be divided, with two companies going to Columbus, Corinth and Holly Springs and four companies and Kautz's headquarters to Grenada. The move was completed on May 5, but it was more than two weeks before Kautz learned the reason for it.

The Reconstruction Act had been passed in March over President Johnson's veto, providing for peace to be maintained by the army until legal governments could be established in the states of the former Confederacy. In accordance with that act, Major General Edward Ord was appointed commander of the Fourth District, composed of the states of Arkansas and Mississippi, with power to appoint a Board of Registration in each county in his district. Ord appointed Kautz inspector for the boards in about fifteen counties in central and northern Mississippi.

Over the next three months, Kautz visited the various boards in his district. The registration process went fairly smoothly with only minimal resistance to the registration of black men in several of the counties. Kautz was empowered to send details of troops when necessary to ensure that the law was obeyed, and did so. Only one major incident occurred when a Mr. Tullidge, a member of the board for Grenada County, published charges against the other members of that board. General Ord subsequently dismissed the board members and named another board in their place. Kautz, knowing Tullidge to be a dishonest man and that the charges he made were unfounded, unwisely wrote a letter to General Ord remonstrating against him for his hasty action.

Charlotte left for Ohio on July 7 and it was anticipated that Kautz would go north to get her about the end of September. By August 15, satisfied that his work with the registration boards had been completed, he wrote a note to Colonel Alvan Gillem, Ord's adjutant, requesting a leave of absence. The following day, he received an order to report to Columbus, Mississippi, to take over the post there. At first bewildered by the order, he soon learned that Colonel Pennypacker was to arrive the following day to take over command of the post at Grenada, making his presence there superfluous.

On August 21, General Ord himself visited Grenada on a tour of inspection and Kautz asked him whether it would be acceptable to take a short leave of absence to fetch his wife. Ord seemed to agree to the leave, but, on August 24, Kautz's request for leave was returned disapproved and endorsed by Gillem, "The services of Genl. Kautz at Columbus could not be dispensed with without injury to the public service." Kautz immediately renewed the application "on the ground that Gen. Ord assured me verbally that I could have a leave the day he was here."[19]

Kautz's wait was short. On September 1, he received a letter from Ord's aide-de-camp, Lieutenant Hugh Brown, stating, "The condition of affairs requires for a time an officer of experience at Columbus, Mississippi. The General commanding directs you proceed and take command of that post. The General further directs me to say that as soon as the exigencies of the service will permit, you will be relieved and your leave of absence will be granted."[20]

Kautz commented, "As the exigency is imaginary and he fixes no definite time, I regard it as only putting me off and evading my wishes about the matter. I wrote him [Ord] a long letter."[21] The letter was a personal one, not directed through channels, and said in part, "I cannot see anything in your letter except a design to put me off and to procrastinate. I never ask an indulgence except when I feel satisfied it can be granted without injury to the service and without imposing on any one, and while I am liable to error, I am also open to conviction in this respect, but the exercise of the arbitrary right to refuse or put off does not convince."[22]

Two days later Kautz left for Columbus and took part in the military commission as ordered. On September 8, his last application was returned disapproved with an endorsement by General Ord that he had answered the application by private letter. Left to brood over his disappointment, Kautz was surprised on September 11 by "an order placing me in arrest and confining me to the limits of the city of Columbus for insubordination for writing a personal letter to Genl. Ord on Sept 1st."[23]

Kautz penned a long letter to General Grant protesting his arrest, but the letter had little effect. The court-martial got underway in Vicksburg on December 2. Members of the court included Colonel Gillem and General Erasmus Keyes, whom Kautz had known in Washington Territory. After the charges and specifications[24] were read, Kautz offered a plea in bar of the trial on the ground that the charges were based on a private letter rather than on an official one and that the letter should not be considered. His plea was denied. The judge advocate then read the various orders and letters on which the charge was based. When a copy of Kautz's letter of protest to General Grant was presented in order to show Kautz's animosity toward Ord, Kautz objected. His objection was sustained. The next day Kautz's defense was limited to reading the motion which he had prepared in bar of the trial and the trial was over. No witnesses were called.

During the second week of January 1868, Kautz was pleased to learn that General Ord had been relieved of command of the Fourth District and replaced by Colonel (Brevet Major General) Gillem. On January 18, Gillem notified him that he had been found guilty and sentenced to an official reprimand in general orders. Kautz was "mortified."[25]

By coincidence, the noon mail brought the result of his court-martial from army headquarters in Washington. The long delay in its arrival was occasioned by the fact that the court-martial and conviction of an officer of Kautz's rank required review at high level and it had been passed on to General Grant. Kautz had, indeed, been found guilty, but Grant had remitted the sentence, saying:

> First, That the accused was justified in assuming a right to reply, unofficially and through other than regular channels, to a communication entitled by General Ord himself as a private letter.
> Second, That while the extracts quoted in the specifications, when taken by themselves and apart from their just connection, seem to lack somewhat of the strict courtesy due from General Kautz to his commanding officer, yet the general tone of the whole letter is so far otherwise as to convince the reviewing authority that General Kautz was not consciously guilty of the disrespect alleged, and
> Third, That not only his eminent services and acknowledged value as an officer, but his habitual and well known observance of the official propriety, entitle him to a favorable consideration of his purposes as manifested in his acts. [26]

Kautz was thus saved from the embarrassment of an official reprimand. He finished his journal note of January 18, "My mortification was greatly relieved by the action of the reviewing authority, remitting the sentence with a handsome compliment to myself and sustaining me almost entirely."[27]

He would later read in the *Ripley Bee*, his hometown newspaper, "General Grant has too high an appreciation of the valuable services of General Kautz to permit a little thing to work his injury, and his remarks are rather complimentary than otherwise. The difficulty between

Ord and General Kautz, in a nutshell, is simply that General Kautz is a soldier and a patriot of the same order of Grant and Sheridan."[28]

On April 14, Kautz noted in his journal, "Charlotte since yesterday has been quite disturbed and sick with loss of appetite."[29] Her symptoms, including vomiting and abdominal pain, worsened, then seemed to abate somewhat, then returned again. On June 1, Kautz wired the governor that someone from the family should come. He received a reply that Mrs. Tod and Dr. Woodbridge, a respected Youngstown physician and close family friend, would leave that afternoon.

By June 2, Charlotte was lapsing into coma and three doctors remained at her bedside with Kautz all day, pronouncing her illness typhoid and her condition critical. At about five in the afternoon, she called for her husband, but did not seem to recognize him. Kautz later wrote, "She made a beautiful prayer in her delirium that unmanned me completely and I left the room and, from the adjoining chamber, I heard her calling her father. 'Oh, Father, Father, come!'"[30]

That night, two neighbors sat with Kautz at his wife's bedside. They fed her stimulants until about four o'clock when she was no longer able to swallow. Kautz wrote, "I saw that she was dying. I called up Dr. Price & he called Dr. Mayer. They both came and pronounced her sinking fast. She was entirely unconscious. I watched by her bed side for a last gleam of light until eight o'clock when she breathed her last, June 3rd, 1868."[31]

34. From Old Mexico to New Mexico

So distraught was August Kautz at Charlotte's death that he was unable to write in his journal for more than a week. Finally, on June 12, he regained his composure sufficiently to fill in the unhappy details. Maria Tod and Dr. Woodbridge had arrived in Columbus about midnight of June 3 and, after a brief but touching memorial service the following morning, Kautz joined them in the long, painful journey back to Ohio with Charlotte's remains. Charlotte was buried at Brier Hill on June 9 and Kautz remained with his in-laws for another week.

When his despondency lifted sufficiently for him to begin to think about his future, he wrote, "I must get something to do that will occupy my mind and prevent me from dwelling on the loss I have sustained."[1]

Postwar duty in the South had been a disappointment. So, June 15 found him on the train to Washington armed with a letter from David Tod to Ulysses Grant asking for a change of duty, possibly to West Point. When he met with Grant three days later he was disappointed to learn that no changes were anticipated at West Point. He then asked Grant "if he would favor a leave of absence or delay in reporting with permission to go to Mexico. He answered that he would, for any length of time I might consider necessary."[2]

On the lonely train ride back to Mississippi, he could think of nothing but his great loss. The train route took him through portions of East Tennessee which were familiar from the campaigns of 1863, but even this was not enough to raise him from his melancholy.

At Columbus he managed to overcome his listlessness long enough to close out his official business, sell his horse, wagon and most of his household furnishings and pack to leave. He found greatest difficulty in packing Charlotte's effects and sending them off by express to Ohio.[3] By July 2 he was on the train for Ohio himself. On the way, he stopped in Covington, Kentucky, to visit Jesse Grant, hoping to meet up with the old man's son, who he knew to be traveling west, but was disappointed to have missed him.

A week at home in Levanna with his family provided some little comfort, but the quiet country life soon became tiresome and he felt the need to find some activity to overcome the inertia which had settled upon him. For some time he had been interested in investing in farm land in Iowa which he was certain would soon gain in value. His present circumstances provided an opportunity to travel to Iowa to do so. Once there, he purchased six quarter sections of land east of Sioux City.

He continued west on the newly constructed Union Pacific. On July 26, near Cheyenne, he met, by coincidence, the special train carrying General Grant on an inspection tour of the Union Pacific.[4] Grant was accompanied by a number of high-ranking army officers, including Generals Sherman, Sheridan, Harney, Gillem, Augur and others. Kautz joined the party as it made its way back to Omaha. For the next three days he enjoyed the company of his fellow officers and was both pleased and annoyed by the throng of spectators who surrounded the train at every stop. Kautz left the special train at Omaha and the following night wrote in his journal, "I have been very low spirited since leaving the Grant party. The excitement of meeting so many old friends and the distinguished character of the party gave me no time for despondency."[5]

Having discovered the palliative for his despondency, Kautz continued to travel and to visit with friends for another month. While in Washington, he met with General William Rosecrans, who had been named Minister to Mexico, although he would not take his post for several months.

Kautz left Philadelphia on the steamer *Juniatta* on September 2, transferred to the *Marseilles* at Havana and arrived at Vera Cruz, Mexico, eleven days later. The overland trip to the City of Mexico by train and stagecoach would take another four days.

Kautz traveled extensively while in Mexico, touring historic sites, including Aztec ruins, but his greatest interest seems to have been the country's mining industry. He visited a number of silver, copper and gem mines and was impressed by the scale and effectiveness of their somewhat primitive mining methods. He invested in precious stones, mostly diamonds, which, it was hoped, would be sold later in the States at considerable profit. As it turned out, the profit was much more modest than anticipated.

Throughout his stay in Mexico, Kautz maintained his habit of frequent letter writing and read the U.S. newspapers diligently. On November 9 he was not the least surprised to learn that Ulysses Grant had been elected president. He was, however, surprised, even shocked, to learn on December 14 that David Tod had died on November 15.

General Rosecrans arrived in early December. Kautz often met with Rosecrans and his wife socially and enjoyed the general-turned-minister's company, but he was somewhat critical of his skill as a diplomat. Toward the end of December, he received an invitation from the Presidential Palace "to take an informal breakfast with Genl. Rosecrans," and later "found that he [Rosecrans] had received a similar invitation to take breakfast with me. Putting the two together, they mean that we are to take breakfast with the President, but they are far from saying so."[6]

The breakfast was an elegant affair attended by President Benito Juarez, his entire cabinet and other government officials. Rosecrans and Kautz were apparently the only Americans present. Kautz said of Rosecrans, "I thought he lacked dignity, a qualification I think very requisite near this government. He constantly spoke the names of the different members of the cabinet without any prefix and frequently used the phrase 'you fellows' which will do for the mess table, but struck me as inappropriate at an entertainment of this kind."[7]

As the time approached for Kautz to return to the States, the stability of the Juarez government came more and more into question. Although Mexico City itself was not threatened, dissident guerilla bands were operating throughout the country. Just a week prior to his planned departure, a regiment of government troops revolted at Puebla on the route to Vera Cruz. Despite the potential risk, Kautz decided to make the trip and reached Vera Cruz without incident. He boarded a steamer there on February 15 and was in New York City the first day of March.

In New York, he met up with B.W. Plumb, the brother of Edward Plumb, the *charge d'affairs* at the Mexico City legation, who had befriended him in Mexico. After taking care of some business matters, he and Plumb hurried off to Washington to attend Grant's inauguration. They viewed the start of the inaugural parade near the White House, then took a streetcar to the Capitol. They watched Grant take the oath of office from a vantage point "between Washington's statue and the front of the Capitol." Kautz added, "The reading of the address did not occupy over fifteen minutes when we all left and returned to our rooms and read the address in the papers as we had not heard a word in the immense crowd."[8] That night, Kautz attended the

Inaugural Ball and came away about 1:30 A.M. without his hat and overcoat, which he was able to recover the next day.

On the following morning, Kautz met his friend Colonel Rufus Ingalls, and they went to the White House to meet Generals Orville Babcock and Horace Porter.[9] According to his journal, "We were fortunate enough to see Genl. Grant. He was at leisure and from him we learned who the cabinet was and also the contemplated changes in the Army."[10]

The changes referred to were the reduction of the Infantry arm from forty-five to twenty-five regiments. Congress had passed legislation authorizing the reduction on March 3, the last day of its session. Grant, strongly opposed to the reduction, would nonetheless comply with the wishes of Congress. Among the regiments eliminated was Kautz's Thirty-Fourth Infantry. He decided to remain in Washington until the order was issued to learn what his "destination" would be.

Kautz called on Grant twice more and spoke with the president at length about his own career and that of his brother Albert. He made one more trip to the White House to visit the president's father, who was in Washington for the inauguration. He said of Jesse Grant, "I found the old man quite feeble and garrulous. He is quite deaf and I think failing very much."[11]

That same day he visited the War Department and learned just enough to feel certain that the reorganization order would not soon be issued, so he returned to New York to visit friends. He learned on March 17 that he had been offered the lieutenant colonelcy of the Fifteenth Infantry, which was stationed in Texas under the command of Colonel (Brevet Brigadier General) Oliver Shepherd. If he should accept, he was to report to Fort Leavenworth, Kansas. He accepted.

Kautz soon learned that the Fifteenth Infantry was to move from Texas to New Mexico. It would take some time to make the move, giving him more time to travel. When he arrived at Leavenworth on May 9, he found Major General John Schofield in command of the Department of Missouri.[12] Schofield permitted Kautz to meet his regiment in New Mexico rather than to join them in Texas. It wasn't until June 10 that Kautz boarded the train at Kansas City. He reached the town of Sheridan, Kansas the following day. As the train moved across the Kansas, prairie, some of the passengers took pot shots at buffalo running beside the train.

The second half of Kautz's 800-mile journey from Leavenworth to the headquarters of the District of New Mexico[13] at Santa Fe was by stagecoach along the old Santa Fe Trail. He reported to Colonel (Brevet Major General) George W. Getty at district headquarters on June 21.

Kautz had expected to be assigned as commander of Fort Stanton, one of four small forts which formed a semicircle protecting, to some extent, sparsely settled northern New Mexico from depredations by the Mescalero Apaches. Instead, Getty ordered him to take command of Fort Craig in place of Lieutenant Colonel (Brevet Major General) Cuvier Grover, who was being transferred to Texas. According to Getty, his stay at Fort Craig would be only temporary until his regiment arrived from Texas. Kautz reached Fort Craig on the afternoon of June 29.

Kautz was at Fort Craig for three and one-half months. It only seemed longer to him. The post had been built in 1854 on a gentle slope less than a mile from the right bank of the Rio Grande. Except for the strip of green beside the river, the surrounding country was harsh desert. The fort had been abandoned for a time, but was reopened at the end of the Civil War. Little maintenance had been performed on its low adobe buildings over the years and the roof of at least one of the storehouses had long since fallen in. The finest building on the post was the commanding officer's house, and Kautz moved into one of its two bedrooms while Colonel and Mrs. Grover occupied the other. The post was home to Company E of the Third Cavalry and Company D of the Thirty-Eighth Infantry, a colored regiment which had been eliminated in the army reorganization and was waiting to march off to Texas to become part of the Sixteenth Infantry.

On the day he arrived, he wrote in his journal, "As I expected, there is not the slightest practical benefit to the service or to any body in my coming here."[14] As it turned out, he was correct. After officially taking command of the post from Colonel Grover on July 19th, he settled into a daily routine which rarely varied. Once he summed up the monotony of his routine by saying, "The same reveille sounded as usual, the same [bugle] calls and the inevitable [retreat] gun.... No event occurred to give prominence to the day above the majority that are passing away in my monotonous stay here."[15]

The monotony ended on October 4 with the arrival from Texas of Colonel Shepherd with four companies of the Fifteenth Infantry. Three days later, three of those companies marched off for posts farther north, leaving one company to replace the colored soldiers of the Thirty-Eighth Infantry who left for Texas the same afternoon. It took Kautz a few days to close out his business at Fort Craig and get packed. He was off on October 12 for his permanent post at Fort Stanton.

35. Fort Stanton

As the crow flies, Fort Stanton is eighty miles due east of Fort Craig, but the proverbial bird would stand a good chance of dying of thirst before reaching his destination. The terrain over which he would by necessity fly is as uninviting as any in the United States. Even some of the place names applied to landmarks on his flight path by early Spanish-speaking settlers (Jornada del Muerto, the Malpais[1] and Oscuro Mountains) serve as a warning to the wary human traveler to keep out. In the 1870s, most travelers from Craig to Stanton moved south along the Rio Grande to Fort Selden, then turned northeast on a route approximating present-day US-70 to Stanton, a total distance of more than 200 miles.

At first, Lieutenant Colonel Kautz considered taking the Fort Selden route but opted for a shorter route across the Malpais, traveled only once by a man named Milligan, which cut the distance in half. Accompanied by a small escort and two wagons containing his baggage and some leaky water casks, he crossed the desert, which he called "dreary and desolate in the extreme,"[2] in five days. He fell exhausted into the bed of First Lieutenant Casper Conrad,[3] who commanded the post in place of Captain Chambers McKibbin,[4] who was away on leave.

Kautz took command of Fort Stanton on October 18. Although he had been led to believe it was a finer facility than Fort Craig, he found it hardly better.[5] Like Craig, it was a two-company post, manned by First Lieutenant Howard B. Cushing's[6] Company F of the Third Cavalry and newly-arrived Company I of his own Fifteenth Infantry which, commanded by McKibbin, had just completed its march from Texas. The fort had been built in 1855 to guard the Mescalero Apache Indian Reservation just to the south on the Rio Ruidoso (aka Rio Hondo). It had been continuously occupied in an effort to protect the few Mexican and Anglo ranchers and miners who lived in the area from the Mescaleros. The fort was located near the Rio Bonito, a small tributary of the Rio Ruidoso which, like the latter, had its headwaters in the San Andres Mountains just to the west. Kautz was favorably impressed by the scenery, but was much less pleased by the post itself, saying, "It is much more pleasant here in the surroundings, especially the scenery, but I cannot say so much for the quarters. They are quite an eyesore to me in their arrangement and plan.... In so romantic a country as this, I do not see how anyone can help building in accordance with the scenery."[7]

At first he attempted to settle into a daily routine similar to that at Fort Craig, but found too many interruptions at the busier Stanton. He did, however, manage to get in an occasional game of billiards, usually with Lieutenant Conrad, at the post store operated by Emil Fritz and Lawrence Murphy.[8]

On a Sunday afternoon in mid–November, a rancher named Robert Casey "came to the post and reported that his cattle, about one hundred and fifty head, had been taken out of his corral the previous night and driven off, it is supposed by Indians."[9] Kautz ordered Lieutenant Cushing with thirty-two members of his company in pursuit of the Indians carrying fifteen days' rations.

On November 23, he wrote in his journal, "Lt. Cushing returned with his command about noon ... having recovered the lost cattle and captured about fifteen or sixteen mules and horses and a child and returned with the loss of but one man wounded. He claims to have killed a number of Indians and to have driven them and that they greatly outnumbered his command. He found them in the Guadalupe Mountains and thinks he marched about three hundred and seventy miles."[10]

Kautz was ordered to Fort Craig to attend a court-martial and got away on November 28, "accompanied by a guide, a corporal and two men with two pack mules,"[11] and returned to Stanton on December 10. He made the return trip in less than three days over an even more direct route through the Malpais than he had followed two months before. While away, he wrote to district headquarters for authorization to send Cushing on another scout. He received authorization on December 15 with permission to provide rations for any citizens desirous of accompanying the scout. Kautz was at first skeptical of the success of the mission, but, as preparations for Cushing's departure were underway, he seems to have become more optimistic.

Cushing's column left the post late on December 19 with forty men of his company and about thirty volunteers with a pack train carrying twenty days' rations and extra ammunition.[12] He traveled deep into the Guadalupe Mountains. On December 26, just across the Texas border, he found a *rancheria* of forty to fifty lodges. His troopers charged into the canyon, killing a number of the Mescaleros and scattering the rest. Cushing's men spent the remainder of the day burning all of their lodges, clothing, weapons and equipment and tens of thousands of pounds of dried meats and other foodstuffs, their entire winter supply. The only casualty in Cushing's column was Lieutenant Franklin Yeaton,[13] who suffered a severe wound to his chest and a lesser one to his wrist.

Cushing pushed farther into Texas with about half his command and, after picking up the trail of some of the Indians, found another encampment almost as large as the first along Delaware Creek. After the Indians scattered, he destroyed it. Kautz penned an endorsement to Cushing's report recommending brevet promotions for Cushing and Yeaton, but none was forthcoming.

While Cushing was away on his second scout, Kautz, seeing that the winter would provide few chances for his customary rides or walks and feeling the need of exercise, set up a carpenter shop in his quarters where he spent hours almost every day. He even constructed a turning lathe with help from the post blacksmith. He had not worked with wood since his days at Fort Chehalis, so he started slowly, making a few picture frames, but soon moved on to making furniture. This was not his only project. In January 1870, he supervised the construction of a dam on the Bonito above the post and an acequia through which water was pumped by a wind-driven auger. On March 2, after months of complaining to regimental and district headquarters, he received orders to complete construction of the post. He drew up plans and work began later in the spring.

On February 10, the post's haystacks caught fire under suspicious circumstances, consuming almost all of the available forage. When a board convened in May to investigate the cause of the blaze, one of the investigating officers was Captain (Brevet Major) Frederick Coleman, whom Kautz had met at Fort Craig in November. When Coleman was ready to return to Craig, Kautz persuaded him to go by wagon over the route used on his recent visit to Craig. Kautz went along with a work crew which, using shovels and sledges, leveled a passable wagon road through the Malpais. Kautz later prepared a map and description of the road and it became the preferred route between the posts.[14]

Late in January 1870, Kautz got word that Lieutenant Cushing's company was to be transferred to Arizona to be replaced by a company of the Eighth Cavalry, which was then in Arizona. The troopers of the Third Cavalry marched off on February 17, but were not replaced until

April 13. The lack of a cavalry arm in the ensuing three months posed a problem. In February, destitute Mescaleros began reporting in to the Fort Stanton Reservation[15] on the Ruidoso in small numbers. Later, even some Arapahos and Comanches from Texas came in, all of which gave Indian Agent Argalus Hennisee something to do. More importantly, there were frequent reports of livestock being stolen by Indians who, we must conclude, were merely trying to save their families from starvation. Without a cavalry arm, pursuit of these "hostile" Indians from Fort Stanton was impossible.

When the forty-seven men of Company B, Eighth Cavalry arrived on April 13, Kautz could see that they were not the equal of Cushing's company. The regiment had been recruited in California in 1866 and 1867, and most of the men had been unsuccessful miners or drifters or worse. The officers of Company B were Captain William McCleave, a native of Ireland who had worked his way up through the ranks, and Lieutenant Orsemus Boyd, a recent West Point graduate, who was accompanied by his wife. Kautz said of the new arrivals, "In the new society we have acquired at the post, Mrs. Boyd is much the most agreeable and refined."[16] Despite predictions to the contrary, the company performed well while under Kautz's command.

If Kautz had been unhappy with the monotony of Fort Craig, he seemed no more pleased with the markedly increased activity at Stanton. He complained all winter in his journal of his desire to have a different assignment in the army or work outside the army. It seems likely, also, that he was interested in finding another wife. In May, he applied for a leave to go east to look for other work. The leave, for six months, was granted in June, but he had to wait for Captain McKibbin to arrive back at the post from a trip east to get his wife. McKibbin arrived on July 2 and Kautz was gone four days later.

Kautz traveled extensively through the East during the latter half of 1870, visiting family and friends and investigating, unsuccessfully, military and nonmilitary opportunities. He spent most of the month of September with his mother-in-law, Maria Tod, and unaccountably developed a deep romantic attraction for Grace Tod, his dead wife's younger sister. For several weeks he mulled over what to do and, finally, penned a proposal of marriage which he mailed to Grace from Moweaqua, Illinois. Her answer arrived at Levanna, Ohio, on the same day that he did. He wrote, "It is a cold and unfeeling rejection and will aid me greatly in overcoming this unhappy passion."[17] His first reaction was one of anger, which was followed by many weeks of anguish and despondency. That despondency did not prevent him from riding up to Ripley with his entire family to vote for James Denver for Congress. When he departed from Levanna two weeks later, he added, "I never left home in such a state of mind."[18]

He arrived back at Fort Stanton on November 18 and seems to have put the disappointments of his extended trip behind him. He learned that Captain McKibbin and Captain McCleave had been active in his absence, mounting two extended scouts looking for hostile Indians. They found none. In October, McKibbin had organized an expedition, including all of McCleave's company as well as about thirty cavalrymen sent from Forts Selden and Craig and some of McKibbin's infantrymen mounted on mules, about 100 men in all. They had marched all through the Guadalupe Mountains and, although they had surprised one large encampment of Mescaleros, they accomplished little more than the capture of three squaws and five children. They arrived back at Stanton four days before Kautz, the men disappointed and exhausted and their mounts jaded.

On November 22, Kautz had a talk with one of the three captured Indian squaws who was the wife of Jose La Paz, a minor chief of the Mescaleros. He learned that the Mescaleros had not fully recovered from Cushing's work of the previous winter and were apprehensive that another winter offensive might destroy them. He arranged for McKibbin to escort her as far as the Pajarita Mountains to see if she could contact her people and convince them to come in to the reservation. She returned on December 14 on foot and quite fatigued, having lost her horse, and informed Kautz that she had contacted them "and they consented to come in but it will take some time to get them together."[19] One of the other squaws, whom Kautz called "Timber Head," said that she was confident that she could find the Mescaleros, so Kautz sent her out two days later to try to do so.

On the afternoon of February 6, some Mexicans brought the exciting news that some of the Indians were approaching on the Ruidoso River. Apparently Timber Head had found La Paz and his band camped on the Pecos River and was bringing them in to the fort. Emil Fritz and Captain McKibbin volunteered to meet them with presents. It seems that one of the presents offered by Fritz that night must have been whiskey because, as the small group of the Indians arrived the next day, La Paz was so drunk that Kautz had no chance to speak with him. He did, however, meet with La Paz on February 8 and explained his status. Apparently Kautz offered protection for the Indians on a reservation and promised that they would be fed by Fritz and Murphy. Four days later, Kautz provided La Paz a mule and rations so that he could go after the remainder of his people.

They came slowly at first but, by the time Kautz left Fort Stanton in 1872, a census of the Fort Stanton Reservation counted 830 Mescaleros and more than a thousand other Indians. The Indian problem in southern New Mexico was solved for the time being, thanks in part to Kautz's efforts.

Early in the previous December, orders were received to prepare to enlarge Fort Stanton to a four-company post. Even in the bitter cold of that winter, Kautz got the work started. By the first week in April 1871 he was able to move into new commanding officer's quarters. For almost half of the year of 1872, however, he was away from Fort Stanton on short trips attending courts-martial, inspections or investigations at some of the other posts in New Mexico and, in keeping with his growing interest in mining, he visited the mines at Nogal and Silver City. On one such trip, he spent almost the entire months of October and November at Fort Union attending courts-martial.

On October 11, the same day that news of the great Chicago fire reached him, Kautz also learned that there was to be an opening at the Army Recruiting Station at Newport Barracks, Kentucky. He immediately wrote to General Sherman requesting assignment to that duty and, two days later, wrote to Phil Sheridan asking him to lobby for the appointment. On April 10, 1872, he happily received orders to report to Newport Barracks. He left Fort Stanton a week later.

36. Newport Barracks

The transcontinental railroad, first authorized by Congress during the administration of Abraham Lincoln, was completed in 1869 when construction crews of the Union Pacific and Central Pacific Railroads met at Promontory, Utah. By the time the ceremonial golden spike was driven at Promontory, many branch railroad lines had sprouted along the main line. Such a road was the narrow-gauge Denver & Rio Grande, which, its ambitious developers hoped, would some day reach all the way to Mexico City. Although that hope was never realized, by April 1872, the D & RG was completed from Denver to Colorado Springs. August Kautz was relieved to learn that he could meet the D & RG at Colorado Springs, thus cutting almost in half the disagreeable stage ride from Fort Union to the nearest railhead.

It appears Kautz was not expecting to return to New Mexico. Before bidding goodbye to Fort Stanton he sold off all his household furnishings. Although he seemed anxious to get away from Stanton, he took his time getting to Newport, stopping, among other places, at his parents' home in Levanna. As he left for Newport, he noted, "As I was not going far away this time, the leave taking was not difficult."[1] He took command of Newport Barracks on May 28, 1872.[2]

The post was situated on six acres on the east bank of the Licking River at the point where that stream empties into the Ohio. The Licking separates the city of Newport from its sister city to the west, Covington. The brick buildings of the post, surrounding a parade ground, were somewhat run-down, but were a considerable improvement over Forts Craig and Stanton. The commanding officer's quarters, a two-story building of ten rooms, was located on the river side of the parade ground with a large porch overlooking the river and the city of Cincinnati beyond.

The duties of the commanding officer were few, consisting of the usual post paperwork and of certifying, after a physical exam by the post's doctors and an interview with the commander, that each of the recruits was fit for infantry service. Always an early riser, Kautz rarely worked past 10 A.M. except on Sundays when, weather permitting, dress parade and band music were held on the parade ground, much to the delight of crowds of local citizens and visitors.

The recruits received little or no training at Newport Barracks. From time to time, detachments of recruits would be escorted to the various regiments by officers of the regiments or by those stationed at the post. Kautz was aided in his work by the post adjutant, Casper Conrad, who had been ordered to Newport Barracks shortly before Kautz. One of the first orders which Kautz issued sent the entire recruit detachment across the river to Spring Grove Cemetery to help decorate the graves of soldiers who had died in the Civil War.[3]

The business of furnishing a few rooms of his large house—furniture, carpets, china, et. al.—occupied Kautz's time for several weeks and cost most of his pay for several months. Fortunately, he received an allowance from the Quartermaster Department to "expand or repair"[4] his quarters.

If Kautz had suffered from a lack of "society" beside the Rio Bonito, he made up for it on the shores of the Ohio. After less than two months at Newport, he noted, "My service here will not admit of much work. My time will be too much taken up with society."[5]

During his first six months at Newport, Kautz made three visits up river to visit his family and, at various times, almost all of his Brown County relatives stayed with him at the barracks. Even his mother, who rarely ventured from her home, was among the fifteen or twenty family members who arrived on the boat to enjoy the fireworks and festivities on the Fourth of July. For much of this time, Kautz's brother Albert was unassigned and awaiting orders. He was living with the family of his wife Esther in Ripley, and Albert and Esther were frequent overnight guests at the barracks.

The mouth of the Licking River as it enters the Ohio, ca. 1870. On the right is Newport Barracks. The commanding officer's quarters is the leftmost of the buildings.

In mid–July, Kautz spent a pleasant week with the Tod family in Youngstown and noted that his meeting with Grace Tod "awakened nothing more than kindly and friendly feelings."[6]

Cincinnati was the most German city in the nation and the most metropolitan city west of the Appalachians, and Kautz took full advantage of the libraries, theaters, both English and German, and other amusements the "Queen City of the West" had to offer. He and fellow officers at Newport Barracks, such as Lieutenant Conrad and post surgeons Peter Moffatt and Ebenezer Swift, often visited the "Over the Rhine" district of the city and were frequent patrons of the Fifth Street Beer Gardens in the heart of the city. Cincinnati was also a major transportation hub and Kautz served as a gracious host, offering lodging at his house to a long list of army officers passing through the city. General Sherman and President Grant were among important visitors to the city to be called upon by Kautz and serenaded by the Newport Barracks band.

Among the many important local citizens with whom Kautz visited and became well acquainted were Israel Garrard, who had served under Kautz in the Second Ohio Cavalry, Judge Stanley Matthews,[7] and August Tobbe, the Catholic bishop of the Diocese of Covington. All three were regular visitors at Newport Barracks. Kautz also made visits to Jesse Grant, who was

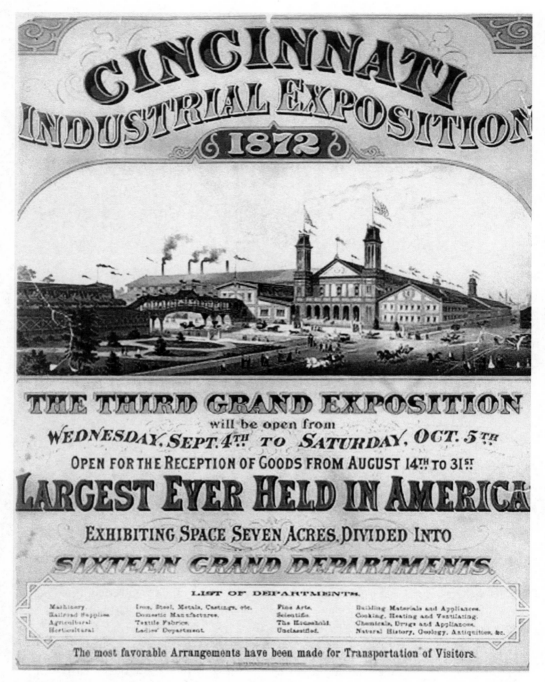

While at Newport Barracks, Kautz was a frequent visitor to the 1872 Cincinnati Industrial Exposition and served as a judge in one of its competitions.

a resident of Covington, and sadly noted the deterioration in the old man's health. Hannah Grant, who had not been particularly friendly toward Kautz in the past, was most appreciative of Kautz's interest in her husband and brought the president's father to visit Kautz at the barracks on several occasions.

In September and October, Kautz made at least twenty trips across the river to see and study the exhibits at the Cincinnati Industrial Exposition and once was called upon to be a judge in one of the exposition's competitions dealing with military equipments.[8] During the month that the exposition was open, the flow of visitors who came for the exposition, but stayed with Kautz as overnight guests, increased markedly. In anticipation of this increased traffic, Kautz had furnished two additional bedrooms in his quarters, but even this added space proved inadequate and he was forced to sleep in his library more than once.

A few days in November were spent in Dayton attending a reunion of the Army of the Cumberland. Although it afforded an opportunity to spend some time with his best friend, Phil Sheridan, and to rub shoulders with a great number of other officers, Kautz seemed more impressed with a chance meeting he had with Miss Vinita Ream at the Soldier's Home in Dayton.[9]

Although his stay at Newport Barracks did not represent an important period in August Kautz's military career nor help to further that career, it would prove to be a landmark time in his personal life, as we will soon see.

37. Fannie Markbreit

Three days after August Kautz arrived at Newport Barracks, he complained in his journal that "Old Joe," the cook, failed to prepare sufficient food for dinner. It was Kautz's own fault. Joe had cooked for Kautz and himself, but Kautz had neglected to inform the cook that he was having guests for dinner, Lieutenant Casper Conrad and his wife and a guest of the Conrads, Miss Fannie Markbreit. Kautz had never met Conrad's wife, who had been living in Columbus, Ohio, while her husband was stationed in New Mexico. A gregarious individual, Mrs. Conrad had acquired a sizeable circle of friends since coming to Cincinnati, among them Fannie Markbreit. Kautz mentioned in his journal that night that Miss Markbreit was the half-sister of his acquaintance Frederick Hassaurek.[1] On the following Sunday, Kautz remained in his quarters and he noted that he "was entertained by Miss Markbreit whose visit still continues."[2]

It was three more weeks before Kautz got an inkling as to why Miss Markbreit was staying with the Conrads. His journal tells us, "Miss M. seems to me to be more or less in the way and I do not understand why she is spending her time here. I have suspected that it is at Mr. & Mrs. Conrad's instigation with a view to my becoming interested."[3] Kautz was correct in his suspicion. Finally, just before leaving on one of several trips to Levanna, he wrote, "Miss Markbreit is still a guest with Mrs. Conrad.... I find Miss M. improves on acquaintance, but still she is far from being my idea of a woman."[4] He returned from Brown County a week later, accompanied by his sister Sophie, and he took Sophie calling with him. It seems more than a coincidence that one of the calls was to the home of Frederick Hassaurek, where they met Miss Markbreit and her mother and "passed a pleasant evening."[5]

Over the next two months, Kautz had many opportunities to spend time with Fannie. After a visit at the home of Fannie's sister, Mrs. Wolfgang (Jennie) Schoenle, he noted, "I had a pleasant evening and Miss Fanny [sic] continues to improve in my estimation of her character. I must be on my guard before I become too much interested."[6]

At no time during the course of their courtship did Kautz fully admit in his journal that he had been the pursued rather than the pursuer. On the last day of the Cincinnati Industrial Exposition, he picked Fannie up at her sister's home in a borrowed carriage and took her on a drive through the suburbs and back to the exposition. During the course of the day, he "intimated" that he might ask Fannie to marry him. The following evening, he wrote in his journal that he had a "very confidential talk" with Lieutenant Conrad that left him "so dissatisfied" with the indecisiveness of his visit with Fannie "that, notwithstanding the rain storm that threatened, I visited her again this morning and proposed to her. She has asked until Wednesday to consult her mother and brother.... I am quite relieved that I have made the proposal. I trust the action is wise and that the result may be a happy one."[7]

The next day, Kautz left for Ripley to vote in local elections, but his mind remained on Fannie. When he returned on Wednesday, he was "gratified by Miss Markbreit's acceptance"[8] and he celebrated by escorting Fannie, her mother, and her sister Jennie to a comedy at the German

Theater. Things were not entirely settled, however, because the following day, Kautz wrote in his journal, "I met Miss Fanny at the Mercantile Library[9] and we had a long talk.... I learned a painful fact that the new love will not tolerate the old and I cannot talk with her whom I love most now about her whom I loved most in the past."[10] Fannie must have made this demand rather emphatically and, perhaps, with a touch of anger for, not long after, he commented, "The antagonism, I find, is not so serious as I supposed and her temper fierce, but harmless and fleeting."[11]

The date for the wedding was set for November 27 and, as preparations were underway, the couple's affection seems, if we can read between the lines of Kautz's journal, to have grown.

During the first week of November, Kautz took the boat to Ripley to vote again — this time for Ulysses Grant for president — then took the train for New York to take care of some business at recruiting service headquarters. While there he bought gifts for his bride and new clothes for himself.[12] When he arrived at headquarters, he tells us, "I called at the Head Qrs. of the Recruiting Service and was completely taken by surprise to receive a telegram forwarded by Mr. Conrad from Newport from the Adjt. Genl. [Edward Townsend] informing me that I am to be relieved from the command of that post on the 1st of Jan. next."[13]

Kautz's surprise was due to the fact that recruit duty was usually for two years and he was to be relieved after only seven months. The telegram from General Townsend, with whom Kautz was on very good terms, was but a warning that he would soon receive the order. Although it was Townsend who would eventually write the order, the decision to do so was General Sherman's, with whom Kautz was not on such good terms. It seems that General John Pope,[14] who had relieved John Schofield in the Department of Missouri while Kautz was in New Mexico and with whom Kautz was definitely on bad terms, had convinced Sherman that he needed Kautz back in New Mexico.

Pope's animosity toward Kautz was based partly on the fact that Kautz had gone over Pope's head in applying directly to Washington to obtain an extension of his long leave of absence in 1870 without Pope's approval.[15] More importantly Pope was seething over an event which had taken place only the previous spring. In his annual report on the Department of Missouri for 1871, Pope had suggested that Fort Stanton was of little importance and should be abandoned. Kautz took exception to Pope's opinion and wrote an official letter to Pope saying that he deemed it his duty to correct Pope's error and adding that "to break up the post is to abandon the country to the Indians."[16] Pope declined to forward the letter and returned it to Kautz. On March 7, Kautz readdressed the letter to the War Department and sent it off through proper channels. When Pope saw the letter for a second time, he rightly saw Kautz's action as a breach of military courtesy and a personal affront to himself. He forwarded the letter to division headquarters where, fortunately for Kautz, Phil Sheridan read it and pigeonholed it. Sheridan's action did not assuage Pope's anger and he apparently requested that Kautz be sent back to duty as a way of getting even.

Immediately after receiving Townsend's telegram, he hopped on a train to plead his case in Washington. At the War Department, according to his journal, "The first man I met was Genl. Sherman. He did not know me at first, but was cordial enough when he called me to mind. He was kind enough to reconsider his intention of ordering me to be relieved on the 1st of Jan." Not fully convinced that his interview with Sherman had had its desired effect, Kautz called on General Townsend, General Sheridan, who just happened to be in Washington at the time, and President Grant to ask their assistance in lobbying for his cause. He concluded his journal entry for that day with, "I ... consider myself fortunate in seeing all my friends and left the city in the evening on the through train much happier in mind than I was this morning."[17]

The military wedding took place at 8 P.M. on November 27 at St. Paul Episcopal Church on Seventh Street in Cincinnati with Reverend William A. Fiske officiating. Besides members of both families, a number of local dignitaries attended, including Mayor Simon Davis. Kautz

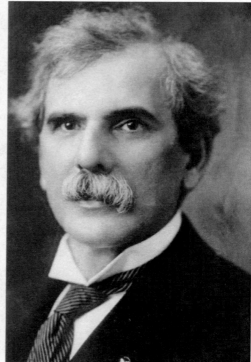

Left: Fannie Markbreit. This photograph was taken about the time of her marriage to August Kautz. *Right:* Leopold Markbreit, lawyer, soldier, ambassador and journalist, ca. 1875. As part owner and editor of the German-language newspaper the *Cincinnati Volksblatt,* Markbreit virtually controlled the German vote in Ohio. He was elected mayor of Cincinnati in 1907 and died in 1909 while still in office. Both photographs are from August Kautz's photograph album, courtesy Virginia (Kautz) Borkenhagen.

was especially happy that his mother and Lou Denver were able to attend. Frederick Hassaurek gave the bride away and Miss Ruth Goodin[18] was her bridesmaid. Major (Brevet Colonel) William Merrill was best man and Casper Conrad, Captain (Brevet Lieutenant Colonel) William Lyster and First Lieutenant James Wheelan served as ushers. There was a small reception after the ceremony although a larger and more formal reception was to be held on December 12. Articles in at least two Cincinnati newspapers commented on how well the officers looked in their new dress uniforms. The *Cincinnati Enquirer* mentioned that "the couple left on the 9:45 train for New York," but the reporter was mistaken in that August and Fannie took so long saying goodbye to their friends that they missed the train and were forced to take a room at the Burnet House.[19]

They did finally get off to New York and, after a week's honeymoon, returned to Newport Barracks on December 7, tired after the long train ride. The following day was Sunday, a day of rest, and Kautz noted in his journal, "The entire day was spent in barracks trying to accommodate ourselves to the new life."[20]

The "new life" included a full social schedule built around Fannie's friends and family including her brother Leopold,[21] who arrived in town on April 16 and lived with the Kautzes from May to July.

The newlyweds held their formal wedding reception on December 12 and, although about half of the invited guests were prevented from attending due to heavy ice on the river, Kautz was satisfied that "it passed off very well."[22]

Early in January, the couple journeyed to Chicago for a three-day visit with Phil Sheridan. Kautz was able to introduce his bride to his best friend and they attended a party, "a grand affair," hosted by Sheridan on the night of January 8. Kautz wrote of a conversation he had with Sheridan that same morning, "Sheridan ... told me that Genl. Sherman had promised Genl. Pope to send me to the Regt. in June."[23]

Toward the end of February, it became obvious that Fannie was pregnant and, when Dr. Swift left for Washington to attend Grant's second inauguration, Kautz asked him to "ascertain our chances of remaining at this post."[24] When Swift returned on March 15, Kautz wrote, "He does not bring any encouraging news from Washington."[25] The next day Kautz penned a carefully worded note to Phil Sheridan asking him to intervene to delay the return to New Mexico at least until the baby was born. Sheridan lost no time in coming to Kautz's aid, writing a personal letter to General Sherman which said in part, "I asked something over a year ago that he [Kautz] might be brought in from New Mexico ... so that he could hunt up a wife and get married.... Now he wants to stay longer than the 1st of June so that his wife can have a baby. The event comes off some time during the summer. If you can do anything for him, it will greatly relieve his anxiety."[26] At the same time Sheridan wrote a short note to Kautz telling what he had done.

Sherman's reply to Sheridan was noncommittal, but it seems his mind was not changed, because three weeks later, Kautz received a letter from Adjutant General Townsend saying, as Kautz reported, "that Genl. Sherman insists on my being relieved on the first of May. Genl. T. says that he will not issue any order until the Secretary [of War] returns to Washington, which will be in a month or so."[27]

Frederick Hassaurek, half-brother of Fannie Markbreit and partner with Leopold Markbreit in the *Cincinnati Volksblatt*, ca. 1875. Both he and Markbreit were briefly law partners of Rutherford B. Hayes prior to the Civil War. From August Kautz's photograph album, courtesy Virginia (Kautz) Borkenhagen.

Kautz heard nothing more for a month but, on May 24, he received a confidential note from Townsend that he was to stay at Newport Barracks for another year. His hopes were raised even higher a few days later. By coincidence, General Sherman was passing through Cincinnati and was staying at the Burnet House. Kautz went to the city to pay his respects to the commanding general and, to his surprise, the subject of his being relieved was not mentioned. The emotional roller coaster continued, however, because, when he returned to his quarters after the visit with Sherman, he found a note from Phil Sheridan stating that General Pope had renewed his application to have Kautz returned to his regiment. Sheridan wrote a follow-up note which Kautz received on June 2. Kautz described it in his journal: "I received a note from Sheridan in which he says he thinks I am all right, but I cannot think so as long as Sherman can have his way."[28]

What both Townsend and Sheridan were referring to in their letters came to light on June 5 when Kautz wrote in his journal, "I was quite surprised to receive an order from the War Dept. appointing me president of a board to investigate and report on military prisons. The instructions indicate it will be quite a permanent affair. This puts us at rest about going to New Mexico for the present."[29] Assignments to temporary duties such as this to the prison board were more often than not made by the adjutant general rather than by the commanding general, so it seems that Edward Townsend had found a way to save his friend from reporting to his regiment at least for a while.

It would take some time for Kautz to contact the other members of the prison board and arrange a schedule for visiting and inspecting the various prisons, so he and Fannie enjoyed the early summer weather by riding out in a newly-purchased carriage, often going out to Avondale to play croquet at Frederick Hassaurek's home.

Kautz continued his frequent calls on Jesse Grant and, on June 29, he noted that Mr. Grant was failing rapidly and that the president was on his way from Washington. Kautz's journal entry of June 30 is a sad one: "I did not learn until this morning that Mr. Grant had died last night at eighteen minutes past seven o'clock. After the duties of the morning, the Dr. [Swift] & I proceeded to Covington and offered our services to the family. The President had arrived. We ascertained that the funeral will take place tomorrow at two o'clock and the Dr. and I are to officiate as pall bearers."[30] The funeral service lasted two hours and, as the funeral procession followed a rather tortuous route to Spring Grove Cemetery, Kautz did not get away until after six o'clock. Kautz said that "some of the pall bearers were quite exhausted,"[31] but he had enough energy left to call on President Grant at the Burnet House later that night.

The members of the prison review board agreed to meet in Boston and Kautz departed on the night train on July 6, noting in his journal that his separation from Fannie would be the first of their married life. When he arrived in Washington the following evening, tired and suffering from a severe headache, he went directly to bed at the Ebbitt House, but not before reading a telegram from Leopold Markbreit informing him that an order had arrived at Newport Barracks relieving him from the prison board and ordering him to join his regiment. He took the time to write in his journal, "The indecision in regard to myself that is manifested by this order is something very disgusting. It makes me very discontented with the service."[32] He slept poorly that night and, although he did not feel up to it, he went up to the War Department to voice his discontent to Secretary of War William Belknap. He learned from Assistant Adjutant General Thomas Vincent that President Grant had gone to his retreat at Long Branch, New Jersey, after his father's funeral and that most of the members of his cabinet, including Belknap, were with him there. Vincent was very kind and suggested that Kautz go to Long Branch and speak with Belknap personally. Kautz was on the afternoon train to New York and took the boat to Long Branch the next morning. As there is no other record of Kautz's interview with Belknap, Kautz's account will suffice to describe what must have been a highly charged encounter: "I met the Secretary soon after my arrival and commenced on the matter of my orders, but he seemed offended at once and repelled me at all points and finally said that he did not see that he was required to answer my question, upon which I left him abruptly. He afterwards came to see me and said he did not wish to discontinue the conversation and he then asked me some questions relating to my personal reasons for wishing to remain at Newport Barracks & he finally yielded to these and said he would suspend the order until fall."[33] After leaving Belknap, Kautz called on President and Mrs. Grant and left Long Branch the next morning still fuming over the treatment he had received from Sherman.

Kautz was back in Washington three days later and went up to the War Department to thank Vincent for his kindness. He also mentioned in his journal that night, "I had a long conversation with Genl. Sherman. He thinks hard of me for avoiding this last order. I defended myself better than I expected and the Gen. could make no response except that he never would give me another order good or bad."[34]

When Kautz arrived back at Newport Barracks, he found an order countermanding the one ordering him back to his regiment.

The most important event of 1873 for Kautz occurred on September 12, when Fannie delivered a healthy baby boy who would be named Austin.

September was also the month of the Cincinnati Industrial Exposition and, between friends and relatives visiting Fannie and the baby or coming to the city to tour the exposition, the guest rooms were constantly full, occasioning Kautz to complain, "Between my relatives and Fannie's, I shall be glad when I get out to New Mexico."[35] Kautz was anticipating orders to go to New Mexico because, even before the baby was born, he had written to Adjutant General Townsend asking to be ordered west with the next detachment of recruits destined for his regiment.

In mid–October, Kautz traveled to Toledo, Ohio, to attend the annual reunion of the Army of the Tennessee, where he spent time with Sheridan and Grant, as well as with other officers he had not seen for years. His main object in attending the reunion, however, was to see General Pope, and the two men met on October 16. Pope's attitude toward Kautz seems to have changed, possibly because Pope concluded that Kautz's connections in Washington were stronger than his own. Kautz wrote of the meeting, "Had an interview with Genl. Pope and he expressed himself disposed to do all he can for me and gave me choice of posts within certain limits. I have chosen Stanton."[36]

After Kautz returned home and had some time to think about it, he changed his mind. He thought he might be happier at Fort Garland, Colorado Territory, than at Fort Stanton.[37] On October 21, he sent a letter to General Pope asking to go to Garland rather than Stanton. He received a reply from Pope's adjutant on October 30 informing him that assignment to Garland would be acceptable. The following day an order arrived from the War Department to report to his regiment with 100 recruits as soon as practicable.

Of course, there was the business of packing up. Kautz managed to sell off more than $500 worth of furniture, some of which, according to Fannie, was the finest they owned. Kautz made a three-day visit home to be with his parents for what he thought might be the last time. On November 7, he relinquished command of Newport Barracks to Major (Brevet Colonel) Joseph Whistler and he and Fannie moved briefly to the Walnut Street House in Cincinnati.[38] On November 10, they, along with 100 recruits, boarded the train for the frontier. They arrived at Fort Garland eight days later.

38. From Fort Garland to Fort Whipple

When the recently-widowed August Kautz was ordered to New Mexico in 1869, he managed to pack all his belongings into one valise, four trunks and two small boxes. Four years later, when he arrived in Colorado, accompanied by a wife, an infant son and a nurse, it required five large wagons to hold their baggage, which included Fannie's piano, a new turning lathe and a carriage which had been purchased in Cincinnati.

That, however, was not the only extra baggage which Kautz picked up along the way. The reader of his journals can easily detect a change in his image of himself and his position in society. This can be seen in his attitude toward servants. In the years following his graduation from the Military Academy, Kautz became accustomed to having a ready supply of domestic help in the form of enlisted men, known as "strikers." It was not until the brigadier's star was sewn on his uniform in 1864 that he felt compelled to hire a civilian manservant and that man, George Washington Lee, became as much a comrade as a servant through the last year of the Civil War. It was with regret that he parted company with George in the summer of 1865. In 1866, Kautz hired a young Cleveland girl, Ellen Denelli, ostensibly as a housekeeper, but actually as a companion for his homesick wife, Charlotte. Kautz treated Ellen as much as a houseguest as a housekeeper and, after her services were no longer needed, he found other employment for her.

After his marriage to Fannie Markbreit, the couple had a succession of unsatisfactory cooks and housekeepers. One of these was the housekeeper Rachel McClintick, who suffered a nervous breakdown, and for whom Kautz arranged admission to the city hospital and, later, to a sanitarium. Kautz felt obliged to continue to visit her until she was well on the road to recovery.

Four days after his arrival at Fort Garland, he noted in his journal that he had hired a cook, Maria Hare, the wife of a soldier at the post. He wrote of her, "She is English and knows her place."[1] His attitude had changed.

Fort Garland was located eighty miles southwest of Pueblo, Colorado, the nearest railhead on the Denver & Rio Grande. Lying in the valley of the Trinchera River, a branch of the Rio Grande, the post could only be reached by crossing 9400-foot La Veta Pass. Although remote, the Trinchera Valley was well settled, primarily by cattlemen and sheep herders.

It was a two-company post, staffed by Captain Horace Jewett's Company D, Fifteenth Infantry and Captain Andrew Caraher's Company F, Eighth Cavalry. Since Colonel (Brevet Major General) Gordon Granger, at the time both regimental and district commander, was on extended sick leave, Kautz served as commander of the Fifteenth Infantry during his stay at Garland. Regimental headquarters was moved from Fort Union to Garland and the regimental band arrived at the post shortly after Kautz, accompanied by the regimental adjutant, Lieutenant Thomas Blair, whom Kautz had known at Fort Stanton.

While her husband busied himself with command of the post, Fannie took charge of the social life. She entertained the gentlemen and ladies of the post and settlers from the surrounding area at dinners or with singing and piano playing in the evenings. Kautz was especially pleased by the multi-course dinner that Fannie and Mrs. Hare served Christmas Day.

Fannie appears to have acted as more than a hostess. Captain Caraher and his wife were not very sociable. Finding that Mrs. Caraher was shunned by the other ladies, Fannie befriended her and, in so doing, brought her into the small social circle of the post, much to Kautz's satisfaction. Fannie also took an interest in other aspects of her husband's life, even learning to ride horseback and fish for trout, both for the first time in her life, leading Kautz to comment, "I am much gratified that my wife seems so contented."[2]

Life was quiet at Garland, partly because of the post's isolation and partly because the only Native American tribe of the area, the Utes, under the leadership of their chief, Ouray, had ceded much of Eastern Colorado and moved to reservations farther west. Kautz enjoyed horseback riding and fishing, but devoted most of his time during the winter to reading, working in his shop or playing with Austin, saying, "I do not often leave the house and do not visit much in the garrison."[3] He added later, "Fannie finds fault and says I stay too much in the house."[4]

Kautz worked diligently to put the regimental records in order, even using eighty-six dollars of his own money in February to purchase a printing press for his office. He also contributed fifty-one dollars to buy instruments for the regimental band. Although the adobe buildings of the post were showing signs of age, Kautz did little to improve them, but he did have Captain Jewett's Company rebuild a boggy portion of the road from La Veta Pass.

Winters in the high valley of the Trinchera provide an abundance of cold, snowy weather, but it was an ideal spot for little Austin. "The climate is highly favorable for children, who seem to escape the fatality that exists in the States. There half the children die before they are two years old, here it is the exception for children to die." He failed to mention, however, that his own health while in Colorado was the best it had been for years.[5] His state of good health was more likely due not to the climate, but to his return to a regular program of exercise and diet which had been neglected during his stay in Newport. Maria Hare's delicious and ample cooking made adhering to the latter somewhat difficult.

Unfortunately, Fannie caught Mrs. Hare in a lie related to some missing bolts of cloth. When her husband, who had taken to drinking heavily, backed her in the lie, Kautz felt obliged to discharge them. Before allowing them to leave, however, he made sure that they were well provisioned. Kautz later learned that they had run up a sizeable bill for food at the post trader's store, food which had never reached the Kautz table.

Somewhat interested in investing in silver mining properties, Kautz made three trips, in January, May and July, to the mountains west of Denver to examine some potential silver lodes, but he was unable to find suitable properties in which to invest. Although he did some woodworking during his stay at Garland, much of the time spent in his shop was devoted to practicing assaying techniques using laboratory apparatus and chemicals purchased in Cincinnati.

Fannie's mother had expressed an interest in visiting her daughter, so Kautz arranged for her to take the train to Denver, where he met her on May 27 during his second trip to the mines. She remained at Fort Garland for the rest of the Kautzes' stay there.

On the first day of April, 1874, Kautz received a letter from his sister Sophie, notifying him that his mother had died on March 23. Dorothea Kautz had been injured in a fall down the stairs at her home the previous summer and had never fully regained her health. The note of condolence which Kautz subsequently wrote to his father proved to be one of the most difficult letters he had ever written.

For quite some time Kautz had been watching his name move slowly up the list of lieutenant colonels eligible for promotion to colonel. He was aware that the retirements of Abner Doubleday and Robert S. Granger in December 1873 placed his name at the top of the list. In February

Fannie Kautz's mother, Johanna (Abele) Markbreit, ca. 1875. From August Kautz's photograph album, courtesy Virginia (Kautz) Borkenhagen.

1874, it was rumored that Colonel James Bomford of the Eighth Infantry had come before the retiring board and, in March, the name mentioned was that of his classmate, Charles R. Woods of the Second Infantry. At the time the Eighth was stationed in Wyoming Territory and the Second was in the Pacific Northwest, and Kautz pondered the advantages and disadvantages of assignment to either of these regiments. On June 17, he returned from a day of fishing to read in the newspapers that his name had been placed in nomination before the Senate as colonel of the Eighth Infantry. Two days later he read another newspaper report that the Eighth Infantry was to be transferred from Wyoming to California. He wrote in his journal, "I may, therefore, expect to be stationed at Angel Island in San Francisco Harbor. Fannie is delighted at the prospect."[6] He did not, however, mention how Fannie reacted on June 21 when he received a copy of the order directing the Eighth Infantry to proceed not to California but to Arizona Territory. On July 8, when he returned from the third of his trips to the mines, he found in the mail his commission as colonel of the Eighth Infantry *vice* James Bomford. As soon as it became apparent that he would be ordered to Arizona, Kautz applied for an extended leave of absence in order to go east to visit his family and friends and to arrange his business affairs.

On the evening of July 30, a ball was held by the people of the village of Culebra, south of Fort Garland, to thank the Kautzes for the many kindnesses they had performed while at the post. The dancing lasted until well past midnight and both Kautz and his wife awoke the following morning sick from their dissipation of the night before.

Over the next week, they were able to sell off the household furnishings they did not wish to take to Arizona, although Kautz was unable to find a buyer for his two horses. As the small wagon train carrying them and the remainder of their possessions pulled away from Fort Garland on the road to Denver on August 6, 1874, Kautz noted in his journal, "Most of the people of the garrison accompanied us to the Eight Mile Hill where they took leave of us."[7]

Colonel Kautz made most of the trip from Fort Garland to Denver on horseback while his family rode in the comfort of the post ambulance at the head of a small caravan carrying all their earthly possessions. For the further comfort of the ladies, it was a somewhat leisurely trip with stops at Pueblo to visit friends and at Manitou Springs to join the tourists enjoying the hot mineral baths.

The morning after their arrival in Denver, Kautz saw the rest of the family off on the train to Cincinnati and introduced them to a fellow passenger, Charlie Blair, his Georgetown schoolmate, now a resident of Fort Scott, Kansas, and interested in politics. He managed to trade his two horses to a local brewer for a town lot in Denver and spent the evening with James Denver, who was visiting the city which he was proud, and a little embarrassed, to acknowledge was named for him.

One more day saw Kautz on his way to Cincinnati by a less direct route, including a visit to some farm land in Iowa which he had purchased in 1868 and an overnight stay at Phil Sheridan's home in Chicago. He reached Cincinnati on August 23.

While in Chicago, Kautz received official notice that his leave had been denied, thus requiring him to limit his stay in Ohio. Three days were spent in Levanna, where he noted, "Father still retains all his vitality and animation and seems contented," and added later, "I missed Mother, but I did not make our visit uncomfortable by recurring to her memory."[8] He also seemed pleased to mention that Fred and his wife, Lucinda, brought their son named Sheridan along when they came to visit him.[9]

Before leaving Cincinnati for San Francisco on September 3, Fannie hired a new nurse to care for Austin. She was a nineteen-year-old black woman, born in Kentucky. Kautz wrote of her, "Our nurse, Julia Pauline Robinson, seems to be an efficient nurse and for a colored girl, is unusually intelligent."[10] A woman she met on the train, citing the high cost of living in the West, tried to convince Pauline to strike for higher wages. After their arrival in San Francisco on September 10, Pauline assured her employers that she had no intention of going on strike. This simple act was only the first of many which, over a period of many years of service, would endear her to the Kautz household and alter Kautz's somewhat jaded opinion of the servant class.

The day after his arrival in San Francisco, Kautz reported to John Schofield, commander of the Division of the Pacific, and received orders to proceed to Fort Whipple, Arizona. While waiting for transportation to Arizona, Kautz enjoyed pleasant reunions with his former classmates, John Mullan, now a successful lawyer; George Mendell, who had recently been assigned the task of redesigning the California coastal defenses; and with John Kelton, who had shown such kindness during Kautz's European tour in 1859. From Mendell, Kautz learned that his West Point roommate, Henry de Veuve, was living at nearby Fort Point. On September 19, he and Fannie called on de Veuve and "found him and his family in very poor circumstances."[11] Two days later, the kind-hearted Fannie took Austin and the nurse to Fort Point and spent the entire day with the de Veuves. She brought them back to the city for dinner and Kautz added about his old friend, "He seems to be as impracticable as ever ... and seems to have a great many prospects, but no success."[12]

On September 24, the Kautzes boarded the steamer *New Bern* for the two-week passage down the coast and up the Gulf of California to the mouth of the Colorado River. There they boarded the river steamer *Cocopah* for the trip to Fort Yuma, the main supply depot for troops stationed in Arizona. They then transferred to the smaller steamer *Gila*, which delivered them farther up the Colorado to the town of Ehrenberg one month to the day after they had left San Francisco.

It took but a day to load their baggage into wagons sent from Fort Whipple. Kautz was thankful it took no longer, writing, "We were not sorry to leave Ehrenberg, which is a dreary, uninteresting place."[13] After a six-day trip over a rough wagon trace, they arrived at Fort Whipple on October 31.

The fort was located on the left bank of the intermittently dry Granite River about a mile north of the town of Prescott. It was a two-company post, its adobe buildings laid out in a quadrangle around a central parade ground. Department headquarters, usually referred to as Whipple Depot, was a separate facility located on higher ground just to the north. Most of the officers of the depot were, however, quartered at Fort Whipple.

Prescott, with a population somewhat more than 1000, almost ten percent of Arizona's population, was the most "Gringo" town in the territory. It had once been the territorial capital, but now much of the town's activity derived from silver and gold mines in the nearby mountains. Only Tucson, the territorial capital, with a population near 3000 and a strong Mexican influence, was larger.

The first persons to greet August and Fannie Kautz were George Crook and his wife, the former Mary Dailey.[14] The meeting was a distinct pleasure for both officers and the Crooks invited the Kautzes to share their quarters on the hill until they could get settled.

Crook had taken command of the department in the spring of 1871. He had been reluctant to take the Arizona assignment, but had agreed to do so at the urging of Arizona Governor Anson P.K. Safford. After meeting with the governor in Tucson, Crook had set out in July 1871 with five companies of the Fifth Cavalry on a reconnaissance to Camp Verde. Twice his offensive operations were halted to permit peace emissaries, Vincent Colyer and General O.O. Howard, who were sent by the Board of Indian Commissioners in Washington, to attempt to implement President Grant's "Peace Policy."[15] Although these men did little to ensure permanent peace, they did lay out a system of reservations for the Apache Indians, including a huge reservation for Cochise and his Chiricahua Apaches in the southeast corner of the territory between the San Pedro and San Simon Rivers and enclosing the Dragoon and Chiricahua Mountains.

It wasn't until September 1872 that Crook's campaign got started in earnest. By the following April, he had induced, through force and intimidation, all of the various bands of Apaches, with the exception of the Chiricahua, onto reservations. Much of Crook's success can be attributed to two innovations. First, he organized companies of Indian scouts, each under command of an army officer, to fight alongside his own troops. Secondly, he employed trains of pack mules rather than army wagons, thus allowing his flying columns to follow the enemy into mountain recesses where they had heretofore found refuge. By the time Kautz's Eighth Infantry arrived, the territory enjoyed a state of relative peace, interrupted only by occasional excursions of small numbers of renegades from the reservations.

As had been the case in New Mexico, the companies of Kautz's regiment were scattered at various posts through the territory, leaving Kautz little work except the preparation and maintenance of regimental paperwork. With both department and regimental headquarters present at Fort Whipple, the large contingent of officers present allowed for a very active social life. Dances, called "hops," were held every Wednesday night and card parties and other events occurred almost nightly. Two of Kautz's classmates, John Chandler and Andrew Evans, were on Crook's staff and rooming together. Kautz spent a number of pleasant evenings at the quarters of the "two crusty old bachelors"[16] talking over old times.

Arizona Territory was remarkably quiet through the remainder of the winter. In the first week of January, a scout was ordered by Crook into the Tonto Basin, consisting of two companies of the Fifth Cavalry and a company of Apache scouts, to round up Indians who had ventured from the White Mountain Reservation. Lasting about six weeks, the expedition killed about fifteen of the renegades and captured almost 100. Captain Frederick Ogilby of the Eighth Infantry led the scout, but Kautz was not otherwise involved.

Except for its remoteness from friends and family, Kautz was happy with Fort Whipple, but he was especially well pleased to command the Eighth Infantry, a unit which he valued as one of the finest in the army. He was realistic enough to know that although his future was secure, he had little chance for promotion beyond colonel. "I have now no hope of promotion to any higher grade and feel that my present situation is more fixed than ever before. I cannot be moved about so much. I belong to the Regt. and the headquarters of the Regt. is my home. Should I go off on leave of absence, I know to what place I must return." A few lines later, he added, "There is some expectation that General Crook will leave the Territory before long and possibly I may succeed to the command of the Dept., more because no one else cares to come here. I do not anticipate a pleasant command and I do not crave it."[17]

Crave it or not, on March 11, 1875, General Crook was ordered to take command of the Department of the Platte. Kautz took command of the department at his brevet grade of major general on March 22. His time as department commander would prove the most difficult of his military career.

39. The Department of Arizona

When August Kautz assumed command of the Department of Arizona on March 22, 1875, he wore stars on his shoulders for the first time since September 1866. Although General Sherman attributed Kautz's rise to department command to President Grant's "natural and proper predilection to his old comrades,"[1] it was more likely his reputation as an effective administrator which led to the assignment. Kautz would find George Crook's shoes difficult to fill.

The first months as department head were pleasant enough. On April 11, Fannie gave birth to a healthy baby girl named Frances, who would be known as Frankie.

Kautz put his organizational skills to work almost immediately. After appointing the members of his staff, he set about to organize the Indian scout companies which had been loosely formed by Crook. He equipped each man with a .45 caliber Springfield rifle, cartridge belt, blanket, poncho and canteen.

A major disappointment to Kautz was the loss of the Fifth Cavalry, which had performed well under Crook. One week after Frankie's birth, he was ordered to transfer the Fifth to the Department of Missouri in exchange for the Sixth Cavalry. The vanguard of the Fifth marched off to Fort Union, New Mexico, on May 1. It would be autumn before the bulk of the Sixth would arrive to take their place, leaving Kautz no cavalry and only the foot soldiers of his own Eighth Infantry. Kautz had a low opinion of Sixth Cavalry, no doubt based on its current lack of leadership. Colonel James Oakes had been colonel of the regiment since 1866, but was on sick leave for almost all of the succeeding years. In the Department of Missouri, the regiment had been successfully commanded by Lieutenant Colonel (Brevet Major General) Thomas H. Neill, but Neill was named commandant of cadets at West Point in the spring of 1875. With both of these West Pointers absent, command of the regiment fell on Major Charles E. Compton, an officer with whom Kautz would find fault on several occasions.

Not until the last companies of the Sixth Cavalry were posted did Kautz feel ready to set out on an inspection of the southern half of his department. Leaving Fort Whipple in late September 1875, he inspected Camp Verde, a four-company post forty miles east of Fort Whipple. He then made the long trek across the territory to Camp Apache, the four-company post located on the White Mountain Reservation not far from the New Mexico border. By the time he reached the San Carlos Reservation on the Gila River seventy miles south of Apache, on October 8, he was suffering from a recurrence of malaria and opted to return to Fort Whipple until quinine brought his fever under control. He left Whipple again on November 9 and visited Camp McDowell, forty miles east of the fledgling town of Phoenix, and Camp Lowell, just outside Tucson. He found both of these two-company posts in poor condition. He finished his tour by visiting Camp Grant, a three-company post fifty miles east of Tucson, where Major Compton had his headquarters, and Camp Bowie, another three-company post located in the southeast corner of the territory just east of Apache Pass in the Chiricahua Mountains. Camp Bowie was also the location of the agency for the Chiricahua Indian Reservation.[2]

While at San Carlos, Kautz had his first meeting with Indian Agent John Clum.[3] Clum had taken over at San Carlos in August 1874 with loose instructions from the Bureau of Indian Affairs to move as many of the Apaches as possible to San Carlos. His first act in this regard was the removal to San Carlos of several hundred of the Indians whom George Crook had settled at Camp Verde. Although Clum claimed that the move was made voluntarily, it was actually intimidation by Crook's troopers which made it possible.[4]

Even before Kautz assumed command, Clum had decided to relocate the Apaches at the White Mountain Reservation to San Carlos as well.

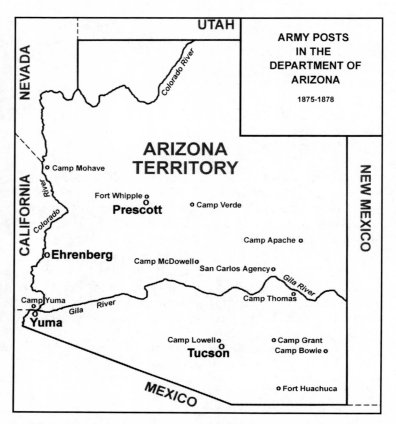

Map of the U.S. Army's facilities in Arizona Territory while Kautz commanded the Department of Arizona.

A disagreement between Indian Agent James Roberts and Lieutenant Frederick Ogilby, who commanded Camp Apache, helped give Clum the opportunity to do so. When Roberts placed restrictions on rations distributed to the 1700 Indians there, Ogilby removed Roberts and took over management of the agency in his stead, charitable acts for which Crook reprimanded him. With Roberts gone, Clum received permission from his superiors to take temporary charge of the White Mountain Agency. Kautz probably would have objected immediately had he known that Clum's main reason for going to the White Mountain Agency was to order the removal of the Indians there to San Carlos, which he did on June 17. When Kautz finally got wind of the move, he wrote to division headquarters objecting strongly. General Schofield passed the letter on to Washington with an endorsement agreeing with Kautz. As it turned out, Clum was only minimally successful in his effort. When Kautz reached the White Mountain Reservation in early October, he found as many as 1200 of the Indians still there, but most of the agency buildings burned at Clum's order.

In Kautz's meeting with Clum at San Carlos on October 8, Clum asked Kautz to remove the company of cavalry and that of Indian scouts stationed at San Carlos. He explained that he had organized an Indian police force and set up a system of tribal courts on the reservation and was certain that no additional help was necessary from the military to keep the peace. Perhaps Clum was right, but Kautz had his doubts. Despite his misgivings, on October 19, Kautz ordered Company L of the Sixth Cavalry from San Carlos to Camp Bowie. The company of Indian scouts, however, would remain.

By that time Kautz had already found himself involved in a war of words with Clum, the Indian Bureau and the Interior Department over the relative importance of the roles of the army and the Indian Bureau in management of Indian affairs and, specifically, over the concept of concentration. Kautz had the backing of his division commander, John Schofield, in the controversy, but the full support of the War Department was lacking. Clum, on the other hand, had found a valuable ally in the person of John Wasson, editor of Tucson's weekly newspaper, the *Arizona Citizen*. Wasson's newspaper had become the unofficial voice of the powerful Tucson Ring, a group of merchants and shippers who earned their livelihoods through providing, at inflated prices, food and supplies to the Indians at San Carlos and to the troops at Camps Lowell, McDowell and Grant. The Indians at the White Mountain and Chiricahua Agencies could be more readily and more cheaply supplied from New Mexico than from Tucson, so it was in the best interest of the Tucson Ring to have as many of the Apaches moved to San Carlos as possible.

The verbal squabble began innocently enough with Kautz issuing reports to his superiors of the near failure of the White Mountain removal and complaining of the underhanded way in which the removal had been carried out despite promises made by Colyer, Howard and Crook several years before. Clum on his part issued exaggerated reports of the success of the removal, claiming that more than 800 Indians had been brought to San Carlos and that more would soon follow. He was careful to note, erroneously, that the removal had been accomplished without the aid of the army. Clum was careful not to mention that, of the 500 or so Indians who had actually been moved to San Carlos, about 200 were Chiricahua, who promptly moved on to the Chiricahua Agency near Camp Bowie. The gloves had come off, however, when, on September 18, Wasson printed in his *Arizona Citizen* a letter from Clum which accused the army of "fraud, hostility and murder." Clum concluded the letter with a statement which he knew would gain the support of the Tucson Ring by saying, "last, but not least, it [the Indian removal] would avert the trade with these Indians from New Mexico to Arizona, where it properly belongs."[5]

Three days later, Wasson sent a copy of Clum's letter to Commissioner of Indian Affairs Edward P. Smith, claiming that the army had been intent on destroying Clum ever since his arrival at San Carlos.[6] Wasson induced Governor Safford to write to Smith also and, although the tone of the governor's letter was far milder than Clum's, he praised Clum highly and stated that "Clum ... is making them [the Indians] contented and therefore is serving the best interest of the people of the Territory."[7]

Kautz wisely avoided responding to these attacks directly but, on the day following his order for the cavalry company to leave San Carlos, he sent a report of his tour of the department to General Schofield in which he suggested that the greatest pressure for removing the remainder of the Indians from the White Mountain Reservation "will come from the residents of Tucson [meaning, of course, the Tucson Ring] ... for they cannot possibly compete with parties in New Mexico for the supply of the Indians."[8] That same day he wrote a long letter to President Grant's private secretary, Orville Babcock, which he knew the president would see, in which he tried to show that concentration was a betrayal of the Indians' trust and that the civilian contractors at Tucson, not wishing to compete with those in New Mexico, were behind the removal.[9]

Meanwhile, Clum had submitted a report to Washington of the prosperity of the Indians at San Carlos and suggested that what progress had been made occurred in the face of opposition by the army. Commissioner Smith forwarded the report to the War Department threatening that "if any trouble shall occur, the responsibility shall remain where it properly belongs [with the army]."[10]

When Smith's letter was forwarded to General Schofield, he responded with an explanation to the adjutant general of the irregular manner in which the removal from the White Mountain Reservation had taken place. He then reminded the adjutant general, "The military commanders will cheerfully execute the executive will when it is properly made known to them. But they do not propose to make war upon peaceable Indians upon the demand of an Indian Agent, nor in obedience to any other authority except that of their lawful superiors."[11] Schofield's letter was made known to Kautz. He would attempt to follow the principle which it clearly stated for the remainder of his tenure as department commander.

There was a lull in the exchanges between the military and the Indian Bureau during the first few months of 1876. On April 12, Kautz learned from Governor Safford that, five days before, a Chiricahua named Pionsenay had murdered a trader, Nicolas Rodgers, and his cook on the Chiricahua Reservation. Rodgers had been selling whiskey to the Indians and it was believed that he was killed because he refused to provide any more to Pionsenay. As Pionsenay fled to the Mexican border, he was joined by a large number of Indians from the reservation fearful of retribution. Kautz responded by ordering additional cavalry to Camps Bowie and Grant, but countermanded the order when he learned that all but Pionsenay and a few others had returned.

About that time, Indians raiding in New Mexico had killed several settlers, and Colonel Edward Hatch, commander of the New Mexico District, reported, probably erroneously, that they were from the Chiricahua Reservation. When reports of these events reached E.P. Smith in Washington along with a letter from Safford claiming, falsely, that the whole tribe had broken out, Smith lobbied Congress to close the Chiricahua Reservation. Congress enacted legislature ordering the removal of the Chiricahua to the San Carlos Reservation on May 1. On May 16, Kautz received an order to effect the removal.

By the end of the month, Kautz had ten companies of the Sixth Cavalry, now commanded by Colonel Oakes, at Camps Lowell and Grant ready to enforce the move. On June 5, Kautz and Clum met at Camp Bowie with Tahza, who had assumed leadership of the largest band of Chiricahua after the death of his father, Cochise. Tahza agreed to make the move. On June 7, Juh, Nolgee and Geronimo, each a leader of a small band of Chiricahua, promised to go to San Carlos as well, but all three soon fled to Mexico.

Before returning to Fort Whipple, Kautz visited the site on the reservation near the Gila River which Tahza had chosen for his people. Here Kautz ordered Captain Clarence Bailey and his company of the Eighth Infantry to construct and man a camp, later named Camp Thomas, which he hoped would prevent the Chiricahua from leaving the reservation and returning to their old haunts. He was back at Fort Whipple on June 19.

The escape of Juh and the others, which Kautz blamed partly on Major Compton's failure to deploy his three-company battalion of the Sixth Cavalry into the San Simon Valley as ordered, was a disappointment to Kautz. More importantly, it gave the members of the Tucson Ring an opportunity to renew their attacks.

On August 21, a petition was circulated in Tucson and signed by a number of merchants and government officials (including the governor), demanding that Kautz resign. The petition, accompanied by a long disgraceful attack on Kautz's character and his failure to act, written by a Dr. King, was printed in the *Arizona Citizen* and a copy was mailed to Secretary of War James Cameron.

Secretary Cameron never saw the letter. It was intercepted by General Sherman and sent through General Irvin McDowell, who had replaced John Schofield, to Kautz for his comment. At the same time, Kautz received a letter from Governor Safford falsely claiming more depredations and killings. Having only the month before received and forwarded a report by Department Inspector General Major James Biddle confirming his own suspicion that Chiricahua depredations were almost nonexistent,[12] Kautz wrote to the governor stating that not one citizen had come forth with any specific information to support the allegations and asking the governor to confirm or deny the seemingly unfounded claims. The governor did not respond.

Over the next few months Kautz's attention was drawn away from events in southern Arizona to the capture of renegades from the San Carlos Reservation who were causing minor problems far to the north in the Tonto Basin and around Camp Verde. Many of these were Indians who had left the reservation to hunt in order to feed their families. Kautz ordered a number of scouts from Camps Verde, McDowell and Apache to round up these renegades. The most notable of these expeditions, led by Major George Brayton, spent most of the months of January and February 1877 in the field and killed or captured about forty Indians.

It wasn't until mid–February that reports of depredations coming from his own officers at Camp Bowie induced Kautz to note in his journal, "There seems to be more of it than I expected."[13] Kautz was suspicious that these depredations were being committed, not by Indians from Arizona, but by Warm Spring and Chiricahua Apaches who were crossing the border from New Mexico and returning in many cases to the protection of the Ojo Caliente Reservation there. His suspicion was partly based on the fact that, in January, Lieutenant John Rucker of the Sixth Cavalry had followed the trail of a band of Chiricahua across the border and, after a sharp fight, captured a nephew of Geronimo. His suspicion was confirmed when, on March 18, he received a telegram from Lieutenant Austin Henely of the Sixth Cavalry, who was stopping at Fort Craig. Henely reported that he had seen Geronimo at Ojo Caliente with 100 stolen horses and demanding rations from the agent.

As the weather began to warm, depredations in the San Pedro and San Simon Valleys were becoming more numerous. Scouts by Lieutenant Rucker and others had followed the trails of raiders into New Mexico, but were unable to punish the offenders. In response, Kautz requested permission to enlist a fourth company of Indian scouts and also authority to construct a new camp, which he would later name Camp Huachuca, deep in Chiricahua country near the Mexican border.

Governor Safford was not so slow to act. As early as February 6, he sent a message to the Territorial Legislature claiming that twenty murders had been committed in the past six months[14] and induced the legislators to authorize a company of militia composed of thirty whites and thirty friendly Indians. The company was mustered on February 22 and soon took the field armed with weapons supplied grudgingly by Kautz. Kautz wrote in his journal, "The Governor's course is meeting with general condemnation. He has misrepresented and entrapped the legislature into very obnoxious legislation."[15]

The same day that Kautz made that note, a letter from the governor appeared in the *Arizona Citizen* dealing primarily with Kautz's mismanagement of the department. The letter was far milder than his message to the legislature and added near the end, "I do not care to get rid of any one."[16]

Kautz prepared an equally "polite" reply which appeared in the *Prescott Arizona Miner* on March 9 and put much of the blame for the Indian problems on the Indian agents, specifically those at San Carlos and Ojo Caliente. On the day he completed the letter, he noted, "I am quite sick of the job I have had writing down the lies that Safford has sent forth against me. I hope my labor will be read and appreciated by the public."[17]

Apparently the Indian Bureau shared Kautz's views that the problem was in New Mexico rather than in Arizona. On March 20, John Clum was ordered to proceed to Ojo Caliente with his Indian police to arrest any Chiricahua Indians there. On April 21, he arrested fourteen Chiricahua at Ojo Caliente, including Geronimo. Unfortunately, he had sent almost all of his police force back to San Carlos before he received further instructions to close the Ojo Caliente Agency and remove all of the Indians there, mostly Warm Spring Apaches led by Victorio, to San Carlos.

In order to facilitate the move, Clum petitioned New Mexico District Commander Edward Hatch to supply two companies of cavalry to act as escorts for the more than 400 Indians

(Victorio and his band of Warm Spring Apaches had escaped into Mexico) who were to be moved. Hatch agreed, but he wired Kautz to have troops and wagons at the border to relieve his own men when they arrived about May 4. Kautz did not receive Hatch's message until May 3 and wired Captain William Wallace at Camp Bowie to come to the relief of Hatch's men. Wallace was able to reach Clum by telegraph at Silver City, New Mexico, and asked the agent when and where he expected to cross the border. Clum, in his ongoing effort to embarrass Kautz, answered, "For the information of the Department Commander, I wish to say, no escort has been asked for from Arizona, nor will any be accepted."[18]

If the egotistical young agent considered this a battle won, he did not realize that he was fast losing his war with Kautz. On April 9, Kautz had written to Adjutant General Townsend for permission to station an officer and a small escort at San Carlos and at the other reservations within his jurisdiction, noting that such assignments were permitted by law although contrary to current policy. Kautz derived great satisfaction on June 9 in appointing Lieutenant Lemuel Abbott to the job at San Carlos with specific instructions to report any irregularities he might note in agency management. On June 22, Clum threatened to resign if an officer should come to the reservation. After Abbott's arrival on July 1, he rode away from the reservation without bothering to tender a letter of resignation.

The first week of April had brought to Kautz's desk two additional attempts of the Tucson Ring to have him relieved. On April 7, he read a letter written to the editor of the *New York Herald* written by a man named J. Lillie Mercer. The letter had been written on February 22 and contained such language as "On General Kautz' head rests the burden of every drop of human blood that has been shed by the murderous Indians since he took command." It was such a vicious attack on Kautz that it is a wonder that the *Herald* was willing to publish it. Kautz was no doubt pleased when both Prescott newspapers, the *Arizona Miner* and *Arizona Enterprise,* came to his defense with strong messages on their editorial pages in his favor.

Two days before he read the *Herald* item, Kautz's official mail contained a copy of a letter which Safford had written in early February to ex-Governor Richard C. McCormick, now Assistant Secretary of the Treasury, soliciting McCormick's influence in Washington to have Kautz relieved. The letter, which increased the number of alleged murders to thirty and was accompanied by a copy of Safford's February 6 message to the legislature, had been seen by President Hayes's Secretary of War George McCrary and came down through channels to Kautz's desk asking for his comment. Kautz's journal calls Sherman's endorsement of the letter "flattering,"[19] but it was more a sarcastic response to Safford's message, saying in part, "If Governor Safford is right ... I advise we withdraw all troops from Arizona ... and allow Governor Safford to try his hand at this game with the Apaches."[20]

Kautz's comment was a rehashing of the Indian problem citing mismanagement by the Indian Bureau and interference by the Tucson Ring and asking a court of inquiry if any action against him were anticipated because of Safford's letter. By the time Kautz's response reached Washington, Carl Schurz's Interior Department was admitting and working to correct the deficiencies of the Indian Bureau and Anson Safford had resigned as governor, claiming ill health as the reason.[21]

On May 3, the best families of Prescott held a ball in honor of General and Mrs. Kautz at the new public school in town. The affair was attended by all the officers of Fort Whipple and some from Camp Verde in their finest dress uniforms. A long article in the *Arizona Miner* described the gala event in detail, including the sumptuous dress of Fannie and some of the other ladies. Kautz had gotten wind of the event only a week before and he prepared a short speech several days in advance. According to the *Miner*, "Gen. August V. Kautz, the hero of the evening, thanked his friends in an appropriate manner."[22] On learning that he still held the confidence of the people of Prescott, Kautz was moved to tears, saying in his journal, "I came near breaking down in my little speech."[23]

Medical news took up much space in Kautz's journal as both smallpox and scarlet fever appeared in Prescott in February and March, taking the lives of a number of children in town and causing considerable alarm at Fort Whipple. Six-months-pregnant Fannie came down with an undisclosed illness in late March and with "something like intermittent fever"[24] in April, each of which kept her in bed for several days and caused Kautz much apprehension. The worst came, however, on June 12, when Fannie went into labor in the morning and was delivered at 7 P.M. of a stillborn baby girl.

The following day Kautz noted in his journal, "My wife is doing as well as possible.... About half past three, Miss Titus and Maj. [Thomas] Wilhelm accompanied me to the cemetery & we buried the remains of my child, which Fannie had christened this morning by the Chaplain by the name of Lillie.... There was a croquet party on the hill in the evening.... I went up and got some ice cream for Fannie."[25]

The day after he buried his daughter, Kautz rode into Prescott and called on newly-arrived Territorial Governor John Philo Hoyt and Territorial Secretary John Jay Gosper. He noted in his journal, "I was well pleased with them and they seem disposed to do the right thing."[26] Time would prove him correct.

Another new face in Arizona was that of Inspector William Vandever of the Indian Bureau. Vandever, a former congressman from Iowa, had served with distinction under General Sherman all the way from Vicksburg to Bentonville. He had been appointed to his post in the Indian Bureau by President Grant in 1873 and was sent to inspect the San Carlos Reservation in April 1877.

Vandever spent enough time with Agent Clum and with Governor Safford to become thoroughly indoctrinated into their views. Although it was beyond the scope of his assignment, Vandever took it upon himself to write "unofficially" to Secretary of War McCrary on May 3 "at the suggestion of Governor Safford" that Apaches had been waging a "murderous war" in southeastern Arizona and that General Kautz had "refused to believe that outrages had been committed." He went on to say that the people of Arizona "desired [that] ... General Hatch, commanding in New Mexico, or some other active officer be substituted for General Kautz." He concluded that it was also his own opinion that Kautz should be relieved, but "without injury to his feelings."[27]

Six weeks later Vandever planned a visit to the closed Ojo Caliente Reservation, but canceled his trip because of the activity of hostile Indians in the upper Gila River Valley. He fired off a telegram to the Commissioner of Indian Affairs stating that murders were occurring almost daily, making it impossible to travel, and adding that the military were "inactive."[28] Vandever had exaggerated the number of murders, and also failed to note that the upper Gila Valley lay entirely within the District of New Mexico, commanded by General Hatch, whom he had recently suggested as a replacement for August Kautz in Arizona.

Vandever's letter and telegram soon found their way to General Sherman's desk, and he forwarded his old comrade's correspondence to Irvin McDowell in San Francisco with the endorsement, "If Gen. Kautz is inactive ... I must yield to the pressures and advise a change of Commanders," and he named several possible replacements.[29]

McDowell demonstrated his loyalty to his subordinate by flatly refusing to replace Kautz without convening a court of inquiry, adding that Kautz was administering the department as well as or better than any other officer who might succeed him.[30]

Kautz seems to have been kept aware, at least in part, of what was going on, probably through John Kelton in San Francisco, because he wrote in his journal, "I received a telegram this evening indicating that I am still the object of attack of the Indian Bureau and that Genl. McDowell has taken up the cudgel for me."[31]

After receiving McDowell's firm reply in Kautz's favor, Sherman let the matter drop, although there is evidence that he had decided to do so even before he heard from McDowell, possibly for no other reason than that he was repulsed by the thought of bowing to a civilian agency in the management of army affairs.

Dutch Kautz had weathered the storm. Clum was gone. Safford was gone. He knew that he still had enemies in Tucson and that those enemies had friends in Washington, but so did he. He felt he could breathe a little easier and he tried to get back to his old routines. He would soon learn that he had an enemy in his own camp who was more dangerous to his career than the Tucson Ring, the Indian Bureau and the Apaches combined.

40. A Damper on the Party

On February 20, 1877, General Kautz wrote in his journal, "Capt. Eagan arrived with his family from the end of the RR."[1] Captain Charles Patrick Eagan had been appointed captain in the Commissary Department at the recommendation of Lieutenant Colonel William McKee Dunn, then assistant judge advocate general. He was subsequently assigned as chief commissary officer of the Department of Arizona by Commissary General Robert Macfeely, Kautz's friend since his days in Washington Territory.

Eagan performed his duties efficiently and, at first, he and Kautz got along quite well. Kautz even accepted Eagan's advice occasionally. Eagan also sought Kautz's advice, including the advisability of sending a letter of complaint he had written to General Macfeely. By that time, however, Kautz was becoming annoyed that Eagan was taking up his time in long conversations as well as by Eagan's tendency to meddle in matters which Kautz thought should not concern him. Kautz wrote, "There is considerable feeling against Capt. Eagan with the officers. He is making himself very offensive by his extreme views and his interference with the people's business."[2]

If Eagan had a close friend at Fort Whipple, it was Major Charles Reynolds, the department quartermaster. According to Kautz, "They are quite discontented here."[3] In July, both these officers sat on the court-martial of Captain Charles H. Campbell of the Sixth Cavalry.[4] Kautz had preferred charges against Campbell for misappropriation of company funds, making a false report and disrespect for a superior officer. Campbell was found guilty but, to Kautz's surprise, was sentenced only to be reprimanded. Kautz felt that Campbell deserved to be cashiered, saying, "The court has not acted with judgement in the case and I shall be compelled to disapprove of its actions."[5] Although his review of the case was unfavorable, he did not recommend a change of sentence.

Fannie Kautz had become depressed after the loss of her baby in June and wanted to go east to spend some time with her family. As early as June 19, Kautz wrote, "It would be so much better if she would have the patience to wait until I could go with her."[6] She did not get away, however, until August 18, escorted by Lieutenant George Anderson of the Sixth Cavalry, who was on his way to West Point. Kautz planned to join her later in Cincinnati.

Meanwhile, although Charles Campbell had gotten off easy in his recent trial, Lieutenant Austin Henely had preferred additional charges of misuse of government property and stealing from the company fund — very serious charges. Campbell's second trial got started October 9. Fort Whipple Surgeon Major James McKee was the presiding officer and Lieutenant Henry Kingsbury of the Sixth Cavalry was judge advocate. Campbell chose Captain Eagan as his defense counsel.

In an unusual but brilliant move, Eagan called Kautz as an expert witness, purportedly because of his recognized knowledge of "Customs of Service." Eagan's actual motive was to trap Kautz into admitting that it was his "custom" to use government equipment for his own private purposes and that Campbell had been following the example set by his commanding officer. As convening officer, Kautz would not have been expected to take part in the trial at all. When Kautz took the stand on October 13, Eagan began his examination with routine questioning, then asked whether the use of small quantities of government equipment was in fact "a violation of the true meaning of the 8th Article of War."

Judge Advocate Kingsbury objected to the question, but Kautz answered, "I think it is."

Then Eagan dropped his trump card: "Have you a spring wagon ... and team of four or more mules with harness, set aside for the exclusive use of yourself and personal staff officers?"

Kingsbury objected immediately. Dr. McKee, seeing in which direction the questioning was leading, recessed the court and, without bothering to dismiss the witness, instructed Campbell to change his line of defense or seek another counsel. Campbell chose the latter course and was given several days to find new counsel.[7]

By the time the court reconvened, Kautz was well on his way east to meet Fannie. After a busy week in Cincinnati and a quiet three days in Brown County, Kautz and his wife were off to Washington. They arrived at the Ebbitt House late on November 6.

On November 8 and 9, Kautz met at length in Sherman's office with a delegation of Arizonans, including former Governor McCormick and Arizona Territorial Delegate to Congress Hiram Stevens,[8] to discuss the Indian situation in Arizona. We might assume from Kautz's journal comments that he made at least some points with McCormick and Sherman, if not with Stevens. As evidence that he did so with little acrimony, he and Fannie were invited to a party at McCormick's home on Sunday evening, November 11.

Kautz also met with the Commissioner of Indian Affairs, the Secretaries of the Interior and War, and President Rutherford B. Hayes in regard to Indian issues. Among other meetings was one with his friend Commissary General Robert Macfeely, in which Captain Eagan was the main topic of conversation, and social calls with Fannie on General and Mrs. Macfeely, James Denver, Congressman James A. Garfield of Ohio, Senator Stanley Matthews and First Lady Lucy Hayes.[9] He and Fannie were back in Cincinnati on November 22.

Kautz received the proceedings of the Campbell court-martial on November 25. Captain Campbell had been found guilty and sentenced to be dismissed from the service. Kautz wrote his review of the case, recommending approval, and mailed it to the Secretary of War's office the next day. He would later regret his haste.

The Kautzes arrived back at Fort Whipple on January 9. Two days later, Kautz received two items in the mail which gave him what he called "some annoyance."[10] Kautz's annoyances included a brief extract of Judge Advocate General Dunn's opinion in the Campbell case handwritten by Adjutant General Townsend. The other was an article in the Prescott *Arizona Enterprise* of January 9 written by Associated Press writer David R. McKee, who was married to Dunn's daughter, Fanny. The article went into much greater detail than did Townsend's extract, stating in part that President Hayes had set aside the entire proceedings at the recommendation of Judge Advocate General Dunn and that it was a rebuke to Kautz for his actions during the trial and for his reviewing of the case while out of the department in Cincinnati.[11]

Kautz could agree with Dunn that there were irregularities in the trial, but he felt that those irregularities might warrant reconvening the court or, at most, ordering a new trial. McKee's article stated, however, that Dunn's action annulled the proceedings and discharged Campbell from further arrest or custody. Kautz was understandably upset. Kautz was convinced that Dunn had been swayed by pressure from Eagan. What Kautz did not know, and Dunn later admitted, was that David McKee's advice also influenced his decision.[12]

On January 12, Kautz wrote, "I am preparing a reply to the Judge Advocate General's opinion ... and I have determined to make an official application to have Capt. Eagan relieved from my staff on account of his antagonism."[13] Inundated by the backlog of paperwork which had accumulated during his absence and suffering from debilitating daily headaches, Kautz made slow progress. He sent the application for Eagan's transfer through channels to Adjutant General Townsend on January 16. He enclosed an acrimonious eight-page letter to Eagan's superior, Commissary General Macfeely, which was highly critical of Eagan, but unnecessarily critical of Dunn and Campbell as well, including, "Campbell is utterly worthless as an officer. I have had a great regard for his father and if there were any hope for his son I should certainly have tried to save him."[14]

Kautz had difficulty organizing the third item, his reply to the judge advocate general, to his satisfaction. When it was completed, it was in the form of a letter to Adjutant General Townsend in which he claimed that Dunn had misrepresented the facts in the Campbell case. He did not get it into the mail to Division Headquarters until January 30, three days after he had received an official copy of Dunn's opinion and learned that it was not supposed to be made public.

If Macfeely was moved in the least by his old friend's letter, it is not reflected in his dispassionate endorsement to the official application for Eagan's transfer: "As Captain Eagan has performed his duty ... in an efficient and satisfactory manner ... I do not recommend his transfer." He added that any unmilitary conduct by Eagan could be handled with a court-martial.[15]

Macfeely forwarded the application along with Kautz's letter to Secretary of War McCrary who passed it along to General Sherman. When Sherman received it on February 4, he added the following endorsement: "As a rule we should always sustain the Comdg. General of a Department, but in this case I am forced to the conclusion that there has been too much controversy, both with civil and military officers, and that a change of Dept. Commanders is advisable. I recommend that the 8th & 12th Infantry interchange Posts, and that Colonel & Bvt. Maj Genl O.B. Wilcox be appointed by the President to command the Department of Arizona."[16]

The usual Wednesday night hop took place at Fort Whipple on February 6, 1878. Kautz wrote in his journal that night, "There was quite a party gathered at the hop room as usual and we had taken our places for the first dance when I received a dispatch informing me that the 8th Infantry was to interchange with the 12th which threw a damper on the party." The next day, he wrote, "During the afternoon I rode to town and found the Eagans had been round informing the people of the good news. Eagan claims that he did it." He added the next day, "Eagan has very few friends to be happy with over what he considers his success."[17]

Eagan later became Commissary General during the Spanish-American War. In that capacity, he was suspected of taking bribes from suppliers, notably in the purchase of millions of pounds of tainted canned meats. He was tried and convicted of conduct unbecoming an officer and sentenced to be dismissed from the service. Although his sentence was commuted by President William McKinley, he resigned in disgrace. He died in 1919, a bitter and friendless man.

41. The Most Important Court-Martial Since the War

The news of the change of stations of the Eighth and Twelfth Infantry Regiments was premature. It was decided in Washington that the move would be prohibitively expensive, so only the regimental commanders would change stations, each accompanied by his staff and band and one company of his regiment.

Kautz did all he could to remain in Arizona. He had his reply to Dunn's opinion and his letter to Townsend printed in a pamphlet which he mailed not only to Townsend, but to every division, department and regimental commander in the army and to several War Department officials. He also wrote letters to Macfeely, Sherman and the president, and telegrams to the latter two. Others were working in Kautz's interest as well. Territorial Secretary John Gosper wrote a letter to the president accompanied by a petition against removal signed by more than fifty of Prescott's influential citizens, including Benjamin Morgan, who had replaced Charles Eagan as Charles Campbell's defense counsel.

When Sherman received Kautz's communication, he telegraphed a cryptic reply: "The President issued the order. No injustice; you have served your three years. Wilcox is your senior in rank and length of service."[1] By the time Gosper's letter reached Sherman's desk, he endorsed it in part, "The whole matter has long since been determined."[2]

And so it had. Kautz received from Sherman the official order transferring him on February 20. He was to go to Angel Island. By the time the order was received, Kautz was already reconciled to the move, although he said that "Fannie takes it to heart."[3]

On February 8, 1878, an editorial in the *Arizona Citizen* (now owned and edited by John Clum) commented on Kautz's removal: "Gen. Kautz is relieved and so is Arizona. The great commanding Fossil is about to receive government transportation to some remote point where his inefficiency and imbecility wont [sic] be noticed."[4]

The *Arizona Sentinel* was hardly more kind, saying, "He has been a heavy load for the army to carry.... We are tempted to say something bitter ... but ... were asked to let the poor man down easy. We will do it. He will never again obtain an important command. Promotion is henceforth beyond his reach."[5]

The *Prescott Arizona Miner* was far less critical, stating, "Gen. Kautz, in stepping down ... hands the offices of the Department over to Gen. Wilcox [sic] in a healthy and quiet state.... It is only to be hoped that he will prove equally competent and administer the affairs intrusted to him with that zealous, watchful care that has been characteristic of his predecessor's administration."[6]

It was late in the day on March 4 when Colonel Orlando Willcox arrived accompanied by his aide, Lieutenant Harry Haskell. Willcox took command of the department the following day.

Kautz and his family were able to get away from Whipple on March 12. By that time, the Southern Pacific rail line had been completed as far as Yuma, allowing them to reach Angel Island by March 21.

The following morning, Kautz went to his office to assume command and "found many letters.... The most important document was a copy of a telegram from Genl. Sherman to Genl. McDowell informing him that I am to be court-martialed at Omaha about the first of May on charges preferred by Judge Advocate Genl. Dunn."[7]

At a loss to know on what grounds he was being tried, Kautz went to the Presidio on March 23 and had John Kelton, McDowell's adjutant, send a telegram to Sherman asking that the charges be forwarded at an early date so that he might have his witnesses summoned. A response came three days later from Adjutant General Townsend stating that the charges had been mailed and were based on what Townsend termed "publishing the Pamphlet Strictures on the Judge Advocate Genl."[8]

Kautz set about in earnest to prepare his defense. When he finally received an official copy of the charges on April 2, he did not find them very serious. The charge was "Conduct to the prejudice of good order and military discipline," based on the specification that it was "wholly irregular and unmilitary" for him to have published and circulated the extracts of the Judge Advocate General's opinion in the Campbell case, which were not to be released publicly, and that he "did, in the said publication [his letter to the Adjutant General], criticize and controvert the views and conclusions which ... he had been officially informed constituted the action taken in the case of the said Campbell by the President of the United States."

Kautz was so confident in his own ability to defend himself that he considered it unnecessary to be represented by counsel. He would represent himself. He surprised General McDowell on April 8 with his list of witnesses, "the President, Secretary of War, General of the Army and Judge Advocate General."[9]

The approaching trial drew much interest throughout the army, partly because it involved a controversy between a high-ranking officer of the line and the head of one of the War Department's staff bureaus. Kautz did little to lessen that interest by sending copies of the charges and specifications to many of his army friends.

The day after receiving the order to report to Omaha, he read a long editorial in the *Army & Navy Journal* which discussed the points of the case. The editorial ended with the statement, "Judge-Advocate-General Dunn has taken the initiative in this matter and he will be sustained by nineteen-twentieths of the officers of the Army."[10]

Kautz disagreed. He noted that this was an unusual course for the editor to take and added, "I am thinking over ... the unfriendly attack in the *Army & Navy* ... and am satisfied that it has emanated from the Judge Advocate Genl's Bureau."[11]

Phil Sheridan seems to have derived some amusement from his old friend's situation, writing to Sherman, "Old Kautz will worry that court for at least three or four months."[12]

Sherman answered that he thought that Brigadier General Christopher Augur, the president of the court, would not allow the trial to drag out, adding, "I wish Kautz well, but he would not take my hints or advice, and the more I tried to caution him the more stubborn he seemed to prove."[13]

When Kautz learned who the members of his court would be his confidence of success increased. He knew General Augur well and trusted him to be open-minded. His friends, George Crook and Rufus Ingalls, were to be members. Also on the eleven-member panel were Colonel Charles Kilburn, assistant commissary general under Macfeely, and seven other colonels, all of whom were regimental commanders like himself and likely to be somewhat sympathetic to a line officer. Major Horace B. Burnham was to be judge advocate.

When he arrived in Omaha on the last day of April, Kautz was not surprised that President

Hayes, Secretary McCrary and General Sherman were not there, but he was both pleased and surprised that General Dunn was present, although Sherman had excused him.

Kautz was up early May 1 preparing his plea in bar. Just before the court met at noon in a parlor of the Grand Central Hotel, he was served with an additional specification, stating essentially that his criticism of Dunn was unmilitary. He asked for a recess until the following morning to prepare a special plea in bar to the new specification. A local newspaper described the scene: "The present court martial is the most important of any held since the war of the rebellion, and the officers are of higher rank. The members ... are the finest looking body of military men ever assembled in Omaha."[14]

When the court reconvened at ten the next morning, Kautz presented his plea in bar, claiming that there was no military offense to be found in the specifications. In his plea, he introduced a circular written by General John Schofield in 1876 which also objected to the views of the judge advocate general in another case, then commented, "I have not heard that General Schofield has been court-martialed."[15] He then went on to explain that he had distributed his pamphlet only within military circles even though he had first learned of the action of the judge advocate general by reading a report of it in a San Francisco newspaper. He said, "The law of self-defense would have fully justified me in publishing my reply in the public press." In regard to the second part of the specification, he added, in part, "I claim that the virtual assumption that I was criticizing the President is not justified.... I do not see how I can be held for criticizing the President's views by showing how the Judge-Advocate-General misled the President.... The tenor of the allegation seems to be that the Judge-Advocate-General is a privileged officer whose actions cannot be questioned."

With his attempt to bar the trial denied, Kautz pled not guilty to the charge, but guilty to almost all of the specifications. The trial then got under way when Burnham called two witnesses, both departmental adjutants, who testified unconvincingly that they considered Kautz's mailing of his pamphlet irregular if not unmilitary.

The next morning Kautz read the accounts of the trial in the local newspapers and mailed a great number of copies to his friends. He noted that the reporter for the *Omaha Republican* had concluded his article, "The bearing of General Kautz in conducting his case ... is such as to commend him to the respect and sympathy of all who watch its proceedings. He conducts his case unassumingly, but with rare shrewdness and tact, and he is evidently making a favorable impression alike upon soldiers and civilians among us. His 'plea in bar' yesterday was a weighty, telling and persuasive one, and the brevity, force and urgency with which he responded to the objections of the Judge Advocate were certainly admirable. Though it is his privilege to have counsel, it is his choice to conduct his own case and plead his own cause — which he evidently holds to be righteous and just."[16]

Much of that day was taken up with the testimony of General Dunn. He was questioned at length about his opinion in the Campbell case, but was forced to admit in the end that he had had a difference of opinion with General Sherman over his decision to overturn the result of the case before passing it on to the president.

After the court adjourned, Kautz went to General Crook's headquarters and they discussed their common interest in mining but, apparently, not the court-martial. That night the mayor of Omaha hosted a lavish reception at the hotel for the distinguished members of the court; it lasted until 1 A.M.

On the morning of May 4, Major Burnham announced that the prosecution's case was closed. Kautz then asked, perhaps tongue in cheek, whether the witnesses he had requested had been summoned. General Augur answered that the court saw no need for them. Kautz then introduced a number of documents into evidence, including the proceedings of the Campbell case and the letter which General McDowell had written at the time of the Campbell case authorizing Kautz to travel to Cincinnati. Kautz stressed to the court that the letter was in no way a leave of absence and that it stated that he would be expected to keep in touch with his department while in the East.

The following day, Sunday, Kautz commented in his journal, "I begin to think that this trial will be to my benefit whatever may be the finding of the court. The public sympathy is in my favor."[17]

In Washington, General Sherman seemed to share Kautz's optimistic view. Based on what he had read about the trial to this point, he said that "the Court would probably find the Judge-Advocate-General guilty."[18]

Monday morning saw Kautz continue his case by reading from the proceedings of the Campbell case. Things heated up on Tuesday. Major Burnham attempted to reopen his case by calling for testimony from Lieutenant Kingsbury and Major Martin, both of whom had arrived from Arizona. After being cautioned several times by General Augur that he could not do so, "he threw in the sponge and requested until the following morning to make his reply."[19]

Kautz noted, "His conduct today prejudiced his case very much."[20]

On Wednesday, May 8, Kautz took but twenty minutes to read his closing statement, which the *Army & Navy Journal* called "a carefully prepared, dignified document — short, but to the point."[21]

On May 9, Burnham delivered his two-hour-long rejoinder, "a huge document containing many words and some personalities."[22] The court then deliberated for more than two hours before adjourning *sine die*.

That night Kautz wrote, "My mind was greatly relieved. There was much disgust felt at the manner of Burnham's delivery which would have done justice to a police court. My case has not suffered at his hands. He had no idea of the case."[23]

Kautz was on the train for San Francisco on May 11. On the way, he stopped off at Colfax and took the narrow-gauge railroad to Nevada City to visit the Murchie mining properties which he and Crook had discussed in Omaha the previous week. Despite Crook's enthusiasm, Kautz was not impressed. He then went on to San Francisco and arrived at Angel Island on May 17. Eight days later, he had an opportunity to read the May 18 issue of the *Army & Navy Journal* which we have quoted above. He commented, "The *Army & Navy Journal* now takes the other side and has much to say about my case, proving my side."[24]

It was not until May 29 that Kautz read the results of his trial in the *Alta California*. As he had expected, he had been found not guilty of the charges. It was a total victory except for one minor detail. General Sherman, the reviewing officer, had written in his review, "The proceedings ... are approved. Colonel Kautz stands acquitted, and will resume command of his regiment." Then Sherman launched a two-page diatribe on "the honor and dignity of the Army ... respect for the lawful decisions of constituted authorities" and "cheerful obedience ... not the obedience of the slave, but of the knight." He concluded with: "Therefore, although the Court-Martial in the case of Colonel Kautz finds 'no criminality' in his publication, the General is constrained to say that it was more than 'irregular;' it was improper, and must not be taken as an authorized precedent."

After reading Sherman's remarks carefully, Kautz was moved to say, "He has done himself more harm than he has me."[25]

42. Benicia Barracks

Before the Kautz family left Arizona, the brevet major general was able to write, "I have overcome all regret at leaving and am looking forward to a pleasant time at Angel Island."[1] A week after reaching the island, he added, "We shall probably become as much attached to this place as we have been at Prescott."[2]

Kautz proved incorrect. Within three months he was directed to move his headquarters from Angel Island to Benicia Barracks, thirty miles northeast of San Francisco on the north shore of Carquinez Strait, the channel through which the Sacramento River empties into San Pablo Bay.

The order for Kautz's removal from Arizona had come directly from General Sherman, but it was Irvin McDowell who chose Benicia Barracks for the Eighth Infantry's headquarters. Kautz accepted this last move philosophically, attributing it to McDowell's tendency to micromanage affairs within his Division of the Pacific.[3]

By early autumn all but one of the companies of the Eighth Infantry were out of Arizona and Kautz found himself in command of a regiment scattered from Fort Yuma and San Diego in southern California to Forts Bidwell and McDermit on the Oregon border.

Kautz's adjutant, Lieutenant (Brevet Major) Thomas Wilhelm, served Kautz well, leaving little more for him to do but sign rolls and reports. This left Kautz complaining in his journal that he had nothing to do and added once, "There is little for any one to do here and I scarcely know how to keep all hands usefully employed."[4]

Several companies of the Eighth Infantry saw field service against the Bannock Indians in Idaho in 1878, but they were under the command of General O.O. Howard. Kautz accepted this anomaly readily. He knew that frontier warfare, as often as not, was the business of individual companies operating independently, leaving the regimental commanders little more to do than to command the posts which they occupied. And so it was with Kautz while at Benicia Barracks.

He was occasionally rankled when even this limited responsibility was taken from him under General McDowell's command. McDowell had a tendency to meddle in affairs of the post which were Kautz's responsibility. Kautz was patient with McDowell, knowing that the general had stood behind him through his troubles in Arizona. He excused the general when he wrote, "The Division Commander desires to be just and tries to do what is right, but so unsuccessfully that I am often excited to antagonism.... He prefers to command my post virtually and allows me no discretion. If he prefers to do my duty for me I shall not object until he holds me responsible for his own mismanagement.... I am, however, so satisfied of his honesty of purpose and desire to do the right thing that I am loth to add to the perplexities his course brings upon him."[5]

In September 1878, it was learned that General Sherman and his aide, Alexander McCook, would be arriving in San Francisco from Arizona on an inspection tour. Mrs. Kautz urged her husband to call on the commanding general and Kautz agreed to go. He said of the meeting in Sherman's private car, "The Genl. received me very cordially and invited us [Fannie was with him] into his car. He was cheerful and interesting in his talk."[6]

Kautz was so pleased with the meeting that he remained in the city in an attempt to cultivate friendly relations with Sherman. He spent several hours in the evening in Sherman's rooms with Mendell and McCook. The meeting with his two friends and the commanding general was so pleasant that Kautz celebrated by going to the Tivoli and "witnessed the music, told stories and drank beer until the place closed."[7] The next morning he awoke with a severe headache which he attributed to the beer.

The following month, Kautz was called upon to testify before the joint committee of Congress studying the feasibility of transferring the Indian Bureau from the Department of the Interior to the War Department. That committee had been formed as a stipulation of the Army Appropriations Bill that year. Members of the committee traveled throughout the country interviewing army officers and Indian agents as well as a few Indians and other concerned citizens. On October 30, 1878, Kautz met John Kelton at the Palace Hotel in the city. Kelton accompanied him to the committee room, where he was interviewed by Senator Thomas C. McCreery of Kentucky and Congressman Andrew R. Boone, also of Kentucky.

When asked by Senator McCreery to give his opinion of the proposed transfer, Kautz answered curiously, "My opinion is that it would be beneficial to the Indians of the country and to the government to make the transfer of the Indian Bureau to the War Department. As commander of the Department of Arizona, I was an advocate of the transfer, but as a post commander in a subordinate capacity I am not an advocate of the transfer."[8]

When McCreery asked him why the different opinions, he answered, "As department commander I was responsible for the peace of the Territory of Arizona, and if I could have had control of the Indians I could have preserved that peace much better than not having control of them. As post commander I should have no such responsibility, and there is a certain taint connected with the management of the Indians."

McCreery then asked why he thought it would be more economical to transfer the bureau. He answered, "I believe it is possible, with unrestricted powers on the part of the Army, to make the Indian entirely self-supporting. I believe the agents can be dispensed with entirely," and added that his opinion was based on twenty-six years as an officer, all on the frontier except during the Civil War.

When McCreery asked on what facts Kautz based his opinion, he answered, "I have put myself on record in my annual report of last year. I sent a copy to each member of this commission."[9]

McCreery asked Kautz to summarize the information contained in the report. Kautz then went into a long explanation of the overestimates by the Indian agents of the number of Indians on the Mescalero Reservation in 1869 and those on the San Carlos Reservation from 1875 to 1877. He then commenced to explain how the almost self-supporting Indians on the White Mountain Reservation were forced to remove to the San Carlos Reservation, where they became completely dependent on rations furnished by the agency.

Congressman Boone interrupted with, "They did not raise anything?"

Kautz answered, "No sir; did not raise anything. When those Indians were under the charge of General Crook ... they were in a fair way of being self-supporting. They were being made to work by the troops. I think that is the only way the Indian can be made self-supporting — by force."

After a few more comments by Kautz, Senator McCreery came back to this same point: "If they had the alternative — labor or starvation — most of them would work?" To this, Kautz responded in the affirmative.

A few more exchanges occurred before McCreery came back to the subject of the White Mountain Indians: "They did not raise anything toward their own support, according to the last report?"

Kautz answered, "No, sir." Then he added, "I would call the attention of the commission to my report.... I have taken very positive ground there in relation to this matter. The decided stand I took in my annual report I am satisfied brought about my removal from the command of that department through influences originating in the Interior Department. I was regarded, I presume, as antagonistic to that branch."

Seeing that Kautz had strayed from the purposes of the committee, Boone changed the subject. "I want to ask you a general question.... There are a large number of white men who are attempting to speculate upon the Indians. Are these not on their lands and encroaching upon them?" When Kautz answered that they were, Boone went on, "State whether or not that class of men ... are very much opposed to the Indian management being transferred to the military department."

"Yes, sir; they are."

"Can you give the reason of that?"

"The reason is they have a great many more officers to corrupt in the Army than they would have under the Interior Department," Kautz replied, and added, "I do not like to say anything more for the Army than for any other class of human beings, as far as that is concerned."

After another question on the difficulty of corrupting army officers, Boone allowed Kautz to return to the subject of his removal by asking, "I would be glad if you would tell the commission whether or not ... your removal was urged by that class of men on account of the fact that an agent countenanced their efforts at peculation."

Kautz responded, "I believe that was the reason of my removal."

Although Kautz was probably wrong on this last point, he was able to get in one last dig against the Tucson Ring.

The work of the Joint Committee went essentially unnoticed in Washington.

In November of that year, Kautz met George Crook and several other officers at the Murchie Mine. Kautz was pessimistic about the prospects of the mine. Nonetheless, he spent much of his pay over the next several months to purchase 900 shares of Murchie stock to add to 587 he had purchased previously.

Kautz's mining speculation was not limited to the Murchie. Shortly after he left Arizona, he had purchased 300 shares of the Tip Top Mine and, in March 1880, he and several San Francisco friends bought the Rowe Mine, incorporated it and offered its stock publicly. Both of these Arizona properties shared one thing in common with the Murchie Mine. All were dismal failures and cost Kautz many thousands of dollars. Fortunately, his real estate investments were more successful and continued to appreciate and, in July 1879, he sent $500 to Edward Huggins to purchase property in the city of Tacoma. Interestingly, Fannie encouraged her husband in his investment schemes, hoping he might be sufficiently successful to afford a trip to Europe.

The two-story commanding officer's quarters at Benicia were spacious enough to accommodate the Kautzes, Miss Emma Titus, Pauline and Pauline's mother Emeline Monroe,[10] with ample room for guests who arrived from the city. Kautz's light workload provided numerous opportunities to go to the city, and both he and Fannie were regulars at the Palace Hotel and at the theaters in the city. Despite the thirty-mile journey from Benicia to division headquarters at the Presidio, the Kautzes developed a close relationship with John Kelton and his wife Josephine, and the Kautz and Kelton children were often playmates.

Fannie tried to drum up interest in a theatrical group at Benicia, but was frustrated after one production by a lack of acting talent (or, possibly, a lack of interest) among the officers and their wives. Seemingly in response, in the spring of 1879, she turned to painting as an artistic

Fannie Kautz at her easel, ca. 1885. Fannie took up painting seriously while at Benicia Barracks and continued painting for the rest of her life. From August Kautz's photograph album, courtesy Virginia (Kautz) Borkenhagen.

outlet and took weekly painting lessons from Juan Buckingham Wandesford, a well-known California artist. Fannie had been introduced to Wandesford by another student, Lucy Tichenor, wife of Henry B. Tichenor, whom Kautz had known at Port Orford years before. Tichenor had amassed a fortune in the lumber business along the Navarro River north of San Francisco.

The Kautzes took three long camping trips in the summer and fall of 1879, one of which was a three-week trip in October to the Navarro River area north of San Francisco, where Henry Tichenor owned vast timber lands. This gave Fannie an opportunity to practice sketching from nature while her husband fished and hiked. On each camping trip, they were accompanied by Major Wilhelm and a small detachment of teamsters to manage the wagons, pitch tents and prepare meals.

Perhaps the highlight of Kautz's stay at Benicia was an extended visit by Ulysses Grant to California. The ex-president arrived on September 20, 1879, on the steamer *Tokio* on the last leg of an around-the-world tour. The next morning Kautz called on Grant in his room at the Palace, where he also met the general's wife and his son, Ulysses. He said of Grant's visit, "The enthusiasm that has greeted Genl. Grant is a surprise even to the people of California themselves. Even the Confederates are outdoing themselves." On September 24, the Kautzes were invited to a reception given for Grant by General McDowell, but failed to attend because the trunk containing Kautz's dress uniform and Fannie's gown got lost on the way from Benicia to the city. Kautz's "annoyance and irritation were too great to be described." Later that evening he called on Grant to apologize for his absence and arranged for Fannie to have a private meeting with the Grants the following morning.[11]

Later the Kautzes attended a farewell reception for Grant hosted by railroad baron Charles Crocker at his mansion on Nob Hill. The awe in which Kautz held the president is obvious in his simple statement in his journal, "Genl. Grant as he shook hands with me called me August."[12]

Soon after Grant's visit, Kautz learned from Division Adjutant John Kelton that General McDowell planned to move Eighth Infantry Headquarters back to Angel Island along with one company of the regiment, but the move did not come about until March 1880. In the meantime, Thomas Wilhelm had been promoted to captain and given command of a company, and Kautz had the rare opportunity to exercise some authority by choosing Wilhelm's Company to join him on the island.

As the *Arizona Sentinel* had predicted two years earlier, Kautz had been let down easy. However, he was satisfied that, although neither his career nor his fortune had "made material progress," they had suffered "no serious losses."[13] For the first time since his days at Fort Stanton, he had time to enjoy the outdoors, if only briefly, and he reveled in the progress his children were making. It seems his major regret lay in his failure to devote sufficient time to writing and had still not completed his *Reminiscences of the Civil War*.

On March 2, 1880, the Kautzes were finished packing for the short trip down the bay to Angel Island.

43. Angel Island

Beautiful one-square-mile Angel Island was only five miles from downtown San Francisco. It was a regular stop on boat tours of San Francisco Bay and a popular weekend getaway for San Franciscans and for visitors to the city. On Saturdays, the *James B. McPherson*, the little steamer employed by the army, was often loaded to capacity with picnickers and other locals coming to enjoy dancing at the post or just trying to escape the dust of the city. Consequently, it was a rare Saturday night when the guest rooms at the commanding officer's quarters at Angel Island were not occupied. The *McPherson* seems to take on a personality of her own in her comings and goings and occasional breakdowns as chronicled by her most frequent passenger in his journal.

A busy social schedule at the island and in the city placed a severe strain on Kautz's finances, already burdened by the poor performance of his mining stocks. In addition to his investments in the failing Murchie and Rowe mines, Kautz had paid John Plume of San Francisco several thousand dollars to purchase 300 shares of stock in the Tip Top Mine in Arizona. In April 1880, he learned that Plume had not bought the stock but had pocketed the money. Kautz generously allowed Plume to repay the debt in installments. Plume died in April 1884, still owing $700.

After moving to the island, Fannie continued her painting lessons until the first week of June 1880, when a well-advanced pregnancy put an end to these weekly trips to the city. A baby girl, named Navarra for the river near which she was conceived, was born on July 14. Although the baby was fine, she was relegated to a diet of condensed milk formula by complications which kept her mother feverish and confined to her bed for more than a month. In mid–September, when the *McPherson* delivered President and Mrs. Hayes to the island to the sound of a twenty-one gun salute, Fannie still could not leave the house. Her husband was pleased to note that the president and his lady were kind enough to call on Fannie before General McDowell hustled the party off, carrying Kautz as well as the regimental band with them.[1]

Over the years, Edward Huggins had kept Kautz informed about the progress of his sons, Nugen and Augustus. Kautz had learned that Kitty had turned her life around: she was married in 1875 to a man named William Diggins and was able to send the boys to school at Union Academy in Olympia for several years. In 1879, they were members of the first class at the Indian School founded by Melville Wilkinson at Forest Grove, Oregon.[2] Both boys had been retained as instructors in the second year of the school's existence. In fact, in October 1880, Kautz sent Nugen money to purchase clothes so that they might be dressed appropriately for their new positions. In April 1881, hearing that Wilkinson was in San Francisco, Kautz managed to meet him to discuss the boys. Kautz said Wilkinson "was enthusiastic in his praise of them and told me I ought to be proud of them."[3]

Irvin McDowell was retired in October 1882 amid a bevy of parties and receptions, and John Schofield took command of the department. Kautz's relationship with his old friend remained cordial, if somewhat distant. As he wrote, "The change has not benefited us in any

View of Angel Island from Pier 41 in San Francisco in 2000. The inset photograph, ca. 1885 from the Martha Summerhayes book *Vanished Arizona*, shows the steamer *McPherson* from about the same point.

Officers' Row at Angel Island with a number of the post's children posing for the camera. Photograph by Major Thomas Wilhelm. From August Kautz's photograph album, courtesy Virginia (Kautz) Borkenhagen.

way.... Genl. Schofield takes no interest in the Division or Dept. as he does not expect to remain here long.... Kelton runs the department and I think has all the say in matters of detail."[4]

In June 1882, the Kautzes received a visit from Fannie's mother, Fred Hassaurek and Hassaurek's teen-aged children, Frank and Minnie. It was a pleasant reunion until Hassaurek announced that he would be departing at the end of July to get married and planned to take a honeymoon in Europe, leaving his children in the care of the Kautzes. According to Kautz, they were unruly children, having been raised for the most part by their oversolicitous grandmother. Kautz suspected that they were having a bad influence on his own children and was so anxious to return them to their father's care that he gave in to Fannie's pleading and agreed to take a long-delayed trip to Europe.

After spending time with family in Ohio, the Kautzes, along with the Hassaurek children, sailed for Europe on April 5, 1883. The European tour began with a month-long stay with Wolfgang and Jennie Schoenle in Barmen, Prussia (present day Wuppertal, Germany), where Wolfgang had been serving as U.S. Consul since 1878. Although the German-speaking Kautzes were hardly noticed by the inhabitants, Pauline was "the excitement of much wonder among the natives. Crowds follow her and block the way."[5]

To Kautz's relief Fred Hassaurek arrived in Barmen to take Frank and Minnie to his residence in Paris. The Kautzes then left their own children under Pauline's care with the Schoenles, allowing them the freedom to travel.

Kautz seems not to have enjoyed a subsequent tour of German cities and was especially disappointed with a one-day stop at Ispringen, where only a few old men remembered him. Most of the summer was spent in Austria, including the whole month of July taking the waters at Carlsbad. Much time was spent with Fannie's uncle, Vincent Abele, and other members of

This somewhat whimsical portrait of the Kautz family taken in San Francisco shows Pauline Robinson in the center of the family. The little girl in the left foreground is probably one of the daughters of John Kelton. *Left to right, seated*: Margaret Kelton, Pauline Robinson, Navarra Kautz; *standing*: Austin Kautz, August Valentine Kautz, Fannie Markbreit Kautz, Frankie Kautz. Courtesy Donald J. Robinson.

the Abele family.[6] Included was a week-long visit with Fannie's cousin Julia (Vincent's daughter) in the village of Freudenthal, where Julia's husband, Gustav Stimpfl, was proprietor of the Freudenthal Glassworks.[7]

There was additional touring in Germany and eastern Europe, but eventually Kautz had to return to duty. Finding good schools in Dusseldorf, he moved his family into a house there and sailed for New York on October 27, satisfied that his children were well on their way to learning the language. Fannie got started with painting lessons again and even Pauline got into the act by taking singing lessons.

Kautz met a great number of old friends in New York. He was most pleased with a visit with ex–President Grant at his Wall Street office, saying, "He received me very kindly and talked pleasantly on commonplace affairs."[8]

His next stop was in Washington, where he stayed with his brother Albert and his wife Esther, in a house which they shared with Esther's brother Joseph and his family. Kautz went up to the War Department to congratulate Phil Sheridan, who had taken command of the army only two weeks before. The following evening was spent at Sheridan's home with members of Sheridan's staff, and Kautz was invited to lunch with Sheridan and his wife on November 16. Before leaving for the west, he wrote in his journal, "I find it very interesting to meet people that I have not seen for so many years," but added, "It is also very distressing to see to what status some have risen."[9]

Left: On his return from Europe in 1883, Kautz stopped at the home of Phil Sheridan in Washington to congratulate his old friend at being named commander in chief. It was here that he first met Sheridan's wife, the former Irene Rucker. This photograph was taken at the time of Sheridan's marriage in 1875. *Right:* Irene (Rucker) Sheridan at the time of her marriage in 1875. She was the daughter of Major-General Daniel Rucker. Both photographs are from August Kautz's photograph album, courtesy Virginia (Kautz) Borkenhagen.

Kautz arrived back at Angel Island on November 30, 1883, to find that General John Pope had just taken command of the Division of the Pacific in place of Schofield. Although his relationship with Pope had been strained in the past, the two men seemed to get along well.

Over the next year, Kautz's lifestyle was far more Spartan than heretofore. He unpacked only enough furnishings for a few rooms in the house and took his meals at the bachelor officers' mess. He rarely entertained, usually not even attending weekly hops. He went to the city infrequently and, rather than pay for rooms at the Palace or Occidental Hotel, he usually stayed in a spare room at the home of John and Mary Swift, a room he came to call "my room."[10]

On December 29, Kautz purchased a Remington typewriter for $97.50. The same day, he received a letter from his wife stating that she planned to put the children in school at Barmen while she traveled to Italy with Lucy Tichenor.[11] It took the usually adept Kautz two days of fumbling to type a reply to his wife's letter but, within a week, he was typing all of his official and private correspondence. From 1885 until his death, his journals were also typed.

The purchase of the typewriter was made in anticipation of having time in his family's absence to pursue some literary work. He had almost completed his *Reminiscences of the Civil War* just before leaving for Europe and had planned for years to write several military manuals, including a manual for boys planning a military career. Despite his resolve to do so and his frequent chiding of himself in his journal, he never got around to starting anything. By midsummer he became deeply depressed. He could not even work in his shop. He noted, "The sense of growing old is upon me and I am afraid I am not good for much more in this life."[12]

His failure to write, however, was not all that was bothering him. The compulsory retirement act had produced a number of openings for brigadier, but, as far as he could tell, his name had not been mentioned.[13] One example occurred in March when his West Point classmate David Stanley was promoted to brigadier on the retirement of Ranald Mackenzie. Stanley was well up the list of colonels from Kautz and was deserving of the promotion, but it was obvious that politics had played a part in attaining his star.

It is possible that Kautz's depression had little or nothing to do with these matters, but rather with the absence of his family. In mid–October he received a letter from Fannie informing him that she would be sailing for the States on October 11. In a flurry of activity, Kautz began unpacking furniture to fix up the house. Within a week he was able to write in his journal, "I spent the greater portion of the day ... at work in the shop and for the first time in the past year worked with some of my former interest."[14] After Fannie's return on the last day of 1884, he seemed his old self again. He especially enjoyed a two-week visit from Leopold Markbreit in February 1885, during which his friend John Swift held a reception for Markbreit at the beautiful Cliff House, attended by a host of prominent Californians.

In June 1885, trouble between Indians and settlers in southern Oregon prompted General Pope to order Kautz to Fort Bidwell to inspect the post and to ensure that the post commander, newly-promoted Captain Gordon Winslow, was prepared in case more serious clashes should occur. Kautz left for Bidwell on June 11, but before doing so, he arranged for his wife to go by steamer to the Columbia River to meet him after his business at Bidwell was completed. Finding both Winslow and his wife Elizabeth "very helpful and kind" and the post in good order, Kautz made the overland trek to the Columbia River in eleven days, meeting Fannie at The Dalles on June 27.

Nostalgia drips from the pages of Kautz's journal as he describes stops at Vancouver Barracks, the train ride to Tacoma and the opportunity to introduce his wife to old friends Rodney Glisan, Lewis Hunt, Warren Gove and Edward Huggins. There were also emotional meetings with old soldiers who had served under him at Fort Steilacoom. He found that the fort itself, which the army had abandoned twenty years before, had become a mental asylum and the buildings which he had designed and built were occupied by "the insane of the territory."

Kautz's daughters, Navarra (left) and Frankie, taken in Barmen, Germany, and mailed to August Kautz in the summer of 1884 by his sister-in-law Jennie Schoenle. From August Kautz's photograph album, courtesy Virginia (Kautz) Borkenhagen.

On the evening of July 1, his two sons Nugen and Augustus came to the Tacoma Hotel to see him and he wrote that night in his journal, "They are well developed men and from all I can learn, are well regarded by all who know them."[15]

The following day he wrote, "I hired a horse and, under the guidance of Augustus, I rode out to Puyallup Reservation and quite a number of Indians, who recognized me and seemed pleased to see me, met us on the way. I found the house of the boys quite primitive, but they have located on a very valuable tract of land and, by industry, they will in time have a good home. They seemed gratified by my visit and I satisfied that I went out to see them."[16]

On July 4, the Kautzes took a steamer for the short trip to Olympia, and Kautz remarked, "I recalled the fact that thirty-two years before I went to Olympia to participate in the celebration of this day."[17] The last stop on Kautz's tour of memories was at Vancouver Island to see William Tolmie. Kautz said, "I found the old gentleman ... unable to recognize me at first. He was highly pleased to see me and we had an hour's talk that was principally devoted to reminiscences of the past," as was Kautz's journey.[18]

Nugen Kautz, in 1880 when he was an instructor at the Forest Grove Indian School in Oregon.

Not long after returning to Angel Island the Kautzes were saddened by the deaths of Ulysses Grant and Fred Hassaurek. To add to Kautz's sense of loss, on October 1, John Kelton left for Washington, assigned to the adjutant general's office. After the Kautzes saw the Keltons off on the train, Kautz wrote, "I am sorry to see Kelton go, but I am reconciled with the hope and belief that in him I shall have a friend at court who may be of great service to me.... He has been a source of providence to me on more than one occasion in the course of my life."[19]

It would seem that Kautz had given up the thought of promotion. When it became apparent that two brigadier positions were due to open in March 1886, he wrote, "I presume I shall be compelled to enter the contest to a limited extent, so much at least as will bring my claims to the notice of the appointing power. I had hoped to become conspicuous as a Col. who has not made an effort for self-advancement."[20] Soon after that, he sought the counsel of John Swift. Swift apparently changed Kautz's mind. "He told me that I didn't stand a chance of getting the promotion unless I started immediately for Washington and presented my claims and influence at headquarters. He maintained that all other influences were useless and any work done at this distance from Washington was thrown away. He supported his views so logically that I resolved to ... start as soon as I could.... I had no difficulty in getting Gen. Pope to consent to my proposition and also his advice to do so as it was my only chance of success."[21] Kautz was on the train east two days later, arriving in the capital on March 4.

The following evening, he wrote in his journal, "I was greatly occupied today and became quite interested in my new vocation of lobbyist, and am rather satisfied with my day's work."[22] He should have been. Before the day was over he had called on Kelton and Sheridan at the War Department and had gained the promise of Secretary of War William Endicott that his claim would be considered fairly and fully. He then made the rounds of Washington meeting a number of influential persons, all of whom offered to do all they could in his behalf. He even received the promise of Senator Leland Stanford of California that the entire California delegation in Congress would meet with the president to offer their support.

After four more days of vigorous campaigning, Kautz had received the endorsement of persons as diverse as James Denver, Senator James Fair of Nevada, and Louis Schade, editor of the *Washington Sentinel*. On March 9, he attended a reception in the East Room of the White House to which all army officers were invited and came away satisfied that President Grover Cleveland at least recognized his name.

Augustus Kautz as a young man, ca. 1890. Courtesy Historic Fort Steilacoom Association.

After another week of lobbying, Kautz waited in Washington to learn the result of his efforts. He had interviews with Phil Sheridan and was invited to Sheridan's home on several occasions, but eventually was convinced that his friend of almost forty years was not among his supporters. When he heard from John Kelton on March 20 that Colonels Thomas Ruger of the 4th Infantry and Wesley Merritt of the cavalry[23] had received the available nominations, Kautz left for Cincinnati, noting, "I was more cast down than I thought I would be."[24]

By the time he arrived back on Angel Island, Major General O.O. Howard had been appointed to replace the retiring John Pope, but he had not yet arrived to take command. What had arrived, however, was a rumor that the Eighth Infantry was soon to be ordered back to Arizona. At first, Kautz scoffed at the rumor, but four days later, he wrote, "We received news today confirming the rumor that the 8th Infantry is to go to Arizona to relieve the 1st. The ladies and officers of the post are very much excited over the news and think the Regt. is very badly treated. I am urged to protest and it is possible that I may do so.... I am most hurt at the possibility that Sheridan is unfriendly to me, for, if he had not been, he would have said something to me."[25] The move was to take place on June 1, but was postponed to July 1 because there were insufficient funds in the War Department coffers to support the transfer of troops until the beginning of the next fiscal year.

Kautz finally had an opportunity to meet with General Howard on April 21 and informed him that the officers of the regiment considered it an injustice to be sent back to Arizona for a second tour. When Howard advised Kautz not to protest against the movement, Kautz responded that he had no intention of doing so.

General Nelson Miles, now in command of the Department of Arizona, decided at Kautz's urging that regimental headquarters would be posted at Fort Lowell near Tucson. When, on May 29, Fannie began packing her trunks, Kautz rebuked her, saying, "I cannot see the wisdom of packing so long as there is no order and the First [Infantry] has not obtained the consent of Geronimo to leave Arizona."[26]

By the time Kautz began his own packing, he seemed reconciled to the fact that he might spend the six years of service remaining to him as a colonel. Although he was concerned about his advancing age, his health was good. He had been bothered only occasionally by headaches in the past few years and he was able to control his chronic dyspepsia by careful dieting and the use of a variety of patent medicines and regular exercise. His finances had also improved. He had a positive bank balance for the first time since returning from Europe.

It was July 5 before the Kautzes were able to get away from Angel Island. As the *McPherson* pulled away from the island to take them to Oakland for the train to Tucson, Kautz mused, "Our departure was characterized by the usual amount of emotion, kissing, handshaking and waving of handkerchiefs, while the Band added to the excitement with its music and 'The Girl I Left Behind Me.' I was not indifferent to the event, as I have not been in the best of spirits at the prospect of leaving the most delightful post I have ever been stationed at, and I was quite conscious that I may never have such another, and in all probability I shall never see Angel Island again."[27]

44. Fort Lowell

During the Eighth Infantry's stay in California, its colonel followed events in Arizona Territory with great interest. As early as May 1878, Lieutenant Earl Thomas of the Fifth Cavalry and his wife visited the Kautzes and, according to Kautz, "The Thomas's have much to tell about Prescott & Fort Whipple. Things are not very lively there and there seems to be some discontent at the new regime." He added, "Wilcox [sic] will probably not last very long."[1] The prediction would prove incorrect.

As additional companies of the Eighth followed their colonel to California, Kautz heard additional comments about Willcox's mismanagement from his own officers, but he felt that "some of the things ... are certainly absurd and ridiculous."[2] Perhaps his mind was finally changed when, on December 16, he read Willcox's annual departmental report which was highly critical of Kautz, saying, among other things, that Kautz had neglected southern Arizona while in command of the department.[3] Kautz's comment was characteristically dispassionate, "I have met with Genl. Wilcox's [sic] report.... He has no consideration for his predecessor & makes misstatements of facts."[4] It took Kautz a full week to compose a letter taking exception to Willcox's report, and he sent it to General Townsend on the day after Christmas. Although Sherman saw Kautz's letter, he did not send a copy to Willcox for his comment.

For the next three years, Kautz scoured the San Francisco newspapers for news from Arizona. He read reports of incursions by Warm Spring and Chiricahua Apaches into Arizona and New Mexico from their hideouts in the mountains of Mexico, of desertions of Indians from the San Carlos Reservation, and of a mutiny by a company of Indian scouts on Cibecu Creek near Fort Apache which took the lives of one officer and four men of the Sixth Cavalry. Although Willcox was not responsible for much of this trouble, his responses were often indecisive and included pleas to the War Department for reinforcements. Twice Kautz was ordered to send troops of his Eighth Infantry to Arizona, leaving Angel Island almost deserted. In April 1882, when mismanagement by the Indian Bureau caused the Chiricahua bands under Geronimo, Juh and Nachez to bolt from the San Carlos Reservation, Kautz noted in his journal, "The papers report some more Indian depredations and Wilcox [sic] will not fail to cry for help as heretofore."[5] He was correct for a change. On May 1, John Kelton informed Kautz confidentially that two additional regiments of infantry were being sent to Arizona from the Department of Missouri.

Occasional rumors spread among the officers of the Eighth Infantry that Kautz would be ordered back to Arizona. In February 1882, Lieutenants Henry Kingsbury of the Sixth Cavalry and Charles Baily of his own regiment arranged a meeting between Kautz and Governor Frederick Tritle of Arizona Territory regarding his availability to make the move. The two junior officers even induced Kautz to write to Grant and Sherman, both now retired, to lobby for his appointment. He seemed genuinely disappointed by Lieutenant Baily's notification that Tritle had "lost his enthusiasm,"[6] and by a "characteristic" letter from Sherman which "did not encourage me about going to Arizona." Kautz added sarcastically, "I do not think that he [Sherman] is very friendly to me."[7]

Because the companies of the 8th Infantry were widely scattered, Kautz kept a framed picture of each of his officers on the wall of his office. The frames were made by Kautz in his own shop. From August Kautz's photograph album, courtesy Virginia (Kautz) Borkenhagen.

Probably both Tritle and Sherman had learned that General Sheridan had already contemplated replacing Willcox with the army's most effective Indian fighter, George Crook. The failure of Willcox to control the Chiricahua outbreak of the summer of 1882 gave Sheridan the excuse he was seeking. In September, he ordered Willcox and his Twelfth Infantry to the East. Crook took command of the department on December 4.

Within a month of Kautz's return from his 1883 European tour, Crook had succeeded in bringing all but a few hostile Apaches back to the reservations. His tools were the same that he had used ten years before — use of Indian scouts, a show of force when necessary and absolute honesty with his enemy. Unlike his two predecessors, however, Crook took to the field himself, leading one lengthy expedition far into Mexico.

The period of relative peace that followed is reflected in Kautz's journals. There is absolutely no mention of Arizona for almost three years until May 1885, when he wrote, "The Indians have broken out in Arizona again. Geronimo and 50 of the Chiricahuas.... This is very unexpected and will require explanation to make known the cause."[8]

The cause was a disagreement between the Indians and Agent C.D. Ford, appointed at San Carlos in November 1884. The result was a long summer of campaigning for Crook's cavalry (and for 200 additional Indian scouts authorized by the War Department). Large numbers of the Indians fled the reservations into Mexico. In November 1885, a relatively unknown Indian named Josanie led a band of fewer than twenty Chiricahua out of Mexico and plundered through Arizona before making an incredible attack on Fort Apache in which at least twenty Indian scouts and several civilians were killed.[9] Before Josanie returned to Mexico via New Mexico in December, nearly fifty people had died, only one of whom belonged to Josanie's band.

So great was the public outcry at Josanie's raid, including that of the Tucson Ring, that Sheridan himself came to Arizona. Sheridan attached the District of New Mexico to the Department of Arizona, giving Crook command of 1000 additional troops.

Back in California, August and Fannie Kautz spent a quiet Christmas at home in 1885. Martha Summerhayes and several of the officers joined them for an excellent dinner. Even the children were permitted at table because Lieutenant John Summerhayes and Mrs. Baily were attending to Lieutenant Charles Baily, who was critically ill. Two days later, Kautz wrote in his journal, "We learned by the papers that the Gov. of the Territory has applied to the Sec. of War for troops to protect the Indians on the Reservation from the whites.... I was asked by Gen. Pope if I would be satisfied to have Col. Bryant go in command of the battalion of the 8th if it should be required to go. I answered that I should be entirely satisfied to have Col. B. go in command. The instructions received have created quite a commotion at the Post."[10]

Orders arrived the following day for seven companies of the Eighth Infantry to proceed to Arizona under Bryant. Kautz, although he felt the move unnecessary, responded quickly to the call to arms. The following morning, he was at the wharf to see the *McPherson* carry the troops off. Their departure was quiet. The band was not permitted to play due to the illness of Lieutenant Baily. Baily died the following night. For the most part, only the women of the regiment were left to attend the funeral on New Year's Day.

Early in February, Kautz wrote, "The papers this morning report that Hieronimo [*sic*] the Apache chief has surrendered unconditionally which would indicate a speedy return of the troops. The ladies of the post are quite cheerful over the news."[11] Unfortunately, the news was premature. Lieutenant Marion Maus of the First Infantry had met with Geronimo and other renegades in Mexico and had sent word that the Indians were willing to meet with General Crook in "two moons" to discuss terms of surrender.

Kautz was on his way back from Washington on March 25 when the meeting between Crook and Apache Chiefs Geronimo, Nana and Nachez took place in the mountains of Sonora,

Mexico. An agreement was reached two days later requiring that the Indians be exiled to Florida for two years before being allowed to return to the reservation.[12]

Crook then hurried back to Fort Bowie, leaving Lieutenant Maus to conduct the Apaches back to Arizona. The procession began the long trek with the renegades and their families in the rear. On March 28, they met a trader named Bob Tribollet who, perhaps at the instigation of the Tucson Ring, sold the Indians enough liquor to get them drunk and entertained them with stories that they would be murdered as soon as they crossed into Arizona. When the Indians sobered up next day, Geronimo and twenty other warriors and some of their women disappeared into the Sierra Madre Mountains.

On March 30, Crook telegraphed Sheridan with the news. For two days, a series of telegrams passed between the two generals, increasingly more caustic. On April 1, Crook, satisfied that Sheridan did not support him, asked to be relieved. Sheridan obliged. He appointed Brigadier General Nelson A. Miles in Crook's place. Two weeks later August Kautz received the order sending him to Arizona. Of course, most of his regiment was already there.

Kautz knew that Miles had the reputation for being ambitious in the style of the late George Custer, furthering his career through a combination of personal bravery, careful use of political influence and the knack of being in the right place at the right time as long as a newspaper reporter was close at hand. If Kautz had heard the widely-told tale that Miles had married the niece of General Sherman more as a career move than for true love, he did not mention it in his journal.

Shortly after Miles was appointed, Kautz reported in his journal, "News in the papers of fresh depredations by the Apaches in the Santa Cruz Valley ... indicates Geronimo is going to try what sort of metal [*sic*] Miles is made of."[13] Kautz was privately critical of Miles for discharging all of Crook's Indian scouts, noting, "Gen. Miles has not been following Gen. Crook's method."[14] Kautz was pleased, however, that Miles allowed him to choose, after some telegraphic bickering, which post he would desire for headquarters of his regiment and which companies would be stationed at that post. He chose Fort Lowell and the companies of Captains (Brevet Majors) Daniel Wells and Thomas Wilhelm.

Today historic Fort Lowell is located in the suburbs of the city of Tucson but, when Kautz arrived on July 7, 1886, it lay six miles beyond the northeastern reaches of the bustling little frontier town. A major thoroughfare, Craycroft Road, now passes across what was once the western end of the parade ground. Beside the road in a city park is the six-room commanding officer's quarters, restored into a small museum. Beside the entrance to the park is a much-larger-than-life bronze statue of a mounted cavalry bugler, reminding us of what Kautz knew all along, that Indian warfare was the work of men on horseback. His infantry would serve only to support the cavalry while in Arizona—important work, but far from romantic.

By the middle of July, five companies of the Eighth Foot were at Fort Bowie under Colonel Bryant with several more at Forts McDowell, Mojave and Grant. Others, such as Captain Whitney's A Company, were spread along the Southern Pacific rail line, which now crossed the state from Yuma to Deming, New Mexico. Kautz was 800 miles closer to the renegade Apaches but, for all practical purposes, he might as well have been back at Angel Island. There is no evidence that, while at Fort Lowell, he gave a single order to anyone beyond the seventy-two-square-mile limits of the post, nor did he receive many.

After a month at Lowell, however, Kautz received an early morning telegram stating that General Miles was in town and wished to see him. When he arrived, he found the department commander still in bed. Their meeting lasted several hours, after which Kautz noted, "I did not discover on what particular account the Gen. wished to see me. I think he is simply making friends and creating strength to his position." Kautz learned that Miles shared his own low opinion of Adjutant General Richard Drum, who had replaced Edward Townsend, and Miles

The commanding officer's quarters at Fort Lowell, Arizona, as it appears today.

suggested that the Eighth Infantry had been sent to Arizona because of Drum's hostility toward Kautz or his regiment. Kautz found that hard to believe, but added, "I deem him [Drum] capable of such an act if he has the opportunity."[15]

Life at Fort Lowell was dull compared to that at Angel Island. For exercise, Kautz often rode across the usually-dry Rillito River to the mountains beyond to search, somewhat successfully, for artifacts of the prehistoric peoples who had lived there. When Captain Wilhelm became bored with camp life and wished to make a scout, Kautz rode east into the lofty Santa Catalina Mountains for several days to help Wilhelm locate a satisfactory campsite for his company.

Early in September, conflicting reports began to arrive at Lowell that Geronimo had surrendered. It was not until later that Kautz learned the full story. Late in August, Lieutenant Charles Gatewood, formerly Crook's commander of Indian scouts, had been sent into Mexico with two Indians who were friendly to both the army and to Geronimo in an attempt to locate the hostiles and negotiate a surrender. Gatewood managed to meet with Geronimo, Nachez and the others on August 26, 1886, near where a company of worn-out troopers under Captain Henry Lawton had made camp. It seemed to Gatewood that his mission would prove a failure until Geronimo was told that his wife and the family of Nachez had already been sent to Florida. That piece of information alone probably decided the issue. The following morning, Geronimo rode into Lawton's camp and agreed to surrender to General Miles.

As Gatewood and the Apaches moved slowly northward, followed at a distance by Lawton's troopers, Miles, fearing the embarrassment suffered by Crook, waited near Fort Bowie until the party had passed well over the international boundary. Once escape had been rendered impossible, he met with Geronimo and accepted Geronimo's unconditional surrender, promising that Geronimo and his followers would be sent to Florida with their families and would later be allowed to return to Arizona.[16]

News of the surrender reached Tucson on September 6. Kautz's involvement in the surrender was to provide the Eighth Infantry band, a cannon and a brief speech at the celebration which took place in town.

With the Apache Wars at a seeming end, Kautz turned his attention to the brigadiership to be vacated in October. He wrote letters to request the aid of some of his former supporters such as Markbreit, Denver, Senator Stanford and Secretary Schurz. He also decided to get Nelson Miles on his side and, on September 16, he took the train to Albuquerque where Miles had moved his headquarters. He met Miles after a late dinner on the 17th and found him drinking heavily to aid his digestion. After leaving the general's room at 3 A.M., Kautz said, "He talked quite freely and drank freely and trusting to the proverb, 'in vino veritas,' I was gratified that he was entirely in sympathy with me in the object of my visit and assured me that he would do all he could for me."[17] Kautz spent much of the next day with Miles and both men seemed surprised that Miles remembered the conversation of the night before. According to Kautz, "He jokingly charged me with trying to talk him to death last night."[18] Miles reiterated his promise to help out and even took a copy of Kautz's service record to keep in his pocketbook if needed. There is no evidence that Miles kept his promise. Kautz seemed not at all surprised to read an Associated Press report on October 14 that Orlando Willcox had been appointed brigadier in place of Joseph Potter, who had been appointed on April 1, 1886, and retired on October 12.

On October 27, all at Fort Lowell were surprised to learn, as Martha Summerhayes describes so well in her little book, that the Eighth Infantry was ordered to Fort Niobrara in the Department of the Platte.[19] On November 22, Kautz turned command of the post over to Major Henry Noyes of the Fourth Cavalry and the Kautzes stayed for two nights in the San Xavier Hotel, where a surprise party was held in their honor. As Kautz was driving away from the post, he noted that there was snow on the Santa Catalina Mountains. He would soon have his fill of snow.

45. Fort Niobrara

Shortly after returning to Angel Island from Europe in 1883, Kautz had written, "The unusual glow in the west, usually most intense just before dark, is observable here from my quarters. It is most like the alpenglow and seems, according to the papers, to be very general all over the earth. I noticed it on the plains first."[1] Kautz may not have known that he was witnessing the effect of the volcanic cloud cast into the upper atmosphere by the eruption on the island of Krakatoa in July 1883. The cloud so occluded the sun's rays that it produced a drop in average global temperatures of several degrees in succeeding years. The Eighth Infantry had not finished unpacking at Fort Niobrara when they felt the full impact of that colder weather.

By the day after Christmas, Kautz's thermometer recorded -15 degrees. On New Year's Day, 1887, the first of a series of devastating blizzards swept across the plains. Temperatures of twenty to thirty degrees below zero were commonplace that winter and for the following three winters. Railroad schedules were disrupted. Entire herds of cattle either froze or starved to death. Beef and produce prices soared. So many farmers were forced to default on their loans that banks failed. Except for the inconvenience of delays in the delivery of mail, doors blocked by snowdrifts and the need to wear an overcoat and overshoes in his office, Kautz was hardly affected.

Fort Niobrara had been built only ten years before on a bluff beside the Niobrara River. It was a large post built to protect settlers in Nebraska from the Brule Sioux Indians on the Rosebud Indian Reservation across the South Dakota border. The post accommodated eight companies, although now somewhat crowded with six companies of the Eighth Infantry and three troops of the Ninth Cavalry.[2] A typical frontier town, Valentine, had sprung up on the railroad a few miles from the fort. The Brule, a branch of the Lakota people, had been at peace for years and, except for providing a small patrol to observe the weekly issue of rations to the Indians, the army had little contact with them.

The duties at the larger Niobrara were more demanding than those Kautz had become accustomed to in California and Arizona. Despite the weather, he seemed content to have made the move, especially since he was serving under George Crook.

In February 1887, Kautz was ordered to Fort Duchesne, Utah, to preside at the much-publicized court-martial of Major Frederick Benteen.[3] After the trial, Kautz met his wife for a trip east to visit family. While in Louisville visiting the Schoenles,[4] he had an attack which, although never diagnosed by the doctor, was no doubt a minor stroke with symptoms of paralysis of the left side of his body, dizziness, slurred speech and blurred vision. He was back to duty by the end of March, but it was August before he could write, after a long horseback ride, "I certainly feel much stronger, particularly in mind, than I ever expected to feel again. I feel that I am getting back to my former condition."[5]

In 1887, the Kautzes decided to send their two older children east to school. Since Fannie was temporarily laid up with a broken leg, Kautz made the trip himself, depositing Austin at the Kenyon Military Academy in Gambier, Ohio, and Frankie at Markbreit's home in Cincinnati.[6]

Austin Kautz as a student at Kenyon Military Academy in 1887. From August Kautz's photograph album, courtesy Virginia (Kautz) Borkenhagen.

The subject of promotion came up again in the spring of 1888. It seemed apparent that Major General Alfred Terry would be forced to retire because of disability. Kautz showed a bit of renewed interest, but did little to promote himself. His journal contained the notation, "There have been a number of applications for my Photograph from Journals, particularly Harper and Frank Leslie, which would forecast that something is in store for me that will justify giving my likeness to the public such as my promotion or death. I prefer to think it may be the former."[7] When Terry was retired, Crook was promoted to major general and Colonel John Brooke of the Third Infantry received the brigadiership *vice* Crook and took command of the Department of the Platte.

In April 1890, Benjamin Grierson was promoted only three months before he was scheduled to retire. Because there was a new Republican president, Benjamin Harrison, a new army commander, John Schofield, in place of Phil Sheridan,[8] and a new adjutant general, John Kelton, in the office formerly occupied by Richard Drum, Kautz saw the possibility of promotion. Still he did little to promote himself.

When it came time for Grierson to retire, Kautz was severely disappointed when he learned that Alexander McCook, whose record Kautz felt was inferior to his own and whose name was below his in seniority, had been promoted over him. Kautz wrote a letter to McCook, whom he truly liked, congratulating him but voicing his own disappointment. Kautz described McCook's reply, "Gen. McCook claims that he did not do anything that a gentleman and a soldier could not do, but admits, 'I used all the influence known to me that I thought would control in the matter.'" Kautz determined at that time to fight as hard as he could when the next vacancy occurred.

Kautz had viewed the death of Phil Sheridan with mixed emotions. He was deeply touched, however, during this period by the deaths of his father in February 1888 and of George Crook in March 1890.

While at Fort Niobrara, Kautz got around to doing some writing. He published four articles in *Century Magazine*. Two, "What the United States Army Should Be" and "Our National Defense," which appeared in 1888, were treatises on changes he felt would be beneficial to the army. One of the major points espoused, a revolutionary view at the time, was the provision of schools for enlisted men, most of whom were either poorly educated or illiterate. Among those who opposed the idea was his own departmental commander, John Brooke, who wrote a highly critical letter to Kautz on the subject. A heated exchange followed which ended with neither man giving ground.

The relationship between the two men deteriorated even further when, during summer maneuvers, a brigade made up of the Seventh and Eighth Infantry Regiments under Kautz's command defeated a two-brigade army commanded by General Brooke.

The ill feelings came to a head, however, the following June as the result of an insignificant incident. Kautz had written an endorsement to a court-martial involving a private of his regiment. He received a letter from department headquarters stating that the commanding general "does not deem your statement as at all warranted by the facts in the case," and ordering him to alter his endorsement. Kautz, was both "annoyed and mortified" to receive such an order. He answered, "To such a reply from the Department Commander to one in my position, there is nothing further for me to do except to await his charges against me for misrepresentation."[9]

Four days later, Kautz received another letter, "Your strict adherence to the orders given in a letter from these Headquarters of June 17, 1890 will fulfill all your obligations in the case ... and will preclude the possibility of a like correspondence in the future."[10] At the same time, Kautz was caught in the middle of a disagreement between Captain Wilhelm and the regimental adjutant, Lieutenant Wilds Richardson, over Richardson's release of a man whom Wilhelm had placed in the guardhouse. Kautz seems to have ended the controversy by "sending for the man of Maj. Wilhelm's Co. and admonishing him as to his duties to his company commander."[11]

During the sixteen years that Kautz commanded the 8th Infantry, the only times the entire regiment came together was on summer maneuvers in 1888 and 1889. Major Thomas Wilhelm took this picture of the officers of the regiment near Fort Robinson, Nebraska, in September 1889. The boy in the lower right is Austin Kautz. From August Kautz's photograph album, courtesy Virginia (Kautz) Borkenhagen.

Not until that matter was settled was Kautz's mind clear enough to realize that to respond to Brooke's last message would do more harm than good. He was surprised a month later to receive an order from Brooke's departmental headquarters to turn the command over to Lieutenant Colonel Alfred Smith[12] and consider himself under arrest. Even before he had learned what charges Brooke was contemplating, Kautz filed charges against his commander of "conduct unbecoming an officer and gentleman in falsely and knowingly and without cause or provocation accusing me of having made statements not warranted by the facts in the case."[13]

So matters stood for a while until John Schofield interceded in the matter and convinced both men to drop their charges.

Kautz was occasionally annoyed by the appearance at the post of minor Sioux chiefs asking him to interfere in affairs on the Rosebud Reservation. In the bitter cold of New Year's Day, 1887, a Brule chief named Two Strike had brought a contingent of Indians to the post to perform the well-known Omaha Dance. The following day, Chiefs Two Strike, Little Eagle, Living Bear and Yellow Horse (the son of principal chief Swift Bear) spent the entire morning relating their grievances, including encroachment of whites on their lands and a shortage of money and of food. Kautz's reply was that the army had no surplus rations or funds to offer and referred them back to the Rosebud agent, L.B. Spencer, with letters explaining their grievances. Other similar visits followed. In the autumn of 1888, a delegation of Indians, including Two Strike and Swift Bear, were called to Washington to negotiate the cession of some lands to white settlement. Yellow Horse came to the post to ask Kautz if he knew when his father might return. Of course, Kautz had no information to offer. Yellow Horse was adamant in claiming to Kautz that the Brule would give up no more land. In April 1879, Kautz wrote in his journal, "Old Two Strike and Crow Dog were in to see me this morning.... They want a new Agent,[14] and they have had a great many deaths among them and regard a Sun Dance as necessary to pacify the Great Spirit, and want to go off to the Crows to have one."[15] Kautz was, therefore, quite aware of the growing tension which existed on the reservation, but felt secure enough in the peaceful intentions of the Indians to allow his two young daughters and a friend from Cincinnati to go to the reservation on the first of July, 1889, to observe the issuance of beef rations and to witness the Omaha Dance.[16]

Kautz had been in the east on New Year's Day of that same year and had witnessed an eclipse of the sun with great interest. Little did he know that in far-off Utah, a heretofore unknown Paiute Indian shaman named Wovoka had seen the same eclipse while suffering the delirium of fever. When he awoke, he claimed that he had a vision in which God spoke to him of a time when a Messiah would come among them, all the white men would be swallowed up by the earth and the Indians would be free to enjoy the land as they once had done. Combining Native

Despite the growing tension on the Rosebud Indian Reservation in the summer of 1890, Kautz allowed his daughters to attend the issuance of beef rations to the Indians there. While there, the girls witnessed the Omaha Dance. Here they are shown with dancers to their left and right and in the background. The unidentified Caucasian on the left may be Indian Agent J. George Wright. Photograph taken by Major Thomas Wilhelm. From August Kautz's photograph album, courtesy Virginia (Kautz) Borkenhagen.

American beliefs with those of Christian ideology, he admonished his people to resist the white man's domination, to remain pure themselves and to dance a new dance, which came to be called the Ghost Dance. In time, Wovoka's new religion spread, with minor variations, all across the plains. Nowhere did it take hold so strongly as among the impoverished Sioux Indians on the reservations of the Dakotas. There the converts were led to believe that if they wore a garment called a ghost shirt, they would be protected from the bullets from the army's guns. By the late summer of 1890, thousands of Indians on the Pine Ridge Reservation were doing the Ghost Dance and many had gone into the Black Hills to await the coming of the promised Messiah.

It wasn't until October 6 that an unconfirmed rumor reached Kautz that there was trouble brewing on the Rosebud Reservation as well. The following day, however, he had visits from a number of Indians, including a minor chief named Thigh, denying any trouble and complaining that the Indians at Rosebud were hard up for provisions.

By mid–November it was confirmed that the Ghost Dance was being performed at Rosebud. On November 18, a dispatch was received to send two troops of cavalry and three companies of infantry to the reservation in order to protect the agent. Colonel Smith, who was to command the operation, was ordered to "exterminate any Indians who oppose him."[17] Three days later, Kautz received a report from Rosebud that more than 500 warriors had become religious enthusiasts and Colonel Smith was asking for reinforcements. Over the next week, a battalion of the Twenty-First Infantry arrived in Valentine to report to Rosebud and the entire Seventh Cavalry Regiment passed through town on the way to Pine Ridge, where additional trouble was threatened. Kautz noted that settlers from isolated farms were moving into town for safety. Soldiers and civilians alike were preparing for war.

Meanwhile, Fannie Kautz had taken the children east to go to school and was living at the Elsmere Hotel in Washington. Much to Kautz's disgust, she was lobbying for her husband's promotion. Her motive, however, if we can believe Kautz, was not a star on her husband's uniform, but rather a move away from Fort Niobrara, possibly to Washington Territory or to anyplace else with a more pleasant society. By the end of October, Fannie had met with the Secretary of War and even had a brief interview with President Benjamin Harrison but, in her letters, she did not seem hopeful.

On November 13, Kautz received a puzzling telegram from his wife: "President Board to examine Arms Powder etc, America and Europe." He soon learned officially that he had been ordered to preside over a board to recommend a magazine rifle for use by the army. He would be going east as well.

Kautz departed Fort Niobrara on December 8, having been in command of the Eighth Infantry for sixteen years, more than a quarter of that distinguished regiment's history. The day before he boarded the train at Valentine, he received a message that Two Strike had promised to bring his Indians in to the Pine Ridge Agency.

Three weeks later the affair of Wounded Knee cost the lives of 300 persons, mostly Indians, and brought the Ghost Dance movement to an abrupt end. Kautz was saved from the embarrassment of being involved in that tragic event.

46. Washington, D.C., and New York

The Board to Recommend a Magazine Rifle held its meetings in New York, but Colonel Kautz stayed with Fannie at the Elsmere in Washington in order to be close to the seat of power when another vacancy for brigadier should occur. It was known that General John Gibbon would retire in April 1891. Meanwhile, he could commute to New York for board meetings. He arrived in Washington on December 13, 1890, but hardly had time to unpack before he was off to New York.

In four days of meetings little was accomplished beyond organizing and adopting rules before adjourning for the holidays. Kautz stopped at Cornwall to get Austin before returning to enjoy the holiday season in the capital. He would write in his journal, "We are all engaged in preparation for Christmas, my part of it being to furnish the funds."[1]

That seemingly offhand remark had more meaning than we might suppose. Ever since he had returned from Europe in 1883, he had been chronically short of cash. His colonel's pay was supplemented somewhat by dividends received on a large block of *Volksblatt* stock purchased years before and by rent paid by tenants on his farming properties, but the failure of his mining ventures, taxes and assessments on his real estate, educational expenses for the children and frequent travel kept his bank balance near zero. In addition, he often had to admonish his wife for her lavish entertaining and her generosity toward others less fortunate than she. Kautz himself was hardly blameless in this last respect. While in California, he had, with little complaint, given several hundred dollars to his unfortunate classmate, Henry de Veuve, and, during his last visit to Brown County, he had transferred the home farm back to his father and convinced the old man to will it to his brother Louis.[2]

He had long since given up on mining investments and determined to stick to real estate. While in Nebraska, he had purchased a block of town lots in Valentine and farm property near Fort Niobrara, but decided that land in Washington Territory would represent a more valuable long-term investment. In the spring of 1888, he had borrowed $10,000 from Leopold Markbreit on his *Volksblatt* stock and traveled with Captain Egbert Savage of his regiment to Washington. In a two-week orgy of buying, Savage purchased $4000 worth of property in Seattle, and Kautz spent the $10,000 he had borrowed for property in Tacoma and Seattle plus $6000 of his brother George's money and several hundred dollars which had been entrusted to him by Thomas Wilhelm and John Summerhayes.

Kautz felt at the time that his real estate holdings would guarantee financial security for his family in case of his untimely death, but he wasn't out of the woods yet. In March 1890, his loan from Markbreit was due to be paid back at the same time that taxes were due on his Seattle property and his bank account was overdrawn. Threatened with insolvency, he was frantic. He was saved by an offer from one of his lieutenants to purchase $2000 worth of his Seattle property, another of $4000 for forty acres he owned near Fort Niobrara, and a generous offer from his brother George to lend him $12,000 "on my own terms" to repay Markbreit, all in one day, prompting him to write, "It is very remarkable how all this comes in one day, after I have been so long in great anxiety of mind."[3]

The holiday season in Washington brought the anxiety back. "I am troubled how to raise sufficient money for current expenses. The bills are coming in and I have exhausted my bank account."[4]

Financial matters were not all that was on his mind. During the holidays, he began laying the groundwork for his campaign for promotion. On Christmas Eve, he called on Senator William McKinley of Ohio and, on New Year's Day, he attended receptions for the president, vice president, secretary of war, commander of the army and the adjutant general. He also called on Mary Crook and found her "much broken and distressed."[5]

Kautz was much distressed himself when his son dropped out of school and returned to Washington with no plans for the future. Through the influence of Henry Krehbiel, music critic of the *New York Tribune*, Austin was placed in a music school.[6] Kautz was not certain how long that would last because Austin was already talking about going to a business college.

The rifle board would not meet again until March, so Kautz set about in earnest to work for the vacancy which would take place on Gibbon's retirement on April 20. Fannie's choice of the Elsmere as their residence was fortunate. Two fellow tenants were Assistant Secretary of War Lewis Grant and Elijah Halford, President Harrison's private secretary and closest adviser.[7] The Kautzes and Halfords would become close friends and Halford did all he could to promote Kautz's cause. Others who lobbied for him were Senator McKinley and Bellamy Storer, recently elected congressman from Cincinnati. He met with Secretary of War Redfield Proctor several times and was convinced that the secretary would not support him. He did feel, however, that John Schofield would be a strong supporter, increasing his confidence in his promotion.

When the board met on March 2, it was at Springfield Arsenal in Massachusetts. When Kautz arrived back from Springfield on March 8, he was surprised to meet his wife at the station on her way to Cincinnati. She had learned the day before that her mother was dying and she was rushing to be at her mother's bedside. Mrs. Markbriet breathed her last on March 30.

As the time approached for General Gibbon's retirement, Kautz was told by Elijah Halford that General Schofield was dead-set against old men being made generals, which was contrary to what Schofield had previously told him. Lewis Grant, however, said that he had seen no recommendation from Schofield in writing and, as Kautz noted, "seemed to suggest that I had better secure such recommendations."[8]

Of course, Kautz was in Schofield's office next morning. He wrote that night, "I gathered that he is not on record in favor of myself or any other officer.... He is as much in my favor as he is for anyone.... I am disappointed, but it is not so bad as if he were opposed to me."[9]

Kautz's disappointment was allayed somewhat that evening when Senator McKinley informed him that he had met with the president and spoke in favor of Kautz's promotion and would do so again the next day. That did not prevent Kautz from writing the following night, "I am rapidly losing faith in men, particularly politicians."[10]

Mrs. Halford had just arrived from Indiana with the rest of their family, but she suddenly became quite ill and Pauline was "requisitioned" to nurse her. Despite his concern for his wife, Halford continued to work for Kautz's promotion and promised, on April 11, to try to get the Secretary of War on his side.

Kautz was then off to New York for a brief board meeting. He spent enough time with Austin to be satisfied with the boy's progress. While in New York, he received word that Mrs. Halford had died. When he returned to Washington on the 17th, he found that Fannie had been very helpful to the Halfords and had offered the use of their own rooms in "their great distress."

On April 20, the day of John Gibbon's retirement, Kautz went to the War Department to see Kelton, but found him absent. Kautz gave up and went to lunch. He met Lewis Grant at lunch and, according to his journal, "As I came out he stopped me and handed me a paper saying it was not important and that I could read it at my leisure. I saw at once that he was speaking facetiously, and I said it may not be of any importance to you but it is very important to me, for I recognized at a glance that it was my letter of appointment to the grade of Brigadier General."[11]

For the next three days numerous telegrams arrived congratulating him and letters started coming from all parts of the country. Callers poured into Kautz's rooms at the Elsmere to offer their congratulations and were served punch by Fannie and Pauline. Kautz wrote, "They did not take their departure until the bowl was dry and midnight had arrived." He added, however, that some few had difficulty "concealing their chagrin."[12]

On April 24, he noted in his journal, "I am informed by the cashier that I have overdrawn my account at the Citizens Bank."[13] The $1000 per year raise just received would come in handy.

47. Vancouver Barracks

If Brigadier General Kautz was elated by his recent pay raise, he was even more puffed up by the congratulatory letters which continued to arrive for weeks. The junior officers of the Eighth Infantry sent him an ornate sword inscribed with their names, which Fannie promptly put on display in the lobby of the Elsmere. Kautz was deeply touched by Mary Crook's offer to send the epaulets which had belonged to her dead husband.

There was hardly time to write thank-you letters, however, before orders arrived sending him to serve on a court of inquiry at Fort Walla Walla, Washington. In April 1891, a soldier named Miller had been fatally shot in a barroom argument by a local citizen named H.J. Hunt. In retaliation, about forty soldiers from the fort broke into the town jail, removed Hunt and hanged him. President Harrison ordered the court of inquiry. After a week of hearings, the court concluded that Colonel Charles E. Compton of the Fourth Cavalry, who commanded Fort Walla Walla, played no role in the lynching, but had done little to prevent it. A number of the soldiers were later tried by military courts.

Kautz arrived back in Washington on June 12. The next morning he called at the White House to thank President Harrison for his promotion. According to Kautz, "I told him that I had only called ... to thank him. In speaking of the fact that I had just returned from the Court of Inquiry at Walla Walla, he ... said that he could not tolerate the conduct of troops, who were there for the purpose of preserving order and maintaining the law, that they should become the violators of the law instead of the preservers of it."[1]

Kautz met with Halford, Proctor and Kelton later the same day expressing his desire to get the Department of the Columbia and was told that a decision would be forthcoming. With his family comfortably located in Cincinnati, Kautz determined to move to New York to be on hand for meetings of the rifle board. The board, however, was meeting infrequently, waiting for a rifle testing range to be constructed at the army's facility on Governor's Island. With little to do and uncertain about his future, Kautz expressed his impatience by writing, "It is not pleasant to be situated as I am at present, separated from my family and not knowing what we are to do."[2]

Kautz's boredom came to an end on July 3 when he received a telegram from Kelton that he had been assigned command of the Department of the Columbia. His work with the board was at an end.[3] After stopping in Washington to pick up his official orders, he was in Cincinnati on July 8, where he found his family ready to depart. They were on the train three days later.[4]

It was a leisurely journey. They stopped in St. Paul to pick up Mary Crook and spent a week with her touring Yellowstone before proceeding on to Tacoma. Kautz spent two days at Vancouver Barracks inspecting his future quarters and officially taking command of the department, then returned to Tacoma, where he showed his children sights related to his early days in the Northwest. He was especially pleased at their interest in the buildings which he had built at Steilacoom more than thirty years before. The family eventually took their first meal in their spacious quarters at Vancouver Barracks on August 11 and were serenaded that night by the Fourteenth Infantry band.[5]

Kautz spent the remainder of the summer inspecting the posts within the department. He spent so little time at Vancouver Barracks that he noted, "We are getting acquainted gradually with the people of the Post, but the progress is slow." He added, "Regiments and Posts have their traits of character and we have yet to find out in what respect this differs from those we have known."[6] He need not have worried about a lack of society at the post as he and Fannie were hosts to a steady stream of house guests who stayed for periods ranging from a few days to several months.

Although the responsibilities of the department commander were great, his actual duties were insignificant, but time-consuming. The post was commanded by the colonel of the Fourteenth Infantry, leaving Kautz to deal only with departmental affairs. Constantly interrupted by house guests, he struggled to complete his annual departmental report.

Domestic problems, however, seem to have been of greater concern to the general. In August, Pauline went on strike and refused to work. She moved to town, threatening to return east. She was induced to return only if the Kautzes hired a Chinese cook, leaving her only the duty of serving at table. In October, Kautz managed to have Austin admitted to Stanford University, but, based on his son's performance in the east, he was skeptical of his success. About the same time, he became aware that Frankie was infatuated with Lieutenant Wilds Richardson one of Kautz's aides. Since the two were living in the same house, they had many opportunities to be alone together, leading Kautz to comment, "My wife it seems has taken Mr. Richardson and Frankie to task for undue intimacy and told me of the result in Frankie's presence and she did not deny it.... While I was conscious of the danger of having young officers in the family, I had hoped that she was superior to the average girl and had ambition that would prevent her

The Kautz family lounging on the back porch of the commanding officer's quarters at Vancouver Barracks, Washington Territory, in 1891. From August Kautz's photograph album, courtesy Virginia (Kautz) Borkenhagen.

from becoming commonplace."[7] Despite counseling by both her parents, Frankie did not get over her infatuation quickly.

A visit from Colonel William Carlin in October was prompted by his desire to have Kautz lobby for his promotion when Kautz retired. Kautz would later put in a good word for Carlin, but, at the time of the visit, it prompted him to comment, "I am getting painfully conscious of the near approach of my retirement. I hope the change will be sufficiently novel to distract me from dwelling on its melancholy aspect."[8]

And he didn't. He simply started packing up a few weeks later.

On January 4, Fannie received a telegram that her brother-in-law, Wolfgang Schoenle, had died the night before and that the funeral was to be held on January 5, the day of her husband's retirement. Fannie bit her lip and went through the events which filled that day. In the afternoon, the post commander held a dress parade in Kautz's honor and it was followed by a superb reception attended by the officers of the post and many of the townspeople. It lasted until 2 A.M. Almost overcome by emotion, Kautz was called upon to give a short speech which was recorded for posterity by the *Army & Navy Journal*. It concluded, "If I were like the farmer's worn-out wagon, which, when the wheels had become worn and the spokes are getting loose and threaten to fall out, he takes it to the blacksmith shop and retires it, it comes out again nearly as good as new, with another career of usefulness before it. If this kind of retirement could be made to apply to my case, it would be highly satisfactory. As it is I must enter my new career and endeavor to find in new interests a new ambition. It is gratifying to me, however, that I am assisted out in such a brilliant manner. I am going out, like a comet, in a great blaze of light, and I assure you that I appreciate it very highly, that I am truly grateful and thank you very much."[9]

At noon on January 5, Kautz assembled all of the officers of headquarters in his office to take official leave of them. Major Ward, the departmental adjutant, read a "little flattering address," which led Kautz to remark, "There seems to be a very general regret at my departure, and I am pleased to know that my retirement is a matter of regret with those with whom I have been serving so short a period."[10] After lunch, he went into town in full dress uniform to have his photograph taken.

So ended the military career of the boy who had sat in a tree house high above the river fearing that the world might pass him by. He had summarized that career in his journal only a few days before: "With my retirement here at this Post the circuit of my military life will be completed. I joined my regiment at this Post from the Academy, and, as Brevet Second Lieutenant, began my career as an officer of the Army and, on the 5th of next month, I will close it at this same Post where I began, with the rank of Brigadier General. My career has not been brilliant but sufficiently successful to be gratifying to much more ambitious men than I have been. While I may not have availed myself of all the opportunities that I have had, I cannot reproach myself with having prodigally wasted any."[11]

48. Retirement

Kautz still had unfinished business. Two days after his birthday, he wrote the order taking leave of the department and ordered his two aides back to their regiments. Lieutenant Koehler left the next day, but Kautz was a bit perturbed that Richardson seemed in no hurry to get away, writing, "I suspect that he is loth [sic] to give up Frankie," but adding, "Girls never marry their first serious lovers, and this is my principal hope."[1]

The business of packing — "breaking up," he had always called it — kept the retired general occupied for more than a week. He determined to go to Puget Sound to check on the progress of his nephew's medical practice and to examine his real estate holdings before meeting his family in San Francisco at the end of the month. When Fannie and the girls departed on January 14, he noted, without further comment, that Lieutenant Richardson left with them.

While in Seattle and Tacoma, Kautz took time to exchange reminiscences with Edward Huggins, Granville Haller and others before boarding the train for San Francisco. A short stay in San Francisco permitted him to meet old friends and to take the train to Palo Alto, where he learned that his son was doing exceedingly well at Stanford. Unfortunately, he missed an opportunity to say goodbye to Pauline, who had returned to her home in Lexington to be with her ailing mother.

The Kautzes went east also, spending most of the months of March and April with family in Ohio. In April, they received word that Pauline was to marry a man named Andrew Streffeler in Lexington on the 14th. Kautz's only comment was, "I never believed that she would be so unwise as to marry a white man."[2]

Kautz's pension provided only $343 per month, so it was a relief to be living with relatives and avoiding the expense of hotel or boarding house charges. Fannie wanted to go to Europe again, however, using as her reason a desire for the girls to continue their education on the Continent. Living off relatives had allowed her husband to put aside a little money and, when he managed to sell a quarter section of farm land for $2800, he gave in to his wife's pleading and agreed to go.

Kautz left Cincinnati for New York alone to make travel arrangements and, when he went to the depot nine days later to meet his wife and daughters, he was surprised to find Lieutenant Richardson, now assigned to the faculty of the Military Academy, in the city to meet the train as well. Although Richardson spent the evening with the family, Kautz gave him no opportunity to be alone with Frankie and the forlorn lieutenant was able to do little more than wave from the pier as the Kautzes departed on the steamer *Friesland* the following day.

Kautz seemed disappointed with this European tour. Concerned about expenses and, subsequently, often staying in second class accommodations, he had to disapprove repeatedly of his wife's extravagance. After landing in Antwerp, the family toured through Germany before staying for the entire month of June at Carlsbad. They then spent three weeks with Fannie's cousin, Julia Stimpfl, before moving on through Switzerland and Italy. By prearrangement,

Kautz left his family at Genoa and returned to the States. Before leaving her, he received Fannie's promise to adhere to a budget of $300 per month.

When Kautz arrived in New York on November 3, he seemed not at all surprised to find Wilds Richardson at the wharf to greet him. Although the Lieutenant "said not a word about Frankie," it was obvious that she was on his mind because he was planning a trip to Italy the following month. Inasmuch as Richardson's arrangements had been made, Kautz "said nothing to discourage him."[3] It seems Frankie said nothing to encourage him after he arrived in Europe.

It would be more than a year before Fannie and the girls came back to the States, giving Kautz the freedom to move about at will. After a brief visit to Albert at the Boston Naval Yard and two months in Washington, D.C., he left for Tacoma in the first week of 1893. He seemed genuinely pleased to be able to spend some time with his sons, Augustus and Nugen, and to meet their wives. Both men were successful farmers on the Puyallup Reservation. Augustus had married Maria Kirschner, the daughter of a discharged soldier. Nugen was married to Eleanor Elizabeth Olney, a first cousin of Franklin Olney, who had married Phil Sheridan's daughter, Emma.

As early as February, Kautz met with newly-elected Congressman William Doolittle of Tacoma in an attempt to have Austin appointed to West Point. Doolittle held a competitive examination for the positions at the Military and Naval Academies on April 29. Austin came up from Palo Alto to take the exam, coming in second out of a large number of applicants. The top scorer, a boy named Pierce Murphy, received the West Point appointment.[4] Doolittle, it seems, had taken an interest in a young man named Andrew Hosher, an orphan who was living in poverty with an uncle. Hosher had not scored well on the exam, but Doolittle still wanted to do something for the boy while not shunning Austin. Accordingly, he gave Austin and his father a difficult choice. Austin could accept the alternate position at West Point, thus relying on Murphy's failing the entrance exam, or Doolittle would give Austin the appointment to the Naval Academy if, and only if, Kautz would pay $300 per year for Hosher to attend Stanford in Austin's place. After consulting with Austin, Kautz accepted the latter offer. All met on May 6 and agreed to the proposition. Austin was on the train for Annapolis the following night.

In the absence of his family and with no permanent home, Kautz seems to have wandered aimlessly for much of the remainder of 1893. There were sojourns with relatives in Ohio, Pennsylvania and Illinois and with Austin at Annapolis in addition to two extended trips to the Columbian Exposition in Chicago. Most of that time, however, was spent in Washington, D.C., where he lived in a boarding house on Corcoran Street as frugally as he seemed capable of doing. Even the Chicago trips were accomplished economically, staying primarily with a lieutenant who had served under him in the Eighth Infantry.

Fannie, unfortunately, did not share her husband's parsimonious nature. He was appalled to learn that she had spent over $3000 in the first five months of the year, necessitating the sale of another of his Illinois parcels in order to bring her and their daughters back from Europe.

In July, Kautz was "much pained" to read in the papers of the death of John Kelton.[5] Kelton had retired the previous year and taken the position of commander of the Soldier's Home in Washington. The newspapers reported that Kelton had left his large family almost penniless, but, when Kautz later visited Josephine, he was relieved to learn that that was not the case.

While living in Washington, Kautz managed to complete and publish several magazine articles. He also arranged with the J.B. Lippincott Company to revise his *Customs of Service* books, but found it impossible because the War Department was in the process of issuing a new set of army regulations which would soon supercede any changes he might make. By the end of the year he was able to write, "I shall continue to write as much as I can, but I find great difficulty in accomplishing anything for the reason that I am not satisfied with what I do. What I do seems so commonplace that it is disappointing to me. My capacity to write has not increased with my power to criticize, and I cannot satisfy myself."[6]

It was not until December 30 that Fannie and the girls arrived back in New York on the steamer *Ems.* Kautz was pleased to note that even Navarra had learned to speak German fluently. When they reached Washington two days later, the first person to call on them was Wilds Richardson. Although Richardson was shunned by all the family except Kautz himself, he was a frequent caller until departing for West Point on February 2. No more was heard of him after that.

Kautz stayed on at the Corcoran Street house until May 1894 before moving to Cincinnati, where he and his family stayed at the home of Jennie Schoenle on Bigelow Place in the fashionable suburb of Mount Auburn. The entire months of July and August, however, were spent at the old homestead in Levanna. For the first time in more than thirty years Kautz was content with the relaxed pace of life in the country, attriuting it to the fact that he was growing old and adding, "One of the great luxuries here is the capacity to sleep.... It is much cooler here and we are free from the dirt and odours of the city, and we have no temptations to stay up late of nights, nor to seek distraction elsewhere because there is none in the neighborhood."[7]

That lack of distraction allowed Kautz time to catch up on his correspondence. On July 30, he received a letter from Pauline, who had returned to Fort Niobrara and was working for the post commander at $25 per month in order to raise money to pay off a mortgage on her mother's home in Lexington. She asked Kautz to lend her $150 for the purpose. Although Kautz wrote in his journal, "I strongly suspect that she is not stating all the facts correctly,"[8] he sent the money immediately. Two weeks later her thank-you arrived, stating that she was starting a mess for the single officers at the post.

Austin Kautz in the uniform of the United States Naval Academy at Annapolis, Maryland, 1895. From August Kautz's photograph album, courtesy Virginia (Kautz) Borkenhagen.

At about the same time, Fannie became severely ill with abdominal pain and vomiting, the cause of which several local doctors were unable to diagnose. Although she was near death for several days, she recovered sufficiently to be carried back to Cincinnati at the end of the month. For weeks after returning to the Schoenle home she was bedridden and able to rest only by receiving large doses of morphine which Kautz administered by injection. Although she was seen by a number of doctors, no consensus could be reached as to the cause of her illness. Finally she was examined by a surgeon named R.B. Hall, who diagnosed a fibroid tumor of her right ovary, the rupture of which had produced the near-fatal illness in August. He recommended surgical removal of the tumor in order to prevent a recurrence of the previous episode.

At first Fannie was skeptical about Dr. Hall's recommendations, which included discontinuance of the morphine upon which she had become so dependent. Kautz wrote that he answered her skepticism with sarcasm, saying, "I suggested to my wife that if she wanted a different diagnosis, all she had to do was to send for a new doctor."[9]

Fannie eventually gave in and Dr. Hall operated on October 26, removing a two-pound tumor from her right ovary. It was almost a month before she was allowed to sit up in bed and she finally left the hospital on December 2. On the last day of the year Kautz wrote in his journal that she had been out of the house only twice since her operation.

As Fannie slowly regained her strength, she was once again struck by the wanderlust, and Kautz agreed to allow her to continue her recuperation at the seashore. On January 15, the Kautzes arrived at the Hygeia Hotel, a spa near Fortress Monroe, Virginia. After a month there, they moved to Annapolis to be near their son, and Kautz was proud to note that Austin was progressing well in the top third of his class.

Kautz had long since decided to sell all of his Midwestern real estate holdings in order to concentrate on managing those he owned in Washington State. Even though the country was in the throes of a severe depression, he had already managed to sell his Illinois farm for $10,600 and, in the first week of 1895, he received more than $2800 for one of his parcels near Storm Lake, Iowa, both very good prices. In addition, the wealthy Hanna Brothers of Cleveland had paid him $2000 for the right to develop his Gopher Mine in Arizona with an option to buy it for $5000 in a year. At a time when many of his contemporaries were suffering severe financial setbacks, he had, over the previous two years, managed to pay off more than $9000 of debt and felt strongly that he was on sound financial ground. With Fannie's approval, he decided that they should move to Seattle so that he could manage his real estate there from close up.

They said goodbye to Austin on May 13 and, after a brief stop in Cincinnati, arrived in Seattle on June 9. A week later they were able to move into a substantial house at the corner of 11th and James Streets. Although the house was rented, this was the first time in their married lives that the Kautzes had a house which they could call their own home. While Fannie, now fully recovered from her surgery, busied herself decorating the house in a manner she considered appropriate for a retired general, Kautz shuttled back and forth between Seattle and Tacoma examining his extensive real estate holdings.

Kautz seemed well satisfied to be retired. A year before, he had quoted General Robert Williams's characterization of retirement as "official and social death," but disagreed with Williams, writing, "One of the most gratifying things to me is that I am not at all troubled by the fact that I am now upon the retired list.... This is no doubt due to the fact that I have many things to occupy me, and I really have all I can do to attend to my own private affairs."

Further on in that same journal entry he spoke of his own health, saying, "My own health continues good. I can take long walks with much satisfaction. I have no aches or pains and sleep well for six and seven hours of the twenty-four. I am no more of a dispetic [sic] than I have always been, although to be comfortable I must take more care in eating than was necessary in my younger days.... I seem to be nearing my end as gradually and satisfactorily as was the case with my father, and I certainly can not ask for more."[10]

Late in August, Kautz accepted an invitation from John H. Wholley[11] to an excursion to Snoqualmie Falls, twenty-five miles east of Seattle. On August 27, the party, consisting of Wholley and his wife, the Kautz family, the Haller family, Rob Schoenle and a few other friends, rode to the falls in a private rail car provided by a railroad executive. At the falls, Kautz was not so brave as to climb down over the rocks to the base of the falls as did some of the younger members of the party, but was easily able to handle the trail from the top of the falls to the base and back. He enjoyed the experience immensely.

On the last day of the month, he wrote in his journal that he was suffering from indigestion which he attributed to the exertion of the climb and the cold lunch served on the train a few days before. Over the next three days, he noted that he was very uncomfortable with pain in his lower abdomen, but went about his business and finished his journal entry on September 3 on a hopeful note, "Should I feel well enough in the morning, I will go to Tacoma."[12]

Those were the last words he wrote. Some time later, his daughter Frankie typed a two-page addendum to his journal which we copy here almost in its entirety:

> My father died September 4th at ten o'clock in the evening and the account of his last hours will close a journal kept for 43 years.
>
> As can be seen from the closing lines of his story, he had not felt any serious indications of approaching illness; indeed to me he had never appeared in better health, or in a more contented frame of mind, than in the few weeks before his death.

Left: Frankie Kautz, age 20. Photograph taken in 1895 in Seattle. Courtesy Donald J. Robinson. *Right:* Navarra Kautz, age 15. Photograph taken in 1895 in Seattle. From August Kautz's photograph album, courtesy Virginia (Kautz) Borkenhagen.

The newspaper clippings will give a fairly accurate account of his illness; it only remains to add the few more intimate recollections of his last hours. He went to bed Tuesday night feeling very well and awoke at 12:30 in violent pain. Mama awakened my cousin, Dr. Schoenle and together they labored for his relief during the rest of the night and the following day. The greater part of the time his suffering was so severe that nothing else was to be thought of, so that we were not ever prepared by the probability of death. After an injection of morphine at 5 P.M., Papa showed such apparent improvement that we became quite hopeful. He lay quietly holding one of our hands and opening his eyes every now and then to see who was in the room, appearing satisfied if he saw us all. He asked a few questions, although the difficulty he had in breathing prevented him from talking much. At about seven he expressed a desire for some soup, and took several swallows with relish. We were sure that he was getting better, but Rob only saw the apparent improvement that comes before death, however, he expected him to live through the night. He did not show any signs that he knew that he was about to die, but seemed contented to be relieved from pain. He asked Mama to wind up the clock and watched her as she did so. He wondered what he had done to bring on such an attack, and when Mama asked him once when he appeared uncomfortable: "What is the matter?," he answered with a return of his habitual humor: "That's what the Doctors would like to know." It was a great effort for him to move, but he expressed a desire to turn on his side. "Wait," Mama exclaimed, "I will call Rob." "No," he said, "You can help me," and those were his last words. At nine I had gone down stairs to see Mr. and Mrs. Wholley and Mr. and Miss [Charlotte] Haller, who by the kind provision of Providence were with us in our trouble, and while I was sitting with them, Varra ran into the room and threw herself sobbing into Mrs. Wholley's lap. I hurried back to Papa's room, passing Rob on the stairs, who said to me "Hurry up!" and we both entered the room in time to see Papa take his last breath. Mama was calling to him to speak to her again and Rob said, "It is all over, Aunt Fanny," and a few minutes after they took us out of the room. His last moments were peaceful and the expression after death was one of rest and contentment.... If he had known of his approaching end he could not have left his affairs in more perfect order, nor could he have left us a more valuable substitute and consolation than his journal, in which we can read every thought, desire and intention of his mature life.[13]

Afterword

The dyspepsia which had bothered Dutch Kautz through much of his adult life had finally taken its toll. A post-mortem examination showed that he had died of a perforated duodenal ulcer. He was buried temporarily in a plot in Lake View Cemetery in Seattle owned by Granville Haller, but, in compliance with a request he had made before his death to be buried near Philip Sheridan, his remains were removed to Arlington National Cemetery and placed only a few feet from the grave of his old friend. The gravesite provides a panoramic view across the Potomac of the National Mall. An ugly little thorn apple tree lies between the two graves, overshadowing that of Kautz, signifying, perhaps, the rift which had occurred between the two generals late in their careers.

After Kautz's death, Fannie lived for a short time in Seattle. With a pension of $50 per month, she later lived with her son's family in Washington, D.C., and died of cancer on August 11, 1913, at the home of her daughter, Frankie, in Wenonah, New Jersey. She is buried with her husband at Arlington.

Austin Kautz graduated from the Naval Academy high in his class. He had a very successful naval career which was aided by a close friendship with Undersecretary of the Navy Franklin D. Roosevelt. He married Louise Hovey, a member of a prominent New England family, and had one son. Austin died in Berlin, Germany, in 1927 while stationed as Naval Attaché at the U.S. Embassy. He was buried at Arlington just down the hill from his father.

Both Frankie and Navarra lived long and prosperous lives, Frankie dying in 1962 and Navarra in 1970.

Nugen Kautz left the Puyallup Reservation some time after his father's death and lived in Portland, Oregon, where he worked for the government. He died in Portland in 1938. Augustus remained on the reservation where he had a large family. He died in 1935. Many of his descendants still live on or near the reservation.

Kautz's brother Albert rose to the rank of rear admiral in command of the Pacific Fleet. He retired in 1902. For a short time, he was Minister to Samoa. He died in 1907 and is buried with his wife, Esther, at Arlington, only a few feet from his brother.

George Kautz remained a successful banker in Moweaqua, Illinois, and was buried there after his death in 1919. Fred Kautz was a tobacco farmer for the rest of his life. Louis Kautz supplemented his farming income with income from a general store in Levanna. For a while he was postmaster of Levanna. Fred died in 1909 and Louis in 1923. Both are buried in Pisgah Ridge Cemetery near their parents.

Leopold Markbreit continued, through his editorship of the *Cincinnati Volksblatt*, to be a silent force in national politics, championing the careers of both William McKinley and William Howard Taft. He was elected mayor of Cincinnati in 1907 and died in 1909 while still in office. His sister Jennie did not remarry. Both are buried with their mother and their half-brother Frederick Hassaurek in Spring Grove Cemetery in Cincinnati.

Few things are written about the career of August Valentine Kautz. Scribner's *Dictionary of American Biography* said of him, "Kautz was a great student, methodical, industrious, possessed of unusual energy and powers of endurance." Richard Z. Starr, in his definitive history *The Union Cavalry in the Civil War*, called him one of the finest administrators in the army. Historian Henry Simmons says, "He proved to be one of the best officers in the Union army." In his book, *Frontier Regulars*, historian Robert M. Utley called his Eighth Infantry Regiment a "regiment of special character."

Perhaps the most telling description of Kautz comes from Wilds Preston Richardson, an officer who served under Kautz in the Eighth Infantry from 1884 to 1892, but had personal reasons to be antagonistic toward his former regimental commander. Richardson wrote,

> In person General Kautz was of medium height, strong build, with a fine head and kindly eye; of a quiet demeanor and most abstemious in his habits of life. In character he was free from even the suspicion of anything like smallness ... and courageous to the very last degree in maintaining what he considered right.... Free from small vices himself, he was equally free from prejudice against those who did have them, and who differed from him in their views upon the conduct of life. Independent in his own opinions, he freely acknowledged that right to everyone else. He measured men by no fanciful standards, but by how they accomplished the tasks set before them. Frugal and economical by nature, preferring self-denial to indulgence, no one, on the other hand was ever readier to loosen his purse strings in answer to any reasonable call. These were eminent traits in his character; a rigid system of life for himself and generosity in all things toward his fellow man.[1]

Chapter Notes

Chapter 1

1. August V. Kautz, *Autobiography (1828–1847)*. Hereafter: Kautz autobiography.
2. W.H. Beers, *The History of Brown County, Ohio*.

Chapter 2

1. Ulysses S. Grant, *Personal Memoirs*.
2. Kautz autobiography, p. 12. "I erected a retreat on the trunk of an old elm tree, that stood about half way up the hill on the edge of the woods and rose thirty or forty feet, amid its leafy foliage.... I spent many hours reading and writing. Although I could not be seen by anyone standing below, I commanded a view extending for several miles up and down the river."

Chapter 3

1. Luther Giddings, *Sketches of the Campaign in Northern Mexico in Eighteen Hundred Forty-Six and Seven*, pp. 39–40.
2. Giddings, p. 57.
3. Ibid., p. 82.
4. Ibid., pp. 98–99.
5. Both Quitman and Butler would be contenders for nomination for the vice presidency on the Democratic ticket in 1848. Butler won the nomination, but lost the election.
6. Kautz autobiography, p. 49.
7. Giddings, p. 185.
8. Beers, p. 351.
9. Giddings, pp. 243–4.
10. Grant's *Memoirs* have been printed in several editions. Page numbers vary in the different editions.
11. Kautz autobiography, pp. 57–58.

Chapter 4

1. Fifty-six men had begun as fourth-year cadets in the summer of 1848. Thirteen resigned or were dismissed for academic or disciplinary reasons.
2. *Official Register of the Officers and Cadets of the United States Military Academy: 1849, 1852.*
3. Mahan graduated from West Point in 1824. He spent 40 years (1831–1871) as professor of civil engineering and military engineering at the Academy. He was the recognized authority on military engineering of his time. His writings were considered standards in his field long after his death.
4. Andrew Wallace, "Soldier of the Southwest: the Career of General A.V. Kautz, 1869–1886," p. 25.
5. Theophilus F. Rodenbough and William L. Haskins, eds., *The Army of the United States: Historical Sketches of Staff and Line with Portraits of Generals-In-Chief*, pp. 452–62.
6. George Crook, *General George Crook, His Autobiography*, p. 3.
7. Ibid., pp. 5–6.
8. Columbia Barracks was soon renamed Vancouver Barracks and, later, Fort Vancouver.

Chapter 5

1. Edith Haroldsen Lovell, *Benjamin Bonneville: Soldier of the American Frontier*. Bonneville graduated from West Point in 1815. He had gained a measure of fame when, in the 1830s, he led an extensive exploration of California, Oregon, Washington and Utah, which he financed himself.
2. Frances Kautz, ed., "Extracts from the Diary of Gen. A.V. Kautz," *The Washington Historian* 1, p. 115. This is the first citation in this book from Kautz's journals. Apparently Kautz commenced recording daily events in journals as early as 1846. The earliest one in existence is the journal commencing June 1, 1857. On that date, Kautz states that this is the third volume of his journals. The first two volumes were lost when a canoe containing all of Kautz's baggage capsized in the Chehalis River. He rewrote the third volume. He apparently attempted to reproduce at least portions of the first two volumes also. His daughter Frances published some of this material in *The Washington Historian* in 1899.
3. Ibid., p. 115.
4. Ibid., p. 117.
5. Ibid., p. 116.
6. United States Congress, *Senate Executive Journal*: August 1, 1854.
7. Grant, *Memoirs*, p. 133–4.
8. Frances Kautz, "Extracts," vol. 1, p. 118. Quotes in the next five paragraphs are also from this source.
9. This is probably Patkanim or Pat Kanim. Patkanim was a chief of the Snoqualmies.

Chapter 6

1. Houston T. Robison, "The Rogue River Indians and Their Relations with the Whites" (master's thesis, University of Oregon, 1943), chapter 4.

2. *Oregon Historical Quarterly* 7 (1907): Letter, J.W. Nesmith to Joseph Lane, April 20, 1879.

3. James Grant Wilson and John Fiske, *Appleton's Cyclopedia of American Biography*, 6 vols.

4. On that same day, Captain Andrew J. Smith arrived with Company C of the First Dragoon Regiment, which had hastened from Fort Orford, on the Oregon coast.

5. Robison, chapter 4. The Cis-ti-costas were Indians who lived along the trails leading inland from Fort Orford.

6. Ibid., chapter 4.

7. Kautz was fond of Wool. It may be recalled that it was Wool who mustered Kautz into the service in 1846. Wool was decidedly sympathetic to the plight of the Native Americans. Kautz was quickly coming to share this opinion.

8. U.S. House Executive Document No. 76, 34th Congress, pp. 86–87.

9. Robison, chapter 4. These were members of Company M, 3rd Light Artillery Regiment. The company was serving here as infantry. The remainder of the 3rd Artillery was still in the East.

10. Alfred B. Meacham, *Wigwam and War-Path; or Royal Chief in Chains*, pp. 298–299.

11. Rodney Glisan, *Journal of Army Life*, p. 364.

12. Ibid., p. 231.

13. John C. Van Tramp, *Prairie and Rocky Mountain Adventures or Life in the West*, p. 151.

14. Glisan, pp. 240–5.

15. This was the end of a long and perilous journey for Company H. Eight companies of the regiment had started west around the Horn in December 1853 on the steamer *San Francisco*. One hundred of the 500 men perished in a storm. Company H then regrouped and marched overland. They arrived at Benicia Barracks in July 1855.

16. *Official Register of Officers and Cadets*, 1853. Chandler had started at the Academy in Kautz's class. He was set back for disciplinary reasons and graduated in the class of 1853.

17. Glisan, p. 263. Glisan was incorrect. Only Kautz was wounded and no one was killed. Crook, pp. 27, 29. Crook's description of the attack is slightly different, based on Kautz's having told him of the event several days later. (See below.) "It seems he had started from Fort Orford to find a road to the Rogue River country. He met some Indians in the woods, and saluted them with compliments of the season, when they answered his salute with a volley at close range. One ball struck him in the chest, and would certainly have killed him but for two books he had in his pocket. The ball struck the corner of one, going through it, but was stopped by the other, knocking him down. The soldiers started to run, saying the Lieutenant was killed, but he jumped up and prevented the stampede. It was a thick, bushy country and he had no trouble in getting away." *Journal*, October 20, 1891. Thirty-six years later, Kautz met a man named Jacob Dubeck, who had served under him in this brief engagement. Dubeck was with his wife, who claimed to have been instrumental in saving Kautz's life. She had been working at Fort Orford as a hospital matron and had sewn a pocket on Kautz's flannel shirt which had allowed him to carry the two metallic despatch books in his pocket.

18. *Journal*, April 30, 1859, and May 4, 1859. Kautz attributed some of the delay in Smith's final assault to the fact that two of Smith's lieutenants, Horatio Gibson of the Third Artillery and Benjamin Allston of the Dragoons, were so drunk that Smith had to wait for them to sober up before attacking. Kautz made the mistake of telling this story to some of his friends and Gibson's resentment almost led to a duel. See Chapter 12.

19. J.G.T., *Overland Monthly* 5, no. 8 (April 1885): p. 421. This article was written by a man identified only as J.G.T., who served with the volunteers. His estimate of casualties probably refers to the two days of fighting. About the enemy, J.G.T. added this: "All were good shots, and possessed of good rifles, and were quite familiar with the ways of the white man."

20. Crook, p. 27. It was here that Crook learned of Kautz's being struck by a musket ball.

21. Francis B. Heitman, *Historical Register and Dictionary of the United States Army*. Reynolds, an 1841 graduate of West Point, was twice breveted during the Mexican War. He was Commandant of Cadets at West Point when the Civil War began. He rose to the rank of major general in the regular service and, in 1862, was offered command of the Army of the Potomac, but declined. He was killed by a sniper on the first day of the Battle of Gettysburg.

22. Ibid. Augur, an 1843 graduate of West Point, served in the Mexican War and was Commandant of Cadets at West Point early in the Civil War. During that war, he was breveted to major general in the regular Army. He was later colonel of the 12th Infantry. He became brigadier general in the regular Army in 1869.

Chapter 7

1. Kathryn Jacob and Bruce A. Ragsdale, eds., *Biographical Directory of the United States Congress, 1774–1989*. Shields, possibly the only man to ever serve in the U.S. Senate from three different states, was a brevet major general in the Mexican War (and, later, in the Civil War). He was governor of Oregon in 1848 and 1849.

2. Heitman. Wright, an 1822 graduate of West Point, was with the 4th Infantry from 1848 to 1855. In the Civil War, he remained on the Pacific Coast and commanded the Department of the Pacific at the rank of brevet brigadier general. He died July 30, 1865, in the wreck of the steamer *Brother Jonathan*.

3. Ibid. Casey, an 1826 graduate of West Point, was breveted twice during the Mexican War. He was in the 2nd Infantry during and after the Mexican War. He was breveted to brigadier general and major general in the Civil War. He retired in 1868. His son, Thomas Lincoln Casey, had graduated first in Kautz's class (1852) at West Point.

4. Companies A and C of the 4th Infantry, Companies D and H of the 9th Infantry, and Captain Erasmus Keyes's Company M of the 3rd Artillery, which had arrived in November.

5. Jacob and Ragsdale. Stevens, born in 1818, graduated in 1839 first in his class at West Point. His class ranking earned him an appointment to the Corps of Engineers. He served under Winfield Scott in the Mexican War, was severely wounded and was breveted to captain and to major. He was then appointed to the newly-formed U.S. Coast and Geodetic Survey. He resigned his army commission to accept the appointment as Governor of Washington Territory. At the same time, he was named to command a team to survey a northern railroad route to the Pacific Coast. He would serve as governor until 1856 when he was elected territorial representative to Congress (1856–

1860). In 1860, he chaired the pro-slavery Democratic Convention which nominated John C. Breckenridge for president and his close friend Joseph Lane for vice president. At the outset of the Civil War, he attempted to be reinstated in the army, but his political views prevented it. The governor of New York, however, named him Colonel of the 79th New York Infantry ("The Highlanders"). He was subsequently breveted to brigadier general and commanded a brigade. He was killed at the Battle of Chantilly on September 1, 1862.

6. As secretary of the territory, Mason served as acting governor on three occasions. If the date of his birth (1830) is correct, he was a very young man to take over the responsibilities that the governorship presented.

7. The treaty was amended at Governor Stevens's suggestion (under pressure) in January 1857 to provide a larger reservation for the Nisquallies on their precious Nisqually River, but this action was too late to prevent the war that followed or the tragic death of Leschi.

8. Ezra Meeker, *Pioneer Reminiscences of Puget Sound: The Tragedy of Leschi*, pp. 229–262. Meeker covers the events surrounding the Treaty of Medicine Creek in detail.

9. Ibid., p. 244.

10. Ibid., p. 209.

11. Ibid., p. 242. This quote is from an article in the *The Truth Teller*, a one-page newspaper published by Kautz in defense of Leschi.

12. Heitman. Haller had served in the Seminole War and was breveted to captain and to major in the Mexican War. He was promoted to captain in 1848 and to major of the 7th Infantry in 1861. He was dismissed from the service in 1863 for "uttering a disloyal sentiment," but reinstated at the rank of colonel 16 years later.

13. Meeker, p. 280. These were the words of J.W. Wiley, editor of the *Pioneer and Democrat*, an Olympia newspaper which, for all intents and purposes, was controlled by Governor Stevens.

14. Wilson and Fiske. Maloney was unusual among the regular officers on the frontier in that he was not a West Pointer. He had enlisted as a private in the 4th Infantry in 1835. He was commissioned 2nd Lieutenant in November 1846 and was breveted during the Mexican War. He remained with the 4th Infantry and rose to the rank of captain in 1854. During the Civil War, he was promoted to major of the 1st Infantry and became colonel of the 13th Wisconsin Volunteers. He commanded a battery of artillery at Vicksburg, where several plaques on the battlefield bear his name. After the Civil War, he rose to the rank of lieutenant colonel in the regular service.

15. Meeker, p. 313.

16. Ibid., p. 309.

17. Ibid., pp. 547–8.

18. This was done partly in defiance of General Wool, who was still in command of the Department of the Pacific. Wool, who was in favor of a peaceful solution to the Indian problem, had wanted the volunteers placed under the command of the U.S. military, while Stevens wanted to command them. Stevens, with considerable influence in the nation's capital, arranged for Wool to be charged with disloyalty. The controversy between Stevens and Wool was ongoing and was a credit to neither man, especially to Stevens. The details, including a declaration of martial law and suspension of the right of *habeas corpus* by Stevens and his conviction for contempt of court, are beyond the sphere of this narrative. Wool was forced to return east to defend himself. In the end, a congressional investigation ensued and Stevens received a reprimand from President Franklin Pierce for his actions.

19. Meeker, p. 337.

20. Meeker, p. 330–31. Leschi went to the Nisqually reservation at Fox Island to meet with the Indian agent, John Swan, to discuss a peaceful settlement. He said that he "was ready to talk."

21. Ibid., p. 207. Meeker added a footnote stating, "Lieutenant Kautz was the officer at Fort Steilacoom who received the child and sent the little fellow, a boy of five years, to the author [Meeker] for care."

22. Heitman. Keyes graduated from West Point in 1832. In addition to his service in the Northwest, he was military secretary to General Winfield Scott on three separate occasions. Promoted to colonel of the 11th Infantry at the outset of the Civil War, he rose to the rank of major general in the regular service before retiring in May 1864.

23. Keyes, pp. 257–9; Meeker, p. 356.

24. Keyes, p. 259. Keyes is referring to Kautz, Army Surgeon Dr. George Suckley, and Lieutenant George Mendell, Kautz's classmate, who had served as engineering officer during the campaign.

25. Ibid., p. 260.

26. Heitman. Winfield Scott was born near Petersburg, Virginia, on June 13, 1786. He studied law, but was appointed to the army by President Thomas Jefferson. He was a hero of the War of 1812 and, remaining in the army, became commander in chief in 1841. He is given much of the credit for the U.S. success in the Mexican War. He was nominated for president by the Whig Party in 1852, but was soundly defeated by Franklin Pierce. Scott continued as commander in chief until his retirement in October 1861. He died May 29, 1866.

27. Meeker, p. 410.

28. Ibid., p. 412.

29. Ibid., p. 413.

30. Sluggia's reward was fifty blankets. In retaliation for his betrayal of Leschi and the later death of Quiemuth, Sluggia was killed on December 7, 1857, by a Nisqually follower of Leschi named Yelm Jim.

31. *Tacoma Ledger*, April 9, 1893.

32. Frances Kautz, "Extracts," vol. 1, p. 117.

33. Born of immigrant parents, Prosch grew up in New York City. He worked for the *New York Daily Express* for seventeen years before moving to San Francisco, where he became part owner of the *Alta California*. He later published newspapers in Steilacoom, Olympia, Tacoma and Seattle.

34. Heitman. George E. Pickett graduated last in the West Point class of 1846. Twice breveted during the Mexican War, he served in the Ninth Infantry in Washington Territory from 1855 to 1861, when he resigned to join the Confederacy. He was severely wounded in 1862. The high point of his military career was also the high point of the Confederacy, when he led the famous Pickett's Charge at Gettysburg. *Journal*: Various entries. Kautz and Pickett were never stationed together while in Washington Territory, but they carried on frequent correspondence both official and personal.

35. *Journal*, January 4, 1858, and April 12, 1858. Mary Slaughter was despondent after her husband's death and never regained her former joyful spirit. She died in 1861.

36. August V. Kautz, *Customs of Service for Officers of the Army*, pp. 181–88.

37. *Journal*, June 1, 1857.

38. Ibid., December 1, 1857.

39. Ibid., December 23, 1857.

40. Heitman. Thomas Lincoln Casey, after graduating first in the class of 1852 at West Point, remained in the engineers throughout a long career. He became Superintendent of Public Buildings for the government in 1877 and

Chief of Engineers at the rank of brigadier general from 1888 until his retirement in 1895. His most enduring achievement was completion of the Washington Monument. The monument had been begun in 1848, but work was halted for lack of funds in 1857. The monument stood half completed until 1876 when Casey took on the task of finishing it. It took eleven more years.

41. *Journal*, October 27, 1860.
42. Meeker, p. 418.
43. Ibid., p. 418.
44. Ibid., p. 420.
45. Ibid., p. 206.
46. Ibid., p. 423.
47. *Journal*, December 20, 1857.
48. Jacob and Ragsdale. Fayette McMullen, born in Gate City, Virginia, in 1805, served in the Virginia senate from 1839 to 1849 and in the U.S. House from 1849 to 1857. He was appointed governor of Washington Territory by President Buchanan and served from 1857 to 1859. After the Civil War began, he was elected to the Second Confederate Congress. He died in a train wreck in Wytheville, Virginia, in 1880.
49. *Journal*, December 22, 1857.
50. Ibid., December 24, 1857.
51. A.V. Kautz, *Map of Connell's Prairie*. The caption on the map, as drawn by Kautz, was "Plan of Tanolcut Prairie. Showing the improbability that Leschi could have killed A.B. Moses on the 31st October, 1855, the Evidence showing that Moses had left Leschi on the prairie, and met him again in the swamp 68 chains distant. To get there Leschi would have to go 104½ chains, the trail impracticable part of the way for horses. Moses rode rapidly from Leschi to the swamp, where he was killed. Surveyed and measured by Lieut. A.V. Kautz, U.S.A., Dr. W.F. Tolmie and W. Tidd."
52. *Journal*, January 16, 1858.
53. Ibid., January 20, 1858.
54. Ibid., January 21, 1858.
55. Charles Grainger, quoted in Meeker, pp. 453–4.
56. *Journal*, February 19, 1858.
57. It must be remembered that Fayette McMullen, although appointed to the governorship of Washington Territory, was, in fact, a Virginia politician.

Chapter 8

1. Heitman. Parke graduated second in the class of 1849 at West Point. He was in the topographical engineers until the Civil War, when he was named brigadier general and put in command of troops. He briefly served as commander of the Army of the Potomac in Meade's absence. He was superintendent of the Military Academy from 1887 until his retirement in 1889.
2. Ibid. Woodruff, like Maurice Maloney, was not a West Pointer. He had been lieutenant colonel of a New Jersey volunteer infantry battalion during the Mexican War. He was mustered out after the war, but received a regular army commission in the 9th Infantry in 1855.
3. *Journal*, June 18, 1857.
4. Ibid., July 4, 1857.
5. Ibid., August 6, 1858.
6. Ibid., December 2, 1858.
7. Ibid., January 22, 1859, and January 23, 1859.
8. Ibid., February 15, 1859. Cousin Lou was Kautz's cousin, Louise (Rombach) Denver, one of Kautz's most frequent correspondents. She was married to James William Denver, whose career included the practice of law in Ohio,

captain in the Twelfth Infantry during the Mexican War, California state senator, California Secretary of State, Commissioner of Indian Affairs, governor of Kansas Territory and brigadier general in the Civil War. The City of Denver, Colorado (previously in Kansas Territory), is named for him. Kautz and Denver became close friends although they differed drastically on politics. Denver often attempted to champion Kautz's military career. As this entry might suggest, his influence in Washington was considerable.

Chapter 9

1. Frances Kautz, "Extracts," vol. 1, p. 115.
2. August V. Kautz, "Ascent of Mount Rainier," *Overland Monthly* 14 (May 1875): pp. 393–403. The quotations in this chapter are from this account unless noted otherwise.
3. Edward Meany, *Mount Rainier: A Record of Exploration*, p. 1.
4. *Journal*, July 10, 1857. Kautz's journal states, "We took twenty-four crackers each and a few pounds of dried meat. We each took a blanket and I had several other things besides for making observations, consisting of a field glass, a prismatic compass, a thermometer, and spirit lamp besides a large revolver. One of the men, Dogue, carried a coil of small rope and Carroll a hatchet."
5. Ibid., July 11, 1857.
6. Ibid., July 16, 1857. The journal says, "This morning it snowed until eight o'clock."
7. Ibid., July 16, 1857. The journal says, "I continued on for half an hour or more; a strong gust of wind carried away my hat." The hat wound up in a crevasse. He improvised by tearing the sleeve from a red flannel shirt and wrapping it about his head.
8. George Vancouver's party had triangulated the height of the mountain at something above 12,000 feet. The actual height is 14,408 feet.

Chapter 10

1. Fred Lockley, *Interview of Nugen Kautz*, January (about 1920). Nugen Kautz said, "They were married after the manner of my mother's people; that is, my father gave a certain number of ponies, blankets, etc., to my mother's father for her and mother's father gave a wedding feast to which all of my mother's relatives were invited and my mother and father ate from the same dish and drank from the same cup. The recognition by a man and woman before witnesses ... constitutes a marriage ceremony among the Indians."
2. *Journal*, June 1, 1857.
3. Ibid., November 19, 1857.
4. Ibid., September 6–19, 1857.
5. Ibid., January 6, 1858, and February 24, 1858. The boy's name was John.
6. Ibid., December 15, 1858.
7. Ibid., January 14, 1859.
8. Ibid., January 17, 1859.
9. The Lummi Indians lived on the northeast coast of Puget Sound. Their present reservation is near the town of Bellingham.
10. The name, Doctin, would not last. Doctin later changed his name to Augustus and, in later years, his father called him by that name also.
11. *Journal*, February 9, 1859.

12. Ibid., February 11, 1859, and February 17, 1859.

13. Ibid., February 22, 1859.

14. This is Wesley B. Gosnell, the Indian agent at the Nisqually Reservation. Nugen Kautz would later live with the Gosnells on their farm to the south in Lewis County.

15. *Journal*, April 23, 1859.

16. Ibid., April 24, 1859.

Chapter 11

1. *Journal*, April 30, 1859.

2. Ibid., May 4, 1859.

3. Heitman. Kautz had known Benjamin Allston at West Point. He served in the Confederate army from 1861 to 1865 as colonel of the 4th Alabama Infantry.

4. *Journal*, May 28, 1859.

5. Ibid., June 14, 1859.

6. Ibid., June 15, 1859.

7. Ibid., June 21, 1859.

8. Ibid., June 25, 1859

9. Ibid., June 26, 1859.

10. Ibid., July 18, 1859.

11. Ibid., July 23, 1859.

12. Heitman. Loring served briefly as a 2nd lieutenant of Florida Volunteers in the Seminole troubles of 1837. He later served in the Florida Legislature. When the mounted rifle regiment was organized at the outset of the Mexican War, he received an appointment as captain. He rose to colonel in 1856. He resigned in 1861 to join the Confederate Army as a brigadier general and was promoted to major general the following year.

13. *Journal*, August 9, 1859.

14. Sandhurst is the site of the Royal Military Academy, the British equivalent of West Point.

15. *Journal*, August 6, 1859. It was Pierce who had appointed Stevens governor of Washington Territory.

16. Ibid., August 16, 1859.

17. Ibid., August 20, 1859.

18. Ibid., August 29, 1859.

19. Ibid., September 2, 1859.

20. Ibid., September 19, 1859. Kautz called it the Hotel züm Adler.

21. Schoppen: a half pint.

22. *Journal*, September 19, 1859.

23. Joseph Grau's son, George Jacob Grau, had emigrated to Brown County, Ohio, in 1840 and, after his wife died in childbirth in 1853, his daughter Maria lived with the George Kautz family. Kautz had seen six-year-old Maria Grau when he was home on leave the previous spring.

24. *Journal*, September 20, 1859.

25. Ibid., September 24, 1859.

26. Ibid., October 4, 1859.

27. Ibid., October 31, 1859.

28. Ibid., November 1, 1859.

29. Ibid. Almost 30,000 men were killed or wounded at Solferino on June 24, 1859. Combined French and Piedmontese forces fought there against those of the Austrian Empire. The battle was so costly to both sides that a peace treaty was signed unifying the various kingdoms and duchies of Italy into a single nation.

30. Ibid., January 23, 1860. Antonio Canova was a neoclassical sculptor of the late 18th and early 19th centuries.

31. Ibid., February 7 and 18, 1860. Maria Louisa Lander, born in 1826 in Salem, Massachusetts, worked in Rome. Although she was an excellent sculptress with a promising future, rumors of indiscretion lost her the friendship of her fellow artists as well as the chance for commissions. She returned to the United States and died in obscurity in 1923.

Virginia Dare was born on Roanoke Island in 1587. Since the Roanoke Colony disappeared leaving no trace, she no doubt died in infancy. Miss Lander chose to sculpt her as she might have appeared as an adult. As the statue was being shipped to the United States, it sank in a shipwreck off the coast of Spain and lay at the bottom of the ocean for two years. It was exhibited in Boston for years, but Miss Lander was never able to sell it. She donated it to the State of North Carolina in her will. It now stands in the Elizabethan Gardens on Roanoke Island.

32. Heitman. An 1841 graduate of West Point, Garrett took an appointment as brigadier general in the Confederate Army. He was the first Confederate general to die in the war when he was killed at Carrick's Ford, (West) Virginia, on July 31, 1861.

33. Ibid., March 1, 1860. Fletcher Harper, one of four brothers who founded the publishing firm Harper & Brothers, was a native of Long Island, New York. Various business and publishing aspects of the firm were divided by the brothers. At the time, Fletcher Harper was in charge of management of the periodicals *Harper's New Monthly Magazine* and *Harper's Weekly*.

34. *Journal*, March 12, 1860. Born Jean Eugene Robert in 1805, he added his wife's name, Houdin. He was the most famous magician of his day. Years later, a Hungarian-American magician named Ehrich Weiss, wanting to capitalize on Robert-Houdin's name, changed his own name to Harry Houdini. Famous in his own right, Houdini was jealous of Robert-Houdin's fame and published a book revealing many of Robert-Houdin's "secrets."

35. Ibid., March 22, 1860.

Chapter 12

1. U.S. Senate Journal. Assigned to the 1st Artillery on July 1, 1852, and transferred on 10 May 1853.

2. *Journal*, April 7, 1860.

3. Heitman; Wilson and Fiske. Blake had served in the Seminole and Mexican Wars and was breveted major in the latter. From 1840 to the Civil War, he was major of the 1st Dragoons. During the Civil War, he was colonel of the 1st U.S. Cavalry.

4. *Journal*, May 22, 1860.

5. Ibid., May 25, 1860.

6. Ibid., May 27, 1860.

7. Ibid., June 22, 1860.

8. Ibid., July 3, 1860.

9. Ibid., August 1, 1860.

10. Ibid., August 18, 1860.

11. DeLancey Floyd-Jones, *Report of an Expedition*. Kautz's journal expressed similar sentiments.

12. Floyd-Jones, *Journal of the March*. In addition to the 149 to Fort Colville with Kautz, 60 were sent to Fort Walla Walla and 35 to Fort Dalles, making a total of 244.

13. Ibid., October 11, 1860. The Snake Indians had attacked a wagon train of perhaps sixty people, leaving a small number of survivors.

14. Ibid., October 25, 1860.

Chapter 13

1. *Journal*, November 2, 1860.

2. Ibid., November 29, 1860.

3. Ibid., December 4, 1860.

4. August V. Kautz, *Reminiscences of the Civil War*, p. 1.

5. *Journal*, December 5, 1860. Everything at Fort Chehalis was new. The post was opened in February 1860. It would be abandoned in 1861.

6. Ibid., December 26, 1860.

7. Heitman. Edward Conner was an 1857 graduate of West Point. He went east with the regiment in 1861. He accepted an appointment as first lieutenant in the newly-formed Seventeenth Infantry and was promoted to captain, but resigned in 1862.

8. *Journal*, December 15, 1860.

9. Ibid., January 25–26, 1861.

10. Ibid., March 11, 1861.

11. Ibid., March 26–27, 1861.

12. *Reminiscences*, p. 1.

13. *Journal*, January 17, 1861.

14. Robert Underwood Johnson and Clarence Clough Buel, eds., *Battles and Leaders of the Civil War*, vol. 2, pp. 30–39. David Twiggs, whom we met briefly in Chapter 3, had been commissioned a captain in the War of 1812 and his distinguished service included command of the brigade which included the Fourth Infantry at the Battle of Monterrey. His Southern sympathies induced him to surrender his Department of Texas and all of the military stores in that state to the State of Texas on February 18, 1861. He was dismissed from the service on March 1, 1861 and was appointed a major general in the Confederacy's "Provisional Army." Age and infirmity prevented his taking an active role in the Civil War.

15. *Journal*, March 28, 1861.

16. Ibid., April 11, 1861.

17. Mrs. Maloney had been suffering through a very difficult pregnancy and had been quite ill. She was finally able to convince her husband to request a leave of absence. She later suffered a miscarriage, her second.

18. *Journal*, May 1, 1861.

19. Ibid., May 2, 1861.

20. Ibid., May 8, 1861.

21. Ibid., May 13, 1861.

22. Ibid., May 15, 1861. So now we know what happened to Kautz's earlier journals. The third volume, which was begun in 1857 and includes the above excerpted material, was damaged also. Kautz later completely rewrote it. The original does not survive.

23. Ibid., June 4, 1861.

24. Ibid., June 9, 1861.

Chapter 14

1. All regular Army officers remaining loyal to the Union were required to do so.

2. *Journal*, July 9, 1861. Use of the term "(Sixth) 3rd Cavalry" is probably explained by the fact that Kautz recopied this entire journal in 1869. His assignment was, in fact, to the 3rd Cavalry which was later designated the 6th Cavalry.

3. Ibid., August 2, 1861. We might wonder what newspaper Kautz was reading.

4. Heitman. Emory graduated from West Point in 1831. He was twice breveted in the Mexican War. At the beginning of the Civil War, he commanded Fort Washita in Indian Territory. He was the only commander stationed in the South to successfully bring his entire command out of enemy territory safely. By the end of the war, he would command XIX Corps and be breveted to every grade up

to major general in both the regular and volunteer services. He retired a brigadier general in 1876.

5. *Journal*, August 16, 1861.

6. Ibid., July 9, 1861. It was this second call which Kautz read about while at Acapulco in July. Kautz failed to note that the 3rd Cavalry Regiment to which he had been assigned was the "new" cavalry regiment.

7. *Reminiscences*, p. 3.

8. *Journal*, August 28–29, 1861.

9. Ibid., August 29, 1861.

10. Ibid., September 21, 1861.

11. Heitman. Christian Balder emigrated to America at an early age. He enlisted in Company A of the 1st U.S. Cavalry in April 1855. He received an appointment as 2nd Lieutenant in the 6th Cavalry on October 26, 1861. He was killed at the Battle of Gettysburg.

12. *Journal*, November 2, 1861.

13. Robert N. Scott, Henry M. Lazelle, Leslie J. Perry, Joseph W. Kirkley, Fred C. Ainsworth, John S. Moodey and Calvin D. Cowles, *The War of the Rebellion: A Compilation of the Official Records of the Union and Confederate Armies*, 70 vols. Series II, Vol. 3, pp. 703–4. Hereafter called OR.

14. OR (Navy): Series I, Vol. 5, p. 745.

15. *Journal*, November 4, 1861.

16. Ibid., November 5, 1861.

17. *Reminiscences*, p. 4.

18. *Journal*, November 9, 1861.

Chapter 15

1. *Battles and Leaders*, vol. 1, p. 166.

2. *Reminiscences*, p. 6.

3. Ibid., p. 6.

4. Ibid., p. 7.

5. *Journal*, May 6, 1862.

6. Ibid., May 10, 1862.

7. Reminiscences, p. 8.

8. Heitman. Benson spent his entire career in the 2nd Artillery Regiment. He enlisted as a private in 1845 and rose through the ranks. He received an appointment as 2nd lieutenant at the end of the Mexican War. He died August 11, 1862, from wounds suffered on August 5 at Malvern Hill.

9. This is Kautz's estimate of the number captured.

10. OR: Vol. 11, Part 1, Chap. XXIII, p. 685.

11. Ibid., Vol. 11, Part 1, Chap. XXIII, p. 683.

12. Senate Journal, March 9, 1863.

13. OR: Vol. 11, Part 1, Chap. XXIII, p. 687.

14. It is of more than passing interest that Cooke was Stuart's father-in-law.

15. *Journal*, June 18, 1862.

16. Ibid., June 22, 1862.

17. *Reminiscences*, p. 15. Kautz, in his reminiscences and, to a lesser extent, in his journal, goes into great detail about Lawrence Williams's character, including his tendency to take advantage of his classmates at West Point, his poor leadership qualities, his poor judgment, his arrest for suspected communicating with the enemy and suspicion of disloyalty at the White House on May 15, his failure to return to duty after his illness in June 1862, his dismissal from the service in 1863 and his later immoral behavior, concluding with, "He was, when I last heard of him, a perfect wreck mentally, morally and physically."

18. Ibid., p. 17.

19. Rooney Lee was with Stuart in command of the 9th Virginia Cavalry Regiment. He arrived at the White House in time to see smoke still rising from his destroyed home.

20. *Journal*, July 4–5, 1862; *Reminiscences*, p. 19.
21. Ibid., July 4, 1862.
22. Ibid., July 15, 1862.
23. Ibid., July 16, 1862.
24. Ibid., September 29, 1861.
25. *Reminiscences*, p. 21. General Randolph B. Marcy was General McClellan's chief of staff and also his father-in-law.
26. *Journal*, August 7, 1862.
27. *Reminiscences*, p. 23. Kautz failed to mention that the three-day public relations event had cost the lives of four of his troopers.
28. *Journal*, August 23, 1862.
29. *Reminiscences*, pp. 24–25.
30. Ibid., p. 26.
31. *Journal*, September 10, 1862.

Chapter 16

1. *Reminiscences*, p. 2.
2. *Journal*, January 25, 1862.
3. Ibid., July 9, 1862.
4. Ibid., July 10, 1862.
5. Ibid., July 28, 1862.
6. *Reminiscences*, p. 27.
7. Savage went on sick leave in August 1862. He would never return to the army. Kautz continued a correspondence with Savage and his wife Belle for years.
8. OR (Navy): Series I, Vol. 19, p. 146.
9. *Reminiscences*, p. 29.
10. Heitman. Thomas McCurdy Vincent, an 1853 graduate of West Point, spent almost his entire career in the Adjutant General Department. He was breveted brigadier at the end of the Civil War. *Reminiscinces*, p. 28. As a plebe at West Point, Vincent had been a tentmate of Kautz at summer encampment and appears to have been appreciative of the fact that Kautz did not "bedevil" him as the other upperclassmen did. Vincent remembered Kautz's kindness.
11. Isaac Gause, *Four Years with Five Armies*, pp. 208–9.
12. *Reminiscences*, pp. 31–2.
13. Ibid., pp. 32–3.
14. Eventually, the camp would hold 8000 prisoners and, before the war ended, more than 25,000 Rebel soldiers would have spent time there.
15. *Reminiscences*, p. 35.
16. *Journal*, December 19, 1862.
17. George W. Wright, "Hon. David Tod: Biography and Personal Recollections," *Ohio History* 8, p.120. Wright tells an interesting story about Tod and Lincoln. At their first meeting, Lincoln questioned Tod about the spelling of his name. He said he married a Todd and she spelled the name with two *d*'s. Tod replied, "Mr. President, God spells his name with only one *d*, and what's good enough for God is good enough for me."
18. The Confederate Cemetery was left to deteriorate. In 1895, William Knauss, who had served as colonel of an Ohio regiment, saw the condition of the cemetery. Through Knauss's efforts, monuments were placed over all of the graves. A stone wall was built around the cemetery. A stone arch stands over the entrance and a statue of a Confederate soldier is above the arch. Below the statue, a single word is carved: "AMERICANS."
19. Gause, pp. 119–20.
20. *Reminiscences*, p. 37.
21. *Reminiscences*, p. 38. This trip to Philadelphia in mid–February was to visit a publishing house there. It will

be covered in another chapter. He and Sophie also visited New York and Washington.

Chapter 17

1. *Reminiscences*, p. 38.
2. The bulk of the Army of the Ohio was the XXIII Corps commanded by Kautz's West Point classmate, Major General George L. Hartsuff. The four divisions of XXIII Corps were commanded by, in addition to Sturgis, Jeremiah T. Boyle, Henry M. Judah and Julius White, none of whose Civil War career was more than mediocre.
3. Samuel Powhatan Carter was the only man to hold the rank of rear admiral in the navy and major general in the army. He graduated from the Naval Academy in 1846 and rose to lieutenant prior to the Civil War. In July 1861, he was given leave from the navy and appointed brigadier general in the army and sent to Kentucky, where it was hoped his popularity might stimulate support for the Union in his home state. He returned to the navy after the war and was later promoted to rear admiral.
4. *Reminiscences*, p. 38.
5. Ibid., p. 40.
6. Gause, p. 123. Gause said that they were part of Brigadier General John Pegram's Cavalry Brigade.
7. In crossing back, one of the small ferry boats was swept away by the river current and capsized. About forty men were drowned.
8. See OR: Vol. 23, Part 1, Chap. XXXV, pp. 386–9 for Sanders's report.
9. *Reminiscences*, p. 44. Kautz said in his reminiscences, "Pegram, who commanded and was opposed to me in this affair, was a warm personal friend of mine. We had traveled in Europe together.... This was the last time I ever saw him; we parted at the Metropolitan Hotel in Newyork, he going to his Regt. in New Mexico and I to mine in Washington Territory."
10. OR: Vol. 23, Part 1, Chap. XXXV, p. 372: *Reminiscences*, p. 43.
11. *Reminiscences*, p. 43.
12. Ibid., p. 43.
13. OR: Vol. 23, Part 1, Chap. XXXV, p. 370.
14. *Reminiscences*, p. 43.
15. OR: Vol. 23, Part 1, Chap. XXXV, p. 447.

Chapter 18

1. *Journal*, September 27, 1862. Morgan was not present at the Battle of Augusta. His brother-in-law, Colonel (later General) Basil Duke, commanded the brigade which attacked Augusta.
2. Frank Wolford, who was born in nearby Columbia, Kentucky, was a lawyer. He served in the Mexican War, at which time he became a good friend of John Hunt Morgan. In July 1861, he helped recruit the 1st Kentucky Cavalry Regiment and became its colonel. In 1864, Wolford was arrested for making negative remarks about Lincoln's management of the war, but was later pardoned by Lincoln. He served in the Kentucky State House both before and after the war and in the U.S. House from 1883 to 1887.
3. *Reminiscences*, p. 45.
4. Ibid., p. 45.
5. OR: Vol. 23, Part 1, Chap. XXXV, p. 655. In his official report, Judah gave as his reason for withdrawing Shackelford's Brigade, "The road to Columbia was neces-

sarily left to other forces to protect." It is interesting to note at this late date that, if both General Judah and Colonel Wolford had felt "authorized" to move their forces in the direction of Columbia, Morgan's raid would probably have had a far different outcome.

    6. *Reminiscences*, p. 46.

    7. OR: Vol. 23, Part 1, Chap. XXXV, p. 694. General Judah, who should have been in command, was still far to the south with Manson's Brigade. Unable to ford the Green River due to high water, the brigade was out of the chase for now.

    8. *Reminiscences*, p. 46.

    9. Ibid., p. 47.

    10. The *John T. McCombs* was spared because it belonged to a friend of Basil Duke.

    11. *Reminiscences*, p. 47.

    12. Ibid., pp. 47–8.

    13. This was a train of wagons moved from Camp Dennison for safety.

    14. *Reminiscences*, p. 48.

    15. Gause, pp. 150–2.

    16. OR: Vol. 23, Part 1, Chap. XXXV, p. 761.

    17. *Reminiscences*, p. 49. "Maj. McIntyre" was James McIntire, a native of Pennsylvania who had moved to Sardinia in the 1840s. He operated a general store on Winchester Street.

    18. Ibid., p. 49.

    19. OR: Vol. 23, Part 1, Chap. XXXV, p. 764. Kautz's message, dated "Piketon, July 17, 1863 — 9:30 A.M." reads: "General Burnside:

    "I command the advance of Hobson. Have just arrived with 400 men. General Hobson is on the road between Piketon and Locust Grove, about six hours behind, with his main force. I shall move in twenty minutes toward Jackson, where Morgan is now reported to be."

    20. It was fried chicken.

    21. On July 6, Sanders was given command of a "provisional brigade" consisting of the Eighth and Ninth Michigan Cavalry. After chasing down a small party of Morgan's Raiders who went toward Frankfort, Kentucky, he marched his men to Louisville, where they boarded transports for Vevay, Indiana, to try to head Morgan off. Finding Morgan already past that point, he followed after Hobson's forces and overtook them. He finally caught up with Kautz at Piketon, where his two regiments, along with a two-gun section of the 11th Michigan Artillery, were put under Kautz's command.

    22. *Reminiscences*, p. 49.

    23. Ibid., pp. 49–50.

    24. OR: Vol. 23, Part 1, Chap. XXXV, p. 660.

    25. Gause, pp. 154–5.

    26. *Reminiscences*, p. 50.

    27. Gause, p. 157.

    28. Ibid., pp. 157–8. Basil Duke, in his account of the raid, paints an almost identical picture.

    29. Two pieces of artillery were thrown over the bank of the river and were later picked up by the gunboat *Moose*.

    30. OR: Vol. 23, Part 1, Chap. XXXV, p. 664.

    31. Ibid., Vol. 23, Part 1, Chap. XXXV, p. 786.

    32. Ibid., Vol. 23, Part 1, Chap. XXXV, p. 663.

Chapter 19

    1. *Reminiscences*, p. 52.

    2. OR: Vol. 52, Part 1, Chap. LXIV, p. 437. Kautz replaced Colonel Charles J. Walker of the Tenth Kentucky Cavalry (General Order No 21, August 11, 1863).

    3. *Reminiscences*, p. 53.

    4. Ibid., p. 53.

    5. Ibid., p. 54.

    6. Ibid., p. 55.

    7. Ibid., p. 57.

    8. Ibid., p. 58. Sheridan was speaking of the Battle of Missionary Ridge, which lifted the siege of Knoxville and forced Bragg to withdraw into Georgia.

    9. Ibid., p. 59.

    10. *Cincinnati Enquirer*, February 1895. Later in life, Kautz was fond of telling the story of Grant's resignation from the army in 1854: "We were then together out in Oregon, and we all remarked in the officers quarters one night, 'Poor Sam Grant, we will never hear of him again. He will never amount to anything outside of the army.' Part of our prophesy may have been correct, but we heard of him again. Yet, how unlikely it seemed then that he should become General of the Army and President, with power to promote the officers who were discounting his career."

    11. *Reminiscences*, pp. 59–60.

Chapter 20

    1. OR: Vol. 32, Part 2, Chap. XLIV, p. 27.

    2. *Reminiscences*, p. 61.

    3. *Journal*, January 22, 1864.

    4. *Reminiscences*, p. 62.

    5. Ibid., p. 62.

    6. The Giesboro Point facility was a down the Potomac River from Washington with stables sufficient to hold 12,000 horses. Worn-down and diseased horses were sent there to be brought back to health or disposed of.

    7. OR: Vol. 32, Part 3, Chap. XLIV, pp. 255–8. In this report, Wilson specifically mentioned Governor Andrew Johnson's East Tennessee recruits, calling them "worthless." So angered was Governor Johnson that, two years later, when he was president, he withheld a promotion which Wilson richly deserved.

    8. *Journal*, April 8, 1864.

    9. *Reminiscences*, p. 65.

    10. Ibid., p. 65.

Chapter 21

    1. OR: Vol. 33, Chap. XLV, p. 862.

    2. Ibid., Vol. 33, Chap. XLV, p. 862.

    3. Ibid., Vol. 33, Chap. XLV, p. 865.

    4. Ibid., Vol. 33, Chap. XLV, p. 877.

    5. Ibid., Vol. 32, Part 3, Chap. XLIV, p. 366.

    6. Ibid., Vol. 33, Chap. XLV, p. 879.

    7. Ibid., Vol. 33, Chap. XLV, p. 879.

    8. Ibid., Vol. 33, Chap. XLV, p. 895.

    9. *Journal*, April 18, 1864. George is mentioned frequently in Kautz's journals. He must have been a free black man, suggested by the fact that he was willing to go to Virginia. He remained with Kautz until July 1865.

    10. OR: Vol. 33, Chap. XLV, p. 930.

    11. Ibid., Vol. 33, Chap. XLV, p. 932.

    12. Edward P. Tobie, *History of the First Maine Cavalry*. For the 1st D.C., their weapons were a mixed blessing. "They had been sent to the front to serve on foot and, on account of their superior arms, they had been placed in the most perilous positions."

    13. Only one other regiment in the entire army had Henry rifles.

14. Losses in the Battle of Drewry's Bluff in killed, wounded and missing were: Union: 390, 2380, 1390; Confederate: 355, 1941, 210.

15. OR: Vol. 38, Part 1, Chap. L, p. 9.

Chapter 22

1. OR: Vol. 36, Part 2, Chap. XLVIII, p. 171. The Blackwater and Meherrin Rivers, and the Nottoway in between, are branches of the Chowan River. All three drain west to east through south-central Virginia, then bend south and join to form the Chowan River in North Carolina.

2. Ibid., Vol. 36, Part 2, Chap. XLVIII, p. 181.

3. Although named the First D.C. Cavalry, eight companies of the regiment were from Maine and many had been woodsmen in civilian life.

4. OR: Vol. 36, Part 2, Chap. XLVIII, p. 176.

5. Ibid., Vol. 36, Part 2, Chap. XLVIII, p. 262-3. This is from Colonel Tabb's report. He estimated his entire force at about 600 men.

6. Ibid., Vol. 36, Part 2, Chap. XLVIII, p. 172. Kautz made no more of the fact that neither of his brigade commanders had obeyed his orders.

7. Ibid., Vol. 36, Part 2, Chap. XLVIII, p. 185. Spear failed to mention that several private dwellings near the station were also burned, probably by accident.

8. Kautz neglected to mention the additional encumbrance of several hundred slaves who fell in behind his marching column.

9. OR: Vol. 36, Part 2, Chap. XLVIII, p. 263.

10. Ibid., Vol. 36, Part 2, Chap. XLVIII, p. 617.

11. Ibid., Vol. 36, Part 2, Chap. XLVIII, p. 180.

12. Ibid., Vol. 36, Part 2, Chap. XLVIII, p. 173.

13. Ibid., Vol. 36, Part 2, Chap. XLVIII, p. 174.

14. Samuel H. Merrill, *Campaigns of the First Maine and First District of Columbia Cavalry*. Merrill was chaplain of the First District of Columbia Cavalry.

15. OR: Vol. 36, Part 2, Chap. XLVIII, p. 174.

16. Ibid., Vol. 36, Part 2, Chap. XLVIII, p. 175.

17. Ibid., Vol. 36, Part 2, Chap. XLVIII, p. 596.

Chapter 23

1. Ibid., Vol. 38, Part 1, Chap. L, p. 9-10.

2. Ibid., Vol. 36, Part 3, Chap. XLVIII, p. 43.

3. Ibid., Vol. 36, Part 3, Chap. XLVIII, pp. 235-6.

4. Ibid., Vol. 36, Part 3, Chap. XLVIII, pp. 368-9.

5. *Journal*, May 22, 1864.

6. OR: Vol. 36, Part 3, Chap. XLVIII, p. 475.

7. *Battles and Leaders*, vol. 4, p. 534.

8. OR: Vol. 36, Part 3, Chap. XLVIII, p. 705.

9. Ibid., Vol. 36, Part 3, Chap. XLVIII, p. 708.

10. Ibid., Vol. 36, Part 3, Chap. XLVIII, p. 708.

11. Ibid., Vol. 36, Part 3, Chap. XLVIII, p. 705. It is of interest, and of some importance taking into account later developments, that this is the only written order that Butler gave to Gillmore. All other orders to Gillmore and to Kautz were verbal.

12. R.E. Colston, in *Battles and Leaders*, vol. 4, p. 535.

13. Ibid., vol. 4, p. 537.

14. Ibid., vol. 4, p. 537.

15. OR: Vol. 36, Part 2, Chapter XLVIII, p. 309.

16. Ibid., Vol. 36, Part 2, Chap. XLVIII, p. 290.

17. Anthony M. Keiley, *In Vinculis; or The Prisoner of War*, pp. 32–34.

18. *Reminiscences*, p. 76. "It [Keiley's book] was purchased by me nearly a year after in a book store in Petersburg and proved to be an overdrawn, wordy sketch of our attempt to capture Petersburg.... His account of the interview, if not a misrepresentation in many respects, shows that he misunderstood me."

19. OR: Vol. 36, Part 2, Chap. XLVIII, p. 278. In this regard, Butler stated, "It seems to me that an infantry support of 3,500 men deserting 1,400 cavalry and leaving them to their fate in immediate contact with the forces of the enemy, too large for that infantry to attack, according to the theory upon which you were acting, was the most unsoldierly act ever done by a commanding officer."

20. Ibid., Vol. 36, Part 2, Chap. XLVIII, pp. 274–282.

21. Ibid., Vol. 36, Part 2, Chap. XLVIII, p. 290.

22. Ibid., Vol. 36, Part 2, Chap. XLVIII, pp. 282–3.

Chapter 24

1. OR: Vol. 38, Part 1, Chap. L, pp.11–12.

2. Grant's *Memoirs*, p. 573.

3. OR: Vol. 40, Part 2, Chap. LII, p. 46.

4. P.G.T. Beauregard, in *Battles and Leaders*, vol. 4, p. 541. Beauregard estimated the total strength of the defenders at 2200.

5. Dearing was a student at West Point in 1861. He resigned to join the Confederate Army. He had been appointed brigadier general within a few days of Kautz's appointment. He died on April 23, 1865, of wounds received April 6. He was the last general officer of either army to die in the Civil War.

6. OR: Vol. 40, Part 2, Chap. LII, p. 83.

7. Hancock graduated from West Point in 1844. He was breveted in the Mexican War and was thrice credited with saving the Union Army at Gettysburg, where he received a serious wound. His role in Grant's Overland Campaign had been conspicuous. In 1880, he ran for president on the Democratic ticket, but lost to Garfield. He died in 1886, a full major general.

8. OR: Vol. 40, Part 1, Chap. LII, p. 729.

9. Ibid., Vol. 40, Part 2, Chap. LII, p. 643.

10. Ibid., Vol. 40, Part 2, Chap. LII, p. 83.

11. Ibid., Vol. 38, Part 1, Chap. L, p. 14.

12. Beauregard, in *Battles and Leaders*, vol. 4, p. 541; OR: Vol. 40, Part 2, Chap. LII, pp. 60–1. Hancock notified Butler at 5 PM that he had two divisions in line to the left of Smith and that he and Smith had examined the country together.

13. OR: Vol. 40, Part 2, Chap. LII, p. 84.

14. Ibid., Vol. 40, Part 2, Chap. LII, p. 86.

15. Ibid., Vol. 40, Part 2, Chap. LII, pp. 94–5.

16. Beauregard, in *Battles and Leaders*, vol. 4, p. 541.

17. OR: Vol. 40, Part 2, Chap. LII, p. 114.

18. Ibid., Vol. 40, Part 2, Chap. LII, p. 115.

Chapter 25

1. OR: Vol. 40, Part 2, Chap. LII, p. 267.

2. Tobie, pp. 332-3. Tobie is quoting in part from Merrill, pp. 233-4, written 21 years earlier.

3. *Journal*, June 21, 1864.

4. OR: Vol. 40, Part 2, Chap. LII, p. 267.

5. James H. Wilson, "The Cavalry of the Army of the Potomac," p. 59.

6. James H. Wilson, *Under the Old Flag*, p. 456.

7. OR: Vol. 40, Part 1, Chap. LII, pp. 731, 739.

8. Ibid., Vol. 40, Part 1, Chap. LII, p. 731. This detour was made against General Wilson's orders, but Wilson later agreed that it was a proper deviation from orders.

9. Ibid., Vol. 40, Part 1, Chap. LII, p. 739.

10. West had taken over the First Brigade after the death of Simon Mix.

11. OR: Vol. 40, Part 1, Chap. LII, p. 622.

12. Ibid., Vol. 40, Part 1, Chap. LII, p. 731.

13. Ibid., Vol. 40, Part 1, Chap. LII, p. 734.

14. Tobie, p. 336.

15. Ibid., Vol. 40, Part 1, Chap. LII, p. 622.

16. Roger Hannaford, *Diary of Roger Hannaford*, un-numbered pages.

17. OR: Vol. 40, Part 1, Chap. LII, p. 622.

18. Ibid., Vol. 40, Part 1, Chap. LII, p. 765. Farinholt's estimate of Federal dead appears to be high.

19. Ibid., Vol. 40, Part 1, Chap. LII, p. 642.

20. Hannaford Diary.

21. Ibid.

22. Mahone's Division was part of A.P. Hill's Corps. They had been involved in the battle at the Jerusalem Plank Road on June 23. After that battle, Mahone had been left at Reams' Station to protect the Petersburg and Weldon Railroad from both Meade's army and Wilson's raiders.

23. OR: Vol. 40, Part 1, Chap. LII, p. 740.

24. Ibid., Vol. 40, Part 1, Chap. LII, p. 732.

25. Hannaford Diary.

26. OR: Vol. 40, Part 1, Chap. LII, p. 623.

27. *Reminiscences*, p. 81.

28. OR: Vol. 40, Part 1, Chap. LII, p. 732. Kautz estimated that about 1000 men of Wilson's Division were with him and perhaps 500 men from his division were with Wilson.

29. Ibid., Vol. 40, Part 1, Chap. LII, pp. 735, 740.

30. Ibid., Vol. 40, Part 1, Chap. LII, p. 732.

31. Samuel H. Merrill, in Tobie, p. 337.

32. OR: Vol. 40, Part 1, Chap. LII, p. 740.

33. This was Lieutenant Michael Leahy's Battery B of the First U.S. Artillery Regiment. Although ordered by Wilson to abandon his artillery, Kautz attempted to get them out.

34. OR: Vol. 40, Part 1, Chap. LII, p. 735.

35. Ibid., Vol. 40, Part 1, Chap. LII, p. 642.

36. Hannaford Diary.

37. Samuel H. Merrill, in Tobie, p. 337.

38. *Reminiscences*, p. 81. Kautz later said, "I immediately gave orders to Maj. [Samuel] Wetherill [of the 11th Pennsylvania] to take the advance, gave him my pocket compass and directed him to keep to a southeast course in the timber...."

39. OR: Vol. 40, Part 1, Chap. LII, p. 732.

40. Ibid., Vol. 40, Part 1, Chap. LII, p. 643.

41. Ibid., Vol. 40, Part 1, Chap. LII, p. 730.

42. Ibid., Vol. 40, Part 1, Chap. LII, p. 540.

43. *Journal*, July 1, 1864. This is the only time in all his writings where Kautz refers to Grant by his boyhood nickname, Liss.

44. Sheridan, *Memoirs*.

45. Ibid.

46. OR: Vol. 38, Part 1, Chap. L, p. 16; Horace Greeley, *American Conflict*, p. 588. Greeley quotes Grant also, but adds, "Grant sent no more cavalry to the Rebel rear for months."

47. Ibid., Vol. 40, Part 1, Chap. LII, p. 169.

48. Ibid., Vol. 40, Part 1, Chap. LII, p. 28.

49. A conservative estimate of the number of slaves liberated would be 400.

50. OR: Vol. 40, Part 1, Chap. LII, pp. 33–34.

51. Ibid., Vol. 40, Part 1, Chap. LII, p. 733. These figures do not accurately match the totals as reported by Kautz's brigade and regimental commanders. If those figures were to be used, the total of killed, wounded and missing would be 35, 135, and 544. As missing men continued to appear for days after the reports were filed, neither total is accurate.

52. Ibid., Vol. 40, Part 1, Chap. LII, p. 32.

Chapter 26

1. *Journal*, July 7, 1864. Kautz had been disappointed after his railroad raids in May that Southern newspapers had not yet learned his name. Now they even spelled it correctly.

2. *Reminiscences*, p. 82.

3. *Journal*, July 3, 1864. That Mathew Brady photo clearly shows that Kautz had not had an opportunity to visit the barber for some time.

4. *Reminiscences*, p. 83.

5. *Battles and Leaders*, vol. 4, p. 547.

6. *Reminiscences*, p. 83. Hancock's offensive, with its ensuing minor battles, is commonly known as the First Battle of Deep Bottom.

7. *Reminiscences*, p. 87. On September 19, Kautz went into far greater detail on this "misuse" of cavalry in a message to General Gregg's headquarters. See OR: Vol. 42, Part 2, Chap. LIV, p. 933.

8. OR: Vol. 42, Part 2, Chap. LIV, p. 471. On August 25, Kautz's friend, Brigadier General Rufus Ingalls, Chief Quartermaster for the Army of the Potomac, sent a wire to Quartermaster General Montgomery Meigs in Washington detailing the need for horses. He said in part, "I have not heard from Kautz, but presume he will require 1400. Five hundred have been issued to Kautz."

9. OR: Vol. 42, Part 2, Chap. LIV, pp. 164–167.

10. Ibid., Vol. 42, Part 2, Chap. LIV, p. 193.

11. *Journal*, August 28, 1864.

12. *Reminiscences*, p. 84.

13. *Journal*, September 1, 1864.

14. Ibid., September 2, 1864.

15. OR: Vol. 42, Part 2, Chap. LIV, p. 694.

16. *Journal*, September 3, 1864.

17. OR: Vol. 42, Part 2, Vol. LIV, p. 933.

18. *Journal*, September 25, 1864. This was Fred's third child, John Edwin, who died on July 25.

Chapter 27

1. OR: Vol. 42, Part 1, Chap. LIV, p. 20.

2. *Reminiscences*, pp. 88–9. The full text is in OR: Vol. 42, Part 2, Chap. LIV, pp. 1082–8.

3. The major roadways radiating east from Richmond were, from south to north, the Osborne Turnpike (roughly parallel to the James River), the Varina Road, the New Market Road, the Darbytown Road, the Charles City Road, the Williamsburg Road, the Nine Mile Road and the Mechanicsville Turnpike.

4. The only artillery which Butler allowed on the movement.

5. OR: Vol. 42, Part 2, Chap. LIV, pp. 1084–6.

6. *Reminiscences*, pp. 89–90.

7. OR: Vol. 42, Part 3, Chap. LIV, p. 65.

8. Ibid., Vol. 42, Part 3, Chap. LIV, p. 66.

9. *Reminiscences*, p. 91.

10. OR: Vol. 42, Part 3, Chap LIV, p. 66.

11. Ibid., Vol. 42, Part 3, Chap. LIV, p. 98. Grant must have passed the recommendation on to President Lincoln immediately because Lincoln's nomination went to the Senate on October 7. The wording of the promotion was much reduced from Butler's original recommendation to read "to major-general of volunteers for gallant and meritorious service in the present campaign against Richmond, Virginia...."

12. Louise Haskell Daly, *Alexander Cheves Haskell: The Portrait of a Man*. Haskell recovered from his wound, minus his left eye, in time to be present at Lee's surrender in April 1865. *Reminiscences*, pp. 91–2. Kautz wrote, "...as we returned the fire, two of the enemy fell and one of them proved to be Col. Haskell ... as I discovered by the papers and letters taken from his person, together with his watch, which a soldier brought me. He was shot through the face and left for dead. A few days after I learned that he was still alive and would recover, and I sent him his private letters and watch. The soldier who brought me the watch and letters, came and asked me what three stars on the collar of a Confederate uniform indicated.... He then stated that he had killed a Colonel, and handed me the watch and papers referred to." *Journal*, August 17–18, 1866. Haskell wrote to Kautz thanking him for the watch and papers and asked Kautz to provide him with some details of the battle "as he became oblivious at a certain point." Kautz answered the letter the following day.

13. *Journal*, January 22, 1866. Kerr later asked Kautz for a letter of recommendation in order to apply for a commission in the regular Army.

14. Ibid., April 19, 1864; May 19, 1864; July 15, 1864; February 4, 1865. The horse was Kautz's personal horse which was shipped from Columbus the previous April. The horse got as far as Washington, where it became lost among the government horses there. Kautz sent his servant, George Lee, to Washington to retrieve the horse and the faithful George returned with it on July 15. The horse had missed all of Kautz's raids during the early summer. On February 4, 1865, Kautz rode with his friend, Dr. George Suckley, to inspect the hospital at the dismounted camp. While there, he visited his horse, saying, "I visited my horse who was shot in the knee last October. I fear he will not be worth much. His leg is still useless."

15. OR: Vol. 42, Part 1, Chap. LIV, pp. 145–6. The official loss in Kautz's Division was 18 killed, 69 wounded and 142 missing or captured. By comparison, X Corps lost 31 killed, 184 wounded and 14 missing. Confederate losses are unknown, but estimated at greater than 1000.

16. OR: Vol. 42, Part 1, Chap. LIV, p. 824.

17. *Reminiscences*, p. 92.

Chapter 28

1. *Journal*, October 10, 1864.

2. Ibid., October 12, 1864.

3. *Reminiscences*, pp. 92–3.

4. *Journal*, October 21, 1864.

5. Jacob Kautz's three sons were:

Philip (John Philip) Kautz, a member of the 70th Ohio Infantry, who was with Sherman's army in Georgia.

David Kautz, who had been in Fred Kautz's Company G, 59th Ohio Infantry, but had been captured at Chickamauga. After eight months as a prisoner, he had been paroled, but not yet exchanged. Ill with tuberculosis at the time of his release, he was still in the hospital at the army's parolee camp at Annapolis. He never regained his health and died in August 1866.

Jacob Kautz had been drafted into the army in May 1864 and served in the 4th Ohio Infantry in Hancock's II Corps. He had been at Deep Bottom in August 1864. Yet unknown to his relatives in Ohio, Jacob had died of a gunshot wound on October 27, ten days before his father came to visit. Jacob is one of the "Unknown Soldiers" buried at Poplar Grove Cemetery near Petersburg.

6. *Journal*, December 31, 1864.

7. Ibid., December 12, 1864.

8. Ibid., December 29, 1864.

9. *Reminiscences*, p. 95.

10. Ibid., pp. 93–4.

11. George C. Barns, *Denver the Man*, p. 321. In a letter to his wife on January 18, James Denver, a solid Democrat, commented on Butler's removal from command. He called Butler "[o]ne whose life has been a libel of honesty, patriotism and courage. An arrant knave, his shrewdness and energy brought him forward. A grasping, arrogant and unscrupulous tyrant, he plundered and insulted defenseless men, women and children."

12. *Reminiscences*, p. 95.

13. *Journal*, January 9, 1865.

14. *Reminiscences*, p. 98.

15. *Journal*, January 11, 1865.

16. Ibid., January 19, 1865.

17. Ibid., January 29, 1865.

18. Ibid., January 31, 1865.

19. Ibid., February 2, 1865.

20. OR: Vol. 46, Part 3, Chap. LXIII, pp. 55–6. Special Order No. 79, Army of the James.

21. *Journal*, March 24, 1865.

22. *Reminiscences*, p. 102.

23. Ibid., p. 103.

24. *Journal*, March 24, 1865. Kautz had never met Mackenzie until this day. He was one of the army's "boy generals." MacKenzie graduated from West Point in 1862, and his meteoric rise to brigadier general was based on his own accomplishments rather than on political connections. His exploits during the war and on the western frontier after the war should be the material of legends, yet he remains almost unknown by historians. Grant, *Memoirs*, vol. 2, p. 541. Grant considered Mackenzie "the most promising young officer in the army."

25. *Journal*, April 3, 1865.

Chapter 29

1. *Journal*, April 18, 1861.

2. Ibid., November 24, 1861.

3. Ibid., November 27, 1861.

4. Ibid., February 21, 1862.

5. Ibid., July 30, 1862.

6. *Reminiscences*, p. 32. Kautz was aware that there were more than 10,000 companies in the volunteer Army. Most were served by clerks and junior officers without military experience.

7. *Journal*, January 29, 1864.

8. Ibid., September 10, 1864.

9. Ibid., January 31, 1866.

Chapter 30

1. *Journal*, April 3, 1865.

2. *Reminiscences*, p. 105.

3. Ibid., p. 106.

4. *Journal*, April 8, 1865. Lieutenant Samuel M. Brown of the First New York Mounted Rifles was Kautz's aide-de-camp.

5. Ibid., April 12, 1865.

6. Ibid., April 13, 1865.

7. Ibid., April 18, 1865.

8. It was not immediately known but XXV Corps was to be sent to Texas. They were to form an occupying force for that state and were to stand ready to enter Mexico, if needed, where a civil war was taking place.

9. *Reminiscences*, p. 108.

Chapter 31

1. Burnett had left the 2nd Ohio in 1863 because of poor health and was appointed judge advocate of the Department of Ohio. He continued in that position for the remainder of the war.

2. *Journal*, May 9, 1865.

3. *Reminiscences*, p. 108.

4. At the time, the Secretary of State was required by law to call an election in the event of the deaths of both the president and vice president.

5. At the time, only one state, Maine, permitted defendants to testify on their own behalf in murder trials.

6. *Journal*, May 26–27, 1865.

7. Ibid., May 21 and June 15, 1865.

8. Barns, p. 323.

9. Ibid., p. 324.

10. *Journal*, May 23, 1865.

11. Ibid., May 25, 1865.

12. From the transcript of trial proceedings.

13. *Reminiscences*, pp. 110–111.

Chapter 32

1. *Reminiscences*, pp. 37–8.

2. *Journal*, January 23, 1864.

3. Ibid., January 24, 1864.

4. Ibid., March 12, 1864.

5. By this time David Tod's term as governor of Ohio had expired and the family was living at the family's estate of Brier Hill near Youngstown, Ohio. They also maintained a residence in Cleveland.

6. *Journal*, April 17, 1864.

7. Ibid., July 15, 1865.

8. Ibid., March 13, 1869. George would be mentioned only once more in Kautz's writings when, while in Washington in March 1869, Kautz "left a certificate of character for my old servant, Geo. W. Lee."

9. Ibid., September 12, 1865. During the stopover in Cincinnati, he visited Jesse R. Grant, who had moved his tannery and leather business to Covington, Kentucky, some years before. Since they had not met since 1852, Grant did not recognize Kautz at first, but they had a long talk, mostly about Kautz's father and Grant's son.

10. Albert, who was also in Ohio awaiting orders, would soon be married himself, to his fiancee of four years, Mary Esther Hemphill.

11. Letter, Kautz to S.M. Brown, 1st Lt., 1st N.Y. Mounted Rifles, October 5, 1865.

12. *Journal*, October 28, 1865.

13. Ibid., January 10, 1866. Although Kautz held the brevet rank of major general, his permanent rank was captain of the 6th U.S. Cavalry.

Chapter 33

1. Jacob and Ragsdale. While still serving in the Senate, Wilson raised and commanded a volunteer infantry regiment during the Civil War. He was elected vice president in Grant's second term, but died in 1875 before the expiration of the term.

2. *Journal*, April 28, 1866.

3. Ibid., March 23, 1866.

4. Ibid., April 7, 1866.

5. Ibid., June 18, 1866.

6. Ibid., July 29, 1866.

7. Baird was Sheridan's inspector general at New Orleans in 1866 and later became inspector general of the Army before retiring in 1888.

8. Kautz Papers: General Order, July 30, 1866.

9. Monroe was the same man who, as mayor in 1862, declined to surrender the city to Admiral Farragut when ordered to do so by Kautz's brother Albert. He was imprisoned by Benjamin Butler and later released. He regained the mayoralty in the spring of 1866. Sheridan would once more remove him from office.

10. *Journal*, July 31, 1866.

11. Ibid., September 1, 1866.

12. Ibid., September 4, 1866. Crook had recently been promoted to major but, like Kautz, he was hopeful for more. Both were aware that the Army Bill had finally passed on July 28. Sections 3 and 4 of the act provided for the increase of the cavalry wing from 6 to 10 regiments and of the infantry from 19 to 45. Two of the new cavalry regiments and 4 of the new infantry regiments would be colored regiments with white officers.

13. Ibid., September 26, 1866.

14. Ibid., November 28, 1866.

15. Ibid., October 25, 1866.

16. Heitman. Born in Pennsylvania in 1844, Pennypacker raised a company of the 97th Pennsylvania Infantry early in the Civil War. Wounded four times, he rose rapidly in rank. He died in 1916 with the distinction of being the youngest man ever appointed a general officer in the United States service and the youngest man to command a regiment in the regular Army.

17. *Journal*, January 1, 1867.

18. Ibid., April 17, 20, 1867.

19. Ibid., August 24, 1867. Gillem's endorsement failed to mention that Kautz's experience was needed in Columbus to take part in a military commission to try a civilian for the robbery of an express company.

20. *Army & Navy Journal*, February 22, 1868.

21. *Journal*, September 1, 1867.

22. *Army & Navy Journal*, February 22, 1868.

23. *Journal*, September 11, 1867.

24. *Army & Navy Journal*, February 22, 1868. The charge was: "Conduct to the prejudice of good order and military discipline." In summary, the specification was that Kautz, after receiving Ord's letter written by Lieutenant Brown, "did fail to send his reply through the proper channels, but in a letter addressed to the brevet major general commanding did use the following disrespectful and insubordinate language" — (see extract of Kautz's letter above) — "thereby attributing motives to his commanding officer other than that of the good of the service, expressing dissatisfaction to his commanding officer with his orders, and intimating that he expected his convictions consulted before he should be refused a leave of absence."

25. *Journal*, January 18, 1868. A general orders reprimand was a rather harsh sentence in those days.

26. *Army & Navy Journal*, February 22, 1868.

27. *Journal*, January 18, 1868.
28. *Ripley (Ohio) Bee*, March 1, 1868.
29. *Journal*, April 14, 1868.
30. Ibid., June 2, 1868.
31. Ibid., June 3, 1868.

Chapter 34

1. *Journal*, June 12, 1868.
2. Ibid., June 18, 1868.
3. Ibid., June 25, 1868. "I commenced several times to pack Charlotte's things today and abandoned it."
4. The tour was taken more for political than military purposes as Grant was seeking nomination for president on the Republican ticket.
5. *Journal*, July 29, 1868.
6. Ibid., December 29, 1868.
7. Ibid., December 31, 1868.
8. Ibid., March 4, 1869.
9. Both Babcock and Porter were brevet major generals who served on Grant's staff during the Civil War. During Grant's presidency, Babcock was his private secretary and Porter his executive secretary.
10. *Journal*, March 5, 1869. It seems incredible to imagine a president sufficiently "at leisure" on his first full day in office to have time for a couple of army officers of relatively low rank, but these were old friends. Of course, his friendship with Kautz goes back to their boyhood. Ingalls was a classmate of Grant at West Point, served with him in Oregon Territory and had been chief quartermaster of the Army of the Potomac. Grant, in his *Memoirs*, wrote of Ingalls, "There never was a corps better organized than was the Quartermaster Corps with the Army of the Potomac in 1864."
11. *Journal*, March 13, 1869.
12. Schofield had resigned as Secretary of War at the end of Andrew Johnson's term as president. Grant had just appointed him commander of the Department of Missouri to replace Sheridan.
13. The District of New Mexico was one of four subunits of the Department of Missouri, which, in turn, was one of four subunits of the Division of the Missouri.
14. *Journal*, June 29, 1869.
15. Ibid., August 26, 1869. It was during this period that Kautz began writing his *Reminiscences of the Civil War*, which was never published in English, although a German version was released in the 1990s.

Chapter 35

1. The Malpais is an extensive hilly area of giant boulders about halfway between Craig and Stanton, impassable by wagon and nearly so for horses or mules.
2. *Journal*, October 12, 1869.
3. Heitman. Conrad enlisted as a private in the 120th N.Y. Infantry in 1862 and was commissioned after the war. He died a major in the 15th Infantry in 1898. He lived long enough to see his son Casper Conrad, Jr., graduate from West Point 5th in his class in 1894.
4. Ibid. Chambers McKibbin was a younger brother of David McKibbin, with whom Kautz had served in Washington Territory. He would retire in 1902 with the rank of brigadier general.
5. *Journal*, October 17, 1869. "I am not so well pleased with the appearance of Fort Stanton as I expected to be. It

is unfinished and there is very little prospect of finishing it at present."
6. Heitman. Cushing had enlisted in the 1st Illinois Artillery in 1862 and received a commission in the 4th U.S. Artillery in 1863. After the war, he was transferred to the 3rd Cavalry. He was killed in action against Apaches at Whetstone Mountain, Arizona, in March 1871.
7. *Journal*, October 21, 1869.
8. Fritz, a native of Germany, had served under Kit Carson at Fort Stanton in 1862 and was discharged there with the rank of major. Murphy had also served under Carson in Carson's 1st New Mexico Volunteer Infantry and was discharged a major. Fritz and Murphy opened their store near Fort Stanton in 1868. Both also owned ranches and Murphy was a judge of the county in which the fort was located.
9. *Journal*, November 14, 1869.
10. Ibid., November 23, 1869.
11. Ibid., November 28, 1869.
12. Ibid., December 19, 1869. Kautz wrote, "About thirty citizens collected to accompany Mr. Cushing.... There is a great deal of delay but before night set in the post was clear of the crowd that had collected. There was a great deal of whisky drinking and some of the party were scarcely able to leave the post."
13. Heitman. Yeaton was the only other West Pointer at Fort Stanton, having graduated in July of that year. Kautz visited him almost daily in the post hospital and, later, in his quarters. Although his chest wound improved, it never completely healed. He eventually was strong enough to depart Fort Stanton in May 1870. He died of his wound in August, 1872.
14. Today's traveler could not use this route as it crosses the off-limits White Sands Missile Range, passing within a mile of the Trinity Site, where the first atomic bomb was exploded seventy-five years later.
15. The reservation was also from time to time called the Tularosa Reservation. Today it is known as the Mescalero Indian Reservation.
16. *Journal*, April 17, 1870.
17. Ibid., October 8, 1870.
18. Ibid., October 22, 1870.
19. Ibid., December 14, 1870.

Chapter 36

1. Ibid., May 27, 1872.
2. Newport Barracks was founded in 1803 as an arsenal. It became a recruiting station in the 1820s. Repeated floods of the Ohio in the 1880s forced the abandonment of the post in 1895. The site is now a city park, made a less enjoyable spot to view the Cincinnati skyline since construction of a flood wall during the 20th century.
3. *Journal*, May 30, 1872. During a previous visit to Cincinnati, Kautz had described the park-like Spring Grove as the most beautiful cemetery he had ever seen. On June 30, 1866, the ladies of Cincinnati organized a brief ceremony beside the grave of Cincinnati's poet-general, William H. Lytle, to honor the fallen dead of the Civil War buried there. The principal speaker at the ceremony was U.S. Congressman Rutherford B. Hayes. In succeeding years, the ceremony was repeated and, from those beginnings, our present Memorial Day Holiday has developed. Spring Grove is the burial site of more Civil War generals than any other cemetery in the nation.
4. Ibid., June 4, 1872.
5. Ibid., July 20, 1872.

6. Ibid., July 11, 1872.

7. Matthews would serve later in the U.S. Senate and served on the Supreme Court from 1881 until his death in 1889.

8. The Cincinnati Industrial Exposition, held annually from 1870 to about 1880, was the premiere event of its type during the early years of the Industrial Revolution. In 1879, the entire world took notice when the exhibit halls were lighted by Thomas Edison's electric lamps.

9. *Journal*, November 21, 1872. Miss Vinnie Ream was the only woman and the youngest person ever to be commissioned by the U.S. government to produce a statue in Washington, D.C. She became a controversial figure when, at the tender age of 18, she received the commission for the statue of Abraham Lincoln which now stands in the rotunda of the Capitol. She also did the statue of Sequoyah in the Statuary Hall of the Capitol and the giant statue of Admiral Farragut, also in Washington. Later she gained a reputation for visiting disabled veterans of the Civil War at various soldiers' homes throughout the country. Although little known today, she deserves to be recognized as one of the early pioneers of the women's movement in the United States.

Chapter 37

1. Friedrich (Frederick) Hassaurek was born in Vienna, Austria, in 1832. His father died when he was a child and, after his mother remarried, he was brought to the United States. He practiced law and, later, became part-owner and editor of the *Tägliches Cincinnati Volksblatt* and, through the paper, was a strong political voice among the large German population of Cincinnati. He was one of the founders of the Republican Party in Cincinnati and was a delegate to the party's national conventions in 1860 and 1868. He served as Minister to Ecuador from 1861 to 1868.

2. *Journal*, June 2, 1872.

3. Ibid., June 21, 1872.

4. Ibid., June 23, 1872.

5. Ibid., June 29, 1872.

6. Ibid., August 30, 1872.

7. Ibid., October 5–6, 1872.

8. Ibid., October 9, 1872.

9. This library, devoted primarily to business, is still in existence. Kautz had joined the Young Men's Mercantile Library Association several months before.

10. *Journal*, October 10, 1872.

11. Ibid., October 28, 1872.

12. Kautz was accustomed to buying his uniforms at Brooks Brothers in New York, usually by mail order. A new-style dress uniform had been authorized earlier in the year with the epaulets removed from the shoulders. It seems likely that he purchased such a uniform to be worn at his wedding. He had his new clothes altered to fit as soon as he got back to Cincinnati.

13. *Journal*, November 11, 1872.

14. John Pope graduated from West Point ten years before Kautz. He was twice breveted during the Mexican War and once more during the Civil War, but his poor performance at the Second Battle of Bull Run had almost ended his otherwise creditable career and relegated him to desk work until his retirement as major general in 1886.

15. *Journal*, November 3, 1870. Kautz described Pope's response to his request for a further extension as "an ungrateful quibble," and added, "He declines to favor me in my trouble and so I am now absent without leave."

16. National Archives, Record Group 98, Fort Stanton Letters: Letter, Kautz to Pope, January 24, 1872.

17. *Journal*, November 12, 1872.

18. Ruth Goodin, the daughter of Samuel H. Goodin, was Fannie's best friend.

19. *Cincinnati Enquirer; Cincinnati Commercial*, November 28, 1872.

20. *Journal*, December 8, 1872.

21. S.B. Nelson and J.M. Runk, *History of Cincinnati and Hamilton County*, pp. 540–1. Leopold Markbreit, with his half-brother Frederick Hassaurek, was part-owner of the *Cincinnati Volksblatt*. He was born in Vienna in 1842. He studied law under his half-brother and in April 1861 went into law practice with Rutherford B. Hayes. The partnership was dissolved several months later when both men volunteered for service in the Civil War. Markbreit rose from sergeant to captain of the 28th Ohio Infantry, but was captured in December 1863. Imprisoned in Libby Prison, he was placed in a dungeon deep under the prison in retaliation for General Burnside's threatened execution of four Confederate soldiers who were arrested attempting to recruit behind Union lines in Kentucky. He was exchanged, but not released until a letter from Hassaurek to Abraham Lincoln in October 1864, threatening the loss of Cincinnati's German vote, forced Lincoln to act in Markbreit's favor. (Abraham Lincoln Papers: Letter, Hassaurek to Lincoln, October 15, 1864.) By now well-known nationally, he was appointed by President Grant as Minister to Bolivia in 1869 and was recalled in 1873 because of the political stand which the *Volksblatt* had taken in the presidential election of 1872. Remaining politically active, he was elected mayor of Cincinnati in 1907 and died in office in 1909. Charles Richard Williams, ed., *The Diary and Letters of Rutherford B. Hayes*, p. 8. Letter, R.B. Hayes to S. Birchard, April 10, 1861: Hayes called Markbreit "a bright, gentlemanly, popular young German."

22. *Journal*, December 12, 1872.

23. *Journal*, January 8, 1873. Sheridan Papers: Letter, Sherman to Sheridan, December 9, 1872. Sheridan's opinion was based on a letter from Sherman in which it was stated that Kautz would be allowed one year "from the date of leaving his Regiment. Genl. Pope," he added, "can count on getting his services at that time."

24. *Journal*, March 1, 1873.

25. Ibid., March 15, 1873.

26. Sheridan Papers: Letter, Sheridan to Sherman, March 21, 1873.

27. *Journal*, April 18, 1873.

28. Ibid., June 2, 1873.

29. Ibid., June 5, 1873.

30. Ibid., June 30, 1873.

31. Ibid., July 1, 1873.

32. Ibid., July 7, 1873.

33. Ibid., July 9, 1873.

34. Ibid., July 12, 1873.

35. Ibid., September 28, 1873.

36. Ibid., October 16, 1873.

37. Fort Garland, although located in Colorado Territory, was included in the New Mexico District and one company of the 15th Infantry was stationed there.

38. Colonel Whistler and his wife had arrived at Newport Barracks on January 12 and had been waiting very impatiently for almost a year to move into the commanding officer's quarters.

Chapter 38

1. *Journal*, November 22, 1873.

2. Ibid., December 31, 1873.

3. Ibid., December 30, 1873.

4. Ibid., February 8, 1874.

5. Ibid., December 31, 1873. Although only occasionally mentioned in this text, Kautz had suffered for years from frequent exacerbations of the malaria he had contracted in Panama. In addition, he had recurring headaches, often debilitating and lasting for days to weeks. The fact that they were occasionally preceded by neurologic symptoms such as blurred vision suggests that they were migraine. He treated himself with large doses of quinine for short or long periods of time, which usually aborted the malarial episodes, but did little for the headaches.

6. Ibid., June 19, 1874.

7. Ibid., August 6, 1874.

8. Ibid., August 27, 29, 1974.

9. Sheridan's full name was Phillip Sheridan Kautz. Fred and Lucinda Hill had been married in 1859. Of their four children, only Louise survived childhood. Sheridan died in 1883 at the age of seventeen.

10. *Journal*, September 4, 1874.

11. Ibid., September 19, 1874.

12. *Journal*, September 21, 1874. Heitman: After graduating from West Point, de Veuve resigned his commission after only one year of service. He was a captain of engineers in the Confederate Army during the Civil War.

13. *Journal*, October 26, 1874.

14. George Crook and Mary T. Dailey had been married in August 1865, explaining why Crook was unable to attend Kautz's wedding to Charlotte Tod.

15. Grant initiated his "Peace Policy" soon after taking office in 1869. The policy took control of all western Indians from the hands of the army and turned it over to the Indian Bureau. The bureau was directed by a Board of Indian Commissioners and acted under the Interior Department. The commissioners of the Indian Bureau were appointed from religious organizations in the hope that negotiation, rather than force, could bring peace to the territories.

16. *Journal*, December 4, 1874.

17. Ibid., December 31, 1874.

Chapter 39

1. Sheridan Papers: Letter, Sherman to Sheridan, undated.

2. The military posts Kautz visited were called camps. Most would later be designated forts.

3. Born in New York in 1851, Clum attended Rutgers and was the first meteorologist at the War Department's Meteorological Station at Santa Fe. He was named agent at San Carlos through the Dutch Reform Church and served there from 1874 to 1877. Later, he edited the *Arizona Citizen* and founded the *Tombstone Epitaph*, served as postmaster and was elected mayor of Tombstone. From 1881 to 1909, he was a postal inspector and spent much of this time in Alaska Territory. He spent his last days on a citrus farm in California.

4. Hiram C. Hodge, *Arizona as It Is*, p. 176. "The military under Crook were commanded to assist in doing what the General had promised should not be done. The General, like a true soldier, obeyed the orders of his superiors, though it must have been extremely humiliating to him to do so."

5. *Arizona Citizen*, September 18, 1875.

6. National Archives, Record Group 75, General Correspondence of the Office of Indian Affairs: Letter, Wasson to Smith, September 21, 1875.

7. Ibid., Letter, Safford to Smith, September 21, 1875. It seems likely that, in his reference to "the people of the Territory," Safford was thinking of his friends in the Tucson Ring.

8. National Archives, Record Group 94, General Correspondence of the Adjutant General's Office: Report of August V. Kautz to the assistant adjutant general, Division of the Pacific, October 20, 1875.

9. National Archives, Record Group 75, General Correspondence of the Office of Indian Affairs: Letter, Kautz to Babcock, October 20, 1875. The fact that this letter is found in the records of the Office of Indian Affairs suggests strongly that Clum and his allies read it.

10. National Archives, Record Group 94, General Correspondence of the Adjutant General's Office: Letter, Clum to Smith, November 1, 1875, and Letter, Smith to Secretary of War, December 8, 1875.

11. Ibid., Letter, Schofield to the adjutant general, January 5, 1876.

12. Ibid., Report Inspector General, Department of Arizona, September 1, 1876.

13. *Journal*, February 9, 1877.

14. *Arizona Citizen*, February 10, 1877. An article in the *Citizen* falsely claimed ten new killings. Actually there had been none.

15. *Journal*, February 14, 1877.

16. *Arizona Citizen*, February 14, 1877.

17. Ibid., March 4, 1877.

18. National Archives, Record Group 94, General Correspondence of the Adjutant General's Office: Enclosure telegram, Clum to Wallace, in letter, McCrary to Schurz, June 5, 1877.

19. *Journal*, April 5, 1877.

20. National Archives, Record Group 94, General Correspondence of the Adjutant General's Office: Sherman's first endorsement March 9, 1877, of letter, Safford to McCormick.

21. It is more likely Safford resigned to avoid moving to Prescott with the territorial government in June. It is curious that Kautz did not mention the resignations of either Clum or Safford in his journal.

22. *Prescott (Arizona) Miner*, May 5, 1877.

23. *Journal*, May 3, 1877.

24. Ibid., April 14, 1877.

25. Ibid., June 13, 1877. Miss Titus is Emma Titus, a friend of Fannie from Cincinnati, who came west to find a husband and remained in the Kautz household until May 1879.

26. Ibid., June 14, 1877.

27. National Archives, Record Group 94, General Correspondence of the Adjutant General's Office: Letter, Vandever to Secretary of War, May 3, 1877.

28. Ibid., Telegram, Vandever to Commissioner of Indian Affairs, June 13, 1877.

29. Ibid., Sherman's endorsement to telegram, Vandever to Commissioner of Indian Affairs, June 13, 1877.

30. Ibid., Telegram, McDowell to Secretary of War, July 10, 1877.

31. *Journal*, July 16, 1877.

Chapter 40

1. *Journal*, February 20, 1877. By this time the Southern Pacific Railroad had been completed from Los Angeles almost to Yuma.

2. Ibid., May 5, 1877.

3. Ibid., July 21, 1877.

4. Campbell was the son of Archibald Campbell, whom Kautz had known on the Northwest Boundary Commission in 1858.

5. *Journal*, August 3, 1877.

6. Ibid., June 19, 1877.

7. National Archives, Record Group 153, Records of the Office of the Judge Advocate General: Record of the trial of Colonel August V. Kautz, May 1, 1878. The records of the Campbell case were included in the later trial of Kautz. See next chapter.

8. Jacob and Ragsdale. Stevens had previously been "engaged in general merchandising and supplying forage for the Army." He was no doubt a member of the Tucson Ring.

9. Lucy Hayes was the first presidential spouse to be called "First Lady." It may be recalled that her husband had once been a law partner of Fannie's brother, Leopold. Although Fannie was a child at the time, she had met Mrs. Hayes then.

10. *Journal*, January 11, 1878.

11. *Prescott (Arizona) Enterprise*, January 9, 1878.

12. There is no doubt that McKee held animosity for Kautz. He was a friend of Eagan, but he was also a friend of John Wasson of the Tucson Ring. There is strong suspicion that he had played a role in having J. Lillie Mercer's very damaging letter to the *New York Herald* published the previous March.

13. *Journal*, January 12, 1878.

14. National Archives, Record Group 94, General Correspondence of the Adjutant General's Office: Letter, Kautz to Macfeely, January 18, 1878, enclosed with Kautz's application for Eagan's transfer.

15. Ibid., Third endorsement by Macfeely to Kautz's application for Eagan's transfer, February 1, 1878.

16. National Archives, Record Group 94, General Correspondence of the Adjutant General's Office: Fourth endorsement by Sherman to Kautz's application for Eagan's transfer, February 4, 1878.

17. *Journal*, February 6–8, 1878.

Chapter 41

1. *Prescott (Arizona) Enterprise*, February 13, 1878. Kautz did not mention receiving this telegram, but it was copied in the newspaper the day it was sent.

2. National Archives, Record Group 94, General Correspondence of the Adjutant General's Office: Sherman's endorsement to letter, Gosper to Hayes, March 4, 1878.

3. *Journal*, February 15, 1878.

4. *Arizona Citizen*, February 8, 1878; *Arizona Sentinel*, February 16, 1878.

5. *Arizona Sentinel*, February 16, 1878.

6. *Prescott (Arizona) Miner*, February 18, 1878.

7. *Journal*, March 22, 1878.

8. Ibid., March 26, 1878.

9. Ibid., April 8, 1878.

10. *Army & Navy Journal*, March 30, 1878.

11. *Journal*, April 7, 1878.

12. Sheridan Papers: Letter, Sheridan to Sherman, April 13, 1878.

13. Ibid., Letter, Sherman to Sheridan, April 20, 1878.

14. *Omaha Herald*, May 2, 1878.

15. National Archives, Record Group 153, Records of the Office of the Judge Advocate General: Proceedings of the Court-Martial of August V. Kautz. Unless otherwise noted, quotations in the remainder of this chapter are from this source.

16. *Omaha Republican*, May 3, 1878.

17. Ibid., May 5, 1878.

18. *Army & Navy Journal*, May 18, 1878.

19. Ibid., May 18, 1878.

20. *Journal*, May 7, 1878.

21. *Army & Navy Journal*, May 18, 1878.

22. Ibid., May 18, 1878.

23. *Journal*, May 9, 1878.

24. Ibid., May 25, 1878.

25. Ibid., May 30, 1878.

Chapter 42

1. *Journal*, March 12, 1878.

2. Ibid., March 28, 1878.

3. Actually, McDowell had been directed to move an artillery regiment out of rented quarters in San Francisco to Angel Island.

4. *Journal*, October 9, 1878.

5. Ibid., December 31, 1878.

6. Ibid., September 26, 1878.

7. Ibid., September 27, 1878.

8. Kautz's full testimony can be found in U.S. Senate Miscellaneous Documents, 45th Congress: Report of the Committee to Study the Feasibility of Transferring the Indian Bureau to the War Department, pp.193–196.

9. Ibid., February 10, 1878. "I mailed a great many of my reports to members of Congress today."

10. Pauline's mother, Emeline Monroe, had joined the Kautz household at Fort Whipple and served as cook and laundress until February 1881.

11. *Journal*, September 20–25, 1879.

12. Ibid., October 21, 1879.

13. Ibid., December 31, 1879.

Chapter 43

1. Hayes, then nearing the end of his term, was the first sitting U.S. president to visit the west coast.

2. Lieutenant Melville Wilkinson of the 3rd Infantry had received an appropriation of $5000 to found a school for Indian children at Forest Grove. In the first year, he had eighteen children in his classes, including the Kautz boys. In subsequent years, both funds and attendance greatly increased. Moved to Salem, Oregon, and renamed Chemawa Indian School, it later had an enrollment of 1000.

3. *Journal*, April 6, 1881.

4. Ibid., December 31, 1882.

5. Ibid., April 17, 1883.

6. Uncle Vincent was Vincenz Freiherr (Baron) von Abele. He had retired from the Austrian Army in the fall of 1882 with a rank of *Feldzeugmeister* (equivalent to major general).

7. Freudenthal glass was produced from 1716 to 1942 and, for most of those years, the factory was owned by the Stimpfl family.

8. *Journal*, November 12, 1883.

9. Ibid., November 16, 1883.

10. John Swift was a lawyer who had served for years in the California Assembly. He was appointed Minister to Japan in 1889 and died there two years later. Kautz considered Swift one of the most intelligent and interesting persons he had ever known and had valued his friendship since meeting him in 1878.

11. Kautz had learned of the death of Henry Tichenor in March. Three months later, the Widow Tichenor and her mother left on a tour of Europe, much of which was spent with the Kautzes.

12. *Journal*, July 27, 1884.

13. The act, passed several years before, required that all officers be retired on their sixty-fourth birthdays.

14. *Journal*, October 26, 1884.

15. Ibid., July 1, 1885.

16. Ibid., July 2, 1885.

17. Ibid., July 4, 1885.

18. Ibid., July 6, 1885.

19. Ibid., October 1, 1885.

20. Ibid., February 22, 1886.

21. Ibid., February 24, 1886.

22. Ibid., March 5, 1886.

23. Kautz later learned that it was Joseph Potter of the 24th Infantry rather than Merritt who had gained the second nomination. This was more to Kautz's liking because Potter was to retire in October, producing another opening.

24. *Journal*, March 20, 1886.

25. Ibid., April 16, 1886.

26. Ibid., May 29, 1886.

27. Ibid., July 5, 1886.

Chapter 44

1. *Journal*, May 25, 1878.

2. Ibid., August 23, 1878.

3. See National Archives, Record Group 94, General Correspondence of the Adjutant General's Office: Annual Report of the Adjutant General, 1878.

4. *Journal*, December 16, 1878.

5. Ibid., April 19, 1882.

6. Ibid., February 16, 1882.

7. Ibid., February 22, 1882.

8. Ibid., May 21, 1885.

9. Ibid. This is the only time in the history of frontier warfare that a U.S. Army fort was attacked by Indians.

10. *Journal*, December 27, 1865.

11. *Journal*, February 3, 1886.

12. About 75 Chiricahua and Warm Spring Apaches had already been escorted to Florida by Lieutenant Colville Terrett and Company D, Eighth Infantry.

13. *Journal*, April 28, 1886.

14. Ibid., June 5, 1886.

15. Ibid., August 7, 1886.

16. This promise proved false. Geronimo remained a prisoner of war in Florida and, later, Alabama and the Indian Territory of Oklahoma. He died in Oklahoma in 1909 without ever again having set foot in Arizona.

17. *Journal*, September 17, 1886.

18. Ibid., September 18, 1886. Miles also told Kautz that Kautz was his choice to succeed him in command of the department.

19. Martha Summerhayes, *Vanished Arizona*, pp. 242–3.

Chapter 45

1. *Journal*, December 15, 1883.

2. Four companies of the 8th Infantry were at Fort Robinson in northwestern Nebraska and two at Fort Bridger in Wyoming Territory.

3. Benteen was convicted on several counts, including drunkenness on duty, and sentenced to be cashiered. President Cleveland reduced the sentence to a year's suspension at half pay.

4. After his tour as consul in Barmen, Wolfgang Schoenle took a job as editor of the *Anzeiger*, a German-language newspaper in Louisville.

5. *Journal*, August 5, 1887.

6. There would be additional trips east for Fannie or August or both to deliver or pick up their children. The following year, all three went to school in Cincinnati and in 1889–90, Austin transferred from the school in Cincinnati to "Lieutenant Charles Braden's school" at Cornwall on the Hudson, New York, later New York Military Academy.

7. *Journal*, April 1, 1888.

8. Ibid. It is unfortunate that Philip Sheridan's death is but parenthetical in this history. On hearing of his death Kautz said, "I have but one regret in relation to it, that he did not live to give me an opportunity to remind him how he had failed to utilize his brilliant record which he achieved in the war, either for his own good or for the service.... When he succeeded to the command of the Army I hoped much for him for I was one of his most ardent admirers and regarded his record as the most brilliant that the war produced."

9. Ibid., June 19, 1890.

10. Ibid., June 23, 1890.

11. Ibid., June 25, 1890. Such an admonishment by a respected colonel would probably have been viewed by most private soldiers in 1890 as a worse punishment than a tour in the guardhouse. Kautz was not certain that he had placated both Wilhelm and Richardson. *Journal*, June 23, 1890. Fannie Kautz seems to have viewed what was happening in a different light. According to her husband, "My wife maintains that the Regt. is going insane on account of the ... isolation of this post in such a climate for such a long continuous period."

12. Alfred T. Smith was named lieutenant colonel of the regiment in December 1888 when Montgomery Bryant was promoted to colonel of the 13th Infantry.

13. *Journal*, July 21, 1890.

14. They got the new agent, J. George Wright, later in the year. Kautz would learn that they were even less pleased with him, primarily because of his young age.

15. *Journal*, April 17, 1889.

16. The friend was Maria Herron, the daughter of a prominent Cincinnati lawyer, John Herron, who, like Leopold Markbreit, was a former law partner of President Hayes. The year before, Maria's older sister Helen had married William Howard Taft.

17. *Journal*, November 18, 1890.

Chapter 46

1. Ibid., December 23, 1890.

2. Louis had been part owner of a lumberyard on the riverfront in Cincinnati (present-day site of a football stadium), but severe flooding in 1884 wiped him out.

3. *Journal*, March 12, 1890.

4. Ibid., February 7, 1891.

5. Ibid., January 7, 1891.

6. Under his mother's tutelage, Austin was already an accomplished pianist.

7. Halford had previously been editor of the *Indianapolis Journal* and was a friend of Leopold Markbreit. Markbreit had asked Halford's aid in Kautz's behalf

several years before, so Halford was already interested in Kautz's promotion.

8. *Journal*, April 6, 1891.
9. Ibid., April 7, 1891.
10. Ibid., April 8, 1891.
11. Ibid., April 20, 1891.
12. Ibid., April 21, 1891.
13. Ibid., April 24, 1891.

Chapter 47

1. *Journal*, June 13, 1891.
2. Ibid., June 21, 1891.
3. The board continued to meet for more than a year before settling on a Danish rifle which would serve the infantry through World War I.
4. With them was Kautz's nephew, Rob Schoenle, recently graduated from medical school. Kautz had agreed to supply funds to get his nephew started in medical practice and Rob, at Kautz's suggestion, had chosen Seattle as a promising location.
5. The Kautz household included, besides Pauline, the two aides-de-camp to whom a brigadier was entitled, Lieutenant Wilds P. Richardson of the 8th Infantry and Lieutenant Lewis M. Koehler of the 6th Cavalry.
6. *Journal*, September 4, 1891.
7. Ibid., September 25, 1891.
8. Ibid., October 24, 1891.
9. *Army & Navy Journal*, January 28, 1892.

10. *Journal*, January 5, 1892.
11. Ibid., December 31, 1891.

Chapter 48

1. *Journal*, January 8, 1892.
2. Ibid., April 8, 1892.
3. Ibid., November 3, 1892.
4. George Washington Cullum, et al., eds., *Biographical Register of the Officers and Graduates of the U.S. Military Academy at West Point, N.Y.* Murphy graduated in 1897, 19th in a class of 67.
5. *Journal*, July 18, 1893.
6. Ibid., December 31, 1893.
7. Ibid., July 8, 1894.
8. Ibid., July 30, 1894.
9. Ibid., September 29, 1894.
10. Ibid., December 31, 1893.
11. Wholley was a West Point graduate who had recently taken a teaching position at the University of Washington.
12. *Journal*, September 3, 1895.
13. Ibid., Addendum.

Afterword

1. Cullum, vol. 6.

Bibliography

Arizona Citizen.

Arizona Sentinel.

Army & Navy Journal.

Atlas of Brown County, Ohio. Philadelphia: Lake, Griffing & Stevenson, 1876.

Bancroft, Hubert Howe. *The Works of Hubert Howe Bancroft.* Vol. 30, *History of the Pacific Northwest-Oregon and Washington.* San Francisco: The History Company Publishers, 1888.

Barns, George C. *Denver the Man: The Life, Letters and Public Papers of the Lawyer, Soldier and Statesman.* Wilmington, OH: privately published, 1949.

Barrett, Stephen M., ed. *Geronimo's Story of His Life.* New York: Duffield & Co., 1907.

Beers, W.H. *The History of Brown County, Ohio.* Chicago: W.H. Beers & Co., 1883.

The Biographical Encyclopaedia of Ohio of the Nineteenth Century. Cincinnati: Galaxy Publishing Co., 1876.

Brown County, Ohio, Office of the County Recorder, Transfer of Deeds (1819–present).

Brown County, Ohio, Probate Court Records, Records of Births (1819–1867).

Cincinnati Enquirer.

The Columbia Encyclopedia. 6th ed. New York: Columbia University Press, 2001.

Crook, George. *General George Crook, His Autobiography.* Edited by Martin F. Schmitt. Norman: University of Oklahoma Press, 1946.

Cullum, George Washington, et al., eds. *Biographical Register of the Officers and Graduates of the U.S. Military Academy at West Point, N.Y. From Its Establishment in 1802 to 1890; With the Early History of the United States Military.* 8 vols. Boston and New York: Houghton Mifflin, 1891–1940.

Daly, Louise Haskell. *Alexander Cheves Haskell: The Portrait of a Man.* Wilmington, NC: Broadfoot Publishing Co., 1989.

Davis, Britton. *The Truth About Geronimo.* New Haven: Yale University Press, 1929.

Explorations and Surveys for a Railroad Route from the Mississippi River to the Pacific Ocean-War Department. Washington, D.C.: Government Printing Office, 1860.

Faulk, Odie B. *The Geronimo Campaign.* New York: Oxford University Press, 1969.

Floyd-Jones, DeLancey. *Journal of the March of Major Blake's Command of Four Companies of U.S. Recruits from Fort Benton to Fort Walla Walla, Washington Territory over the "Fort Walla Walla to Fort Benton Wagon Road" between the 7th Day of August and the 4th of October, 1860.* Washington, D.C.: War Records Office, National Archives.

_____. *Report of an Expedition made by a Detachment of U.S. Recruits Under the Command of Major Blake, 1st Dragoons, from St. Louis, Mo., to Fort Benton, Nebraska Territory, via the Missouri River, during the Summer of 1860.* Washington, D.C.: War Records Office, National Archives.

Ford, Henry A., A.M. Ford, and Kate B. Ford. *History of Hamilton County, Ohio.* Cleveland: L.A. Williams & Co., 1881.

Fort Stanton Letters. Record Group 98, National Archives, Washington, D.C.

Gause, Isaac. *Four Years with Five Armies.* New York: The Neale Publishing Co., 1908.

Giddings, Luther. *Sketches of the Campaign in Northern Mexico in Eighteen Hundred Forty-Six and Seven.* New York: George P. Putnam & Co., 1853.

Glisan, Rodney. *Journal of Army Life.* San Francisco: A.L. Bancroft & Co., 1874.

Grant, Ulysses S. *Personal Memoirs.* New York: The Century Co., 1885.

Greeley, Horace. *The American Conflict: A History of the Great Rebellion of the United States of America, 1860–'65.* Hartford: O.D. Case & Co., 1866.

Hannaford, Roger. *Diary of Roger Hannaford.* Library, Cincinnati Historical Society.

Hardin, Martin D. "Across the New Northwest in 1860." *The United Service Magazine* 6: pp. 576–88 and 7: pp. 186–97.

Hardin, Stephen L. *Texian Iliad: A Military History of the Texas Revolution.* Austin: University of Texas Press, 1994.

Heitman, Francis B. *Historical Register and Dictionary of the United States Army.* Washington, D.C.: Government Printing Office, 1903.

Henry, Robert Selph. *The Story of the Mexican War.* Indianapolis: The Bobbs Merrill Company, 1950.

History of the Pacific Northwest, Oregon and Washington. Portland, OR: North Pacific History Co., 1889.

Hodge, Hiram C. *Arizona as It Is; or The Coming Country, Compiled from Notes of Travel During the Years 1874, 1875 and 1876.* New York: Hurd and Houghton, 1877.

Horwitz, Lester V. *The Longest Raid of the Civil War.* Cincinnati: Farmcourt Publishing, Inc., 2001.

Howe, Henry. *Historical Collections of Ohio*. 2 vols. Cincinnati: C.J. Krihbiel & Co., Printers & Binders, 1888.

Ingersoll, Ernest. "In the Wahlamet Valley of Oregon." *Harper's New Monthly Magazine*. New York: Harper & Bros., October 1882.

Jacob, Kathryn A., and Bruce A. Ragsdale, eds. *Biographical Directory of the United States Congress, 1774–1989, Bicentennial Edition*. Washington, D.C.: U.S. Government Printing Office, 1989.

Johnson, Robert Underwood, and Clarence Clough Buel, eds. *Battles and Leaders of the Civil War*. 4 vols. New York: The Century Co., 1887.

Kappler, Charles J., ed. *Indian Affairs: Laws and Treaties*. Washington, D.C.: Government Printing Office, 1904.

Kautz, August V. "Ascent of Mount Rainier." *Overland Monthly* 14 (May 1875): pp. 393–403.

_____. *Autobiography (1828–1847)*. Unfinished handwritten manuscript, Library of Congress, Washington, D.C.

_____. *The Company Clerk: Showing How and When to Make Out All the Returns, Reports, Rolls and Other Papers, and What to Do with Them*. Philadelphia: J.B. Lippincott & Co., 1863.

_____. *Customs of Service for Non-Commissioned Officers and Soldiers; as Derived from Law and Regulations and Practiced in the Army of the United States*. Philadelphia: J.B. Lippincott & Co., 1864.

_____. *Customs of Service for Officers of the Army; as Derived from Law and Regulations and Practiced in the United States Army*. Philadelphia: J.B. Lippincott & Co., 1866.

_____. *Letters to First Lieutenant S.M. Brown, First New York Mounted Rifles, 1864–1865* (nine letters). Library, Cincinnati Historical Society.

_____. *Map of Connell's Prairie, Washington Territory, 1857*. Steilacoom Historical Society.

_____. Papers of. Library of Congress, Washington, D.C.

_____. *Personal Journals, 1857–1895*.

_____. *Reminiscences of the Civil War*. Unpublished manuscript transcribed from the original handwritten manuscript by Mrs. Austin Kautz and presented to the Army War College Library in July 1936; Library of Congress.

Kautz, Frances, ed. "Extracts from the Diary of Gen. A.V. Kautz." *The Washington Historian* 1–2. Tacoma, WA: The Washington State Historical Society, 1899–1901.

Keiley, Anthony M. *In Vinculis; or The Prisoner of War, Being the Experience of a Rebel in Two Federal Pens*. New York: Blelock & Co., 1866.

Keyes, Erasmus D. *Fifty Years' Observation of Men and Events*. New York: Charles Scribner & Sons, 1884.

Kirchenbuch, 1644–1962, Evangelische Kirche Ispringen. Microfilm record of baptisms, funerals and marriages. Salt Lake City: Church of Latter Day Saints.

Lincoln, Abraham. Papers of. Library of Congress, Washington, D.C.

Lockley, Fred. *Interview: Nugen Kautz*. Portland, Oregon: Oregon Journal, undated. (Courtesy University of Oregon Library.)

Long, E.B., with Barbara Long. *The Civil War Day by Day: An Almanac, 1861–1865*. Garden City, NY: Doubleday & Company, Inc., 1971.

Longstreet, James. *From Manassas to Appomattox: Memoirs of the Civil War in America*. Philadelphia: J.B. Lippincott, 1896.

Lossing, Benson J. *Lives of Celebrated Americans Comprising Biographies of Three Hundred and Forty Eminent Persons*. Hartford: Thomas Belknap, 1869.

Lovell, Edith Haroldsen. *Benjamin Bonneville: Soldier of the American Frontier*. Salt Lake City: Horizon Publishers, 1992.

Marshall, S.L.A. *Crimsoned Prairie: The Wars between the United States and the Plains Indians During the Winning of the West*. New York: Charles Scribner's Sons, 1972.

Meacham, Alfred B. *Wigwam and War-Path; or Royal Chief in Chains*. Boston: John P. Dale & Co., 1875.

Meany, Edward. *Mount Rainier: A Record of Exploration*. New York: The McMillan Company, 1916.

Meeker, Ezra. *Pioneer Reminiscences of Puget Sound: The Tragedy of Leschi*. Seattle: Lowman & Hanford, 1905.

Merrill, Samuel Hill. *Campaigns of the First Maine and First District of Columbia Cavalry*. Portland, ME: Bailey & Noyes, 1866.

Nelson, S.B., and J.M. Runk. *History of Cincinnati and Hamilton County, Ohio: Their Past and Present*. Cincinnati: S.B. Nelson & Co., Publishers, 1894.

Newell, Gordon. *"So Fair a Dwelling Place": A History of Olympia and Thurston County, Washington*. Olympia: Olympia News Publishing, 1950.

Nishimoto, Bonnie. *The Arnheim Lutheran Church Parish Register*. Woodbridge, VA: published privately by Bonnie Nishimoto, 1988.

Official Register of the Officers and Cadets of the United States Military Academy. West Point, NY: 1849, 1852, 1853.

Oregon Historical Quarterly 7 (1907).

Overland Monthly 5, no. 8 (1885).

Peral, Miguel Angel, ed. *Dictionario Biografico Mexicano*. Mexico City: Editorial P.A.C., 1944.

Powell, William S., ed. *Dictionary of North Carolina Biography*. 4 vols. Chapel Hill, NC: University of North Carolina Press, 1979.

Prescott (Arizona) Enterprise.

Prescott (Arizona) Miner.

Reid, Whitelaw. *Ohio in the War: Her Statesmen, Her Generals, and Soldiers*. 2 vols. Cincinnati: Moore, Wilstach & Baldwin, 1868.

Reports of Explorations and Surveys to Ascertain the Most Practicable and Economical Route for a Railroad from the Mississippi River to the Pacific Ocean, 1854–55. Vol. 6. Washington, D.C.: A.O.P. Nicholson, Printer, 1857.

Ripley (Ohio) Bee.

Robertson, William Glenn. *Back Door to Richmond: The Bermuda Hundred Campaign, April–June, 1864*. Newark: University of Delaware Press, 1987.

Robison, Houston T. "The Rogue River Indians and Their Relations With the Whites." Master's thesis, University of Oregon, June 1943.

Rodenbough, Theophilus F., and William L. Haskin, eds. *The Army of the United States: Historical Sketches of Staff and Line with Portraits of Generals-In-Chief*. New York: Maynard, Merrill & Co., 1896.

Roper, John L., Henry C. Archibald, and George W.

Coles. *History of the Eleventh Pennsylvania Volunteer Cavalry.* Philadelphia: Franklin Printing Co., 1902.

Sanger, George P., et al., eds. *Statutes at Large, Treaties and Proclamations of the United States of America.* 18 vols. Boston: Little, Brown & Co., 1845–1875.

Scott, Robert N., Henry M. Lazelle, Leslie J. Perry, Joseph W. Kirkley, Fred C. Ainsworth, John S. Moodey, Calvin D. Cowles. *The War of the Rebellion: A Compilation of the Official Records of the Union and Confederate Armies.* 70 vols. Washington, D.C.: U.S. Government Printing Office, 1880–1901.

Sheridan, Philip H. Papers of. Library of Congress, Washington, D.C.

_____. *Personal Memoirs of P.H. Sheridan, General, United States Army.* New York: Webster, 1888.

Simmons, Henry E. *A Concise Encyclopedia of the Civil War.* New York: Bonanza Books, 1965.

Speer, William S., and John H. Brown, eds. *Encyclopedia of the New West.* Marshall, TX: United Biographical Publishing Company, 1881.

Summerhayes, Martha. *Vanished Arizona.* Philadelphia: J.B. Lippincott Company, 1908.

Sypher, J.R. *History of the Pennsylvania Reserve Corps.* Lancaster, PA: Elias Barr & Co., 1865.

Tacoma Ledger.

Thompson, Carl N. *Historical Collections of Brown County, Ohio.* 2 vols. Piqua, OH: Hammer Graphics, Inc., 1969.

Tobie, Edward P. *History of the First Maine Cavalry.* Boston: First Maine Cavalry Association, 1887.

Tolmie, William Fraser. "Journal of William Fraser Tolmie." *The Washington Historical Quarterly* 1 (October 1906): pp. 77–81.

Tucker, Marcia Willoughby. *Day Island: A Glimpse of the Past.* Seattle: Rhododendron Press, 1997.

United States Census, Brown County, Ohio (1850).

United States Census, Hamilton County, Ohio (1830).

United States Congress. *Senate Journal, Bills and Resolutions.* Washington, D.C.: Government Printing Office, 1774–present.

United States Senate, Miscellaneous Documents, 45th Congress. *Report of the Committee to Study the Feasibility of Transferring the Indian Bureau to the War Department.* Washington, D.C.: Government Printing Office, 1879.

Utley, Robert M. *Frontier Regulars: The United States Army and the Indian, 1866–1891.* New York: Macmillan Publishing Co., Inc., 1973.

_____, and Wilcomb E. Washburn. *American Heritage Library of Indian Wars.* Boston: Houghton Mifflin Co., 1977.

Van Tramp, John C. *Prairie and Rocky Mountain Adventures or Life in the West.* Columbus, OH: Signer & Condit, 1870.

Wallace, Andrew. "Soldier in the Southwest: The Career of General A.V. Kautz, 1869–1886." Ph.D. dissertation, University of Arizona, 1968 (printed by University Microfilms, Inc., Ann Arbor, Michigan, 2003).

Warner, Ezra J. *Generals in Blue.* Baton Rouge: Louisiana State University Press, 1964.

_____. *Generals in Gray.* Baton Rogue: Louisiana State University Press, 1959.

Warner, Mikell de Lores Wormell, trans. *Catholic Church Records of the Pacific Northwest.* Saint Paul, OR: French Prairie Press, 1972.

Williams, Charles Richard, ed. *The Diary and Letters of Rutherford B. Hayes, Nineteenth President of the United States.* 5 vols. Columbus: Ohio State Archeological and Historical Society, 1922.

Wilson, James Grant, and John Fiske. *Appleton's Cyclopedia of American Biography.* 6 vols. New York: Appleton & Co., 1889.

Wilson, James Harrison. "The Cavalry of the Army of the Potomac." *Papers of the Military Historical Society of Massachusetts.* Boston: 1913.

_____. *Under the Old Flag: Recollections of Military Operations in the War for the Union, the Spanish War, the Boxer Rebellion, etc.* New York: D. Appleton, 1912.

Wright, George W. "Hon. David Tod: Biography and Personal Recollections." *Ohio History* 8: pp. 107–131.

Index